MARRIAGE COUNSELING:
A CASEBOOK

MARRIAGE

COUNSELING:

A CASEBOOK

ASSOCIATION PRESS, NEW YORK

The Theory and Practice

of Marriage Counseling

Including 41 Typical Cases

Contributed by Members

of American Association

of Marriage Counselors

Edited for American Association of
Marriage Counselors by

Emily H. Mudd, Ph.D.   Abraham Stone, M.D.
Maurice J. Karpf, Ph.D.   Janet Fowler Nelson, Ph.D.

MARRIAGE COUNSELING: A CASEBOOK

Copyright © 1958 by

American Association of Marriage Counselors, Inc.

Association Press, 291 Broadway, New York 7, N. Y.

Third Printing, October, 1959

Library of Congress catalog card number: 58-6469

55

Printed in the United States of America

American Book–Stratford Press, Inc., New York

References to opinions, authorities, books, pamphlets, tests, and schedules in the various chapters are in each case the responsibility of the author of the chapter or the contributor of the case and, therefore, do not necessarily carry the endorsement of the AAMC as such.

ACKNOWLEDGMENTS

We wish to thank the Editors of *Marriage and Family Living* for permission to use materials in Cases 9, 34, and 36, earlier versions of which were published in the Journal.

David R. Mace has graciously given permission for us to quote at length in Chapter 2 from *What Is Marriage Counseling?,* Public Affairs Pamphlet No. 250.

We appreciate also the permission granted by Harcourt, Brace and Company, New York, for our adaptation in Chapter 2 of the poem "Epithalamion" by Jan Struthers which appeared in her volume *The Glass Blower and Other Poems.*

Our thanks are extended to Dr. Robert W. Laidlaw and to J. B. Lippincott Company, copyright owners, for excerpts quoted in Chapter 15 from Dr. Laidlaw's chapter in *Understanding Your Patient,* edited by Samuel Liebman, M.D.

Thanks also go to Mrs. Marjorie R. Olton, office executive of the AAMC, without whose co-operation on details, big and little, this book could not have been completed so effectively. We are indebted, too, to our typist, Miss Doran McKeever, legal secretary of Cleveland, Ohio, for her skill and her loyalty to the project.

THE CASEBOOK COMMITTEE

vii A SPECIAL ACKNOWLEDGMENT

For the Association

A SPECIAL ACKNOWLEDGMENT

We dedicate this book to the memory of Dr. Robert
Latou Dickinson in appreciation of all that he did through systematic research to advance the understanding of marital relationships and for his sharing with the Association much un-
published data gathered in his gynecological practice and as a
pioneer in marriage counseling. Dr. Dickinson was one of the
Founders of the American Association of Marriage Counselors
and throughout the years he was an inspiration to the membership. His memory serves as a stimulus continually to increase
knowledge and to improve service in marriage counseling.

This volume brings to fruition the intention of the American
Association of Marriage Counselors which on December 7,
1951, voted the appointment of a Casebook Committee. At that
time the Executive Committee enthusiastically received Dr.
Emily Mudd's suggestion that such a casebook, properly com-
piled, could be very helpful in teaching and training individuals
who are professionally concerned with the practice of marriage
counseling and in interpreting to intelligent people its process
and meaning.

A preview of the script leads us to feel that the committee has
accomplished a formidable task in a highly satisfactory manner.
We want to thank its members for their diligence, perseverance,
and final accomplishment. In a multidisciplinary organization
such as ours, with the attendant differences in training and experience, it is not easy to meet the requirements for publishing
a representative casebook. What was initiated as a casebook
committee finally became the board of editors and as such are

presented to the readers. We want also to express deep appreciation to those members who co-operated in providing the case material which is the core of the volume.

For the Association
LESTER W. DEARBORN, *President*

FOREWORD

This book illustrates and implements one of the original and continuing aims of the American Association of Marriage Counselors—namely, the achievement of perspective, new skills, and insights for the members through the exchange of clinical information and the pooling of experience. The particular concept of a casebook derived from suggestions and requests for such a book by AAMC members themselves. The Executive Committee discussed these suggestions in 1950, and in 1951 an appropriate committee was appointed by Dr. Robert W. Laidlaw, the president of the Association. This Casebook Committee consisted of Dr. Emily H. Mudd, who was the first chairman; Dr. Abraham Stone, Dr. Maurice J. Karpf, and Dr. Laidlaw, ex officio. Subsequently, Dr. Stone accepted the chairmanship in 1952–53 while Dr. Mudd was president; and in 1954 Dr. Mudd again accepted the chairmanship. In 1954 Dr. Janet Nelson was added to the Committee. Early in its deliberations the Committee decided that the purpose of the casebook was to serve those who are professionally active in the field of marriage counseling rather than to be a popular treatise on the subject. The Committee also decided that the book should not stress or sponsor any particular philosophy or technique or particular aspect of marriage counseling. This decision seemed in consonance also with the present stage of development of marriage counseling, which is still largely experimental requiring a free, untrammeled, and uncongealed atmosphere for the greatest progress. These decisions were approved by the Executive Committee, and the Casebook Committee set to work with these two principles in mind.

The Committee worked carefully to devise ways and means

ix

of developing a broadly representative presentation of material, in no sense a literal duplication, in terms of problems, type of counseling, or other aspects of any one counselor's practice. One of the requirements for consideration by the Membership Committee of the American Association of Marriage Counselors was the submission of two full case summaries of situations counseled by the applicant. The Committee thus had a potential source of case material for possible use, providing the members concerned consented to the release of their cases. The entire membership was circulated for suggestions as to procedure and asked to submit one or more cases illustrative of a counseling problem and the process by which it was handled. From the richness of material returned, the Committee thoughtfully selected, not just the "best" cases, but those representative of various professional backgrounds, points of view, techniques, and problem areas. The resulting collection of premarital, single, and marriage-adjustment cases is thus broadly representative of the over-all field of marriage counseling. It is not necessarily typical of the proportionate caseload of any individual member which inevitably varies with his or her professional background, working affiliation, and personal interests.

The procedure for the selection of cases was taxing and rigorous not only for the AAMC membership but also for the Casebook Committee. Each individual case submitted by a member for possible inclusion in the book was read and voted on individually by all four members of the Committee. Only cases which were approved by a majority of the Committee were tentatively accepted. These were then returned to the counselor who presented them with, when indicated, suggestions for revision. Upon resubmission they were again read individually by each committee member. Final decision for inclusion required unanimous committee approval.

The first reading of the assembled cases submitted, faced the Committee with a number of new problems. As was anticipated —indeed, as is true of all symposia—the cases varied in style, approach, depth and perceptiveness of treatment, and adequacy of presentation. The Committee was forced to choose between an enforced and artificial uniformity and consistency of treatment, on the one hand, and the suggestiveness and educational advantage of a multidisciplined approach, on the other. Again it chose the latter as having the greater promise at this juncture for a potential contribution to marriage counseling. The contributors prepared their own material in accordance with a broadly conceived outline which did not diminish the salient features of each problem or its particular handling by the counselor.

A similar problem related to editorial or critical comment since it seemed certain that the book would be used as a text or for reference purposes. Here again the Committee decided (and we hope wisely) that the original purpose would best be served by offering only an occasional note or comment. It was decided to have a brief introductory comment before each major section of the book and to let the case material speak for itself.

The final selection of cases includes contributions from all the major professions from which marriage counseling derives— medicine, psychiatry, psychology, sociology, family life education, the ministry, social work, and the law—and presents many, if not most, of the problem areas most frequently encountered. However, the per cent contributed by each major profession does not follow the breakdown of AAMC membership. An appreciably higher proportion of cases came from members in the behavioral and social sciences than from members in the field of medicine and the ministry (whereas the membership actually includes about an equal proportion of physicians, including psychiatrists and social workers, the next highest representation being ministers, psychologists, and sociologists). The emphasis, in requesting cases, on describing the *process of counseling* undoubtedly introduced a selective factor. It is conceivable that this higher proportion of case contributions from the fields of psychology and sociology may be due to the fact that training in these professions leads to easy familiarity with the recording of case notes into a form which presents the process of counseling. And institutions in which social workers are employed still require the keeping of detailed records, interview by interview. On the other hand, practitioners of medicine, trained to help disturbed patients in a direct and practical manner, and ministers, trained to comfort and support their parishioners by human sympathy and faith, are less likely to keep step-by-step records of what the counselor does, how he does it, and the emotional overtones and interaction between the counselee and himself. These cases also come from a variety of settings: the social-casework type of agency, college or university counseling service, Planned Parenthood center, educational institute, family counseling service, marriage counseling agency per se, as well as from the private practice of AAMC members. In this group of forty-one cases, twenty-five were seen in agency or university settings, and sixteen in private practice. In twenty-six instances the case histories were contributed by male, and in fifteen by women, counselors.

The first detailed outline was prepared by Drs. Karpf, Mudd, and Stone. The first draft of Chapter 1 was prepared by Dr. Nelson. Dr. Karpf prepared the first draft of Chapter 2, Drs. Mudd and Stone the first draft of Chapters 15 and 16. As the burden of the technical work involved in the collection and editing of cases increased, Dr. Nelson was appointed editorial assistant to the Committee, a position made possible through funds made available by the Association. She, therefore, initially edited and ordered the cases and prepared the comments on Part II, Sections 1, 2, and 3 for consideration by the Committee. However, the whole manuscript in literal detail, including introductory notes and comments, is the product and responsibility of the entire Committee. The completed manuscript was reviewed in 1957 by the president of the Association, Mr. Lester Dearborn, the secretary, Dr. Robert Harper, and the legal counsel, Mrs. Harriet Pilpel. These officers reported to the Executive Committee of the Association on September 20, 1957, their approval of publishing the manuscript, and the Executive Committee empowered the Casebook Committee to proceed, listing the chairman and the committee members as editors.

The Committee recognizes and hereby acknowledges with sincere appreciation the co-operation of the entire membership. It is especially grateful to the following members whose cases make up Part II. A large majority of the membership voted to thus list the names of the contributors in the Foreword rather than to present the cases signed by the individual counselor. This procedure allowed for greater freedom for the counselor in presenting his or her material and protects more adequately the anonymity of the clients. In all cases, identifying items of name, location, age, and the like have been carefully disguised.

Cases are presented by the following AAMC members:

*Barrabee, Paul S., Ph.D.
Blood, Robert O., Jr., Ph.D.
Bridgman, Ralph P., B.D., M.A.
Burton, Genevieve, Ph.D.
Busching, Howard C., Ed.D.
Dearborn, Lester W., B.S.
Eckert, Ralph G., Ph.D.
Ehrlich, Gerald, Ph.D.
Ehrmann, Winston
  Wallace, Ph.D.
Ellis, Albert, Ph.D.
Froscher, Hazel Bazett, M.A.
Gottlieb, Bernardt S., M.D.
Gottlieb, Sophie B., M.A.
Grant, Henry M.
Harper, Robert A., Ph.D.
Hill, Reuben, Ph.D.
Jackson, Hazel C.
Karpf, Maurice J., Ph.D.
Kassan, Martin, M.A.

Kerckhoff, Richard K., Ph.D.
Klein, Margery S., M.S.W.
Marion, Beatrice C., M.A.
Marsh, Earle Millard, M.D.
Moorhead, Muriel, M.S.W.
Morgan, Mildred I., Ph.D.
Mudd, Emily H., Ph.D.
Nash, Ethel Miller, M.A.
Pyner, Rita R., M.A.
Schiller, Patricia, LL.B.
Shields, Frances E., M.D.
Skidmore, Rex A., Ph.D.
Spencer, Douglas, Ph.D.
Stern, Alfred, M.D.
Stokes, Walter R., M.D.
Stone, Anthony R., M.S.S.W.
Tingue, Arthur M., S.T.M.
Turner, F. Bernadette, Ph.D.
Woodward, Luther E., Ph.D.

CASEBOOK COMMITTEE:

Emily H. Mudd, Ph.D., Chmn.
Maurice J. Karpf, Ph.D.
  * Deceased.

Abraham Stone, M.D.
Janet Fowler Nelson, Ph.D.

Contents

PART ONE

MARRIAGE COUNSELING AND THE CONTEMPORARY SCENE

1. Marriage in the United States Today

This casebook, although it presents a wide variety of problems in the whole area of marital and premarital adjustment, is nevertheless basically concerned with the counseling process, as described by one or another marriage counselor. Just as the membership of AAMC is interdisciplinary in composition, so, logically, must the point of view of this book be eclectic in character. It is hoped that readers will be stimulated to re-examine their own techniques by careful consideration of the wide variety of problems, processes, and results presented.

Needs of marriage and family living have to be considered in relation to the times in which they are observed. They are determined by cultural attitudes as well as by world events. They often reflect the conflict between former established family patterns geared to an earlier economy and the needs of today's rapidly changing social scene. The transition from an established, to a new and as yet untried, value system constitutes one of the most important challenges that marriage faces today.

In this century, revolutionary discoveries and global interaction have had a terrific impact on our lives. The social aspects of the business cycle, which used to concern us so much, seem almost trivial when compared to two world wars, the cold war, the draft, and prodigious advances in science and technology. Modern technology has invaded not only the factory but also the home, and many skills required of husbands and wives are quite different from those learned in their parental homes. Furthermore, the division of labor between men and women is no longer so clearly marked. It is much more blurred, workwise and homewise.

Urbanization in all its forms has been another important factor in changing family life. Tremendous progress in communication and transportation has taken place. This has had its impact not only at the level of world diplomacy but in terms of a teen-ager's "date." We have become an urban-industrial people, the majority living in cities, many of us in small apartments. We are highly mobile. Our families are smaller—not only in terms of fewer children but, although there are proportionately more oldsters, there are fewer grandparents living with us.

It would be comforting to think of marriage as a haven to which one could retreat from the strain and conflict of daily living. But contemporary marriage is not a thing apart. It is a way of life within which we must cope with the uncertainties and complexities of the Atomic Age.

Specifically, changes in age of marriage, size of completed family, and length of life have greatly affected patterns of family formation and have introduced complicated problems of personal as well as family development.

The average young man in the United States in 1950 entered marriage for the first time at about the age of 23 years, and his wife at about the age of 20. Both the groom and the bride in 1950 were more than a year younger, on the average, than those who entered their first marriage the previous decade. This decline stands in contrast to the fact that during the entire 50-year period from 1890 to 1940, the average (median) age at first marriage for grooms had declined only about two years, and that for brides only about one-half year according to the best available estimates.[1] This shift to earlier marriage is dra-

[1] Paul C. Glick, "The Life Cycle of the Family," *Journal of Marriage and Family Living* (hereinafter designated as *Marriage and Family Living*), Vol. XVII, Feb., 1955, No. 1, pp. 3-9.

matically highlighted if we consider the statistical extreme. In 1951, 2.1% of all men under 20 were married, whereas in 1940, only 1.4%. The corresponding figures for women are 13.7% (1951) as compared to 9.8% (1940). This is a sharp rise in only eleven years. It would not have to be carried far into the future to have 5% of the men and 20% of the women, under twenty, married.[2] Absolute age is important here, but of equal significance is the decline in the age gap between median age of husbands and wives in the last fifty years—2.8 years in 1948 in contrast to an estimated 5 years in 1890.

We have also moved from a large- to a small-family system. The average number of children born per married woman in the United States was about 2.35 in 1952 as contrasted with 5.4 in 1890. The statisticians tell us that this is all part of the over-all picture of the 150-year decline in the average size of the completed family. There are important fluctuations and variations to be noted, however. For instance, there was a marked increase in the birth rate during the first years of World War II which tapered down in 1943–44, rose again to an all-time high following demobilization, and then again began to taper off. However, the birth rate has reached successively higher levels for each year from 1950 to 1955. And in 1955, it was one-seventh above the immediate postwar peak recorded in 1947.[3] There is some evidence too that a healthy selective factor is operating. The Planned Parenthood Federation of America reports that it is in the families of six children or more that the decrease obtains and that an actual increase is observable in the middle-class groups. It has been suggested by reliable authorities that during the next decade or two the average num-

[2] See Lester A. Kirkendall, *Early Marriages—How Shall They Be Regarded,* Public Affairs Pamphlet No. 236, 1956 (22 East 38 Street, New York, N. Y.) Note also the following facts:
The Metropolitan Life Insurance Company estimates that in 1955, 3.3 per cent of males under 20, and 16.7 per cent of females under 20, were married. *Statistical Bulletin,* Vol. 37, May, 1956.
[3] Metropolitan Life Insurance Company, "The Birth Rate: Recent Trends and Outlook," *Statistical Bulletin,* Vol. 37, Oct., 1956.

ber of children per completed family is likely to rise moderately and the proportion of women who remain childless throughout their reproductive years is certain to decline. This is due largely to the wider acceptance of the concept of planned parenthood as well as advances in the care and treatment of the infertile couple.

There has also been an increase in life expectancy, a remarkable achievement of the medical and related sciences. The marriage of persons who today marry in their twenties is statistically capable of lasting forty-one years. Two generations ago, because of later marriage, more children and earlier death, there was a fifty-fifty chance that one spouse would die at least two years before the last of five children married. Today when one's two or three children leave home for college, career, or marriage, one-third of one's married life (fourteen years on the average) is still ahead.[4]

Paralleling this marked difference in size and structure of the family, is the rapid emergence of women as persons—politically, socially, economically. In the United States, this dates from the feminist movement which reached its peak circa World War I, and the acceleration, and acceptance, of women's widespread employment in World War II. There are today more married than single women gainfully employed. In 1950, before the Korean War, almost one-fourth of all married women living with their husbands, earned some outside income.[5] In spite of these statistics, the marriage and/or career debate is still with us as a source of emotional conflict.

Sexually, too, women have come into their own. No longer is sex for women a taboo subject, or an experience to be only "dutifully" accepted. Today, women have begun to realize their capacity to enjoy sex and respond to it under circumstances of

[4] Paul C. Glick, "The Life Cycle of the Family," *op. cit.*
[5] Stella B. Applebaum, *Working Wives,* Public Affairs Pamphlet No. 188, 1955.

their own choice. The potential for enrichment of the marital relationship is great; but it is not without its problems in a society where there is still a considerable lag between conventional patterns of conduct and the newer and more flexible attitudes.

That the family is indeed less stable as a result of all these rapidly shifting social and economic forces is often "proved" by recourse to divorce statistics. What exactly is the situation?

By whatever method of computation we use—divorce in terms of total population, comparison of number of divorces to number of marriages in any given year, or the more realistic approach of examining divorce in relation to that segment of the population, which is exposed to the risk of divorce, that is, the married population—our divorce rate is high. There were 10.3 divorces per 1000 married females, fifteen years and over, in 1950, compared to 8.7 in 1940, 8.0 in 1920, and 4.0 in 1900.[6] However, within this picture of over-all increase, there is evidence of marked fluctuation. The divorce rate is sensitive to many social and economic factors. The depression low-point in 1932 was 6.1 (though this was still twice as high as it was in 1920.) It reached a peak following World War II, when in 1946 the divorce rate per 1000 married females over fifteen years of age, was 17.8. As of 1955, the divorce rate was not only not increasing but showed some signs of at least temporary decrease. However, it is still high. It has been variously estimated that between one-fourth and one-fifth of the marriages contracted since World War II will end in divorce.

It is also important to consider at what period in marriage divorce is most likely to occur. We have known for some time that the probabilities of divorce are greater in the early years of marriage. Marital stability would seem to be a function of time. With the possible exception of the middle years, when the

[6] Public Health Service, *Vital Statistics of the U.S.*, 1950, Washington 25, D.C.

children have left home, and marital adjustment may be further complicated by difficulties associated with the menopause, this has held true whether the divorce peak was reportedly at seven years of marriage, at five, or more recently, two. In 1950, the percentage of all divorces granted in the United States decreased by single years of married life until the nineteenth year, when it increased somewhat.[7] Furthermore, although the divorce rate has increased at all levels, it has been greatest at the earlier years of marriage. To absorb the full impact as Dr. Bossard indicates: ". . . such data must be considered cumulatively. That is to say, each year's total must be added to those of the preceding years if one is interested in the total number of persons involved Thus in the eight-year period 1946–1953 inclusive, a total of 3,442,000 divorces were reported as granted in the United States. Multiplied by two, this means that about seven million matrimonial mates passed through the experience of divorce during the eight-year period." [8]

Does all this carry only negative implications? Certainly it does reflect the difficulties of maintaining the *status quo* in family life during the process of rapid social and economic change. Perhaps it is also in part due to a gradual change in our divorce laws. The laws on divorce have become more liberal—with serious discrepancies existing from state to state—to the extent that they permit divorce on grounds that imply no real guilt; yet, increase in the divorce rate has been much more rapid than the change in the divorce laws.

Also there is today greater acceptance of the possibility of divorce, and with the acceptance of this possibility divorce has lost some of the feelings of failure and guilt that formerly obtained. This has been repeatedly noted by our social scientists. One of the most recent studies, based on opinions of eighteen "experts" (students of the family) reports the increasing divorce

[7] *Ibid.,* 1953, p. 30.
[8] James H. S. Bossard, "Divorce: Some Selected Repercussions," Ch. 9 in *Man and Wife,* ed. by Emily H. Mudd, Ph.D., and Aron Krich, Ed.D. (New York: W. W. Norton & Company, Inc., 1957).

rate and changing attitudes toward divorce first in a list of significant change in the American family.[9]

May not this higher divorce rate also reflect a new emphasis, a new value, that we place on marriage? It is no longer in any accepted sense an "endurance race." Our demands for personal satisfaction, for a *good* marriage, are greater. Even from the point of view of the children, who always pay the highest price for marital failure, we are beginning to realize that the way a divorce is arrived at can do much to modify the hurt—that is to say, insightful acceptance of individual responsibility for the adult failure, consideration and love for the children as persons and not just unhappy pawns in their parents' conflicts. Moreover, we are beginning to suspect that a marriage that is doggedly maintained "for the sake of the children" may create severe psychological problems, not only for the parents but, through them, for the children. It has been said that children may be better off as orphans of divorce than as members of a family always at war with each other. This in no way denies the trauma of divorce and the inevitable conflicts and negative repercussion for all concerned. It calls attention to the fact that the trauma can be less intense and the scars less lasting.

Social research is also concerning itself with the whole problem of remarriage. This is an important consideration, for a recent census survey reveals that about 75 per cent of those who got divorces between 1943 and 1948 were already married again (in 1948). Of those divorced between 1934 and 1943, approximately 86 per cent had remarried by 1948.[10]

Not so much is known about the success of these remarriages. There is some evidence to show that second marriages are somewhat more likely to end in divorce than first marriages. And an unresolved neurotic pattern, carried over from one marriage to another, bodes little good to the second venture. On the

[9] W. F. Ogburn and M. F. Nimkoff, *Technology and the Changing Family* (Boston: Houghton Mifflin Company, 1955), Ch. I.

[10] Paul C. Glick, "First Marriages and Remarriages," *American Sociological Review,* 14:730, Dec., 1949.

other hand, a recently published study emphasized that second marriages can be good; some indeed are highly successful.[11]

None of this is to say that divorce is "good." But the modern emphasis is not necessarily to preserve the (legal) family at all costs, but to promote the adequacy and satisfactions of family members in and through the marriage. To the extent we value the voluntary aspects of modern marriage, recognize the basic importance of deep respect for the needs and personality of each partner, accept the fact that marriage is a vital institution of society which is terminable if the values of constructive personal relations cannot be achieved, we shall do far more to raise the standards of marriage than by relying on negative controls. One does not preserve the values of marriage merely by preserving the form.

Marriage Counseling—an Aid to Strengthening Family Life

Marriage counseling is indeed an "expression of our times." More and more individuals and families who might perhaps be able to work out their adjustment to their environment in a less complex society, find the stresses and strains of modern-day living too intense, too complicated, and too demanding for them. They do not know how to use their potential inner strengths and resources to be able to cope adequately with the conflicting and competitive demands for their attention and energies. Nor do they have the knowledge and experience needed for an objective analysis of the disturbing elements, an evaluation of the destructive and constructive factors at work, and a marshaling of the positive forces for solving the problem or problems which face them. The individuals involved feel a deep need, therefore, to seek the aid of professionally skilled outsiders, uninvolved and more "objective" persons for help in their difficulties.

To be sure, marriage counseling has been carried on through the ages, by families and friends, doctors, ministers, teachers—

[11] William J. Goode, *After Divorce* (Glencoe, Ill.: The Free Press, 1956), Ch. XXII.

informally, semiformally, and more recently formally. Yet in one sense it is new—new in the sense of a developing awareness of its own special area within the whole field of education for marriage and family living. It is new in its insistent emphasis on high professional standards of training, experience, and performance. At this stage of its development it is not a new profession per se, in any technical, academic sense. But it is an emerging area of specialized skill in many professions. And because it is interdisciplinary in character, it offers optimal advantages for research and new learnings in the various fields of medicine, psychiatry, psychology and social work as aids in resolving complex problems of personal relationships.[12]

In this country, the formalization of marriage counseling has developed concurrently with the growth of courses in education for marriage and family living in schools, colleges, and universities. Collaterally, family conferences and councils organized for the general dissemination and exchange of ideas, information, and techniques in the different fields of specialization related to marriage and family living almost universally include special committees or sections devoted to marriage counseling.

Specifically, marriage counseling has developed along a number of lines: as a by-product of the daily practice of professionally trained individuals—doctors, ministers, social workers, psychologists, and so on; as a development of already established community services, notably the family-service type agencies, child study and parent education groups, Planned Parenthood centers, social hygiene programs, university counseling services; as a service specifically focused on marriage counseling; and more recently full- or part-time private practice of professionally trained persons in a variety of disciplines, who specialize in marriage counseling. Marriage counseling is becoming more clearly

[12] Emily H. Mudd, Ph.D., "Knowns and Unknowns in Marriage Counseling Research," *Marriage and Family Living*, Vol. XIX, No. 1, Feb., 1957.

defined through examination of the processes involved, and its potentials are becoming more generally recognized.

From the point of view of agencies and organizations, a recent survey of existing services undertaken by the American Association of Marriage Counselors seemed to point to a tendency to what might be termed specialization within specialization.

This tendency to recognize marriage counseling as distinct from other inclusive types of family counseling or family casework services is important to note. (The very process a person goes through in identifying the problem and seeking specialized help is often a first step toward resolution of the problem. Agency structure may thus become a dynamic factor in marriage counseling.) This is perhaps one important factor in the development of marriage councils, unattached to other existing organizations, but supported by a variety of persons, clients, and community organizations and serving as a resource to a total community.

Development of specialized in-service training in marriage counseling, on the postgraduate level is also progressing—all part of the increased emphasis on higher professional standards. There is wide variation in the selection of candidates for training, in procedures, in scope of training programs and in opportunity for academic credit. But again, the fact that there is no stereotype is undoubtedly healthy at this stage of development, predicated of course on the assumption that there is a deep commitment to the proposition that wherever and by whomever marriage counseling is practiced, it should be done under the highest possible standards of professional and personal ability and integrity.[13]

[13] Suggested references for this chapter:
Emily Hartshorne Mudd, Ph.D., *The Practice of Marriage Counseling* (New York: Association Press, 1951), Chs. 1 and 2.
Janet Fowler Nelson, Ph.D., "Current Trends in Marriage Counseling," *Journal of Home Economics,* Vol. 44, No. 4, April, 1952, pp. 253-256.
Abraham Stone, M.D., "Marriage Counseling Today and Tomorrow," *Marriage and Family Living,* Spring, 1940, pp. 39-40.

2. Principles, Processes, and Techniques of Marriage Counseling

Counseling is a generic term and much of what will be said here about marriage counseling will apply in equal measure to other forms of counseling. All counseling aims, at least theoretically, at developing insight into the nature of the problem and the causes or factors which produced it; and endeavors to give the counselee support, encouragement, reassurance, and new perspectives so that he may look upon himself as but one of many who face or have faced similar problems which can be solved under favorable circumstances. To some extent also all types of counseling use similar means to achieve their ends even though they may be quite different in their fundamental and basic theoretical approaches. At one time or another every counselor is called upon to give advice, information, and guidance. Some will use these devices only as a last resort. Others will utilize these methods more freely because they feel that the counselee wants, needs, and is entitled to more direct and immediate help. They believe, moreover, that unless the counselee does get such help he will become discouraged and will discontinue the counseling. The damage to the counselee from discontinuance when he needs counseling, they feel, is bound to be much more injurious than giving such direct help.[1]

[1] See Frederick C. Thorne, Ch. IV in *Six Approaches to Psychotherapy,* ed. by James S. McCarey (New York: Dryden Press, 1955); and also—
Carl R. Rogers, *Counseling and Psychotherapy* (Boston: Houghton Mifflin Company, 1942), pp. 19-28.

Psychotherapy and Counseling

Counseling, in this sense, is also closely related to psychotherapy. Psychotherapy may be considered the more generally inclusive in terms of personality reorganization; marriage counseling, the more specific procedure in its focus on the interpersonal relations between men and women concerned in the marriage. We shall approach the more specialized interest of this chapter— marriage counseling—through a brief discussion of the more general aspects of psychotherapy and counseling.

There are as many conceptions and definitions of psychotherapy as there are schools—one might almost say, individual psychotherapists.[2] A recent and "comprehensive" definition of psychotherapy has it as "a form of treatment for problems of an emotional nature in which a trained person deliberately establishes a professional relationship with a patient with the object of removing, modifying, or retarding existing symptoms, of mediating disturbed patterns of behavior, and of promoting positive personality growth and development."[3] According to Wolberg, there are three major types of psychotherapy: supportive psychotherapy, insight therapy with re-educative goals, insight therapy with reconstructive goals.[4]

Regardless of what one may think of the suitability and applicability of the varying methods and techniques of therapists from different schools of thought to their goals and objectives, several things become clear. First, that the different types of psychotherapy are not necessarily mutually exclusive as to either goals or methods; second, that whereas the goals and objectives are relatively few, the theoretical framework, the methods, techniques, and procedures are many and in some instances substantially different from each other; and third, that in a field where

[2] Albert Ellis, "New Approaches to Psychotherapy Techniques," *Journal of Clinical Psychology,* Monograph Supplement, July, 1955.

[3] Louis R. Wolberg, M.D., *The Techniques of Psychotherapy* (New York: Grune and Stratton, 1954).

[4] *Ibid.,* p. 8.

there are such wide divergencies of practice there is room for, and in fact bound to develop, a wide variety of schools of thought aiming at the crystallization and formulation of philosophies. These schools of thought will furnish a so-called theoretical basis for practice and will confer upon the practitioner the sanction of authoritativeness because of belonging or adhering to the particular school or system.

Some thoughtful therapists are both puzzled and challenged by the divergent or diametrically different schools and theories of human behavior and motivation underlying psychotherapy, especially when all the schools claim success in treating maladjustment. They can only conclude that none of the schools has the whole truth and that the dynamic elements responsible for the success claimed by all the schools may be the features common to all of them. Hence they proceed to select out what appear to them to be those elements which are common to all psychotherapeutic situations.[5] In spite of criticism, eclecticism is not without merit or justification.

Two of these elements seem to be of special importance to marriage counseling and deserve discussion at this point. They are the "relationship" between the counselor and counselee, and the counselor's concept of "personality."

Importance of "Relationship" in Counseling

The relationship between counselor and client, or therapist and patient, is coming to be recognized in this country as central in the counseling or therapeutic process. Different schools or systems of therapy and counseling may evaluate it differently, but all recognize its importance and some deem it basic in the results obtained.[6]

[5] Eugene Ziskind, M.D., *Psychophysiologic Medicine* (Philadelphia: Lea and Febiger, 1954), pp. 282-288.

[6] See the following four references:

Fay B. Karpf, *The Psychology and Psychotherapy of Otto Rank* (New York: Philosophical Library, 1953).

Carl Rogers, *Counseling and Psychotherapy* (Boston: Houghton Mif-

The relationship between counselor and client should not be confused with such concepts as transference or rapport. Thus the term "transference," as used in Freudian technique, refers to displacement of the libido from its infantile love-objects (usually one's parents) to the psychoanalyst in the course of psychoanalytic treatment. This redirection of desires and feelings which are usually retained in the unconscious, may be positive, if they are warm, friendly, and affectionate, or negative if they are unfriendly or hostile.

"Rapport" is a more general term referring to the positive, co-operative association of two persons which makes possible a confidential, sympathetic, understanding, and helpful process in counseling and therapy. "Relationship" as used here refers to the interaction between counselor and counselee which becomes a motivating force in the changes and growth which take place in the counseling procedure. In marriage counseling there is a multidimensional "relationship," that is, the relationship of the counselor to the marriage partners, individually and collectively, and, where necessary, to the children and the family as a "unity of interacting personalities," as well as to the new and developing relationship between the spouses to each other and to the family as a whole. The counselor needs to keep this many-faceted relationship constantly in mind in order to stimulate its development to its fullest potentialities and to utilize it for the growth of the personalities involved.[7]

Personality an Important Concept for the Counselor

The counselor's concept of personality is no less important. The term "personality" and its meaning have been the subject of

flin Company, 1942); and his *Client-Centered Therapy* (Houghton Mifflin, 1951).

Anita Faatz, *The Nature of Choice in Casework Process* (Chapel Hill, N.C.: University of North Carolina Press, 1953).

[7] See: Hilda M. Goodwin, Ph.D., "An Inquiry into the Nature and Use of the Tridimensional Relationship in the Process of Marriage Counseling," Doctoral Dissertation, School of Social Work, University of Pennsylvania, June, 1957.

intense controversy in the socio-psychological literature in the last three decades. It would take us too far afield to sketch even briefly the main considerations and directions of this theoretical ferment.[8] But we cannot fail to indicate here that the counselor's view of personality is of the utmost importance in determining his approach to his client as well as the type of therapy he will utilize. If he looks upon personality as essentially static, biologically fixed and determined by early conditioning, as unchanging and unyielding, he will necessarily be limited in his expectations and goals; and he will assume, consciously or unconsciously, an attitude which will restrict him as well as his client in the solution of the problem under consideration. If, however, the counselor views personality as an unfolding, evolving, ever-growing, and developing expression of almost limitless potentialities and inner strengths which only need assistance to achieve fruition, he himself, as well as his client, will envision broad goals and will marshal the inner resources of the client toward their realization.[9]

This view of personality is, by and large, familiar to counselors and more particularly marriage counselors, coming as they do from the fields of education, social and clinical psychology, social case work, the ministry, and psychiatry. In addition, certain new concepts of personality as nonstatic and dependent upon the frame of reference of the person judging it, have been substantiated by actual research on material collected during marriage counseling with spouses. These findings indicate that the impressions which husband and wife have of each other's personality characteristics, vary as the spouse is influenced by

[8] Cf. Gardner Murphy, *Historical Introduction to Modern Psychology* (New York: Harcourt, Brace and Company, Inc., 1951), pp. 419-430. Also—

Fay B. Karpf, "American Social Psychology—1951," *American Journal of Sociology,* Vol. LVIII, No. 2, Sept., 1952, pp. 187-193, especially pp. 188-189.

[9] Cf. Maurice J. Karpf, *The Scientific Basis of Social Work* (New York: Columbia University Press, 1931), pp. 89-91 and 419.

Gordon W. Allport, "The Trend in Motivational Theory," *American Journal of Orthopsychiatry,* XXIII, 107-119, Jan., 1953.

feelings of love and accord (oneness) or of dislike, discord, or separateness. In other words, partners who feel love for each other tend to see each other's personality characteristics as more similar to their own than partners who are in conflict or feel strong dislike for each other. This holds for couples even though the husband's impressions of himself may not resemble the wife's impressions of herself. In fact, this holds when there are considerable differences in how each partner sees himself. Implications of these findings in terms of concepts of reality and projection are obvious. They have an important bearing on the question of the advisability, and even urgency, of working with both partners in a marriage in order to understand the actual relationship between husband and wife.[10] In the viewpoint of the Committee who prepared this manuscript, dynamic concepts of personality have important creative possibilities for the counselor and make counseling an art replete with potentialities for constructive stimulation and guidance.

Types of Counseling Procedures

As in psychotherapy, there are different schools and types of counseling, and the type used depends upon the orientation of the counselor and the institutions with which he is connected. For our purpose it will suffice to mention briefly only two well-known schools: directive counseling and nondirective counseling, representing the two extremes. Most counseling falls somewhere in between these two extremes. The thoughtful reader of the cases in this volume will have little difficulty in identifying these types as represented by the case material, although it should be borne in mind that very few counselors, except those who are devotees and dedicates, adhere strictly without deviation to either approach.

[10] M. Preston, E. H. Mudd, W. L. Peltz, and H. B. Froscher, "Impressions of Personality as a Function of Marital Conflict," *Journal of Abnormal and Social Psychology,* 47, 326-336, 1952; and—
Nathan W. Ackerman, "The Diagnosis of Neurotic Interaction," *Social Casework,* XXXV, April, 1954, 139-147.

Few counselors will classify themselves as consistently "directive." Those who disagree with this form of counseling claim that it is authoritarian, that its results, although quick, are often transitory, that it does not seem to build up the counselee's inner strength and resources, that it may call forth the resentment, opposition, and hostility of the client. Some also feel that although directive counseling may occasionally be justified in cases of emergency to gain time or to give specific information, it should be resorted to only under circumstances demanding such procedure.

Similarly, comparatively few counselors will identify themselves as entirely "nondirective." This approach, mainly associated with Carl Rogers, actually had its origin in psychoanalysis, Rankian psychology, passivity, and so on. Rogers now prefers to call his procedure "client-centered" counseling or therapy, having more or less abandoned the earlier designation of "nondirective" as inadequate for describing his processes and aims. This does not mean that he rejects the "nondirective" approach. It means, rather, that as he sees it, directive counseling is interested in problem solving, problems of the client, to be sure, but as discovered, defined, diagnosed, and prescribed for by the counselor with the client having little or no initiative or part beyond coming to the counselor. The counselor directs all activity, and the counselee is the passive recipient of the benefits of the counselor's wisdom and experience.

In "nondirective" counseling, the client becomes the active agent; it is he who endeavors to discover, define, and diagnose the problem and who even prescribes the solution. The counselor serves as a catalyst, occasionally reinterprets what the counselee brings forth, and enables him to draw upon his own resources for the solution of his problem.

Client-centered or "nondirective" counseling also has its critics. They recognize its value because it avoids the weaknesses and dangers of the directive procedure. They admit that it tends to utilize the inner resources of the client and provides more ready acceptance of the client on a nonjudgmental basis than the directive approach. However, they maintain that "nondirective" counseling has the weaknesses of its strengths; for example, that to depend solely upon the inner resources of the counselee is to waste a great deal of time, and that the client usually has neither the time nor the finances nor the patience required in this procedure.

As in psychotherapy, so also in counseling, there are those who would call themselves eclectics; and, as in psychotherapy, unless such eclecticism is based on comprehensive knowledge and discriminating choice, it may be little more than a patchwork of expedients and opportunism. However, when it is based on knowledge, discipline, training, and requisite skill, as well as experience, it can be a broad, flexible, and constructive approach to counseling.

Marriage Counseling Differentiated

We have thus far treated counseling and marriage counseling as closely related to psychotherapy. Indeed, there are those who hold that counseling in general, and marriage counseling in particular, is a type of psychotherapy, or at least short-term, conscious, face-to-face psychotherapy.[11] Others seek to differentiate the one from the other.[12] Recently, the New York Academy of Sciences, recognizing the urgent need for clarification of the fields of psychotherapy and counseling, established five Commissions—in Medicine, Psychology, Social Work, Guidance and Counseling, and the Ministry—to explore the subject. The

[11] Earle M. Marsh, M.D., said in a paper before the Marriage Counseling Section of The National Council on Family Relations, July, 1954, at Mills College: "Psychotherapy and marriage counseling, to me, are one and the same. Psychotherapy attempts total personality reorganization; marriage counseling only partial personality reorganization, i.e., enough to make either divorce or continuation of a marriage easier." In *Marriage and Family Living,* Vol. XIV, Feb., 1952, pp. 66-67. See also—
Robert W. Laidlaw, M.D., *Marriage and Family Living,* Vol. XIV, Feb., 1952, pp. 66-67.
[12] Emily H. Mudd, Ph.D., "Psychiatry and Marital Problems," *Eugenics Quarterly,* Vol. 2, No. 2, June, 1955, pp. 110-117.

following statement offered by the Commission in Guidance and Counseling is pertinent here:

> . . . we can express the difference in emphasis then, by saying that counseling looks more often toward the interpretation and development of the personality in the relations characteristic of specific role-problems while psychotherapy looks more often toward the reinterpretation and reorganization of malignant conflictual elements within the personality through the relation with the therapist.[13]

It may also be pointed out that unlike psychiatrists, psychoanalysts, and some clinical psychologists, the marriage counselor deals more often with so-called normal, average people, who, on the whole, manage their affairs quite adequately but occasionally find themselves confronted by a set of circumstances or a constellation of problems which are too much for them, either because of their own emotional involvement, or because they do not possess the necessary information or perspective to handle the situation, or both.

This view of marriage counseling problems leads to several rather important considerations. First, that the marriage counselor who is not a psychiatrist and who has no special training, though holding himself alert to evidence of abnormalities and of hidden motivations, need not always, in fact is not necessarily equipped to, probe too deeply, and should not indulge in extended analyses or attempt fundamental personality changes. In many situations requiring his professional services, he can safely deal with the problems as they present themselves on a reality or conscious level after making certain that he is not dealing with a displacement; that is, that the client is not withholding the real problem from him by substituting a different problem, perhaps one of lesser significance and importance. Second, that the marriage counselor must make certain, so far

[13] William G. Perry, Jr., "On the Relation of Psychotherapy and Counseling," *Annals of the New York Academy of Sciences,* Vol. 63, Art. 3, Nov. 7, 1955, pp. 319-432.

as possible, that he is not dealing with a deep-seated psychotic or neurotic behavior manifestation with which it is beyond his ability to cope. This implies that the marriage counselor should be sufficiently well trained to recognize a neurosis or psychosis when he is confronted with it. This is admittedly not always easy or certain, for there are situations which will puzzle or escape even the better-trained psychotherapist who is not especially versed or experienced in differential diagnosis. It means also that although the nonmedical marriage counselor need not be prepared to handle the deep-seated neuroses or psychoses, he should be prepared to interpret psychiatric service to his client and, where needed, to spend sufficient time to lay the groundwork for a constructive psychiatric referral. In addition, in cases where it becomes evident that the marriage produces, in Karen Horney's term, a real "enslavement for one or both partners," the counselor may have to aid the family members to as nondestructive as possible a severing of their relationship, and to a positive attitude toward the future.

The wise marriage counselor, will, of course, call a competent psychiatrist into consultation whenever it is possible if he is uncertain about the nature of the problem with which he is dealing. Similarly, the conscientious marriage counselor will take proper precautions that he does not overlook or ignore somatic factors and will refer to the medical profession whenever the situation seems to require it.

It follows that the marriage counselor can best make his important contribution by equipping himself to function not as a pseudo-psychiatrist or analyst, but as one who has made a special study of the problems and interpersonal relationships of family life: the bonds, loyalties, and conflicts; the loves, rivalries, and hostilities; the need for identification and independence, on the one hand, and the conflicting desire for independence, on the other; the wish for security and the urge for adventure; in brief, the stresses and strains involved in membership in a marriage and a family and the psychosocial factors and influences of such membership on the personality.

By way of summarizing our discussion of the differentiation of marriage counseling up to this point, it may be said that the marriage counselor should have, in addition to the necessary knowledge and understanding of the positive and negative influences on the family, special training to be able to differentiate normal from abnormal or deviant behavior mechanisms and to understand the dynamics of human motivation as manifested in the interpersonal relationships in the marriage. This requires as a minimum about the same type of psychiatric knowledge as is included in a standard curriculum for a master's degree in social work. Such knowledge, however, will no more equip the marriage counselor for involved psychiatric analyses and therapy than it does the social worker except where there has been additional and special training. And, like the social worker, the marriage counselor can handle most situations on a conscious level, being ever watchful for indications of more profound disturbances and calling upon the appropriate specialist when necessary.

The foregoing comparison of marriage counseling with social work in terms of the type and amount of psychological and psychiatric knowledge required as a minimum for marriage counseling and the level on which they can function, raises further questions about the other professions engaging in marriage counseling. This is especially true of the professions of medicine, psychology, the ministry, and social work. Some members of these professions carry their marriage counseling load as part of their daily work within their own professional activity. Others, apparently a relatively small minority of the members of these professions, recognize that marriage counseling requires specialized knowledge and skill and therefore believe that marriage counseling can be most effective and will make its best contribution to those who need what it has to offer by developing a new and distinct professional discipline. (There is a relatively large group of people doing marriage counseling without any kind of training for the work who are not members of any professional group. These people would, in all probability, deny any need for specialized training. However, since they are not members of any recognized profession we cannot be concerned with them here.)

A recent survey by Kerckhoff outlines the views of some of these professional groups.[14] Rutledge and Bridgman, in independent studies, present the viewpoint for marriage counseling as a distinct professional discipline.[15] These divergent points of view are being subjected to thoughtful examination and evaluation by committees of the American Association of Marriage Counselors and by individual members of the Association.[16] The issue as to whether marriage counseling is or will become a separate professional entity or will remain a specialized aspect of various disciplines is not yet resolved and may be confidently expected to come up again and again. Whatever the merits of the varying views and however the issues involved may be determined, adequate preparation for marriage counseling, regardless of by whom it is done, is an obvious necessity.

As the case material in Chapters 3, 4, and 5 will demonstrate, marriage counseling consists of three major divisions: (1) premarital counseling, in preparation for marriage; (2) marital counseling on problems and difficulties arising within the interpersonal relations of marriage; and (3) counseling with the unmarried, the divorced, and single persons who as yet are un-

[14] Richard E. Kerckhoff, "Interest Group Reactions to the Profession of Marriage Counseling," *Sociology and Social Research,* Jan.-Feb., 1955.

[15] Aaron L. Rutledge, "The Future of Marriage Counseling," Preprint of *Merrill-Palmer Quarterly,* Summer, 1955. Also—

Ralph Bridgman, "Marriage Counseling as an Emergent Professional Function," Preprint of *The American Family, Its Strengths and Problems,* Ch. X; scheduled for publication, 1956.

[16] Robert A. Harper, "Should Marriage Counseling Become a Full-Fledged Specialty?", *Marriage and Family Living,* XV, Nov., 1953, 338-340.

married. Counseling of any one of these types may be carried out individually or in groups.

Some Important Aims and Steps in the Counseling Process

Given the necessary preparation on the part of the counselor which will enable him to differentiate between normal and abnormal behavior in terms of the client's cultural background, there emerges a set of procedures in the counseling process which serve as basic steps. Although these may be considered elementary by the experienced counselor, they are mentioned here for those readers who are not yet sophisticated in counseling, and who hope to prepare themselves to understand marriage counseling. In addition, for beginning professional workers and for those more experienced who wish to take stock of their work, the following aims and procedures may serve as helpful guides to marriage counseling. It should be emphasized, however, that although these steps are used with each partner in the marriage, in marriage counseling the focus of the counseling is on the interpersonal relationship between the marital partners.

1. Establishment of Rapport: Webster's New International Dictionary defines rapport as "harmony, conformity, accord or affinity, intimate or harmonious relations." Establishment of rapport means, therefore, the development of a close understanding; the development of confidence on the part of the counselee in the counselor. The need for rapport is, of course, obvious if the counselee is to be willing to confide in the counselor and share with him the thoughts, problems, and experiences which have arisen in the marriage relation—the most intimate relationship known to men.

2. Reduction of Hostility: The counselee is frequently oppressed by the feeling of hostility to the person or persons or situation which he believes to be responsible for his problem. It is important for the counselor to provide the opportunity for and to encourage the fullest possible expression of this hostility because little constructive work can be done until the client frees himself from the weight of this load. This is sometimes referred to as ventilation of feeling or catharsis. This process can be begun by the counselor's making the client feel comfortable in verbally expressing his negative feelings toward his spouse or others involved, whether his feelings are based on fact or fantasy.

3. Development of Insight and Objectivity: The third aim in the counseling process is to develop insight and objectivity in the counselee. This is perhaps the most difficult goal to achieve because emotional disturbance, which is almost always present, hinders insight and objectivity. It certainly cannot be accomplished without good rapport between counselor and counselee. Hence it must follow after or at times be developed simultaneously with the establishment of rapport.

4. Reorientation: Once insight and objectivity are obtained, it is not difficult to lead the counselee to a reorientation toward his problem or problems and the situation. This may mean the development of a new or different relationship to the person or persons involved; or it may mean the avoidance or a more courageous facing or transcending of conflictual situations, as the case may require; or it may necessitate changing his role or behavior; or it may require reorganizing existing relationships. In a sense this means aiding the counselee in re-educating himself so that he may be equal to the new conditions of life which he will have to face, and the requirements they will make on his resources.

5. Development of New Objectives and Perspective: As a result of the reorientation, new goals will have to be envisaged in terms of the new relationship to be established. These must be related to the counselee's needs, his abilities, and his resources, both personal and environmental; to those of his spouse and to the marriage itself. Here it may be well to call attention again to the problem-solving capacity of the individual if properly stimulated by a good relationship with the counselor and a modified relationship to the marriage partner.

6. Implementation: The new objectives and relationship will require ways and means of achieving them. These, in turn, will necessitate carefully considered plans which will be based on all the foregoing considerations. It may be well to emphasize that the planning should be done by the client instead of the counselor. The client should experience the thrill of making and executing these first plans and discuss the results with the counselor as a means of gaining self-confidence in his newly acquired strengths and awareness of inner resources.

The foregoing six elements in the counseling process are not independent of each other. They are, in fact, interdependent in time and psychological development and they may be worked on, to a greater or lesser degree, depending upon the situation, almost from the first interview.[17]

Some Suggested Principles and Guides for Marriage Counseling

At this point it seems desirable, even if repetitious to the seasoned practitioner, to consider some of the important principles, techniques, and processes of marriage counseling. In such a young field of specialization there is little likelihood that any set of guides could meet with general acceptance. The American Association of Marriage Counselors has as yet made no attempt to formulate guides for practitioners. However, various members of the Association have from time to time presented their philosophy and methods of marriage counseling.[18] David Mace is

[17] Cf. Louis R. Wolberg, M.D., *The New Technique of Psychotherapy*, p. 3.

[18] See the following six references:

John F. Cuber, "Functions of the Marriage Counselor," *Marriage and Family Living*, VII, Winter, 1945, pp. 3-5.

the author of the first Public Affairs Pamphlet on this subject. In homely, simple words he explains clearly how marriage counseling is done:

> The methods of different counselors vary a good deal of course, but there are basic principles which most accept. One of these is that the counselor's job is not to tell John and Mary Smith what to do, but to help them to find their own solution to their problem. Only a solution that comes from them, out of their own thinking and feeling, is of any use. If the counselor dictated a policy to them, he would be taking over the job of running their lives, imposing his will upon theirs. This he must not do, because the work of the counselor is based upon his respect for the freedom of the individual to manage his own life in his own way, in so far as this is in accord with the welfare of others.
>
> The counselor therefore accepts John and Mary Smith as they are. He makes no attempt to put them under pressure to do what he thinks they ought. Whatever they say, and whatever they do, he continues to respect their individuality. He knows that if he fails to do this he has forfeited the power to help them.
>
> The aim of the counselor is to create an atmosphere in which John and Mary are free to talk of themselves, to bring out their hurt feelings, to unburden their disappointments. He may on occasion see them together, but usually he sees them separately, because if there is conflict between them they will feel freer and more relaxed out of one another's presence.

Dean Johnson, *The Understanding and Use of the Self in Counseling,* Bulletin of the Menninger Clinic, No. 17, 1953, pp. 29-35.

Albert Ellis, "Marriage Counseling with Couples Indicating Sexual Incompatibility," *Marriage and Family Living,* XV, Feb., 1953, pp. 53-59.

Robert G. Foster, "How a Marriage Counselor Handles a Case," *Marriage and Family Living,* XVI, May, 1954, pp. 139-143.

Robert W. Laidlaw, "The Management of Marital Problems in Private Practice." Paper presented at 13th Annual Meeting of the American Psychiatric Society, Chicago, 1957.

Emily Hartshorne Mudd, in *Man and Wife,* a Source Book on Family Attitudes, Sexual Behavior, and Marriage Counseling (New York: W. W. Norton and Company, 1957), Chs. 2 and 19.

Some marriage problems can be cleared up in one interview. But that is very unusual. As a rule a series of separate interviews will be necessary with each of the marriage partners. It takes time for John and Mary to gain complete confidence in the counselor; and it takes time for the counselor to get to know John and Mary well enough to give them all the help they need.[19]

Dr. Mace explains to the layman how marriage counseling works. Because of its obvious importance to the field, the Casebook Committee feels it worth while to stimulate further thoughtful consideration on a professional level of common concepts and experience in counseling. It is in this spirit that the following formulation is offered as background to the case material.[20] Eventually, after suitable study by appropriate committees of the National Association, a list of principles may be adopted and recommended as groundwork for professional orientation and practice in marriage counseling.

1. *Flexibility and an Open Mind Are Among the Essential Prerequisites for Marriage Counseling.*

The counselor should hold himself free from preconceptions as to the cause of the difficulty, should not jump to conclusions, should avoid hasty and unwarranted generalizations, and should scrupulously avoid preconceived and ready solutions. He must be prepared to follow the evidence wherever it will lead him.

2. *The Counselor Should Endeavor to Maintain Objectivity and Be Nonjudgmental and Nonmoralistic in His Attitude.*

Many persons doing marriage and family counseling, especially those who come to it with a definite religious perspective, find it extremely difficult to maintain unbiased and open-

[19] David R. Mace, *What Is Marriage Counseling?*, Public Affairs Pamphlet No. 250 (New York: Public Affairs Committee, Inc., 1957). Used by permission of the author.
[20] Maurice J. Karpf, "Some Guiding Principles in Marriage Counseling," *Marriage and Family Living*, May, 1951, pp. 49-52.

minded attitudes. The problem of right and wrong is almost always present in such counseling, and the counselor is hard put to it to avoid rendering value judgments and taking sides, particularly where extramarital sex relations are involved or where other ethical and religious values enter into the conflict between husband and wife. Nevertheless, the counselor should eschew such judgments and hold himself free from prejudice, if he desires to win and hold the confidence of his clients and to be of help to them. The counselor should be careful, however, not to give the impression to his counselee that he, the counselor, is lacking in such values for himself. He should be aware of his own cultural and emotional biases and the emotional blocks they may produce.

3. *The Problem First Presented by the Counselee Is Frequently Not the Most Important Problem.*

This may be due to ignorance, reticence, shyness, or initial lack of confidence in the counselor. Or it may be due to a lack of insight and understanding, or to a lack of courage or emotional inability in facing the facts on the part of the counselee. Occasionally, it may be due to an unconscious or even deliberate attempt to mislead the counselor and get him to take sides or identify himself with the counselee. It is important for the counselor to bear this in mind, or he may be misled by the surface situation, making the problem much more difficult of ultimate solution.

4. *The Counselor Should Utilize Other Professional Skills Early Enough to Be of Maximum Benefit in the Counseling Process.*

This requires a recognition on the part of the counselor when a situation is beyond his professional skill and competence. It also requires the possession of a sense of professional security with respect to what the marriage counselor is as well as what he is not equipped to do, so that he will not feel that resorting to other professional skills would be considered an admission of incompetence. Failure to recognize his natural limitations may do incalculable harm to the counselee and may bring discredit upon the counselor. This applies especially to the use of medical, psychiatric, and legal assistance as soon as the need for such assistance becomes evident.

5. *Listening Is a Major Part of the Counseling Process.*

There is probably no single phase of the counseling procedure in which counselors differ as greatly as in the degree of their activity and permissiveness. The counselor must bear in mind that the interview serves several purposes, including that of providing a catharsis for the counselee. This is likely to be nullified if the counselee is not given the opportunity and encouraged to talk freely and fully. Besides, if the counselor does too much talking he may stop the counselee from presenting his story in the most telling way, may give the narrative a different and false direction which in turn may mislead both counselor and client.

6. *The Counselor Should Lead the Counselee to Develop His Own Plans Rather Than Plan for Him.*

Here is another area in which counselors differ greatly. It is impossible to say what the correct procedure would be in a given case because it will depend upon the situation and the personalities involved. This, however, may be said with a fair degree of certainty; those plans are best which emanate from the counselee under helpful guidance and suitable stimulation. Furthermore, the counselee is much more likely to identify himself with and execute a plan which he, himself, has made than to participate in a plan which stems from the counselor, regardless of how intelligent and logical it may be.

7. *A Good and Successful Marriage Requires Flexibility and Mutual Compromise.*

Many people who accept the view that compromise is necessary in marriage have a tendency to set rigid and arbitrary standards and limits as to how far they will go in compromising. It is essential to remember that an unyielding attitude or a mechanical and fixed set of rules in what should be a fluid and easy relationship, may lead to disastrous results and that the art of adjustment lies in knowing when to yield and when not to yield. Give-and-take in marriage is a desirable ideal, but it is sometimes better and wiser to give all or take all. The goal should be a flexible arrangement which will take into consideration the values involved in the issue and the personalities, rather than a hard and fast line which is adhered to regardless of the consequence.

8. *Unless and Until Otherwise Determined by Diagnosis of a Competent Psychiatrist or Other Relevant Specialists, Counselor Should Assume That Counselee Is Within Normal Limits.*

Recognizing the ambiguity and the differences in understanding of the concept of normalcy, it is still safer for the nonmedical counselor to think of his client as temporarily beset by a combination of problems which are beyond him, and as in need of objective exploration, guidance, and kindly assistance, than to assume that his behavior is abnormal and proceed to spin fancy theories about the why's and wherefore's of his deviational behavior or that of the people in his orbit. Where the client's actions do not conform to the concept of normal behavior as commonly held, or where the counselor's knowledge and understanding are inadequate to explain or account for the symptoms, difficulties, and problems he faces, the counselor will do much better to seek psychiatric help than to determine that his client is neurotic or psychotic or to be even more specific in his diagnosis. Seeking medical or psychiatric help will be better for the counselee, too, because if his behavior should be due to some physical, mental, or nervous disorder, he will be put in touch with medical aid without losing what may prove to be precious time.

9. *In a Marriage Which Has Little or No Foundation for Future Happiness Careful Consideration Should Be Given as to Whether It Might Be Better Dissolved Early Than Maintained. Where There Are Children New Factors and Values Come into Consideration.*

It will be obvious that the acceptance and application of this view will differ with the counselor's religious orientation. If he is opposed to divorce on principle, then, of course, nothing can justify the breakup of a marriage. It need hardly be pointed out that the counselor should not take the initiative in bringing about the dissolution of a marriage, any more than he should take the leadership in urging that a marriage be undertaken. But he should be fully cognizant of the human values and needs for both husband and wife in the situation and, except for the reservations indicated, should not use his influence to help maintain a marriage relationship that has little or no present positive value for the married partners or any prospects of improvement for the future.

10. *The Counselor Should See Both Partners, and Others If Necessary, in Order to Obtain a Complete and Rounded-Out Picture of the Situation.*

Psychoanalysts prefer to see only the patient they are working with and, with few exceptions, will not see the other party or parties to the conflict. This pattern has held also for many psychiatrists, although in the last decade there have been more flexibility and experimentation by certain groups who interview the spouse or family members when they deem it constructive. The former procedure is due mainly to two reasons: first, these specialists are primarily concerned with the patient's personal adjustment and they aim to aid him in obtaining his maximum self-realization; second, they believe that the patient will feel threatened and that if he knows his spouse or other family members will be seen, he will fear lest his confidence will thus be violated. The marriage counselor, however, aims at treating the situation as a whole, and the interpersonal relationships of the persons involved. He must, therefore, know the picture as it appears not only to the client who comes to see him, but to the spouse who is intimately involved in the situation. Hence he should endeavor to see the spouse whenever possible. Occasionally it may be necessary to see parents or other family members. The counselor must be careful, however, to make it absolutely clear that confidences will be respected and under no circumstances should he reveal to one spouse, directly or indirectly, what he has learned from the other unless, as sometimes happens, one spouse requests the counselor to open up a difficult subject which he has found it impossible to do for himself, or unless both spouses give the counselor blanket permission to use any of their material with the spouse as it might seem helpful. The preservation of the client's confidence is at times extremely difficult and requires the utmost caution and self-discipline on the part of the counselor.

11. *Joint Conferences with Both Partners Can Be Helpful but Are Difficult and Potentially Dangerous. They Should Be Undertaken Only After Careful Preparation.*

Husband and wife may make the wildest accusations and say the most cutting things to each other without necessarily bearing a permanent grudge. Once these things are said in the presence of a third party, even a professional person, they tend to become fixed and to take on a different significance and value. A joint conference can provide just the opportunity for either or both parties to say things to punish and hurt each other which neither will forget because of the presence of a third party. The joint conference can, therefore, become the means of further separating spouses instead of bringing them together. But it can also serve as a time-saver and as a means of clearing up misunderstandings from lack of communication. It can serve as the place where fantasy and reality may meet for the first time. Hence it becomes an important adjunct to counseling techniques but should be used with the utmost care.

12. *The Counselor Should Approach Every New Problem in a Spirit of Humility and in the Conviction That Regardless of How Similar It May Appear to Others in His Experience, It Must Be Studied and Treated As If It Were Totally New and Unprecedented.*

This principle is anticipated, in part at least, in some of the others already stated, but it is so important that it merits repetition and emphasis. The uniqueness of personalities and their interrelationships as well as the complexity and unpredictability of human interaction must ever be kept in mind. Besides, professional personnel dealing with people in trouble must exercise the greatest possible caution lest they act on the assumption that they are endowed with special powers of omniscience. It is sometimes difficult for them to keep from believing in their own superior qualities and to refrain from acting accordingly. It would be well for those who feel this way to remember and try to emulate one very good psychotherapist who prayed each morning that he might resist the temptation to play God and prayed each evening for forgiveness for having succumbed to the temptation.

13. *The Counselor Should Ignore or Violate Any of These Principles Mentioned When the Situation Demands It.*

This brings us back to the point of our beginning—namely, the need for an open mind and flexibility in point of view, approach, and method on the part of the counselor. This is the only principle that should be held inviolate and is a *sine qua non* for marriage counseling. Given a counselor with adequate training, an open mind, an appreciation of the value of the human personality, a dedication to do everything possible to be helpful to his client, and a spirit of humility arising from the awareness of the inadequacy of our present knowledge regarding human behavior and its motivations, the counselee is in relatively safe hands.

The Unknown in Marriage Counseling

In the foregoing list of principles, the Casebook Committee has described what seem on the basis of conviction, to be important guides to consider in the process of counseling. Dr. Mace in the same spirit tells us what he feels leads to success in counseling: "There are three conditions in particular which go a long way toward ensuring the success of marriage counseling. If they could be guaranteed in all cases, the effectiveness of counselors would be very greatly increased. First, marriage problems should be brought for counseling as early as possible." Second, "both husband and wife should co-operate fully in the counseling process," and third, "the couple should be willing to continue with counseling for a reasonable length of time."

Counseling at its best is not merely a matter of solving problems. It is a process in which growth of the personality and of the relationship aims to avoid the recurrence of that type of problem ever again." [21]

We would fail to present an over-all picture if we did not emphasize also the limitation concerning our *actual knowledge* of the value of these or other elements. What actually happens either during or after the attempt is made to help persons troubled with problems of personal or family adjustment is as yet primarily a matter of hypothesis. Beyond a few earnest and careful efforts,[22] as Emily Mudd states, "there is little scientific

[21] David R. Mace, *op. cit.*
[22] See the following seven references:
W. V. Snyder, "A Comparison of One Unsuccessful with Four Successful Nondirectively Counseled Cases," *Journal of Consulting Psychology,* Vol. 11, 1947, pp. 38-42.
Albert Ellis, "Requisition for Research in Psychotherapy," *Journal of Clinical Psychology,* Vol. VI, No. 2, 1950, pp. 152-156.
R. I. Watson and I. N. Mensch, "The Evaluation of the Effects of Psychotherapy," *Journal of Psychology,* Vol. 32, pp. 259-308.

information available concerning what effect a series of interviews with an analyst, a psychiatrist, a clinical psychologist, a social worker or a marriage counselor actually has on the adjustment of a disturbed individual or a distorted situation. A cultish apathy will furnish little eventual protection from the necessity of proving through scientifically acceptable methods that our hypotheses concerning how people are helped can be subjected to verification." [23] National organizations of clinicians from all the professions involved in therapy have a primary responsibility for investigating not only in what proportion of cases the results are helpful but also the how and the why of their procedures.

Perhaps we can do no better at this point than adapt, with some important changes, what Jan Struther has written on the art of Love:

> The raw materials of guidance are yours
> Fond hearts, native wit and mind in tune
> And so, dear innocents, you think yourselves
> Couns'lors, full blown?
>
> Am I, because I own
> Chisel, mallet and stone
> A sculptor? and must he
> Who hears a skylark and can hold a pen
> A poet be?

F. E. Fiedler, "Factor Analysis, Relationships in Psychoanalytic, Non-Directive and Adlerian Therapy," Vol. 14, 1950, pp. 436-445; Vol. 15, 1951, pp. 32-38.

Malcolm G. Preston, Emily H. Mudd, Hazel B. Froscher, "Factors Affecting Movement in Casework," *Social Casework,* March, 1953.

Robert G. Ballard, Emily H. Mudd, "Some Sources of Difference Between Client and Agency Evaluation of Effectiveness of Counseling," *Social Casework,* Vol. XXXIX, No. 1, pp. 30-35, Jan., 1958.

Robert G. Ballard, Emily H. Mudd, "Some Theoretical and Practical Problems in Evaluating Effectiveness of Counseling," *Social Casework,* Vol. XXXVIII, No. 10, pp. 533-538, Dec., 1957.

[23] Emily H. Mudd, "Knowns and Unknowns in Marriage Counseling Research," *Marriage and Family Living,* Vol. XIX, No. 1, Spring, 1957.

If neither's so, why then
You are not yet couns'lors. But in time to come
By constant exercise of skill and wit
By patient toil and judgment exquisite
With knowledge, wisdom and kindly heart
You may, my innocents, fashion
This desire, this ambition, this passion
Into a useful and healing art.[24]

Summary

In this chapter we have traced marriage counseling and its relation to psychotherapy, general counseling, and social casework. The differences in point of view, theoretical background, and implications for practice were briefly sketched; and the potentialities of marriage counseling as an aid to adjustment in a complex interdependent human relationship were indicated. A series of steps in the marriage counseling process and a suggested set of criteria as guides are included.

[24] Adaptation based on "Epithalamion" by Jan Struther, copyright, 1941, by Jan Struther and used by permission of Harcourt, Brace and Company, Inc.

PART TWO

MARRIAGE COUNSELING

CASES

In all cases, as stated in the Foreword (p. xiii), identifying items of name, location, age, and the like have been carefully disguised.

MARITAL ADJUSTMENT COUNSELING

Introduction

Marriage counseling may be defined as the process through which a professionally trained counselor assists a person or persons to resolve the problems that trouble them in their interpersonal relationships. The focus is on the relationship between the two persons in marriage, rather than, as in psychiatric therapy, the reorganization of the personality structure of the individual.

Moreover, since interpersonal relationships do not exist in a vacuum, conflict may appear in many specific problem areas. These may range from the handling of finances to social, cultural, sexual, parental, and in-law difficulties.

In marriage counseling, the major emphasis, to be sure, is on learning to *cope* with the problems, on understanding and dealing successfully with the particular emotional overtones that surround them; but the marriage counselor must also assume the responsibility for providing, when necessary, factual information to lessen the tensions.

The following cases cover a variety of situations involving marital conflict. They have been presented by counselors whose initial professional training differs widely. They also are illustrative of marriage counseling carried on in private practice as well as in established marriage counseling centers; in counseling services of schools and universities, in a Planned Parenthood center, and in a church.

3. Youthful Marriages

Case 1. *Personality Conflict in an Intercultural Marriage*
Case 2. *Wartime Marriage—Three Years Later*
Case 3. *A Young Marriage and a Mother-in-Law*

All three of these reported marriages are relatively "young" marriages, in terms of age of spouses, and in duration of the marriage (3-6 years). The first deals with an obvious cultural difference—nationality background. The second, apparently less striking, is nevertheless, as poorly based in terms of family background and personality adequacy of the spouses. In the third, the mother-in-law problem is recognized as primarily a manifestation of the immaturity and personality maladjustment of the son-in-law. The sociological background of the counselors, lightened by psychological insights, provides three interesting reports.

CASE 1

Problem: Personality conflict in an intercultural marriage
Presented by: A college teacher and marriage counselor (Ph.D. in Sociology) in private practice in large seaboard city

Introduction: Mrs. Anne B had gone to her physician because she had spells of dizziness and burning sensations about her body. An examination revealed nothing wrong with her physically, and the physician referred her to me as a private marriage counselor because he suspected that poor marital relations were tied in with her symptoms. I saw Anne once a week for six months in sessions of one hour each, usually alone but occasionally together with her husband, Joseph.

Anne, aged 26, was born of Irish parents in an Eastern-seaboard city. Of the lower socio-economic class, she left high school at the end of her first year to work at low-paying, unskilled jobs until her marriage six years ago. Her 31-year-old husband is of Italian descent. His education was little more than Anne's, but he has learned the trade of sheet metal worker which provides an adequate living on the scale to which both are accustomed. They have two daughters aged five and three.

The Interviews: During the *first session,* at which time she was seen alone, Anne gave a detailed account of her somatic complaints. These had first appeared after a prolonged series of visits to the dentist. One day she thought she was going to faint while shopping, and this frightened her so badly that she has been afraid to go out of the house alone ever since. She also developed the fear that she would hurt her own children. Anne talked with much emotion, and stated that she hoped she wasn't losing her mind. Near the end of the interview, she complained that she was lonesome at home during the day, that she was lucky to go out in the evening with her husband twice a month, and that she was disgusted with the same old routine all the time.

Anne used the *second session* to tell about her home life before she got married. With much difficulty and tears she told about her mother who was an alcoholic and her father who gambled. Since the father worked at night and the mother usually was away from the house on a drinking spree, Anne frequently was left alone to take care of the house and her younger brother and sister. However, in spite of her best efforts, Anne was always the object of criticism and punishment by her mother, and these rages over the slightest real or fancied error on the part of Anne caused her to live in constant dread of blame.

Furthermore, Anne resented the fact that her mother favored her brother, and it angered her that her mother often would embarrass her in front of other children. However, she never dared express these feelings, and indeed she never could discuss any personal problem with her mother—not even the advent of her first menstruation. Her jealousy of her girl friends who came from happier homes not only alienated her from them but also led her to become sorry for herself.

At the *third session,* Anne said that it made her feel better to be able to talk about herself. She then proceeded to discuss her feelings about her husband and children. She married him in the face of severe criticism by her mother, who objected bitterly to Anne's marrying an Italian. Since her marriage, Anne has been afraid of her husband, even afraid that he might hit her. Accordingly, she has been reluctant to express herself to him and she has kept her thoughts to herself. Despite her inability to communicate, however, she was unable to conceal her antipathy toward sexual relations which she claimed were not enjoyable to her, and her husband was annoyed at her lack of enthusiasm.

Joseph's closeness to his family and his criticism of her family was another source of irritation to her, but at the same time, she was constantly apprehensive lest her family antagonize him. Finally, she complained that her husband insisted he was too tired to take her out in the evening and all they did was to watch TV. Nevertheless, after this indictment of her husband, Anne then admitted that she considered herself to be a poor wife and mother, and she felt both guilty and inadequate when the children were injured or ill.

At the *fourth session,* on my suggestion, both Anne and Joseph were present. Joseph began by assuming a hostile and aggressive attitude. He seemed to be suspicious that a trick was being played on him. A good portion of the session was spent by them in a discussion of their differences of opinion and expounding on what they didn't like about each other. He said that she was a poor housekeeper and didn't cook to please him. In rebuttal, and obviously supported by my presence, Anne stated that the small size of their apartment was an obstacle to good house-keeping, and that their small income hindered her ability to cook the way her husband wanted.

At this point, I talked over the probable reality of their respective arguments. Joseph was surprised and pleased. He had expected that I would be completely on his wife's side, and he lost much of his belligerency at my apparent ability to see some merit in his complaints. At the same time, Anne seized those remarks of mine that appeared in her favor as evidence of continued support from me. I used this situation to make the suggestion that the menu be planned together on Sunday for the entire week. They reacted with eagerness. Joseph was pleased that his wife was willing to do something constructive, and she was gratified that he was willing to co-operate with her.

At the *fifth session* at which both were present, they agreed that the menu-planning idea was a tremendous success. It was a relief to Anne to be safe in the knowledge that her husband would approve of what she was serving to him, although she still didn't like her cooking unfavorably compared with his mother's manner of preparing the dishes that were typically Italian. The discussion then turned to the housekeeping problem. Anne had wasted a lot of time and effort by her haphazard approach to the task. A detailed schedule for each day was worked out and written down on a sheet of paper. When reduced to this form, the housekeeping seemed much less formidable to Anne.

The *sixth session* was with Anne alone. By this time she was elated at the improvement in her relations with her husband. Because she appeared to be receptive, I explained to her the difference in cultural and social values of Irish and Italian families. This information fascinated her and placed in an objective light many of the things her husband did that had bothered her. As a result, she could understand that her husband's behavior with his own family reflected characteristically Italian attitudes he had learned from his parents, and was not necessarily a personal attack of her.

With this as a background, *a number of subsequent sessions* were used to give Anne an opportunity to talk more about herself and her early history. The salient points brought out indicated a generally unhappy childhood and youth. She was ashamed of her family. The drinking, gambling, and arguing by her parents deeply disturbed her. There was no love, no acceptance. Although her father was kinder to her than her mother, he wasn't affectionate and she couldn't feel close to him. Furthermore, she felt excluded from the relationship between her mother and her brother.

Constant criticism and punishment by her mother encouraged her to have a low opinion of herself and an exaggerated fear of committing any error. In this regard, Anne vividly recalled how violently her mother had acted toward her grandmother when the latter lost control of her bowels during her last illness of cancer. Sex was a subject that Anne learned to view with distaste and apprehension. With her parents as models, sexual relations appeared to her essentially as "dirty" even between husband and wife. These attitudes and her obligations at home served to restrict her social life. She never was "one of the gang," never dated with boys, and generally became shy and withdrawn. She began to consider her way of life as a jail from which she had to escape.

Her marriage to Joseph served just such a purpose, but in view of her mother's prejudice against Italians and objection to the marriage, Anne saw herself as committed to something for which she was emotionally unprepared and from which she could not retreat because she had no support from her family. This dilemma was intensified by the strong bond between her husband and his family and by her unfamiliarity with the Italian language and customs which created an atmosphere of "being shut out" when she visited her in-laws.

During this phase of counseling, Anne began to have some insight into her fears of assuming responsibility, of being punished for mistakes, of being rejected by her husband, and into a rather deeply repressed fear of having a "nervous breakdown" as her mother had had at one time. She became aware of her ambivalence toward Joseph, her dependence upon him, and how she was threatened when he was nice to his mother. She started to understand such things as why she found it so difficult to express herself freely to Joseph, why she recoiled from sex, and why she couldn't bring herself to ask her mother-in-law for advice in preparing Italian dishes. In other words, Anne was developing the ability to analyze how her feelings were conditioned by her own experiences, and how some of her husband's behavior was in response to her behavior as well as to his own emotional needs.

On several occasions there were flare-ups of tension between Anne and Joseph because of repetitions of former threatening patterns of interaction. At these times both were discouraged, but not to the point of wanting to give up. In the meantime, there was a steady improvement in many respects. Anne was much more at ease with her mother-in-law. She was less overwhelmed by her household chores, and she surprised herself by actually enjoying taking care of the children. Joseph became less rigid and authoritarian, and with his co-operation their social life became more active and their sexual life more enjoyable. There was little discussion of Anne's symptoms, which had greatly decreased.

The *final month* was devoted to sessions alternating between Anne alone and with both spouses together. As current problems arose, their apparent causes and ways of handling them were discussed. It seemed that Joseph was no longer afraid of appearing "soft" and could afford to show his wife the affection for which she longed. Consequently, every opportunity was utilized to show him what contributions he could make to remove obstacles to a happier relationship. This new attitude of her husband plus her success with the planned menus and housekeeping greatly enhanced Anne's sense of adequacy and security. Although they still had arguments, these were of short duration because, as they said laughingly, they knew that I would approve of the one who acted the more reasonably.

Summary: In brief, this case dealt with a woman who had deep feelings of inadequacy and insecurity as the result of a very threatening early home life. She married a man whose ethnically different cultural values contributed to a strengthening of these feelings. The counseling was directed by stages toward several goals:

1. To allow her to ventilate her feelings and obtain support from me.
2. To enable her to establish a freer relationship with her husband with the help of this support and by my efforts to gain his co-operation.
3. To furnish tangible means whereby she could gain more adequacy and, at the time, cement the atmosphere of willingness on the part of both to co-operate with each other.
4. To give her some objective understanding of the cultural differences between her own ethnic background and that of her husband.
5. And the final goal, to give her some insight into her own personality needs and how they related to those of her husband.

With the apparent attainment of these goals, her symptoms became negligible as the marital relationship improved to their own stated satisfaction.

Follow-up: Two years have passed since I last saw Anne and Joseph. About three months ago I sent her a note inquiring how things were going. In reply, she phoned me and told me that she is happy with her present relationship with Joseph. They still have arguments, but these are neither violent nor of long duration, and her symptoms have practically disappeared. Knowing that I am available for consultation seems to be an important factor in her thinking. Best of all, Anne believes that her marriage is constantly improving. Recently she referred a friend to me, which might signify that she is pleased with the outcome of the counseling.

CASE 2

Problem: Wartime marriage—three years later
Presented by: A teacher-counselor (Ph.D. in Sociology) working in a college setting

Introduction: This is an account of a sick marriage of college students, inaugurated on impulse, without preparation or adequate previous acquaintance, poorly based in terms of family background and personality adequacy of spouses, and sorely strained by the exigencies of three years of married living in five states. Left to themselves the spouses would probably divorce in a few months. But it was their decision to try to hold the marriage together, and they referred themselves to a college teacher-counselor for that purpose.

The Problem as Presented by the Client: The two clients are James S and Mary S who have been married for three years and have undergone destructive quarrels on the average of two a week, sometimes more, rarely less. Neither is satisfied with the marriage, both regret the marriage. They disagree on all vital areas except sex. The parental families have taken sides, and neither spouse feels welcome or at home in the other's home.

The first meeting was at a beach, a pick-up, no courtship possible since James was in service. The relation was idealized by both through letters. They had a few dates followed by a typical gangplank marriage induced by feelings of guilt on Jim's part for intimacies elicited by Mary. Actual marriage was on a dare by another couple over James' protest, and occurred at 4:00 A.M. James says he has regretted the marriage ever since, and his wife has alternated between regret and tenacious insistence that the marriage should be permanent.

After the marriage James' family rebuffed them both, and they went West on a honeymoon trip; also, to look for a job in a plane factory where Jim had made friends while in the Air Force. Neither was well prepared for close intimate contacts —they had long periods of sulking, pouting, and not speaking after violent quarrels over inconsequential matters such as the way clothes were to be packed, or where to eat, or what to eat. Once arrived, both found jobs; but a series of bad decisions by James ended in a financial fiasco and they returned to the Middle West where James entered a school and Mary returned to her family for a limited period. When Mary didn't return as expected, James suggested the advisability of a divorce. Mary, panicky at the thought, begged to be permitted to return. Jim had been faithful to her and thus deprived sexually. He "wanted a woman the worst way" and permitted her to return.

Both enrolled in school the quarter after Mary returned, and the latter did satisfactory work as a freshman. Jim, however, found that his schoolwork deteriorated with Mary's return and he made the most of it in their fights. Following a trailer-neighbor's divorce which shocked them into a more realistic examination of where they themselves were heading, they referred themselves to the counselor for such help as he could give them.

Personal Data Provided by the Initial Interview: James S is 27, an agricultural economics junior at a state university subsidized by the rehabilitation service because of injuries received in the Air Force. He comes of a family of six, farmers, college educated parents, Methodists, but liberal in their relationship to their children—a thrifty and respectable family. James registered in the neurotic bracket on the Thurstone inventory. He is inclined to worry and is overly concerned about his health and its effect on his grades. He is talkative, longfaced most of the time, inclined to feel quite self-righteous.

Mary S is a study in contrasts. She is 22 years old, a freshman, reared in the South in a highly respectable environment. Deserted by her mother when two years old, she was reared by a stepmother and preacher father whose religion and call to the ministry followed a life of "sin"—a free-will Baptist atmosphere of hell-fire and damnation precluded dancing, shows, sports, conviviality of all sorts and channeled all excitement into emotional church services. Mary deserted her religion for a few months when she was in her teens and has been guilt-ridden since. She is fundamentally fun loving, sex loving, and world loving with few self-instilled inhibitions, and is constantly in conflict with herself. Mary presents a history of childhood tantrums, spoiled by her father and indulged in every way. Her devices for controlling her environment are (1) losing her temper, (2) crying and wailing, (3) infantilisms, winsomeness, coquettishness, pouting, appealing to love, and so on. Her score on the Thurstone inventory showed high neuroticism, a study of fears, hates, and unpredictability. One minute she is sweet, winsome, and smiling; the next termagant, stormy, and raging. Her method of fighting is simple and highly direct with few subtleties in manipulation. She clears up spontaneously when she wins, and is loving and affectionate as a reward.

Counseling: The counseling process was carried over six appointments. The counselor saw first one and then the other member of the pair and usually ended each appointment by seeing them together.

Jim and Mary arrived for the first interview, holding hands, making a good front of mutual solicitude, helping one another, looking to the other for clues as to what to say. Mary had read the Groves book (*Conserving Marriage and the Family*) [1] given to Jim when he had made the first appointment, and Jim planned to read it. The counselor suggested that Jim take the book into an adjoining room while he interviewed Mrs. S.

Mary made an excellent first impression, affable, agreeable, and disarming with a straightforward account of the courtship, lack of adequate engagement, mistake of marrying so fast; admitted that she was hard to live with, that they were both very stubborn, and that she had a temper. The worst thing was that Jim wanted her to do things that were wicked, wanted to break down her religion, and he shouldn't, should he?

Mary appeared bewildered with the complexities of married life. Counselor explained that many engaged couples met the problems before marriage which she and Jim had to meet first after their marriage; also that many couples who had been married many years still had areas in which they were working out adjustments. Mary thought maybe if they had had time they would have discovered they were too different to get married. She said they occasionally got to the point where they weren't having many quarrels; then they would try to plan something they hadn't talked over and that would start another quarrel, and the bottom would drop out.

Mary resents the attitude of Jim's family toward her religion, thinks they are fine people, better educated, better off than her folks, but they ought to let her live her own religion and not tease her about not going to shows. If religious questions didn't keep popping up she would have some hope. She resents Jim's idea that she might work for pay. In the South, a woman expects to be supported and she doesn't want to be married to a man who can't support her. Still, she has learned her lesson

[1] Ernest R. Groves, *Conserving Marriage and the Family* (New York: The Macmillan Company, 1944).

and is back with Jim for good, if she can only keep him wanting her; she thinks he would just as soon let her go.

Jim in his first interview talked steadily without interruption for almost two hours. He covered his courtship (his story jibed with Mary's), the marriage, the first year's adjustments and difficulties summarized above. He bitterly described the trap set by his wife in getting him to buy her the engagement ring; she induced him to pet her and then began crying saying she wasn't that kind of girl. He wanted to believe this and proposed to get engaged (he had been released from service just two weeks before and had come directly from service to see this religious, saintly girl he had met on his last leave who wrote such sweet letters about home and family). Less than three days later Mary and another couple proposed going to Kentucky to marry, and again tears prevailed on him, and he acceded, only to regret it. His marriage has been one series of disillusionments about Mary, and about married life in general. Instead of saintly, she is hypocritical and fanatic about surface evidences of religion. Instead of sweet, she is spoiled and selfish. Surprisingly enough, the area he least suspected would be developed was that of sexual response and here they clicked pretty well.

Jim thought he had been attracted to Mary and had idealized her during service because he needed a conscience to keep him from drinking, women, and vice which he felt abounded in the Air Force. He felt cheated when he found she wasn't really a saint. The counselor asked if he should hold that against Mary, since she didn't claim to be a saint, did she? Jim felt she did, and was a fraud. He showed no insight into the idealization or projection processes of the service period. Jim felt Mary just used her religious views to frustrate him, and as an excuse to be impolite to his friends. He said his family regarded her as a religious fanatic. The counselor asked if there might be other reasons for her not going to parties, such as not knowing how to dance or to skate, or being afraid of his friends.

Jim's account of their brawls begins with Mary's inexplicable fits of temper. Then he gets mad, and Mary goes into a numb sulk and won't speak. Neither one sleeps much. He claims he can't predict whether she will love him or "cuss" him for anything he does, which leaves him jittery and uncertain what to say, and he knows he was a fool to let her come back, but he did want a woman badly.

As they left together, the counselor suggested that at the next interview he wanted them to tell him more about their points of common agreement, their similarities, and to see if the list might not be expanded gradually to cover more areas.

As a matter of fact, the next appointment was broken. Jim called to say they were going to a basketball game and having some friends over. Would another night do just as well? The counselor detected some pride on Jim's part that Mary had agreed to go to the game and to have friends in, and agreed to change the appointment.

At the next interview, the counselor asked for a progress report. None was forthcoming from Mary who sat quietly, obviously waiting for Jim. Jim said they were getting along better, but he wasn't doing so well in school, wasn't getting his sleep. Mary showed disgust but still wouldn't talk, waiting for Jim. She winced when Jim talked about grades or sleep.

The counselor asked about the common activities, points of agreement. Mary suggested sexual compatibility, swimming, and ice skating. Jim added possibilities of football and basketball games, and riding, although that was too expensive. He said with some bitterness, dancing would be fun, but Mary's religious ideas got in the way. Mary responded, "Dad says it's okay to go to games now, but not to dances and shows." Jim snorted at mention of her father, says he doesn't see why Mary can't make up her own mind. Mary's eyes go opaque when Jim digs her on certain questions, and she withdraws visibly from the conversation.

The counselor asked Mary if she thought sports and activities were wicked, or was it the people who participated in them? Mary said, "No, but I feel guilty after playing." Counselor inquired how the idea of wickedness and recreation had come to be tied together in church beliefs. Mary said she would feel better if she could talk with a minister who would say it was all right to go to shows and dances. She didn't think just any minister would do, but the Baptist minister might do. Counselor agreed to arrange appointment to get it straight.

Talking with the counselor alone, Mary relaxed and, visibly more at ease, said that she was delighted with the progress they had made, that Jim had bought a box of candy on Valentine's Day, and was more loving. Their only quarrel had been about having a baby, which they wouldn't have talked about if they hadn't felt they were making progress. She was anxious to save the marriage and might compromise on religious teachings to do it; she guessed you were sinning if you didn't do all you could to keep a marriage together even more than if you went out and played.

On the other hand, Jim's progress report was more doleful than Mary's: grades getting worse, losing sleep, wife too grouchy to listen to his troubles, he needs someone to snap him out of it. The counselor suggested that marriage can't cure all troubles, that men find they worry until they work out a plan and do something about it. We all need to take a minimum of responsibility for our own mental hygiene. Jim thought that was what a clinical psychologist in the Veterans Administration had told him too, but he couldn't see how he could help himself much. He needed a good wife to "listen him out," love him, and be sympathetic.

Mary joined Jim to review their needs for one another and the basis for building a stronger relationship. Mary's need for affection and an indulgent parent and Jim's need for sympathy, understanding, and encouragement were brought out in the discussion. Spelled out in activities of listening, loving, genuine expressions of feelings, and protectiveness, the counselor sensed

the tentative acceptance of new roles, at least at the verbal level.
The counselor commented that both had tried hard to reform
the other without too much success. Marriage is rarely a successful reform school; we usually just succeed in spoiling the
relationship. Right now they had to build the relationship so
that they could abide one another when they were "bratty."
Mary veered away from the discussion with the question,
"Shouldn't I drop out of school so Jim doesn't have to work
so many hours at the gym? Then he would get better grades."
Jim said he liked to work, for it took his mind off his troubles.
And besides didn't she want a husband to support her? Mary
said she was changing her mind about that, at least until they
had babies. Both agreed that the basis for the decision would
be Jim's health and the health of their marriage, and that they
would need to think about it.

Discussion of sex compatibility as the session closed revealed
that Mary achieved orgasm through clitoral manipulation and
not through friction following entry of penis. Jim's comment
was, "Nice to know what makes your wife tick, eh, honey?"

At the next interview Mary reported on her visit with the
minister which was satisfactory. She decided to go to a show if
Jim asked her, to try it out. She went to the Winter Carnival
and the Varieties and saw only one vulgar thing in them, didn't
feel guilty afterward—real progress here.

Concerning interpersonal relations, Mary said, "Jim irritates
me, and I fly off before I think. I guess I'm hard to live with,
but I'll get over it. It's Jim who gets mad and stays mad now."
Mary moved deeper, said she had always been selfish, temperamental, was spoiled by her parents. She doesn't remember when
she didn't get her way by crying. The last few days she has tried
being reasonable when she wanted something, and it works just
as well as getting mad. It's when she is in a hurry, afraid she will
be late, or afraid of company coming that she is her worst.
She told of blowing off at Jim because he brought his overshoes
into the trailer just as she was leaving to take a shower. "I

usually start things, I guess I sound like a meany, but you might as well know it, if you are going to help us." Counselor said understanding of this sort often preceded progress in marriage. Mary said, "I think we both probably expect too much of each other." No wiser words had been stated in the counseling process to date.

With Jim's arrival a review of the interview was made and he explained he could take Mary's tantrums better if he could understand why she was mad. Today he was just trying to help her by placing the milk bottles, after wiping them, topdown so they could drain, which was the way she had told him to, and she kicked them across the trailer screaming, "You never do anything right!" Mary flushed and said, "You upset me, because you were doing it different, and I thought you were making fun of the way I do it." Jim, with a hurt look, explained that most of his troubles came when he was trying to make her happy and she misunderstood, maybe that was the reason for his low grades, and that he couldn't sleep. The counselor asked Jim if he realized that reference to low grades and sleep had become his way of fighting back at Mary, a more subtle weapon than the tantrum, but a punishment just the same. Jim looked sick for a minute. Mary said, "That's a sort of mean and deceitful way to fight. I'd rather have someone come out and beat me!" Jim said, "I never thought of it that way."

The counselor worked through three quarrels, the one over the bottle, the shower, and going to Jim's folks, which they had had since the last interview. The deficiency in constructive role playing was apparent, both operating on the personality level of criticism almost immediately after the issue was raised. The reasons for conflict were analyzed, and the prerequisites for successful constructive conflict reviewed: (1) ability to identify hurts, and relay the fact to the other partner, (2) ability to understand hurts in the partner, to realize where the shoe pinches, and (3) the ability to deal with issues and conditions and to weave the conflict from personalities back into issues if the partner goes personal. A battle over handling the in-laws developed at the end of the session and was handled constructively by looking over the alternatives and agreeing upon one they mutually liked. The sense of growth was apparent to both clients and they made another appointment. Levy and Munroe's *The Happy Family* [2] will be their reading, meanwhile.

Conclusions: This case is not yet closed. The marriage is still far from a happy one. The processes of alienation have been largely arrested, and a constructive channeling of the neurotic drives begun. The couple is almost totally deficient in "we" feeling, in complementary personal role playing, and in a common philosophy of life and marriage. Socially the marriage is worth saving mainly because neither partner would be very likely to attain a successful marriage within other combinations. There is some investment in the habits of living together already established. The bases for building the marriage are insufficient to encourage parenthood at this time, but sufficient to work out a companionate marriage. Enrollment in college with common friends, interests, and activities makes a hopeful start in establishing a beneficent circle of "I enjoy you because you enjoy me" to counterweigh the vicious circle of destructive conflict underway for the past three years.

CASE 3

Problem: A young marriage and a mother-in-law
Presented by: A counselor (Ph.D. in Sociology) in the Marriage and Family Clinic of a Southern university

Introduction: Bob came first for consultation, and Joan a few days later. I saw them about thirty times for a total of forty-

[2] John Levy and Ruth Munroe, *The Happy Family* (New York: Alfred A. Knopf, 1956, rev. ed.).

five hours over a period of two years, most of the time individually, but on a few occasions together. Although the prognosis
after the first session seemed very poor and almost, but not
quite, hopeless, the situation did improve. The rate of change,
however, was at times infinitesimally small and at others it retro-
graded. At our first meeting, Bob said that he had almost made
up his mind to get a divorce from his wife since the marriage
was in a hopeless state, but he had decided "as a last resort" to
see if I could help him. Joan felt the situation was serious but
not desperate.

Background Material: Bob was 24 years old. He was a Navy
veteran, but he had had no combat experience. He was slim, of
medium height, and nice-looking. He was rather quiet, shy, and
introspective. Though personally religious, his church attendance was sporadic. He was usually kind and co-operative. He
had a sister who was slightly older. His mother and father did
not have a successful or even a passably acceptable marriage
by everyday standards; it was only tolerable. During the depression, they had had an exceedingly difficult time. His father, a
mechanic, had never been very successful even during periods
of prosperity and, during the depression, his jobs were menial
and sporadic. The mother had also been employed at various
times. Although she was personally kind to her family, she was
not warmhearted, and she developed a hard-bitten attitude toward the rest of the world. The picture that Bob gave of his
father was that of a man who was without spirit, but he was not
bitter toward the world. Bob loved his father, but he did not
respect him. His mother tried desperately to do the best she
could under trying and oftentimes hopeless situations. She faithfully mended clothes, canned the produce of the garden, raised
chickens, and kept a tight fist on the meager family purse. She
doled out money stringently, though fairly, and without be-
grudging its use. Bob's memories of his childhood were ones
of gray drabness.

His scholastic record was average or above. After finishing high school, he worked as a clerk in a grocery and as a plumber's assistant. He joined the Navy during World War II.

In addition to his generally unsatisfactory home life, several other specific experiences also had detrimental effects upon him. During his early teens, he had sexual intercourse several times with his sister. That he had been weak-willed bothered him more than that he had been bad or evil. Masturbation and incest were to him additional indications of his weak character. When he went into the Navy, he wanted to do his bit for his country, and he was patriotic. But after extensive primary training and ship duty on coastal patrol, he could not face the prospects of actual combat. When his ship was ordered to a theater of actual operations, he suffered a "nervous breakdown." This act in his own mind was the most terrible blot on his character. The psychiatric treatment which followed had been palliative rather than curative. His subsequent navy career was spent in the U. S.

During this period, he was stationed in Florida near his home. He began to date frequently a young Jewish girl whose parents were wealthy. They had a violent and passionate love affair. After a few months, she became pregnant. She told her parents. Although she and Bob wished to get married, her parents would not grant her permission. They arranged an abortion, and they prevented their daughter from seeing him again. Bob suffered deeply and even contemplated suicide. (It appears to me in retrospect that this experience may have helped him in the long run as it indirectly demonstrated that he was a man.)

A few months later Bob met Joan. At the time that I first met Joan, she was a nice-looking girl of 21. She was kindly and co-operative, and she tended to accept the world as it is. Although she was often under great strain in her relations with Bob and although she was sometimes petulant, usually with reason, she was fundamentally a cheerful person.

Whereas Bob's family adjustment to life had been a willy-nilly resignation, Joan's parents attacked it with firm determination. Joan's father, Mr. B, had had many economic difficulties during the depression, but he had always approached them with a spirit of optimism. During the pre-war rise in business activity, he began to ascend rapidly the managerial scale, and became sales manager of a large concern. His work took him to all parts of the United States so that he was away from their home in a large Midwestern city much of the time. As the family grew in economic affluence, Joan's mother also traveled much, but she rarely went with her husband. Joan's father was a forthright man, and he and Joan got along well during the little time they were together. Although the relationship between Mr. and Mrs. B was cordial, it was not intimate. It appeared that Mr. B was very happy to be in a work which he enjoyed and which took him away from Mrs. B.

Mrs. B, whom I subsequently met and talked with at length, was a most domineering and dynamic woman. She was that rare combination of feminine attractiveness and athletic ability. Joan never knew exactly why her parents were not more intimate. From indirect evidence gathered from Joan and Mrs. B it appears that Mr. and Mrs. B were not sexually compatible. Mrs. B greatly admired her husband, or at least she made an excellent pretense of greatly admiring him. That he was financially a success, that he always knew what he wanted and went after it, that he provided his family with all the material necessities of life and many luxuries, and that he was a gentleman, were the qualities which Mrs. B constantly extolled to others.

Although Mrs. B had almost a tigress-like love for Joan, she did not want to be bothered with her most of the time, so she sent Joan to boarding school, to summer camp, and to college away from whatever community they were living in. Mrs. B had Joan with her during vacations when they traveled a great deal. Most of the time Joan did what her mother desired, not because she was cowed by her mother, but because what the mother wanted was usually agreeable to the daughter. There was, therefore, a considerable spirit of mutual respect between the two, although their relationship was often rocky and at infrequent intervals even stormy.

In her middle teens Joan became ill and had to withdraw from boarding school for a few months. The illness was chronic and debilitating, but not serious. The mother went to extremes in babying Joan and in making her believe that she was more ill than she actually was. This experience had some bearing on Joan's subsequent marital adjustment because at times she complained of being physically ill or run down during the first two or three years of the marriage when there was no apparent organic basis for it.

Description of Their Courtship and Early Marriage: Bob and Joan met in the closing months of the war when she was on a vacation visit in Florida with her mother. Although they did not fall in love at "first sight," the courtship progressed rapidly toward marriage. Even before marriage they quarreled and had many areas of conflict, but they also had many areas of common agreement and mutual satisfaction. The major fact, however, which held them through the courtship and the early years of a rocky marriage was a mutual respect and esteem which persisted although it grew feeble during the more trying months. They liked to dance and to go swimming once in a while. After some weeks of courtship, Bob told Joan about his affair with Sarah and his cowardice, but not about his incestuous relationship with his sister. For a young girl, she displayed a high degree of sympathy and understanding.

They were both physically attractive to each other, and they began to have premarital intercourse without any apparent conscious plan. She had never had any experience with other boys or men beyond heavy petting on a few occasions and light petting on many. Although she did not have an orgasm during any of the few times they had premarital coitus, she enjoyed the experience. Shortly after marriage, she developed orgasm reaction very soon. Joan had no adverse conditioning about sex.

Her mother had told her about the elementary facts of sex: menstruation, pregnancy, and the male's role in intercourse. This instruction, although brief, was matter-of-fact and sympathetic. Bob's conditioning toward sex was less satisfactory than Joan's. That he had masturbated extensively and committed incest bothered him considerably. The memories of these occurrences tended to aggravate his feelings of inferiority and subsequently to affect indirectly rather than directly his sexual adjustment in marriage.

When Bob was separated from the service, he and Joan decided to get married, and he to go to the university. Joan had completed about two years of college. Although he was four years older than she was, he had never gone to college because, after graduating from high school, he had worked for a while and then he had gone into the Navy. Mrs. B objected at first to the idea of her daughter getting married, but her opposition was not persistent. She eventually gave not only her consent, but also the promise of a small monthly allowance to Joan to assist the couple for as long as Bob was in school. She kept this promise in spite of the fact that at times it appeared that the marriage would not last. Bob's father gave Bob a monthly sum throughout his college career.

At the university, they were able to get an apartment in one of the veteran housing projects. Joan took one or two courses and Bob, of course, a full schedule. At first their marriage went along reasonably well although they had begun to quarrel about various matters to be described shortly. Bob's grades were slightly above average. Whereas, they had been able at first to live on his GI benefits and the small allowance which they received from their families, they found that with the passing months, it became more difficult. Bob began to contract for odd jobs as electrician and plumber. Joan became pregnant inadvertently the first year. Bob, therefore, worked almost full-time for a regular contractor the first summer.

During the second year of school, the economic, scholastic, and mother-in-law tensions grew greater. Bob had difficulty choosing a major field of study; Mrs. B came to visit them every three or four months. She was always critical of various little things he did. As time went on, he became progressively more discouraged. The coming of the baby intensified the economic and emotional tensions and aggravated Bob's feelings of insecurity. The strain of caring for the baby was very great on Joan, and it caused her to be more irritable and short-tempered. Mrs. B's attempt to direct every aspect of the child's rearing during the periods when she was in town completely unsettled both Bob and Joan. Bob and Joan themselves differed about certain aspects of the baby's care, he feeling that she ought to be more methodical and precise.

He was also excessively germ-and-dirt-conscious. In consequence, the traditional male-female attitudes about cleanliness in the household were reversed.

Joan had little or no firsthand experience of cooking, housecleaning, washing, shopping, maintenance of household equipment and supplies, and budgeting. These were mundane matters which her mother scorned and which, except for keeping one's room clean, were outside the realm of life at a boarding school. But her worst offense was that she was her mother's daughter.

The major complaints that Joan had about Bob were that he was not so personally affectionate as he might be, that he did not understand some of her problems in trying to run a household and rear a baby, and that he would not believe that she really did love him more than her mother. Bob had, for instance, wanted her to sever completely her relations with her mother. When she would not, he felt that she loved her mother more than him. In their sex life, Bob made advances to her only once a week or less. It was a satisfying relation for both. It was an occasion when they felt close together, and personally intimate as well as being erotically successful. She had an orgasm almost always. Her only complaint was that he did not want to make love oftener. She stated to me that she would like to have intercourse two or three times a week.

The Counseling: In theory and in retrospect the therapeutic procedure appears logical and simple. Its actual implementation and evolution, however, were painfully slow, and many temporary setbacks and disappointments were encountered.

The basic problem was, of course, Bob's feelings of insecurity and his lack of confidence in himself. The major irritants to his well-being were, in a rough order of importance, the interference from and fear of his mother-in-law, failure to pass one of his courses in German, a different attitude from Joan's about child rearing and about everyday chores of living. The principal assets in the relationship were that they had a certain respect, as well as love, for each other. Furthermore, although they often quarreled bitterly, they were never insulting to one another and they never violated the personal dignity of the other. Joan was emotionally better adjusted, and Bob was more worldly-wise, and he had greater insight except in an all-important few of his own problems. At the time it seemed that the greatest sources of strength and of reconstruction were their mutual respect, Joan's straightforward emotional determination to preserve the marriage, and Bob's rather keen insight in some matters.

The major therapeutic measures that were eventually used with Bob included: (a) catharsis, (b) emotional support, (c) intellectual assistance in studying German, (d) development of insight into his own, Joan's, and Mrs. B's behavior, and (e) reduction of the psychological threat to his ego presented by Mrs. B. Under each a number of variations were used. They were not, of course, all applied simultaneously or continuously. Some were used throughout the two-year period, such as catharsis, and others only at specific periods, such as reduction of mother-in-law threat. The major task that was necessary with

Joan was helping her to develop greater insight into Bob's emotional problems and to utilize even more her latently very strong emotional balance. This quality was already the mainstay in the marriage. But it appeared that it had yet unused potentials which could be put to even greater service. This supposition proved to be correct.

After discovering in two sessions with Bob and one with Joan how painfully disturbed he was, it was decided to help him initially to relieve his personal distress through catharsis and emotional support from me and to take positive measures to correct his deficiency in German.

I found that his approach to the study of German was quite faulty and, as a teacher, I helped him make certain corrections. Arrangements were also made with his own instructor to have a short conference each week. That the German instructor as well as I, showed an interest in him as a person gave him a positive, though small, indication that he really was not so bad and hopeless a person as he had thought.

In our counseling sessions he was also encouraged to talk about himself and his problems. Although told in a subdued voice, his first accounts literally spewed forth in torrents. His story of his own life was pathetic, and his condemnation of his mother-in-law was vitriolic and vehement. That I was not aghast at his tales of horror seemed to surprise him no end. The catharsis produced encouraging, though not spectacular, results. It was constantly bolstered by indirect rather than direct demonstration from me that Bob was a perfectly normal being and in fact that he excelled in many things—his perseverance, his scientific aptitude, and his mechanical skill—and that what he had experienced was not unique or hideous. For example, on the negative side, I was eventually able to get him to understand that all men including the bravest and excluding only insensible fools experienced fear, but because his "emotional resistance" had been lowered he had suffered more. This self-enlightening process had, of course, to be carried out slowly and judiciously.

On the positive side, he was indirectly commended for his special abilities.

After a short period of time more and more effort was directed toward helping Bob to develop greater insight into Joan's personality so that he could see for himself that she was his best friend and that she was doing better in many areas, such as taking care of the home and siding with Bob rather than with her mother on all important issues, than might be expected of so young and inexperienced a girl. In view of her almost complete lack of training, her efforts and success in carrying on under adverse economic conditions were commendable. Bob began to acquire more respect for Joan's household endeavors long before he began to appreciate her greater loyalty to him than to her mother. Whereas the resolution of the former problem was accomplished with more or less continual progress, the latter was characterized by many ups and downs and some severe setbacks.

At one point, for instance, when Bob was in a particularly unsettled state, he tried to get Joan to promise to stop writing her mother or at least to write her not oftener than once a month. She was in the habit of writing her a rather long letter once a week, and a brief note now and then in answer to some specific query. The idea of her writing her mother and especially seeing her do it incensed him. In the next conference with Joan this matter was discussed. Two palliative measures were adopted. One was that she would write her mother when Bob was not at home, and the other was that she would spend less time and effort in discussing and analyzing the content and implications of her mother's letters with Bob. Up to this point she had considered it her wifely duty to have him read her mother's letters and her answers and to discuss in detail the stated and implied meaning of everything her mother said. These measures alleviated, but did not solve, the problem. As far as Bob was concerned, every effort was made to get him to understand that

Joan's writing her mother once a week was a normal daughterly courtesy.

Interview with Wife's Mother: Mrs. B came to visit Joan and Bob a few months after I had entered the picture. This event not only made it possible for me to have an extensive conference with her, but it also marked the major turning point in the case.

The first part of our subsequent meeting could have been the high spot in a melodramatic movie of unusual personalities. It was "thrill packed" to say the least, but more importantly it was revealing. Two new therapeutic moves were made as a result: one with Mrs. B and one with Bob. The appointment was made for mid-afternoon, and the session ran on for the rest of the day. She was most courteous to me and especially grateful that I had taken an interest in her daughter. After the initial exchange of complimentary formalities and pleasantries, she began her devastating castigation of Bob. She called him just about all the derogatory names imaginable without using any profanity except an occasional "hell" or "damn." To her, Bob was "weak-willed," "lily-livered," "a jellyfish," "yellow," "no backbone," "wishy-washy," "lacking in determination," "not a man," "not a fit husband for my daughter," and so on. Divorce, however, was not mentioned once. She took the opportunity to give vent to all her disappointments and frustrations, as Bob had done before, but in quite a different way.

When she had spent herself on this topic, I was able to get her to talk of herself, her husband, and Joan, her own life, and so forth. She was fundamentally a pathetic, lonesome, and bewildered woman. But I was equally certain that her picture of herself in her mind's eye was quite to the contrary. My previous secondhand impression that she had not wished to be bothered with the actual responsibility of rearing Joan although she loved her was confirmed.

During the latter part of our conversation I turned the discussion back to Bob and Joan's marriage. An attempt was made to try to get her to understand that Bob had emotional problems and that an attempt to force him into a certain line of action would have an effect diametrical to that desired.

During our conversation I got the distinct impression that she was violently opposed to divorce. Therefore, since the attempt to inculcate sympathy for Bob did not appear immediately successful, I decided upon a frontal assault by this question, "Why don't you encourage Joan to get a divorce, and you take her and the baby away from Bob?" The question seemed to surprise her greatly, and she blurted out quickly, "I don't want any divorced daughter and fatherless child on my hands!" As we discussed this idea more, the fact that this was a possible consequence of the forces then in operation seemed to have come as a minor shock to her. She also seemed to sense, although she did not voice any confirmation, that her role in the whole relationship might possibly help Joan or Bob or both to decide to get a divorce. After this session there was not a revolutionary change in her behavior toward Bob and Joan, but Joan noted immediately and Bob sometime later that there was a subtle difference which in retrospect marked the turning point. Our conference ended on a cordial note. It was unfortunate that she did not have someone she could talk to freely and often.

Counseling Continued: Knowledge gained in this conference with Mrs. B was also used to construct a new therapeutic approach to Bob's problem. Prior to this time I had tried to help him gain more insight into Mrs. B by seeing that she did certain things in certain ways because she was a domineering mother who was interested in her daughter's welfare on the one hand, but who had not been willing to make some of the usual minimum sacrifices in rearing her. In other words, she was not perfect; she was human and fallible like the rest of us. This approach was helpful, but it was not nearly so effective as that evolved from a greater understanding of Mrs. B. From the time of my meeting with her, I began to build up the idea in his mind that Mrs. B was really a lonesome and pathetic woman. She was a woman to be pitied, not feared. In other words, she was really not a big threat to him but only a small threat, and perhaps not a threat at all. Although he was not able to convert this terrible ogre into a harmless old rag doll, he was able after some months to look upon her as an annoying mother-in-law who could not be loved. From this point on, the sailing was not smooth, but Bob's condition improved progressively.

Throughout this time and the remainder of the two years I continued to work with Joan also. Even though she did not have the aggravated personality problem which Bob did, her task was a difficult one. She had to learn to bear with Bob's many problems, as well as with some of her own, while carrying on the continuous day-to-day tasks of a housewife and mother. Her uncommonly good sense and firm determination to see it through were priceless ingredients in the preservation and reconstruction of the marriage.

As the mother-in-law threat was reduced, greater proficiency in German achieved, more insight into his and Joan's life gained, and self-confidence restored, Bob's whole life became brighter, and the marriage more satisfying. By the time of Bob's graduation, they were well on their way to a normal adjustment.

Follow-Up: Since his graduation four years ago, I have been able to follow the fortunes of Joan and Bob because he comes to see me, sometimes with Joan and the children and sometimes by himself, on an average of once every six months. He has a good job. They have acquired a new car, a house, and another child. They are all quite healthy. Even though Bob will always be somewhat reserved, he is now fairly well adjusted. In fact, the degree of personal and material well-being is far greater than would have been predicted even four years ago, and, of course, infinitely more so than could have been foreseen six years ago. Joan, too, has gotten much more from the marriage.

A good commentary on the change in Bob is his relationship to Mrs. B. When he was a lowly student, she stayed at a hotel when she came to visit. But she spent most of the day at the young couple's apartment in the student housing project where she slew him a thousand times a day. Now during her flying visits every three or four months, she stays with them. These visits are no longer catastrophic for Bob. They are nuisances, but they are tolerable.

EDITOR'S NOTE: This is a good illustration of a combination of practical help, education, and counseling.

4. Dominance and Submission in Marriage

Case 4. *An Older Dominating Wife; an Impotent, "Irresponsible"*
     Husband
Case 5. *Quarreling and Fighting Over Money*
Case 6. *Breakdown in Marital Communication*

These cases may be generally classified as dealing with personality conflict. It is interesting to note the wide variety of specific problems—among others, sex, money, wife's job—with which clients were originally preoccupied. These were, to be sure, handled practically and forthrightly by the counselors, but as the counseling process contributed to greater insight and individual emotional growth, they also became, not in themselves insignificant, but important as areas of difficulty which could be utilized to strengthen the total marriage relationship.

CASE 4

Problem: An older, dominating wife; an impotent, "irresponsible" husband
Presented by: Marriage counselor (Ph.D. in Sociology; graduate degree in Social Work) in Western city

Introduction: Mr. and Mrs. B were referred to the marriage counselor by a judge of the courts in a near-by city. Both partners felt the marital situation had become so acute that the marriage should be dissolved. In an initial interview, Mrs. B said that discovering that her husband was impotent and irresponsible was beyond her "coping ability." Mr. B announced that his wife's domination was too much for him! Although the couple lived some fifty miles from the counselor's office, the counseling period, extending over a year, included 29 interviews with Mrs. B; 59, with Mr. B.

Description: Mrs. B. is a tall, dark-complexioned, angular, independent-appearing woman, with an automatic smile which reminds one of a light turned on and off by a switch. She is an accomplished dress designer and prominent in her community. She is 39 years of age.

Mr. B is a tall, slender, rather "scared"-looking person, with blonde, wavy hair, who gives the impression of being bewildered most of the time. He has thin lips which he screws over to the side of his face during conversation. It appears to be a tic. He is a physical education teacher at a near-by high school; he also runs a farm. He is 29 years of age.

Background: Mrs. B's father was a successful grocer; little reference was ever made to her mother. However, it appears that her parents have a good marriage. Mrs. B seems to have had no traumatic experiences during childhood. She had a married sister ten years her senior who died of cancer seven years ago.

According to Mr. B, he grew up in a home where normal emotional exchange apparently was lacking. He has great hostility toward his father who he felt never appreciated him. He has two younger, unmarried sisters, both of whom he considers "mixed up."

He refers to his father as a man of limited education, who did janitor work most of his working years. Mr. B seems ashamed of his father's background, and is obviously not proud to claim him as a parent.

Premarriage: When the B's married, as reported by Mrs. B, there was quite a furor. Mr. B's parents were not present; however, Mrs. B's parents came for the wedding. Mrs. B's father disliked Mr. B intensely. The two men had fistic encounters as a result of the tension between them. One time they were having a very stormy session, Mrs. B (wife-to-be) interceded in some way and fell on a cement sidewalk. Three days before the marriage, Mr. B told his wife-to-be that he doubted he could go through with the marriage. He was "afraid." Since she insisted that the marriage be consummated, he haltingly went to the altar.

Interview Content: Mrs. B came for the first interview. She seemed very upset as she listed her husband's shortcomings which had become unbearable to her. She was tired of "waiting on" her husband. He came home with new clothes for himself and never suggested that she buy anything. He asked her to contribute $25 per month toward the household expenses, which she resented. He allowed her car to "sit" in the driveway while he parked his new station wagon in the carport. It never occurred to him that her car might need washing too.

She said, "I cracked up two weeks ago." She cried for two days straight before calming down. "I could not stop." He had "no concern for my tears."

At the close of the interview, MC (Marriage Counselor) said, "It isn't necessary to cry over this situation." Through interviews, she and Mr. B could explore the causes for the marital disharmony, and decide, one way or the other, what she wanted to do about them.

Mrs. B's eyes lightened. She said, "Do you think there is some hope?" She was given assurance that if she and her husband were willing to consolidate their efforts in behalf of the marriage, there was hope; however, it was important to determine first whether they actually wanted the marriage to work or not.

When Mr. B came for an interview, he had a supercilious look on his face. He was a very ineffectual-looking man and screwed his thin lips to the side in nervous gesturing. He kept running his fingers through his wavy hair throughout the interview. With all the resistance he could muster, he gave MC the critical eye.

When MC expressed the feeling that he had a side, too, and that she (MC) was equally interested in the problem as he saw it, he was slightly more productive. He quoted Dr. G (a psychiatrist whom he had previously seen) as saying, "If you stay with her, you will hurt her; if you leave her, you will hurt her." He had reference to his sexual inadequacy.

According to Mr. B his wife cried a lot; he didn't understand why. "I feel like a heel." He felt that sex was a problem; however, he gave the impression that he was generally inadequate. He knew the marriage could not continue. He quoted Dr. G frequently to substantiate his feelings.

MC told Mr. B that there were many obstacles to marital success in the situation. MC told him, as she had told Mrs. B, that through counseling, perhaps he would be helped to crystallize his thinking, and that whether the marriage held or not, he and his wife would be more sure of what they were doing.

MC discouraged making another appointment at this time and suggested that Mr. B think it over.

After several weeks, Mr. B returned for counseling. He was still resistive. The marital situation hadn't improved, but he was willing to work at it.

Mr. B spoke of his childhood as responsible for his maladjustment. He seemed deeply resentful of his background because of what it had done to him. He brought out that he did not have a positive feeling toward anyone in his family and particularly not for his father. He again quoted Dr. G. He said that sex meant nothing to him. What information he gave was upon questioning. His whole attitude was one of doubt about the value of professional help; however, of his own accord, he made another appointment.

In subsequent interviews, Mrs. B was very emotional in discussing her husband's inadequacies. She referred especially to his impotency. She felt he should have told her of this before marriage. His table manners were "atrocious." He would only nibble at special dishes she cooked for him. "There is no incentive in cooking or anything else."

MC explored some of the possible reasons that her husband's behavior came as such a surprise to her after marriage. When asked what she had seen in Mr. B in their courtship days, she said that he was a "gentleman" and that they had common interests. (Note: This woman is ten years older than her husband.) She brought out that she felt he had a good "potential" and would develop his personality. According to Mrs. B, she and Mr. B had kissed each other in their courtship days in a rather perfunctory manner. She, however, at no time wondered about his sexual competency.

MC asked Mrs. B if she thought she had a normal interest in sex. She had never, actually, thought of this. She mentioned that she had been engaged to a homosexual at one time and that she had had other men friends, too. She rationalized considerably in giving reasons for discontinuing the friendships with the amorous men.

She showed a need to talk further about her husband's irresponsibility. She again brought out that she wanted "to help him" get some place. When MC asked Mrs. B what she meant by her husband's "potential," it was obvious that she meant that she planned on directing him toward certain goals.

She told how she advised him in business ways. "If it hadn't been for me, he could not have received the loan from the bank. It required my signature. I know that I have more knowledge of business than he does." Since her husband always procrastinated, she said that she had gone to the bank regarding a property they were considering for purchase, instead of letting him take care of it. He resented this. Mrs. B paused for a moment in reflective thought, when MC wondered if Mrs. B might be overdirective. She answered, "Well, I always have wanted my own way." She spoke of her childhood; as a little girl, she described herself as very determined.

Through discussion, it was brought out that Mrs. B was probably somewhat confused herself in the sexual area in that she had tended toward homosexuals; at least she had been engaged to one and had married another with similar tendencies. She thought she might be too independent and not as "feminine" as she really wanted to be.

Mrs. B found counseling helpful. She wasn't sure she wanted to continue the marriage but was convinced that she wanted to improve her own personality.

Mr. B was seen several times when his wife visited her parents in California. He had not been able to make himself write. He said he was tired of being "dominated" and "pushed around." MC encouraged him to write his wife a rather casual letter. It was suggested that he not write anything that he did not mean; however, to allow her to "save face" inasmuch as her parents would wonder why she had not heard from him. MC thought the least he might do would be to lessen some of the embarrassment his wife would naturally feel if she did not hear from him. Mr. B looked surprised. "I never thought of that. I never think of little things like the other husbands do." He considered this a problem in the marriage. However, Mr. B said that he missed his wife. He was not sure, nevertheless, that he wanted to save the marriage. MC asked Mr. B if he had stopped to think that possibly his wife might not wish to remain in the marriage. This seems to have been the first time that it occurred to him that the decision, as to whether or not the marriage would hold, was not his alone. From this time on, it seemed that progress gradually evidenced itself.

He brought out that he had always felt inadequate; however, now he could see how unsharing he had been in the marriage. He said he sometimes wished he had his freedom, and yet wondered if he could get along without his wife.

MC assured him that he probably would respond more easily to treatment now that he recognized that he, too, had something at stake. MC said not to worry about the sex part of the marriage. If he solved some of his other conflicts and became a more mature person, perhaps the intimate aspects of the marriage would improve. He hoped so. At this point Mr. B seemed to want to talk about his reasons for finding sex so unattractive to him in his marriage.

He said that he had homosexual tendencies but they had never become overt. Among his friends, he discussed one or two who had similar tendencies. To him, sex was "repulsive" and kissing meant "nothing." He never was responsive to women but thought "marriage would make me that way."

He told MC that he masturbated several times a week. He admitted that he thought a homosexual experience might be pleasant but never had "gone through with it." After making these comments he seemed unable to discuss the subject further at this time.

When Mrs. B returned, the B's had their ups and downs. Tension was high at times. Mrs. B made emergency appointments when something very upsetting occurred between them. They separated for two days and almost separated on other occasions. The interim moments, however, between their quarrels and threats to dissolve the marriage, were more satisfying than they had ever been before. They both arrived at the conclusion during this period that there was something to salvage in the marriage.

One morning when Mrs. B came to the study, she was furious. "I maintain my own car, contribute $25 to the household expense, and he spends his money on himself." He paid current bills but didn't consider any of her expenses as his concern. MC suggested that the B's make an appointment together regarding a budget. Mr. B resented the idea. He told MC that he couldn't "talk" with his wife around. MC told him that a deadlock in progress had been reached and that such an interview seemed indicated if further progress through counseling was to be expected.

Several interviews were devoted to household budgeting. After the first interview on budgets, which was an exchange of divergent views, objectives were established.

The B's decided to pool part of their earnings, Mr. B's income from teaching and his wife's income from her dress designing. Mr. B was to keep a separate account for his farm. He was to make decisions regarding the farm without Mrs. B's usual veto. She was to be advised of what he was doing, and if any capital investments were made, or any other major decisions, he would talk them over with his wife. Mrs. B decided to let her husband develop the farm according to his own thinking. She was pleased that they would have a budget.

Mrs. B would take care of the mechanics of bill paying. They had had many arguments, previously, about this, since Mr. B ignored accounts.

Both were happy over the budget plan; however, several stormy sessions preceded the final acceptance of some of the suggestions made for handling the money.

When this major problem, "money," was out of the way, other difficulties in the marriage were discussed.

During this period, each verbalized resentment toward the other. Frequent quarrels took place although, between them, there were longer periods of comparative calm. Mrs. B had reminded her husband on several occasions, while shedding copious tears, that she had given up her "family and job" for the marriage. She told her husband that she had nothing to return to, in the event the marriage did not hold. MC thought probably Mrs. B was battling with her "independence" needs. She answered she "probably" was. She began to describe herself as a "dominating woman." Her automatic smile became less frequent.

Mr. B was finding some assurance through MC's encouragement in learning that marriage is a difficult adjustment for many people. When MC said that she did not believe that his wife was marriageable at the time they took their vows either, he seemed somewhat relieved.

Mr. B referred to his mother. He reflected hostility toward her because she "had allowed" his father to treat him as he did. He felt he was very immature and continued to blame his childhood for "making me this way."

Although Mr. and Mrs. B were gaining some insight into the problem, the marriage was still in a very precarious state.

Mr. B's interviews were biweekly for several weeks. He kept his appointments faithfully. According to him, on two short trips from which he had recently returned, he had not missed his wife. He had actually seemed to be relieved. He took care of his own sex needs when he was away from Mrs. B through masturbation. He did not want to write to her. It almost seemed that he could not write.

On exploring possible reasons for his feelings, he again blamed his childhood. MC asked him if he was not using his childhood as a crutch rather than assuming any responsibility for his failures. He thought for a moment and said that this was probably true. MC said that all of us were victims of our childhood, in some ways, but that to use one's childhood as an excuse for poor performance in our adult years was not a very mature way to attack a problem. He knew this. (MC had discovered early in counseling Mr. B that a direct approach stimulated thinking which resulted in more productive subsequent interviews.)

As though trying to assume some responsibility himself for his inadequacy, he mentioned that he was always overlooking some of the little things that would please his wife. He knew that he was not always very considerate.

MC asked Mr. B what the possible reasons might be for his behavior. He said he guessed that he was afraid of his wife. MC asked him to explain this. He brought out that she was not necessary to him in the usual ways husbands and wives were necessary to each other. He spoke of his wife's education and thought that probably he was "jealous" of her success. He added, with emotion, "I intend to be successful in farming in spite of her." He said he did not "feel" anything when his wife was around. He referred to himself as being self-centered, but he would feel disgusted with himself for not thinking of the "little things." He would ask MC for suggestions.

From time to time, MC suggested specific things he might do for his wife, which would please her. He would say with great surprise, "Why, I never would have thought of that." Although he said that he did not care to do these things and that perhaps he would feel more like doing them for some other women, yet, when his wife showed appreciation for anything he might do, this seemed to mean something to him.

He began to question whether, if he were married to someone else, he would be more responsive sexually. MC suggested that many married men who felt inadequate thought that some woman, other than their wives, would be able to give them what they wanted. He might be right.

Concurrent interviews with Mrs. B brought up many specific grievances—her husband's table manners, personal cleanliness, and the like.

She brought out that although she had seen some improvement and knew that Mr. B was responding to treatment and probably doing the best that he could, she doubted that he ever could offer enough to make the marriage worth while. MC said that that might well be true. Mrs. B was asked whether or not she thought further interviews would be helpful, or if she would like to take the whole matter over by herself. She was sure that she wanted to continue counseling.

In discussing some of Mrs. B's complaints with Mr. B, he seemed disturbed over the fact that his wife would not discuss such matters with him. MC wondered if the reason might be that he would only become angry and perhaps not do anything about it anyway. He thought so. MC said, "Have you any idea why your wife may have felt this way?" He knew that he had not been able to discuss very much without becoming upset. He guessed that if he were better able to sit down and talk things over like a more mature person, fewer of these problems would have to be brought to the attention of a marriage counselor.

Subsequently, Mrs. B reported that her husband's table manners were improving; that he had bought her several gifts and that he was showering several times a week. MC thought that possibly she should ask her husband about mannerisms she might have that were annoying to him. It was suggested that all of us have idiosyncrasies, of one kind or another, and that she, perhaps, had been thinking only of the irritants in his personality, and that he might be harboring some resentment about some of hers as well.

MC suggested that perhaps, if she and Mr. B would specify the times during the past week each had found fault with the other's actions, they might be helped to discover some particular need of theirs which motivated their reactions. She could see the merits of this suggestion.

For the following two weeks, Mr. B said that both looked for reasons that they reacted toward situations as they did. She brought out that her husband felt competitive toward her. She guessed that because of the age difference and the fact that she was better known professionally than he, he was trying to prove to himself that he could be successful. She could see his competitive behavior particularly in connection with the farm. It was strictly "a hands off" project as far as he was concerned. MC wondered if his desire to be successful might not be a commendable objective. She had thought of this herself. She also began to see that unless she was directing his life, she wasn't happy. MC thought that Mrs. B might be treating her husband somewhat like students in dress designing. She acknowledged that this very need of hers was one of the basic problems in the marriage. Mrs. B felt, however, that she was less dominating than she had formerly been. She said this with some pride. She seemed pleased to begin to understand herself better.

Before the B's were married, there was a "fellow" by the name of Fred with whom Mr. B had spent considerable time. He was in business in New York and came West for a short vacation. He returned at this time and naturally wanted Mr. B to spend some time with him. Mrs. B, knowing of her husband's homosexual tendencies, and, of course, his sexual inadequacy, became very much upset during Fred's visit. MC tried to allay some of her anxiety by saying it might be rather difficult for Mr. B to break off a friendship of such long standing. MC also suggested that Mrs. B make no comment to her husband regarding Fred. If she were able to refrain from being critical, probably her husband would discuss with her his visits with his friend.

When Mr. B came in for his next interview, he was very much pleased to think that he had "told off" Fred. Apparently in the past, Fred had been the one to advise Mr. B and more or less serve as his therapist. Mr. B, with some pride, had told Fred that he thought he was "mixed up" and that if he were married, he would probably have a less successful marriage than the B's were enjoying. MC asked if he had mentioned Fred's visit to his wife. He said that he had "just last night" talked with her about Fred. "For the first time in our marriage, she listened with understanding." He was so pleased to find that she was not critical and "for once" didn't give advice.

During the next three months, considerable improvement in the marriage was indicated. Every day each was becoming more marriageable. Mrs. B had no further complaints about the budget. The sexual relationship was improving. The B's had given several patio parties in their home which were very successful. They had intimate little chats following these gatherings which both enjoyed. Mr. and Mrs. B considered themselves as more mature and felt they could much more easily share their thoughts and experiences with each other. They began to compare themselves with their friends. They would say to MC, "They need you worse than we do."

It was not until this time, actually, that Mr. B was able to discuss sex easily. During one interview, he pulled a chair up to MC's desk while the counselor drew pictures of the sex organs. He had no idea what the word "clitoris" meant. He did not find his wife repulsive, but on frequent trials at insertion of the penis, he was unable to retain an erection. MC was very encouraging always when he discussed these failures. MC told him that that should not bother him too much as even very virile men, from time to time, were too tired or upset sometimes to be successful. He was glad to know that.

MC used a small doll to help in getting the point over as to the position of the male and female during intercourse. He apparently had not considered his position and said that his wife probably complained of his "dead weight" on her. After he and his wife decided to make a conscientious attempt to improve their sexual relationship, he discontinued masturbation.

After several months, he said that he was actually beginning to enjoy sex with his wife. His ejaculation was quick but MC, again, told him that as he gained confidence in himself, this aspect of sexual intercourse would work itself out. He was given help in understanding the meaning of manual manipulation, so that his wife might be more satisfied. Both were patient with each other. MC's emphasis with Mrs. B through this period was in helping her understand that her attitude while her husband was working through his sexual problem, was as important as therapy. Mr. and Mrs. B came to MC reporting their success, sexually speaking, with the greatest of pride. They began to talk about having a child. The B's felt that further counseling at this time was not indicated, and the case was closed. They wanted to be sure, however, that they could return for a "refresher" interview if necessary.

Counselor's Comments: It seemed that Mrs. B's independence and rather aggressive approach to life was a defense against her own need for love and affection. She lacked femininity which she covered by a kind of superficial affectation as shown by her automatic smiling and facial expression. Mr. B was a very weak individual, who needed a dominating person to direct him, but, by the same token, resented his dependence. Each was basically immature.

It was necessary to help Mr. B understand that his desire to terminate the marriage (reflected in the early interview) was actually a face-saving move on his part. Basically, he wanted marriage, but his inadequacy overwhelmed him. Mrs. B had ambivalent feelings about the marriage. To give up the independence that she had enjoyed was almost too big a price for her to pay.

She compared her husband unfavorably with other men. She lost respect for him on learning he was childish in so many ways. His sexual inadequacy was, ostensibly, her greatest problem. Probably, had Mr. B been a sexually satisfying partner, she would not have married him. Her leaning toward those with homosexual tendencies indicated that she may have been fearful of sex herself. Since Mr. B was so inadequate, she did not have to face her own problems. MC doubts that Mrs. B ever did gain much insight here.

Mr. B, in discovering that he was so unable to be a successful sex partner, tried to overcompensate by being a successful farmer. As he had said one time, "I'm going to make a success of this in spite of her."

Although the prognosis was guarded when interviewing was begun with this couple, and improvement was gradual and intermittent, both were patient and co-operative throughout the counseling period. It is hoped that before long the B's will either have adopted a child or have had one of their own. Parenthood would be a maturing experience for both of them. It is believed that each would be an excellent parent.

From all indications now, this husband and wife are enjoying a kind of companionship which seems almost above average. They have many common interests, enjoy the same friends, and have developed a most satisfying emotional exchange between them.

EDITOR'S NOTE: In this case, the immaturity of both spouses and the struggle for dominance (complicated by the ten-year age difference) are elements in the emotional climate within which a specific sex problem obtained. This case is by no means "short term" counseling (counseling period was extended over a year) and is here reported in considerable detail. The editors feel that the step-by-step counseling process will prove interesting, especially to the professional reader.

It could be noted that the relationship of patience, interest, support between the counselor and these clients was perhaps the most therapeutically important factor in the picture we have of positive growth.

CASE 5

Problem: Quarreling and fighting over money
Presented by: Marriage counselor (Ph.D. in Education; graduate degree in Psychiatric Social Work; ordained minister) in private practice in a large metropolitan city

Introduction: The R family is intact, consisting of the husband, wife, and their children. Mrs. R made the first contact by telephoning for an appointment. She stated that the medical social worker at the county hospital where her daughter has undergone several operations had suggested that she and her husband seek marriage counseling. She described the problem as being concerned partly with finances and partly with more serious problems of quarreling, fighting, and the tension which this creates for all members of the family.

The Problem as Presented by Husband and Wife: Mrs. R, who was first seen in an interview, said that she and Mr. R had been married fourteen years and had known each other nearly two years prior to marriage. Mrs. R's eye was considerably discolored from a recent blow from her husband following a heated argument over finances. This was the first time he had struck her. She complained that Mr. R does not allow her sufficient money with which to buy food and run the household, holding her usually to $35 a week plus the cost of milk although it had been understood that she would receive $50. Yet her husband sometimes puts $10 in the offering plate at church; she cannot get herself as much as a new pair of stockings! Mr. R has a violent temper and uses abusive language which he later denies. Mr. R's father, who is nearly eighty years of age, lives with the family. Mrs. R feels her husband places his father before herself, complains that her father-in-law coughs, that he is careless in his personal habits, and that his care adds considerably to her burden. Mrs. R and her husband have not been living as man and wife for about three months. Prior to that time sexual relations occurred two or three times a week with varying degrees of satisfaction. She stated that her husband tends to be very abrupt in his sexual advances. Mrs. R can't think her husband loves her any more as he is never demonstrative except in connection with the sexual relationship, is stingy with her, and seems to care more about his father than her. During the interview her eyes filled with tears several times. Her general mood was one of unhappiness. She pictured herself as a suffering wife, glossed over any part she might contribute to the family quarrels, and gave the appearance of repressing a great deal of her own anger and hostility. The children seem to constitute no added problem except that one of them, a teen-age girl, has had several operations for an orthopedic condition and is obliged to use crutches for getting around the house and has to have home instructions from school. She reveals genuine interest in this child and her plight and at the same time expressed considerable resentment that when this girl needs one dress the father is apt to buy her two although he objects to Mrs. R spending a small amount for her own clothes.

During the first interview with Mr. R he was quite apologetic about having struck his wife and volunteered that he supposed it was mean of him to withhold knowledge of their finances from her. He had been recording the check stubs in symbols which only he understood so that his wife did not know whether she could draw a check or not. He denied not loving his wife but pointed out that she does nothing to inspire affection; in fact, her behavior drives him the other way. He complained that she gets violently angry and is sometimes spiteful, as on one occasion she turned on every light in the house after an argument over finances. He asked, "Why does she dig into me so much?" Mr. R is aware that the presence of his father in the home complicates the problem, but none of his brothers or sisters are in as good a position to provide a home for the father as he. Moreover, his father paid several thousand dollars as down payment on the home which is in the family's name, with the understanding that this would be his home while he lives. His father treats him with real respect and he has not the heart to turn him out. He complained that his wife dislikes housekeeping and though she provides adequate meals, washes and irons clothes he feels the home needs much more of a woman's touch. He mentioned that a few days before his wife's mother had died she slipped his wife a bankbook with $1000. Mr. R feels that the women in his wife's family gang up on and hold out against the men. He fears that if his wife gets much money in her hands she will hold out in this way. Mr. R has found that his wife tends to conform to social expectations in the presence of people who are outside the family. Consequently he invites neighbors to come into the home almost every evening to play cards or Scrabble or engage in conversation. When neighbors are present his wife does not involve him in quarrels or make critical comments. This seems to be largely a protective pattern and does not stem from any active social interest on the part of Mr. R himself.

The Counseling: During the first interview with each mate explanation was made that the counselor's role is one of helping each mate to understand himself and the other, and to discover the ways in which each perhaps has brought to the current family certain attitudes and feeling patterns which were developed in the course of growing up. It was noted that the counselor would not be giving either of them specific advice of a rule-of-thumb kind. Because the situation was charged with a great deal of emotion on the part of both Mr. and Mrs. R, ample opportunity was provided to each of them to talk out their complaints and express their anger and hurt feelings. After some ventilation of this sort, the counselor inquired about the growing-up experiences of each, and the sort of relationship that had prevailed with reference to parents, sibling, and peers.

Though Mrs. R seemed considerably more repressed during the first interview than did her husband, she was rather more open in her discussion of her own family background and her feelings about it. She described her father as a stern man who for the first twenty years of her life ruled her with angry looks. She said, "He only had to look at me with that look and I did whatever he wanted no matter how unpleasant and did not answer him back." Only later, a few years before her marriage, did she begin to talk back to him and sometimes refuse his bidding. Her father became decidedly depressed after her mother's death and he was not able to work much after that. Her mother seemed to have played a protective role shielding her from the worst of her father's severity and as already noted had given her a bank account of $1000 a short time before her death. Mrs. R has two brothers, with the younger of whom she had been very close prior to her marriage. After the father's death this brother took over all the furniture and possessions of the home and all the bank accounts involving an unknown amount of funds. Both Mrs. R and her older brother have felt bitter about this and neither of them are now on speaking terms with the younger brother. The older brother has threatened that he would not speak to her if she in turn talks to her younger brother. Mrs. R told this with some obvious regret at the disturbed relationship with the younger brother who perhaps otherwise would have been used more or less as a confidant with regard to her own problem.

Mrs. R had two years of college training and was employed for a short while before her marriage. She often talked about getting a job again but was frank to state that her only motivation for this was the money. When asked what she wished for or would like to have changed about the present relationships she said, "I would like my husband to be kind, gentle, and loving to me, not just in connection with sex; and I want him to allow me more money for the house and to buy the children clothes when needed." She expressed doubt whether her husband had ever loved her, said he never kissed her. He had dated her months before he told his mother. There was some discussion of her disappointment that her father was stern and unloving and that she thinks of her husband as being a bit like her father in that he is rather undemonstrative. In a subdued way Mrs. R expressed a great deal of hostile feeling as she talked about both her father and her younger brother and it seemed doubtful as to how responsive she can be to a man in close relationship with her. It seemed likely that in her somewhat rejecting attitude toward males she probably inhibited her own sexual interest, with the result that she rather rarely achieved orgasm in her sexual relationship with her husband and in the main assumed an attitude of tolerating rather than anticipating or enjoying coitus. At the same time she did not seem to be altogether frigid and made favorable comment on those occasions when her husband was surprisingly tender and gentle.

Mr. R was definitely more controlled during the interviews, offering relatively little confidential information regarding his own family background. He noted that his parents had separated when he was in his early twenties but still maintained that his own childhood had been fairly happy. (Mrs. R claims that Mr. R's family life was not at all happy; that there was friction during the years especially over money matters and his father was stingy with his mother.) Mr. R stressed somewhat his regret at not having been able to go to college because of the need to work in order to assist in the maintenance of the large family. He had taken some special training along the line of his work and tried to advance himself in various ways but changed jobs some ten times over a period of fifteen to eighteen years.

Mr. R expressed a great deal of distress over his wife's attitude toward his father. He felt that his wife basically does not dislike the father but is punishing him by urging that he require the father to live elsewhere. Mr. R acknowledged that the home is somewhat crowded and that he should follow through his intention of dividing one of the larger rooms. Mr. R obviously is very responsible in reference to his work and endeavors to secure overtime and extra work to increase the family income. It was clear that during the periods when income is minimal rather than maximal, there is not more than about $35 a week left for food and general household expenses after fixed expenditures—mortgage, taxes, car payment, and so on—are deducted. But during periods when there is substantial overtime or extra work, there is considerable margin above this. His handling of the money seems to stem partly from a family pattern and lifetime concern about cautious spending and partly from a desire to punish his wife or hold her in line when she is irritable toward him and criticizes him. Her criticism hurts his feelings very much and he then "clams up" and burns up inside, except occasionally when his anger bursts forth rather violently. His generosity with his daughter and in charitable contributions when he has funds are denials of a rigidly fixed penurious pattern.

During the first two interviews with Mrs. R and the first rather long interview with Mr. R, besides providing opportunity for ventilation and catharsis, some interpretation of each was made to the other in terms of their experiences in growing up with their respective families and what had become more or less characteristic patterns of thought, feeling, and expectation. Mr. R stated that he considered Mrs. R's father pretty much a crackpot and he could understand how living with him through the childhood and teen years could well have caused his wife a great deal of hurt feeling and tendency to feel hostile toward a male person.

Mrs. R became much more relaxed as interviews progressed and she expressed more freely her very frank feelings of hostility toward her father formerly and currently toward her younger brother and her husband. She seemed to feel that if her husband would show her more consideration and affection and deal kindly with her, she could manage the household satisfactorily. She admitted she does not especially like housework but she has always tried to do her duty and believes she does fairly well considering the limited funds with which she is supplied. It was the counselor's impression that Mrs. R was probably correct in her judgment that she could get along all right if loved and treated kindly.

Effort, therefore, was made to help Mr. R understand his wife's great need for more affection and more evidence of being cherished and counted upon. Since he was already apologetic and repentant about striking his wife, withholding money from her, and quarreling bitterly at times, he seemed to be better motivated than his wife toward trying to effect some changes. He expressed willingness, if not eagerness, to change the general scheme of handling the family finances and asked the counselor's help in working out a suitable arrangement.

There followed a *joint interview* with Mr. and Mrs. R during which there was rather complete discussion of income and expenditures and the formulation of a plan for handling the same. Incidentally, both Mr. and Mrs. R reported that there had been no serious quarrels during the previous week. After some discussion it was mutually agreed that Mr. R would deposit all his salary in a checking account, Mrs. R would keep the checking account, except for the itemized fixed charges amounting to about $150 a month which Mr. R would pay by check at the end of the month. Mrs. R in turn agreed to keep a record of the purchases from the $35 to $50 which she expects to draw from the checking account weekly, and Mr. R agreed to keep a record of his expenditures for travel, lunches, dinner, and so on. Both promised to try to save something from the funds available to them, the savings to be deposited in a joint savings account. Mrs. R made it clear that she would not go through another year on $35 a week and instead would seek part-time employment if that proved to be necessary. Mr. R offered no radical objections to his wife's working but expressed the opinion that they can manage without. The counselor suggested that they give this plan a two-week trial at the end of which they return for separate interviews for the discussion of more personal aspects of their problems. During this joint interview there was also some discussion of the children and their respective needs. Interestingly, the mother provides the boys with their weekly allowance, and the father the girls.

In *Mrs. R's interview two weeks later* she reported that it had been the best two-week period for a long, long time. Mr. R had been much more considerate and kind, he now kisses her goodbye before leaving home and cheerfully says hello when he returns. He has left the checkbook in her hands and she draws $45 weekly for food and household essentials. Each week thus far she had a few dollars left for saving. In this interview Mrs. R noted for the first time that until the past two weeks she had had choking sensations in her throat much of the time. She had been to physicians who at one time thought she had a thyroid difficulty and said she had not told the counselor about this earlier lest he send her off posthaste to a doctor who would again think it was her thyroid. She was well aware that she has this condition only when she has been very angry or is under tension. She reported that at such times her heart pounds at high speed. She is sure this has been entirely due to tension and states that she has been entirely free from this and has slept well during the past two weeks. When they visited her brother's family the latter commented how much happier Mrs. R seemed to be. Mrs. R noted that they had not had a single quarrel in two weeks, and the children had commented that it is so much nicer when their parents do not fight. She said that her husband's father does not bother her so much now when Mr. R is good to her; she feels she owes his father proper care. Mrs. R ascribed the improvement to the help obtained through the counseling. She felt no need to return for further interviews. She said she would rather stay at home and take care of the family than go to work.

In his interview two weeks after the joint interview, Mr. R reported that things had been going fine. He feels very different toward his wife and hopes that it lasts. She does not show tension nor get so angry at him. If her tension should ever mount again as it did a few weeks ago and put her in another of "those depressed moods" he could not stand it. In recent weeks, he has not been dragging neighbors in every evening to help to keep her calm and interested. He expressed the wish that his wife would develop some outside interests that would give her some satisfaction, and that she would show more interest in decorating and tidying up the home but agrees that she does not neglect meals, washing, and mending. Mr. R thought that they could get along now and expressed appreciation of the counselor's help. He expressed concern as to what could be done if his wife ever got in a depressed mood again. Counselor suggested that he seek a new appointment if this happens and counselor would help him to find appropriate resources if needed. Counselor noted that Mrs. R gets depressed only when she has been made angry or is feeling unloved and neglected, and discussed the cumulative effect of the treatment she had received from her father. Counselor suggested that if Mr. R could show more affection and trust his wife a little further in the handling of funds this would make her feel more cherished and appreciated and perhaps give her enough satisfaction so that she will neither develop symptoms nor resort to her former critical attitudes toward him. Counselor was aware that this might place on Mr. R more responsibility than he could carry consistently, but he seemed better prepared to carry it than his wife. Since both Mr. and Mrs. R seemed happy with the outcome and expressed the desire not to return for further appointments, it was left this way notwithstanding the counselor's doubt as to whether the adjustment would be sustained. It was suggested that they seek further appointments if needed rather than allow things to snowball into a serious state of affairs.

Follow-up: A follow-up telephone call a year and a half later revealed that the adjustment did not maintain itself at the high level prevailing when counseling terminated. Mrs. R's largely negative account may have been somewhat exaggerated because the first incident of Mr. R's striking her (during the year and a half) had occurred only a few days prior to this. During a heated quarrel Mr. R had kicked her in the legs, causing some bruising. She still feels that he is somewhat stingy with her, and she especially objects to the violence of Mr. R's occasional temper outbursts. She said that if he ever abuses her again she intends to report the matter to the local priest. She is sure her husband will not like this but feels that that might help since he is quite a religious man and faithful in church attendance and may therefore accept instruction or suggestion from the priest. Mrs. R's physical symptoms return during intervals when she is under tension and is free from them when things are going rather smoothly. She expressed no interest in obtaining treatment for herself and was inclined to blame her husband for the periods when tensions mount.

Counselor's Comment: This case illustrates the dilemma in which the counselor frequently finds himself. In order to avoid continued dependence upon a counselor it is necessary to allow and encourage husbands and wives to manage their affairs as quickly and as fully as they can on their own and give them the freedom of terminating the counseling as soon as they feel they can handle matters. When symptoms drop away and relationships improve as they often do in the first weeks, counseling is apt to be terminated without the basic dynamic factors having been dealt with sufficiently to insure long-term adjustment. There is at least a fair possibility that had this couple continued counseling sessions for at least twice as long as they did, they might have gotten sufficient understanding to have maintained the adjustment better through mutual efforts to meet each other's emotional and social needs after a period of time; or if they had returned for further counseling when tensions again mounted they could probably have been helped to achieve fuller insight into their difficulties and to develop skills in maintaining their relationships on a healthier basis.

CASE 6

Problem: Breakdown in marital communication
Presented by: Marriage and family counselor (MSSW) in private practice in urban area

Introduction: Mr. and Mrs. M came to the counselor's office wanting help with their marriage. Mrs. M had already spent several months attempting to alleviate the tension between them by going to (1) a family service agency, (2) a psychiatric clinic where she received both individual and group psychotherapy, and (3) classes sponsored by the Adult Education Division of the local Department of Education, conducted by the counselor. In recent weeks, Mr. M had become more seriously interested in working on the problem, and he had attended these classes with his wife as he "had the time." In their request for help with their marriage, they agreed that they had spent enough time on "the preliminaries" and were ready to "plunge into a more direct attack on the problem."

First Joint Interview: Although they seemed sincere and co-operative, as soon as they were accepted for counseling, the interview seemed to deteriorate into a battle for the upper hand. Charges concerning old hurts of the past were flung into the face of Mr. M by Mrs. M and he reacted with countercharges and somewhat inappropriate laughter. As the tension built up, Counselor suggested that preliminary individual sessions might be of more help. They calmed noticeably at this, and after ex-changing rather crestfallen glances, Mrs. M said she thought that such a procedure would only prolong the start. Mr. M agreed heartily and asked Counselor what should be done. Counselor suggested that they review briefly their marital situation.

Quite politely, taking turns in the narrative, they told of their marriage of eleven years' duration. They had married after a courtship of approximately one year. Mr. M had been the ag-gressor, Mrs. M stressing that she had been only mildly inter-ested in him. She finally consented to the marriage because she hoped that he would "grow up" over the years ahead. But, she emphasized, the more she tried to help him mature, the less progress he made. During her pregnancy which resulted in the birth of a son, he seemed more immature than ever, often for-getting her altogether while socializing outside the home. Now, their son being 13 years of age, he "always has time for others," but little or none for herself and the boy. The worst hurt of all was the loss of a second child five years ago.

This second child, while still an infant, succumbed to pneumonia "all because he, Mr. M, would not get out of bed to keep him covered during a cold night." Mr. M burst into tears at this, and this seemed to silence Mrs. M who paled and kept her grim, pale face averted. Mr. M recovered his poise sufficiently to explain that he is a "very heavy sleeper" and to reiterate what the physician at the time had said, that the child's death was not really anyone's fault. Mrs. M, tearful herself by this time, pointed out that if she had not been suffering with a cold herself at the time, she would have risen to check on the baby.

Counselor observed that there are many bitter memories of the past that one can use as weapons against the other. Both agreed, and Mrs. M remarked that she had a hard time forgetting. "If only he would change," she pleaded, they could be happy.

His poignant "How do you want me to change, dear?" brought an indignant snort from Mrs. M who quickly stipulated that he could be more punctual, for one thing, spend more time with her and their son, and, while in their presence, keep his mind on their conversation.

Very meticulously, he answered each of these criticisms and pointed out that as a struggling accountant, he had to "get out and make contacts," spend evenings working on financial problems for his clients, and when he had time at home his mind was usually on these matters. She pointed out that he is not really a struggling accountant, since his business has grown considerably in the past few years. She also stated that she was tired of being his secretary since she could not take care of home, their son, and his business contacts too. He replied that it was either this, or he would have to hire a secretary. She retorted that he ought to be able to handle it himself, or at least give her recognition for what she was doing. He said he considered her help "mere legwork" and insisted that there was "nothing to it." She immediately went into detail and pointed up how much there was to it.

The time was drawing to a close, and Counselor reviewed briefly the problem as it was presented—a struggle for mastery, lack of communication due to pattern of constant attack and counterattack, lack of mutual recognition of the assets of each. They both nodded and seemed to acknowledge this summary, and as they were leaving, Mr. M said this was the most talking he and Mrs. M had done "in years." She added, "Maybe we'll learn something this way about communicating."

Second Interview: Mr. and Mrs. M were on time for their next appointment. As soon as the interview began, the same old "dueling" relationship showed up. After a few minutes of this, Counselor asked whether they had discussed the initial session of last week since that interview. They had not. Counselor suggested that they take an evening between sessions for this purpose. Mr. M said, somewhat facetiously, "She'd only beat on me." She came back with "He'd just laugh it off." And the interview again deteriorated into the same kind of contest described in the record of the initial interview. Counselor decided to let this run its course, on the assumption that this was an old tried and true method of relating for them, and being anxious about possible change, they wanted to keep on familiar ground for a while. (This assumption was not stated to Mr. and Mrs. M.)

Toward the end of the hour, Counselor asked what they saw as future steps in the counseling process. Mr. M suggested that they write a list of things that bother each of them about the other. Mrs. M said her list would be "a mile long." Mr. M said his could be done in one sentence—in fact, one word—"love." He explained quickly that he doubts that Mrs. M loves him. She did not meet his pleading gaze, but merely replied that she did not feel enough warmth for him to say she loved him. Yet, for the sake of their son, she did not want to break up the marriage. He brightened at this remark, and commented that he never knew when she might be starting divorce proceedings. She said pointedly that she still has not decided against a divorce. He cringed at this, and with tears in his eyes, asked her to name the conditions and he would meet them in order to try to earn her love. She shrugged her shoulders and said that he had made such statements before. Counselor suggested that they try listening to each other during the week to come, and they said they would try.

Third Interview: The same pattern of attack and counterattack continued in the next interview. Mrs. M had her list of "grievances" in her lap during the session, and Mr. M said he had his in his pocket. However, they had not spent any time discussing this together. Mrs. M explained that they were planning a graduation party for their son, and this was time consuming. Also, they were planning a three-week trip to Florida.

Mr. M brought up the topic of sex. He complained that she would never take part in this with any apparent enjoyment, although she always experienced orgasm. Their position for coitus was unpleasant to him, since they would assume a crosswise position on the bed where, as he put it, "I had the pillow to kiss." She said she did not like his kisses or fondling—but just wanted relief of sexual tension through orgasm about once a month. He wanted sexual relations at least a couple of times a week. She wanted him to use "two condrums" for safety. He wanted some variations in their sex life, for example, fellatio and cunnilingus. These suggested practices repulsed her. She felt that he was too crude sexually, emphasizing that she wants to be courted. He often asks, "If you want it, say so; if not, I'll work." In addition, on the rare occasions when she has agreed to cunnilingus, she has experienced "kidney infections." She blamed these practices for her condition, although their physician had stated that there was no connection between the two.

Since the hour was drawing to a close and this would be the

last session until their return from Florida, Counselor commented again on their need to attack each other and to defend themselves from each other, pointing hopefully to a time when such a pattern would not be so completely necessary. Laughingly, Mrs. M put away her list and said that they would take this up some other time. Mr. M laughed also. In spite of the similar pattern in this interview as in those before, it appeared that there was some lessening of tension.

Summary of Fourth, Fifth, and Sixth Interviews (All Joint): The Florida vacation was "a flop." Arguments, tension, spoiled it, Mrs. M said.

Each blamed the other for having spoiled the vacation, especially for their son, and evasively defended themselves. As they left, Mr. M remarked that it appeared that they were in the "same old rut." Counselor replied that they would remain in that rut as long as they chose to, and suggested again more listening, less harping and nagging (for Mrs. M's benefit, especially). The next appointment had to be skipped because of a PTA meeting they were attending *together* (a rare occurrence, she said).

Seen again, the same pattern of fighting and defending continued, although they reported not so much open conflict during the past two weeks, and they had enjoyed the PTA meeting. Mrs. M brought out that she cannot bring herself to give Mr. M any credit for anything while he, in turn, could not possibly give her the affection she craves, because he cannot see any reward, or possibility of reward. Counselor remarked that this was indeed a great deal to understand, but stressed that unless some of these intellectualized concepts were soon put into practice, the goals of counseling might never be settled.

They arrived at the next interview looking happy. Mr. M reported that they had been looking over real estate together. Not that they were planning to build a house, but even "just talk is wonderful." He said that this indicated to him that she is really planning to continue their marriage instead of breaking it up.

Mrs. M remained silent during his account and, when he finished, she launched into a tirade against him, attacking his poor memory, his irresponsible attitude toward her and their son. She burst into tears. (It was as though she could not bear the idea that there might be anything other than misery between them, and had to emphasize the negative to prove it.)

After the tirade, she told of his having done some woodworking around the home which, incidentally, is a house belonging to *her parents*. She was critical that he did not finish the job (one nail hole was not filled in for the finishing work). Her perfectionistic strivings became more and more open as she talked, making a situation where no matter how well he did something, it was always a failure.

Counselor reviewed this perfectionistic attitude with her and reviewed Mr. M's own need to fight back by leaving things not quite perfect. They both seemed aware of a new focus on each other. It was suggested that they talk this over some more at home, and work on things together, rather than each looking for the defects in the other.

Two Interviews with Mr. M: Mr. M phoned to inform Counselor that Mrs. M was ill. He requested an appointment for himself, stating that he and Mrs. M had agreed to this. In his interview, he reported some progress in communication (they are talking more together and not battling so much). They are not using weapons of past hurts against each other and there has been some improvement in their sexual pattern—including her allowing cunnilingus without "creating a scene," even if she did not really enjoy it. Counselor took the opportunity to orient Mr. M to sexual ethics in terms of acceptable practices to both partners, the need for foreplay, the need for courtship, and so on.

Mr. M dated all their unhappiness to the death of the second child, pointed out that his wife had never forgiven him. Since then their marriage has been a constant rivalry. He requested another session alone for next time. Counselor agreed if this was acceptable to Mrs. M. Mr. M said it was.

He seemed to enjoy the second session to himself and spent a great deal of the time reminiscing about his own personality development, stressing his own early problems in life with constant illness, his inability to continue at school because of illness, his "catch as catch can education," and his feeling of inferiority to Mrs. M who had graduated from college. He could see that much of his behavior was to compensate for the feeling of inferiority. He planned to put this to one side, now, and attempt to think of his wife as a person instead of a rival, he said. Counselor commended him on the goal, but acknowledged that it would not be an easy task. Mr. M said he was determined to make it work, because underneath all this, he really and truly loved his wife, and hoped that she could love him.

He then requested two sessions for his wife by herself, on her instructions to arrange this with Counselor. This was agreed upon.

Two Interviews with Mrs. M: Mrs. M was early for her appointment. She was suffering with some dizziness due to middle-ear infection. She drove a new car to the city after having a parking lesson *from Mr. M.* She started out talking of her son's nervousness, but quickly related it to the tension between herself and Mr. M. She attributed much of the tension between them to their allegiances to their respective families. Counselor brought it back to the present (it appeared that Mrs. M was trying to keep the conversation away from the present).

At this, Mrs. M said that she did not feel that her husband had changed (complied with her demands?). Counselor took the opportunity to review her perfectionism which existed from the very first in their marriage, and to discuss the law of opposite effect with her; for instance, her demands for compliance only result in more rebellion. Suggested giving without demanding or expecting it in return. She could see that marriage was like a chemical experiment (she had a degree in chemistry), and that in many ways, she had been setting it up for explosion.

A few days later, Mr. M popped into Counselor's office briefly to report wonderful news about his wife. "She's wonderful," he said. "I don't know what happened, but it's wonderful!" Counselor could not see him for any planned time, but wished him and Mrs. M luck.

Mrs. M came to her next interview looking radiant. She reported feeling closer to Mr. M than ever before. She had extended herself to show him some affection, and the whole tone of the family had changed. Their son's nervousness has abated, Mr. M took *her side* against a favored uncle of his (which was something she never thought she would see), and so on, and so on. She summed up by saying that she stopped something malignant and started something wholesome. Counselor acknowledged all this and gave credit where due. But also warned of possible occasional setbacks, which, Counselor emphasized, would in no way indicate that all had been lost, but would merely be an indication of the vacillation that comes with any change in pattern of adjustment. She seemed skeptical that any setbacks could happen and said, "I didn't know where I was or what the decision about our marriage was going to be. It is a wonderful feeling to know now that there is a chance for a new, happier life ahead."

Joint Interviews, a Week and a Month Later: The following week, Mr. and Mrs. M came in together again. It was interesting to note that they began the hour with an argument (testing new progress by old patterns?). Counselor tried to help them examine what they were doing by arguing when they came in together. Both seemed unable to grasp what was meant. Counselor suggested that they were testing the newness of their relationship's improvement. However, Mrs. M refused to budge, and Mr. M asked, "What do you want, blood—instead of apology?" They spent the rest of the time going over the argument which concerned some slight difference of opinion as to whether they should force their son to keep to a decision he had made about attending summer camp.

A month later (Counselor had been on vacation), Mr. and Mrs. M reported some progress and some "slipping back." They could now discuss things without losing their tempers. They still have far to go, they agreed, but they have achieved some of the necessary tools with which to work.

Concluding Monthly Interviews: They requested monthly appointments instead of the usual weekly ones. Their search for real estate continues, and they are starting tentative plans about a new home. Their sexual relations are much better, with Mr. M making fewer demands and Mrs. M offering more opportunity for the variations he craves, with some beginnings of enjoyment on her part. Counselor agreed to monthly appointments.

Counselor continued to see the M's at monthly intervals for the next four months. During these sessions, the M's showed evidence of regressing to their old patterns, and expressed interest in more frequent sessions again to "get back on the track." This was arranged.

(The counselor questions whether he had been premature in spacing the sessions at monthly intervals, for they certainly showed no indication of continuing progress until the weekly sessions were resumed.)

One problem that kept coming up during the "second phase," was their expectancy that everything would be "rosy" for the rest of their lives with only the slightest, occasional frictions. The counselor's purpose therefore was to help them try to utilize their conflicting ideas and attitudes constructively. As they practiced "letting the ideas fight" instead of each other, they saw that conflict is part of life, after all. It was during this phase that they talked more and more of their marriage as a permanent arrangement. Mrs. M began to express warmth toward her husband by "omission" (refraining from carping criticism). By degrees, she was able, in a limited way, to express positive warmth for his strengths. He, in turn, seemed more able to take on a fatherly role with their son, and "remember more of the things she needed" (including material things such as flowers occasionally, the bread for the evening meal, as well as praise for her ability to manage the household). He also bought her a car for herself, much to her delight.

Several months later, they proudly announced that they had purchased a handsome piece of land on which they planned to build a new home. Both saw this as the symbol of their acceptance of each other as marriage partners.

Summary—by Clients: In the closing session (a full year after the resumption of weekly interviews) they summarized their progress in terms of having achieved the level of happiness best suited for themselves, acknowledging that they tend to strive beyond their abilities to maintain peace, that they thrive on a certain amount of healthy conflict! Now, they agreed, their marriage was "saved"; their arguments less frequent; the sequels of such arguments of much shorter duration than ever before in their lives. Case closed.

EDITOR'S NOTE: The realistic acceptance by the clients of limited goals is one of the interesting features of this case. It also demonstrates the successful use of repeated joint interviews (a technique usually used sparingly) to open up positive and constructive lines of communication between the partners.

5. Problems of Sexual Adjustment

This group of cases focuses on problems of sexual adjustment. The role of the counselor as educator is unmistakably indicated, but even when information giving is the immediate concern, emphasis remains on the development of a healthy approach to and emotional acceptance of sex. Re-education of faulty attitudes, whether derived from ignorance, misinformation, or crippling experience, is reflected as a major responsibility of the counselor in these cases; catharsis and reassurance emerge as two of the most useful tools.

Furthermore, there is repeated evidence that sexual adjustment is but part of total personality adjustment. Immaturity on the part of one or both spouses will often be reflected in the area of sex. However, although sex problems are indeed sometimes present in basically "good" marriages—marriages reflecting warmth, regard, and respect for one another—they are more likely to respond to simple and uncomplicated treatment under these circumstances.

CASE 7

Problem: A sexually unsatisfied wife
Presented by: Marriage counselor (A.B.; graduate degree, Social Casework) in a nonprofit, nonsectarian marriage counseling agency located in a large metropolitan city

Introduction: Mr. and Mrs. X in this case came to the agency for help around the wife's lack of satisfaction in sexual relations on referral from the American Association of Marriage Counselors. They had been married eleven years, and had two boys, age five and two. In their middle thirties, she was the older by two years. However, Mr. X, tall and thin, and quite good-looking, with light hair graying, seemed the older. He presented a rather distinguished appearance, more that of a professional person than a skilled workman which he was. Mrs. X is a medium-sized woman with good figure. From the standpoint of features, she is quite homely, but her face is fluid, expressive, and she makes the most of what she has by dressing simply and attractively. They seemed devoted to each other and to their children, but Mrs. X seemed more capable of insight, although obviously distressed to have had to come for counseling. He was noticeably shy but seemed eager to work on his problem.

Counseling: In a slow, rather deliberate manner Mrs. X, who was seen first, launched immediately into her story. She seemed to forge ahead with dogged determination. She spoke intelligently and with what appeared to be a good bit of insight, but made many superfluous gestures with her hands. From the start of their marriage, physical difficulties interfered. Intercourse was unsatisfactory to both immediately. Neither had had premarital examinations, and Mr. X had pain with intercourse for which he finally consulted a doctor after their marriage. Mr. X had a varicocele and hernia, and an emergency operation was performed which was a long and serious affair. She had pain too and didn't know why. When she went to a doctor she learned that she too needed an operation. About eight months after marriage one ovary was removed. The first time intercourse occurred after the operation she was fearful lest she have the same difficulty as before. Her husband was very patient and considerate, and sex relations were "fairly satisfactory although she did not experience orgasm." Her doctor had told her she shouldn't have children for a year and that year was an unhappy one for her, because she didn't know what would happen at the year's end. Mr. X had said before marriage that children were of no importance to him, and she almost didn't marry him because of this.

At the end of the year Mrs. X did become pregnant, but two months after conception she began to miscarry and lost the baby. Again there was another year when she was told not to conceive. However, a successful pregnancy was accomplished but she was in bed practically the whole time. From the time of conception she was allowed no sexual contact. The baby was born Caesarian. Later, with a second pregnancy she was allowed more activity but still no intercourse. The second baby was also Caesarian. Her tubes were tied after second delivery as she had already had six abdominal incisions and the doctor was adamant about no further pregnancies. She was relieved and felt that certainly intercourse should be all right since she and her husband didn't even have to bother about contraceptives. She has kept feeling that this trouble is all her fault since Mr. X has been extremely considerate but thinks she is too slow in reacting.

Although there has been difficulty around sex throughout eleven years of marriage, it came to a head the preceding summer. Whenever he approached she would have some excuse—a headache, backache, indigestion. She knew she had to do something because these excuses were seldom more than just excuses. Part of the trouble is that Mr. X had orgasm almost immediately upon penetration. She reached orgasm occasionally only because she continued movement after his orgasm. Following her menstrual period there is increased desire and particularly then is she left "up in the air" when unsatisfied. Perhaps once a month she obtains satisfaction but "it takes so much effort." Mr. X thought he could last longer if frequency was stepped up. They tried this, even three and four times a week but there was no improvement.

They have always been able to discuss their difficulties freely and they decided together to do something about this. After the first miscarriage they had gone to see a doctor but got little from the interviews—were not even examined physically. He seemed to feel that there had been many physical difficulties but that these would right themselves over the years. With no encouragement to return, they had let the situation drag on. Then, more recently, Mr. X again consulted a doctor, had a series of treatments but feels that if anything, the situation is worse. Counselor asked at this point if Mr. X were able to arouse his wife with manual stimulation. She has attained orgasm this way but doesn't think it is right. She wants to have it "the right way." The counselor briefly gave some explanation here about manual manipulation which was somewhat reassuring.

Commenting that they certainly had been through a lot of physical difficulties in their marriage, the counselor wondered how they got along in general. "Very well except for the sexual difficulty which is now beginning to tinge our whole relationship. I no longer know how I feel about my husband—I wonder if I really love him as much as I should. I feel irritated most of the time about very small things. I think I might be irritated even if sex was all right." Why should she allow herself to become aroused when there will be nothing for her? She almost hates Mr. X for arousing her and then leaving her unsatisfied. She cannot pretend any longer that she doesn't care. If they cannot have satisfactory intercourse, why should they have it at all? She thinks he insists so often in order to prove that he can be successful as a man—he puts so much pressure on her to reach a climax. Sex has never been fun to her but she thinks it could be. She feels that Mr. X doesn't really enjoy their relationship either. He complains that the satisfaction is purely physical and so brief that he knows there should be more in it for him too.

Questioned about her preparation for marriage, Mrs. X reported, "My own parents' attitudes upset me greatly. Mother's sex attitude was wrong and she relayed this to me. She's a very bitter woman who merely tolerates sex." Premarital lovemaking with Mr. X was very satisfactory although they never had intercourse. She anticipated therefore that everything would be fine in marriage, and it was a great blow when she found there was pain. If they had had a premarital examination she didn't think they would have married—had she been told that she might not be able to have children and that there would be so much physical difficulty for both. The counselor explained that no competent premarital examiner could have told her dogmatically that she couldn't have children but might have helped to prepare her for the difficulties of childbearing.

Mrs. X also expressed resentment that it was only because *she* blew up that they had sought help. Counselor pointed out that Mr. X is getting some sexual satisfaction and Mrs. X is really the one who feels this thing more keenly. Therefore, wouldn't it be natural that she initiate the step? Perhaps it was quite a bit for Mr. X to come at all and it did show his concern.

Mrs. X readily agreed with this, saying that their doctor had mentioned how considerate Mr. X had been—how so many men would not care whether their wives were satisfied or not. The counselor added that it was sometimes easier for a woman to talk about these things, especially when the counselor was a woman who would be seeing them both. Mrs. X could see this, realized that it seemed to be a severe blow to masculine pride to have to admit that he couldn't satisfy a woman. She seemed to soften toward her husband after this discussion.

The counselor spent the remaining few minutes of this initial interview discussing the possibility of reading of which neither had done much. Mrs. X bought the Butterfield No. 1 pamphlet [1] which she took into the waiting room to read while her husband had his interview. In planning for successive interviews, the counselor assured her something could be gained but briefly explained that about a third of American women never experience orgasm although they are able to get a great deal more from intercourse than Mrs. X now does.

The counselor then saw Mr. X. She expressed her appreciation of the fact that perhaps it was not easy for him to discuss something of such a personal nature with a woman. He agreed that he had been startled when he realized he wouldn't see a man but had been able to compose himself while waiting for his wife.

Explaining that Mrs. X had discussed their physical difficulties the counselor suggested that Mr. X talk about his reaction to intercourse after the herniorrhaphy. There had been no discomfort after the operation but recently a slight irritation. He referred again to the unsuccessful medical treatment and the fact that he has orgasm just as quickly if not more so.

Encouraged to talk about his premarital experiences, Mr. X said he had been "slightly promiscuous" although he had never attempted relations with his wife. When he was satisfied—this wasn't always—it was a purely physical thing and he never considered whether the girl was satisfied or not although he thought that some of the girls had been. He gave serious thought to only one other girl before marriage, and the others he went with mainly because of sexual attraction. He thought his wife more enjoyable and more intelligent than the other girl, however.

[1] Oliver M. Butterfield, *Marriage and Sexual Harmony* (New York: Emerson Books, Inc., 1950, rev. ed.).

Asked if the pain with intercourse had been present before marriage, he replied that it had. Sometimes it was worse because of frustration when desires were aroused and not satisfied. While he was dating Mrs. X he would play around with other girls but in the year and a half before their marriage took place, he had no contact with others and he has had none since marriage. The counselor commented that a year and a half must have been hard for him. He went on to say that he had not resorted to masturbation—had never considered it but now that he looks back on it, maybe it would have been better that way. He said, "I think I'm the only man that can appreciate cramps in a woman." (This was the second statement that identified himself with woman.)

Now Mr. X desires intercourse very frequently and has an erection as soon as his wife gets into bed with him. Only when he is very tired does he not want it. He works five days a week and goes to school three nights. This is his fourth year studying. There are two more years. He is preparing himself "just in case a better opportunity presents itself."

Counselor commented that Mr. X had undertaken a lot, seemed very ambitious, and perhaps there was reality to his being tired much of the time. Did he often find it hard to get to sleep? The only times are when his wife is out in the evening and he goes to bed without her. Then he falls into a kind of half sleep in which two dreams recur. In the one he fears that someone is trying to enter the house and he gives him a thrashing. The person is unidentifiable. In the other dream he is having a beautifully satisfying sexual relationship. This is most frequently with his wife; only sometimes is it an unknown female. The counselor felt he was finding it difficult to talk; but finally he went on to say that in the dream he is able to satisfy his wife by oral contact with her genitalia. She also satisfied him through oral contact. He has wanted his wife to perform fellatio but she refuses. Cunnilingus he has resorted to recently in an effort to arouse her. She doesn't like it but she doesn't object and he doesn't feel comfortable about it. The counselor brought out a research (sex) schedule which she said they would go over at a later date but read him one question which illustrated that this form of sex play was an acceptable technique. Mr. X was quite surprised, having thought it a form of perversion. Other women have had oral contact with him and he has liked it. Asked if there had ever been contact with other boys when he was growing up or with men, Mr. X's immediate reaction was that he never had contact with other men —had never desired it. Then he recalled an experience with another boy his age when he was 12. They played with each other three or four times but thought this was wrong.

Counselor felt Mr. X had been able to be quite frank and recognized his willingness to work on this thing. He felt that this is nothing physical—it is all in his mind and the trouble is mostly his fault since he has orgasm too quickly. The counselor remarked, however, that rarely was any difficulty between two persons the fault of one of them entirely. The important thing to do here was to get to understand the feelings and attitudes on both parts in order to see how they played into this. Mr. X was very willing to return as often as necessary even though it will be difficult for him. It was suggested that he try to read the Butterfield pamphlet too. He seemed most eager to do anything Counselor thought best.

A further suggestion was made—that the frequency of intercourse be cut down for a few weeks. If they had relations not more than twice weekly, in between times he might try to show his wife as much affection as he could without becoming too aroused—and still let her know there were times when he thought he could be affectionate and not insist on relations. He thought this was a good idea and he would try it.

Following the initial separate interviews, Mr. X was seen twice again. Mrs. X was also seen two more times and though counseling ended rather abruptly because of various illnesses in the family, it was apparent from a final telephone conversation with Mr. X that they really did not feel the need for further counseling.

Conclusion: Both Mr. and Mrs. X felt that the sexual difficulty had cleared up and for the first time in their marriage they were experiencing satisfaction in this area. Reading and discussion with the counselor had resulted in freeing Mrs. X from some of her long-held inhibitions, and she was able to permit her husband and herself greater freedom of expression. Perhaps more than anything else contributing to the apparently quick resolution was a good basic relationship in the marriage and a real desire to please each other accompanied by willingness of each to examine his own contribution to the problem. Mr. X described their new relationship as a "second honeymoon" with new-found confidence in each other. It was also apparent that his sexual knowledge had been faulty and he got a good deal out of reading. Mrs. X benefited from discussion of her early impressions of sex as related by her mother and her relationship to her mother in general. Mr. X's experience with counseling was largely one of re-education, but for his wife it was a real emotional experience. She saw sexual maladjustment as being the cause of her parents' unhappy marriage and had been panicky about what would happen in her own. She tried through the years to give her mother the emotional support the mother failed to get from the father and saw that her own marriage suffered as a result. A beginning break with the mother came the spring prior to counseling and was probably also a factor in Mrs. X's readiness to utilize help.

Follow-Up: Though there was no formal follow-up, a professional friend of the counselor who has known Mrs. X for many years and resides in the same community, recently brought the X's up in casual conversation, not knowing they had been clients at the agency. They had joined a dance group to which the friend belonged and were considered a delightful and compatible couple by her and others in the group. About a year after this, a professional acquaintance, working in a casework agency, mentioned Mrs. X to Counselor. This caseworker, a friend of Mrs. X's sister, was approached by Mrs. X for information about child guidance agencies. Mrs. X explained about the help she had received with her marital difficulties and said that because she had found one such experience so helpful she had no fear about using another source of help when it was indicated.

CASE 8

Problem: Personality immaturities focused on sex
Presented by: Counselor (A.B.) in a family relations center in a large metropolitan area

Background Information: Louis is 41. Sandra is 38. They had been married for nineteen years when they first came to the Family Relations Center. They have a son 12 and a daughter 8. They have no contacts with in-laws. Sandra's parents were divorced when she was 5. She was raised largely by an aunt with occasional brief intervals with each parent. Her father was an irresponsible man, her mother was always kind and quite dependent. Louis' parents died shortly before his marriage. They were very strict morally. Both Louis and Sandra are inactive Protestants They send the children to a Methodist Sunday school. They are both from families of long American residence in which various Western European stocks are blended. Each is an only child. Both are college graduates. He is a successful salesman with an income of $8,000 per year. She has never engaged in gainful employment.

Presenting Problem: Louis was referred to the Center by a genito-urinary specialist to whom he had gone because of very quick ejaculations. The specialist reported no ascertainable physical basis for the difficulty.

Summary of First Several Visits to the Center: Louis and Sandra have now been in touch with the Center for two years. Louis has had 38 visits and Sandra 25. In the first six months (21 visits for each) Sandra came with Louis largely so that he would feel she was obtaining assistance as well as he. More counseling time at each visit progressively was spent with Louis as he became able to face his difficulties. Louis reported that throughout his marriage he had always had trouble with getting and maintaining erections as well as with quick ejaculations. His wife often wanted intercourse in early marriage but usually he failed her. He had had no sex relations with anyone other than his wife either premaritally or extramaritally, but he had masturbated "very excessively" (sometimes several times a week) and felt both guilty and inferior because of it.

He had never been willing to go to a physician about his difficulties until three months before coming to the Center he had learned that his wife, Sandra, was associating with another man, John, who had become very friendly with her and the two children and he subsequently went to his family doctor to discuss his condition. Even the children talked about the "friendly man."

John was invited to dinner and, while feeling the effects of considerable liquor, told Louis that he intended to wreck Louis' marriage if possible. Ever since Louis had heard about John he had been unable to avoid being unpleasant toward Sandra and making derogatory remarks about her in the presence of other people. He said he was sure Sandra was much superior to him and that he both loved and admired her.

Sandra came to the Center following Louis' first visit. She felt she had made a great blunder by trying to talk realistically to Louis about her problem. He was in a "turmoil" because she had told him she had met a man, had lunch with him, and wanted her husband's help in getting him out of her mind.

She felt she was married to an adolescent child and that for nineteen years she had always tried to protect him from the harsh realities of life. She had trained herself to be on guard every minute so that his feelings would never be hurt. Their entire home pattern had long revolved around the demands of his emotional immaturity.

She said that when first married she was quite passionately in love with Louis, but he had avoided physical relations even on their honeymoon and had seldom attempted them afterward. After a year or so she felt their sex life should be different and tried to talk with Louis about it. He told her that was something she shouldn't talk about and that it should occur as seldom as possible. She was very naïve at 20 and took his word for it. As a matter of fact, she still thought of him as the head of the house and as the one who knew the answers about life.

Sandra said she hunted up books on how to live a celibate life and practiced the development of rigid self-control. She said she quite effectively learned to block her feelings.

Several years later Sandra met a physician who became her very close friend. She said this man gradually helped her to see the realities of her marriage and to again develop normal sex responses. The man traveled a great deal and in ten years of association they saw each other only for brief intervals about once a year. They kept in touch with each other constantly by correspondence. The man often urged her to divorce Louis and marry him, but she always refused to renounce her obligations. With this man Sandra said her responses to sex relations were always very complete and satisfying although exceedingly infrequent. She said that the stimulation of his spontaneity, wit, and penetrating mental reactions had been a great joy to her throughout their period of association. She spoke of Louis' mental and emotional life as "exceedingly dull, limited, and drab."

After ten years Sandra and the physician finally agreed it was best to end their relationship and to give her every chance to unify her life with Louis. (Louis knew nothing of this ten-year-affair at the time of the couple's first visits to the Center. Nine months later, in a spell of suspiciousness, he searched through an old trunk of Sandra's and found the man's letters. This created a minor crisis at that time.)

Sandra had met John at a party nearly two years before her visit to the Center. They immediately felt strong emotional reactions to each other but nothing overtly occurred between them at the time and she had made up her mind to avoid seeing him again. However, he persistently found ways of meeting her. He insisted that he couldn't help trying to see her although she told him that nothing constructive or permanent could ever come from their association.

John was always light and pleasant in his persistence and she knew she did enjoy meeting him. After nearly a year she went to dinner with him. She felt he had all the "enthusiasm and joy of life" that Louis so greatly lacked. Then, over the past year she had met John by appointment and on two occasions they had intercourse. These experiences had been very complete and satisfying to her as had those with her former physician friend.

The summer before, John had come to her vacation ground. There he met her children. He took them fishing and looked after them and played with them in a way their father had never done. Since that summer, John had been trying actively and persistently to persuade her to leave Louis and marry him. She admitted she had been more tempted to give up her marriage than ever before.

Sandra knew that she really had no grounds for divorce. Louis had always been a kind and good husband and she couldn't bear to hurt him even though she couldn't possibly love him.

She could let Louis copulate with her if she could just remain detached but it was hard to go through his emotional upsets. Louis' concern about his sexual inadequacy had become very great since he was aware of John's existence. She said he persisted in attempting relations night after night only to fail and wind up in tears and self-recrimination.

Throughout the first year Sandra maintained the position that no matter what changes might occur in Louis they could not affect her inability to feel drawn to him physically. However, she said she desired to do anything that would help Louis live a fuller life. The counselor frequently reminded Sandra that feelings often changed. She always replied that she was willing to let her feelings change and that she wished she could be in love with Louis.

Consultation with Louis for some time consisted primarily of his questions as to whether the counselor thought Sandra was going to stop seeing John and his statements of regret that he was not free from his sexual limitations. He wanted the counselor to sympathize with him because he was so greatly wronged when he had always been a faithful husband, a good man. He could not face a divorce and he could not accept the existing situation.

The counselor would assure Louis that from Louis' point of view he had good cause to feel wronged but that there might be other ways of viewing things which would be more likely to solve his problem and make happy living more possible.

When Louis would speak of his sexual difficulties the counselor would discuss various forms of sex behavior as different ways of meeting the needs of the sex drive without any implication of essential evil in any of them. He would talk about sex and its potentialities for both beneficial and harmful results to individuals and to society. He explained the benefits of masturbation at some length to offset the guilt feelings that Louis had in relation to the practice and to convince him that his troubles in marriage were not caused by the practice in itself but might be aggravated by his feelings about his behavior.

This line of thought would lead readily to discussion of emotional patterns in general.

The counselor believed that Louis needed to recognize his feelings of insecurity and fear and to develop a sense of ease about having them.

To help toward this recognition and acceptance the counselor talked frequently about others who had had the same kind of feelings, letting Louis make his own comparisons. The counselor also spoke lightly about how various emotional patterns develop in all of us and how sometimes they are helpful and sometimes they cause trouble. He also pointed out how patterns often start in childhood when they bring satisfactions but later, if continued, only create difficulties. When the counselor could use himself as an example he would do it to encourage the feeling that such emotional patterns are common to humanity and may be discussed objectively.

The counselor also believed that Louis needed help toward accepting himself as a limited human being without any obligations to be perfect or always to be right or always to do things well.

He talked with Louis, using many examples, about how much people reduced their efficiency by being afraid of not doing things perfectly and, conversely, how efficiency can be increased if one can simply do his best with no distracting fears of failure. He talked about the limitations of all human beings and of how unreasonable it is to demand perfection either in ourselves or others. He talked of the value of being able readily to explain any mistake by simply saying that "it seemed a good idea at the time," without feeling a need to prove that it actually was the right or wise thing to do.

Through such discussions, Louis steadily developed a feeling of ease about facing his own difficulties. He would often laugh about the infantile things he had done. At first he would speak of them as "silly" or "foolish" and show a sense of guilt about having done them. Gradually, however, he came to speak of them as quite natural with the background he then had had.

In the course of a year Louis had become able to accept the

idea that to change Sandra's feelings toward him or to alleviate his sexual difficulties he needed to develop greater maturity within himself. He had learned to get much more enjoyment out of life. Sandra told the counselor that family trips or evenings at home were more pleasant and relaxed than ever before.

Consultation with Louis then became more a discussion of choices that might be made both as to behavior and as to feelings and of ways to develop in the direction of the choices made. He acquired habits of looking at and enjoying the outside world rather than dwelling on how he was treated and what others thought of him. He frequently reported to the counselor about some situation in which he had merely smiled although formerly he would have been greatly disturbed in the same setting.

Louis still had periods in which the maladjustment in his marriage caused considerable upset but he more often could direct his thoughts toward the more positive aspects of his situation. His hardest struggle was to accept his sexual limitations. As his worries about them decreased he sometimes performed more adequately, but his repeated failures still threw him into frequent spells of despondency and into intense struggles to prove his sexual competence.

The following extracts from a letter which Sandra wrote to the counselor after about one year of counseling explains something of the situation:

> My dear ———:
> I have the evening off! It deserves the exclamation point, too. Louis is out of town till tomorrow, and I have the same sense of exhilaration I did when I was a little girl and earned a half holiday for having had an "A" report card.
> It is serene here tonight. I am listening to Brahms. The children are asleep and when I've finished yapping at you— I can go quietly, delightfully to bed—alone.
> I am grateful to you for everything you have tried to do for us and for all you have done for Louis. He has lived for so long in a small cell bounded by his own inadequacies and

fears. It is a good thing to watch another human being blossom as he has. In a detached way I can see him grow up, become an adult. I watch him open up to the rest of the world, become kind, understanding to the children and me. I wish I could give a single damn.

I got over minding so many years ago his being all the things that were unacceptable to me, that now when he works so hard at being the nice person he has become, it has no effect.

The physical part of our life together is still a nagging, smothering arrangement. It is always there on the fringe of whatever we do. A joyless arrangement that usually comes to nought and when we go beyond the nought quality, it's like the mountain laboring mightily and bringing forth a mouse.

And I'm never free of it. I go to bed and lie so rigid every muscle aches so that we can pretend the courtesy of being asleep. I know in advance I'll be awakened during the night, and that in the last analysis it won't work and I'll spend some hours encouraging Louis and persuading him that this is a temporary insecurity and not to worry. With always the futile knowledge that it wouldn't make any difference if it did work.

I can't leave this life I've built. The years of working and plowing in my best efforts are in this marriage. It looks good, it is important to many people besides our small family group. It is important to me as a small stand in a confused world.

I have to work out a pattern for living on the gounds I've chosen, I can't leave and I won't, but when I try to send John away I'm lost in all the frustrations of living. Sounds stupid—I should be able to work it out better.

Sandra

In the past year, with few counseling visits, the situation has improved through Louis' continued development of an outgoing personality. He has more fully accepted his sexual limitations and devotes his energies to other aspects of life. When, at intervals of weeks apart, copulation does occur, he is more relaxed and more competent. Sandra reports that on a few occasions, when Louis had been particularly at ease, she has been able to respond to him physically, which she had insisted she would never be able to do. Louis reports that he still has some bad spells but can dissipate them quickly and that he is living a fuller life than ever before.

Sandra still sees John but less frequently. Louis no longer watches her but goes off on business trips without worry. To a considerable degree he has accepted Sandra's need for some other contacts and associations.

It would be hard to find a home with a greater appearance of family solidarity and pleasant atmosphere than now seems to exist. Their marriage is still unsatisfactory sexually, but the maladjustment is much less disturbing.

The Counselor Summarizes: The history describes some changes in personality and relationships. There is evidence, both from the husband's and from the wife's reports, that there was improvement in Louis' general emotional adjustment, that there has been some improvement in sexual adjustment, and that there has been considerable improvement in the family atmosphere.

EDITOR'S NOTE: It would be interesting to discuss this case from the point of view of neurotic interaction. Some counselors might feel that it was distinctly immature of Sandra to feel she *must* continue to carry the burden of this marriage.

CASE 9

Problem: Psychological blocks to marital consummation
Presented by: Psychiatrist (M.D.; LL.B.), specializing in mar-
riage counseling, in private practice in a large city

Introduction: During the course of twenty-five years in a medical practice devoted to problems of sex and the marital relationship I have encountered something over seventy instances of women who have been married two or more years, yet were physically completely virginal, never having consummated sexual relations. In addition to these cases a total of two or three hundred women have been seen who presented a similar problem after some weeks or months of marriage. In none of these particular cases was impotence in the husband a primary factor.

The nature of the problem involved in most cases of this group is illustrated in the following account of a typical case. Names and circumstances have been so masked as to conceal the identity of those involved, but the essential facts are reported accurately.

Mrs. M's husband called from another city for an appointment, saying that he and his wife were in a serious marital difficulty.

First Interview, Mr. and Mrs. M: At the first interview, husband and wife were seen together. The husband was a mature type of graduate college student, just about at completion of his postgraduate training. He was personable, talked easily, and proved in all ways co-operative, intelligent, and considerate. The same may be said of the wife, except that she was somewhat younger and was extremely shy in her manner, to the point of panic when anything relating to sex was mentioned.

Mr. M stated that he and his wife had been married two years and that during this interval they had not succeeded in consummating sexual relations. He explained that from the first Mrs. M had been nervous and fearful about intercourse and that when their initial attempt had proved painful and unsuccessful her anxiety had increased greatly. Other attempts at intercourse were made, all unsuccessful, and with Mrs. M becoming more panicky and hysterically defensive with each experience.

A few weeks after the marriage, while they were in Europe, Mrs. M consulted a gynecologist who is presumed to have performed a hymenal incision and dilation under local anesthesia. This failed to result in successful consummation of intercourse. Additional attempts at sexual relations finally brought Mrs. M to such an overwrought emotional state that for several months prior to consulting me intercourse had been completely abandoned.

Despite severe tension over the sexual-relations problem both husband and wife felt that they had a satisfying general relationship and both appeared eager to obtain professional help with their sex difficulty.

Physical Examination of Wife: A routine pelvic examination of the wife disclosed two things of significance. She was so hysterically defensive about being examined that on the first occasion only the most superficial examination was possible. In addition she was found to have a very narrow and inelastic vaginal entrance; so much so that, except for the history, I would never have suspected the previous surgery and dilation that had been performed in Europe.

Plans for Continued Treatment: Following my physical examination of the wife I outlined to husband and wife a plan which was readily accepted. This was for the wife to remain in my city for several weeks for accomplishment of full dilation of the vaginal entrance, contraceptive instruction, and psychotherapy. Meanwhile the husband was to continue his studies and be rejoined by his wife as soon as the preparation for successful

sexual relations was completed. I felt that this period of separation was desirable because of the acute tensions that had accumulated. This judgment appears to have been sound, for by the
time the short separation was over each person had become less
defensive and there was an evident renewal of good feeling.

Summary of Twenty-one Office Visits by Mrs. M: During the
next two months, the wife made twenty-one office visits. On
each occasion a little dilation was done, combined with a discussion of sex attitudes and instruction in anatomy and contraceptive technique. Some reading was prescribed and was discussed to amplify its personal application. Mrs. M's early life
was reviewed in a brief psychiatric type of history, and active
interpretation was made as to the significance of her background
in reference to her problems of adjustment in marriage.

Her history disclosed that she was raised in a morally rigid
Protestant family where she had been subjected to great senti-
mental overprotection by her mother and had been given the
strongest impression that everything sexual and genital was
utterly loathsome and unmentionable. Her parents appear to
have gotten on with each other in a conventionally acceptable
manner. She felt very close to her mother at the time of marriage.
Many times during interviews with her I had the impression,
despite her excellent intellectual and physical maturity, of talking with a highly defensive, squeamish little girl about five or
six years of age.

She displayed no major psychopathic defensive mechanisms
except her extreme genital squeamishness and an increased tendency toward romantic fantasy outlets. She said that during her
engagement period she felt strongly erotic and was sure that
sex would be a wonderful experience, though she had no co-
herent concept of what it would be like and felt fear closing in
when she tried to think about it in genital terms.

At her first interview Mrs. M was hysterical in speaking of
relations with her husband. She cried out, "I just can't sleep with

him." She immediately added that this seemed a terrible thing to say, because he was so completely kind and considerate. Then she asked, "Do you have others like me?" She was relieved when told that her sort of problem is fairly common and quite solvable.

During this session she wept much of the time and frequently sniffed at a bottle of smelling salts. She said this somehow made her feel better. She admitted it was a habit copied from her mother. This mannerism was discarded after her second interview.

In connection with Mrs. M's sessions on the examining table I wish to make an observation that is characteristic of most cases of this kind. During the early sessions she responded to the lightest touch at the vaginal entrance by both local and general muscular contractions and with hysterical cries that she was experiencing extreme pain. After several sessions she was able to control these reactions increasingly well but interpreted any movement of the dilating instrument as a source of pain. This kind of response clearly seems to be an unconsciously motivated moralistic defense reaction which opposes the instinctual tendency to feel tactile and rhythmic genital stimulation as a pleasure experience. During the last dilations Mrs. M was able to relax and appeared relatively comfortable during the procedure and made no complaint of pain.

At the point where she was taught self-examination of her vaginal anatomy Mrs. M balked severely. She felt that she just could not insert her fingers into the vagina, but after many cautious attempts over a period of days she finally announced with satisfaction that she had achieved the seemingly impossible and felt comfortable in thoroughly exploring her intravaginal self. At this time she made the very significant observation (quoted from my verbatim shorthand notes): "Everything seems much larger, bigger than before; not only the vaginal entrance but all my sexual self seems much larger now and I feel so good about it. I can relax my muscles and easily put two fingers into the vagina. It seems unbelievable, but I'm really doing it."

At this stage, near the end of her sessions, her whole emotional reaction toward the thought of intercourse was quite evidently taking on a new realistic tone, with panic reactions entirely gone.

Instruction in personal anatomy and contraceptive technique took about three times as long with Mrs. M as with the average patient, but at the end she was thoroughly proficient.

Before relations with her husband were attempted he was briefed as to what had been accomplished during their separation, and detailed instructions were given him as to technical approach in consummating intercourse. Mrs. M was made aware of this careful briefing of her husband as a factor in building her confidence.

A few days after rejoining her husband Mrs. M wrote that intercourse had been accomplished without difficulty, although she experienced no erotic pleasure from it. I had cautioned both Mrs. M and her husband not to be upset if her erotic response should not appear at first.

Mr. M Resumes Counseling; Mrs. M Continues: During the next three months Mr. and Mrs. M visited my city prior to the husband's accepting a position abroad. I saw Mrs. M five times for further discussion of her marital adjustment and saw Mr. M twice. Both were pleased with the progress that was being made. They were having sexual relations without anxiety or physical difficulty. Mr. M seemed to present no potency problem, and Mrs. M at last report was achieving some erotic reaction and becoming a more relaxed and active participant in intercourse. Both were satisfied that they have a good future together, and they planned to start a family soon. They are now in a foreign country, and a further progress report is not available at this time.

Discussion of Case by Counselor (Psychiatrist): It will be clear to anyone with psychiatric experience that Mrs. M presented

much more than a simple physical problem and that the mere
supplying of authentic sex information could not have sufficed
for her needs. Her main difficulty may properly be called psychiatric, and I am sure that my efforts with her would have failed
had I not recognized this and blended with the other procedures
a specially adapted kind of psychotherapy. This consisted in an
alert observation of her emotional reactions at every stage of the
procedure and the offering of warm support and encouragement,
while at the same time gently moving her toward coming to
grips with the aspects of sex about which she felt deep anxiety
and panic. Under this approach her anxiety abated rapidly and
as it did so her frozen defensiveness melted and she was able
after each session to become a little more accepting of her natural role until at last she was led to accept sex participation in
an affirmative spirit, with only minor fears remaining. At the
point of successful intercourse the husband became, in effect,
the therapist, and fortunately was able to assume his role well.
Had he lacked the ability to perform his important part Mrs.
M could not have utilized what she had gained through her special preparation.

There must still remain a question as to whether what has
been done with Mrs. M is, in a practical sense, adequate for her
future or whether she may demonstrate later a need for deeper
psychotherapy. I hope not, but am frank to say that I cannot
be sure. Should further problems appear I feel confident that
Mrs. M would, because of what has been accomplished, not
unduly delay seeking my further advice or that of some other
qualified professional person.

I cannot leave this case without noting that many of the Mrs.
M's are quickly deserted by husbands who will no longer en-
dure their wives' frustrating and unreasonable sex behavior. In
other instances an uncomplaining husband of a Mrs. M eventually discloses that his seeming patience is an expression of his
sexual impotence. But there are quite a few men, like the husband of Mrs. M, who combine adequate potency with great

patience and affection for the wife and who can, with the right
sort of professional help, work out a happy marriage in the
face of very discouraging beginnings.

I would note that patients such as Mrs. M are usually far from
easy to handle. They require of the physician-counselor a degree
of tact and patience that is unfortunately lacking in many doctors. Indeed, most of the Mrs. M's whom I see have already
had unsuccessful and unhappy contact with one or more physicians who had run out of patience with them. So I would suggest that in referring such cases it is wise to know your doctor
exceptionally well.

Follow-Up Report: About five years after Mrs. M presented her
problem, she and her husband returned to their home city.
During the next couple of years, she consulted me briefly on
two occasions for routine advice concerning a planned pregnancy
and referral for obstetrical service. She stated that the marriage
was going well.

After delivery of her baby she came in for a routine check
on contraceptive technique. Under pelvic examination, she
displayed considerable apprehension and muscular tension, yet
in a degree quite mild as compared with her behavior of seven
years earlier. A satisfactory check of her contraceptive technique
was accomplished in only two office visits.

During these visits, Mrs. M reported that she now accepts sex
relations but has not yet come to feel much erotic warmth and
has not at any time attained orgasm. She admitted that her feelings about sex are still predominantly squeamish and uneasy.
But she was firm in asserting an affectionate relationship with her
husband and expressed delight with the baby, which she was
breast nursing. She spoke eagerly of plans to have more children. The pregnancy and delivery had been well tolerated, with
the aid of an understanding obstetrician and through membership in a special training class devoted to preparation for
childbirth.

At my last contact with Mrs. M, I would have liked to suggest that she undertake deep-level psychotherapy because of her continued and intractable anxiety about sex participation. However, this proposal could not feasibly be offered since she and her husband were about to leave on a two-year foreign assignment in an area where psychotherapy is not available. It will probably be suggested later.

In closing this report I feel that I should add something about the approximate incidence of "Married Virgins" in counseling practice. It is my impression that about five per cent (one in twenty) of all couples who enter marriage *without routine premarital medical service* will turn up with a "Married Virgin" problem. Only about one per cent (one in a hundred) will go as long as two years without seeking or obtaining relief. These figures are closely supported by data from my particular practice and I believe they have general application if shaded downward just a little.

Clearly enough the case described in this report is of a type not to be handled by the nonmedical counselor without medical consultation. But experience leads me to believe that all counselors may profit by an awareness of the relative frequency of the problem in the experience of medical counselors, and a realization of some of the special factors involved in its successful management.

CASE 10

Problem: Hostility and sexual frustration
Presented by: Counselor (B.S., graduate work in Psychology and Education) in counseling service of an educational agency located in an urban area

Introduction: In my many years of counseling experience, I have tried various patterns of case recording. The method employed in this presentation is not recommended for general recording. It is used here to give an intimate glimpse of the methods employed in the counselor-client relationship to develop rapport, decrease resistance, and encourage ventilation.

Notes were taken and the interview recorded through dictation immediately following each session so that it fairly represents a verbatim report.

Mrs. N comes from a middle-class New England family. When she first came to see me, she was 31 years old and had been married 11 years.

First Interview: After the usual pleasantries, I informed her that if she could tell me some of the facts regarding her problem, I could give an opinion as to whether it appeared to be a problem in which I might be helpful. She hesitated at first and then said, "I don't know how to begin. Nobody seems to understand my problem; the doctors are all puzzled—they don't seem to know what I am talking about. Dr. A seems to know more than anyone else; she said I should talk with you. But I don't know—it is very hard to talk about it."

Counselor—"Well, relax, take your time. Would you rather begin talking yourself, or would you have me ask questions?"

Mrs. N—"Well, perhaps you had better ask me some questions. It may help me get started."

C—"You are a married woman. Does your problem involve your marriage relations?"

Mrs. N—"Yes, that's just it."

C—"Is it a sexual problem?"

She hesitated and fidgeted a bit, and then burst out, "Well, I might as well tell you! You see, I only want it once a month."

C—"You mean that you want to have sexual intercourse only once a month?"

Mrs. N—"Yes—why does a man want it so often? Does he

really have to have it? Is it true that if a man doesn't have it with his wife, he will go to some other woman?"

C—"Well, before I answer all those questions, perhaps I had better have a little more information."

Mrs. N.—"Well, it's this way—I just don't want to be touched. I could kill anyone who touches me, especially my husband, and yet I am sure that I love my husband, and I think he loves me, but I don't know. He won't much longer unless I change. I get irritable and contradictory, and life at home is getting to be unbearable for both of us. What's going to happen to my children?" Here she started to cry, at the same time saying, "I have tried hard not to be this way, but I can't help it—I can't help it!"

Then came a flood of tears and she started fumbling in her pocketbook. I opened my desk drawer, took out some tissues and passed them to her, saying, "You see, I am used to weeping women, and I am prepared."

She smiled through her tears and said, "I hate to be so silly; I wish I could stop."

C—"Don't try. Just relax and cry all you want to—it will do you good."

With this, she smiled, wiped her tears away, and got control of herself.

C—"This condition which you report to me is not uncommon in my experience. In the frequency and intensity of sexual drive, there is great variation. Let's study the situation a little more closely. When you do have intercourse, do you enjoy it?"

Mrs. N—"Yes, once a month I do."

C—"Do you have orgasm?"

Mrs. N—"What do you mean?"

Here I described a characteristic orgastic response of the female: "An increase in tension with an abrupt release causing a convulsive movement of the pelvis and muscular spasms."

"Oh," she said, "I have that—not always, but generally if it is at this time in the month."

C—"Tell me more about that. What time in the month do you seem to desire intercourse?"

Mrs. N—"That's the funny part of it. It's the day right after my period. I can hardly wait for my husband to come home. We generally wait, however, until bedtime. The next day, I still have some desire, but much less, and the third day, less still."

She then said that from that time on, she reacted with hostility toward any approach of her husband. This even included his kissing her, because, she said, "If he kisses me or touches me, I know what he will want to do, and I hate it!"

At this point, Counselor said, "Let's consider the normalities of your situation—you are sexually aroused immediately following your period. That is very common in the female, and I would say, myself, that was very normal. And I would say that the fact that your interest on the two following days is somewhat less could also be considered normal. But the fact that following that, you find any physical contact intolerable and show such decided signs of hostility is something that we must look into."

Mrs. N—"Do you think my husband is normal or is he over-sexual? He wants it two or three times a week. I think perhaps he would do it every night if I would let him."

C—"Two or three times a week sounds very normal to me. I think most husbands his age would want it that frequently; and I am sure that a great many wives would feel disappointed if their husband didn't."

Mrs. N—"You mean there are *women* who really want it that often?"

C—"Yes, a great many do; but of course, a great many don't—it all depends on the woman. But in happy marriage adjustments, the wife is usually responsive to her husband's needs, and enjoys the relationship herself."

Mrs. N—"I didn't know that. I have a woman friend who says
  she doesn't like it either."
C—"There is no information that is more unreliable than what
  one woman tells another about her sex life!"

I went on to say, "Do you think that it is possible that you
don't want your husband to touch you because you're afraid
that it will arouse you, and you don't want to be aroused? In
order to get a better understanding, I would like to have you
answer a few questions."

Here, I began an inventory of her sexual experiences. She
denied masturbation, denied any sexual experience in childhood;
however, the emotional reaction to these questions left some
doubt in my mind as to the truthfulness of the statement. She
denied that she had had sexual intercourse with any other male
but her husband, but admitted that they had had sexual intercourse before their marriage, about which she felt very guilty.

I then gave her some information concerning masturbation,
its frequency and considered normality, and spoke of fantasy
as usually being a component part of the experience.

Without any further prompting, she said, "Well, I have some
very funny ideas. For years, I have often thought about people
being cruel." She then described a fantasy of a sado-masochistic
nature: "I imagine that I am taken out to some place off in the
woods, tied to a tree, and whipped with a switch."

The hour was about up, and I was getting ready to make
another appointment when she said, "What we have just talked
about makes me think of something else. It is about another
woman."

C—"Yes, what did you want to tell me about her?"
Mrs. N—"My husband—the woman works where he does. He
  claims that he liked her a lot, but had no relations with her
  —I don't think he did, but I don't know. But then, that is all
  over; she wouldn't dare come near him again, not after what
  I did!"

C—"Why, what did you do?"

Mrs. N—"I wrote to her and demanded that she come to my home and see me, but she didn't do it. So, knowing that she would be going down to the theater on a certain night, I went down there and met her in the lobby. She wanted to go out somewhere else to talk but I said, No, that I had given her that chance and she didn't take it, so now she could stand right where she was and take it!"

As she said this, her facial expression indicated a sadistic satisfaction, from the episode, just thinking about it.

Then she continued, "Believe me, I have thought of a lot of things I would like to do to *her*!"

C—"Such as what?"

Mrs. N—"I have thought I would like to stick a knife into her —I don't mean to really injure her, but to hurt her."

Here, I gave her reassurance and told her I had had many reports like that, and that people often thought of doing things which they had no intention of really doing and wouldn't even if they could. However, I said it was a matter concerning which I would talk with her the next time, but that we must stop now, for another client was waiting.

The conference had lasted 1 hour and 20 minutes. She said she felt better and was anxious to come back as soon as she could. A busy schedule made it impossible for me to see her for two weeks.

Second Interview: Client said that since seeing me, she had been so happy with her husband that it seemed like a miracle. "In all my married life, I have not been so happy as I have been for the last two weeks!" Although this was halfway between her periods, she had found a desire for intercourse and hadn't found it repulsive when her husband had attempted it. As a matter of fact, she had had satisfactory intercourse three times since the last conference.

(It seemed to the counselor that this was one of the cases where catharsis and reassurance were going to be almost immediately effective.)

At this session she disclosed the following: She told of a girl friend of her own age, who was dominated by her brother some years older than she; in fact, she said he "ruled the roost." She told of an incident where this girl was slapped by the brother and sent to bed for saying something that he didn't like. The girl was afraid of him and did as she was told.

On several occasions, this girl was sent to bed or refused permission to go out, but although Mrs. N felt sorry for her friend, and hated the brother, she still was fascinated by these scenes of dominance and submission.

She still claimed she could not remember any incidents of masturbation but stated that she used to squeeze her legs together and got a certain sensation but didn't know that that was masturbation. "But I know my little boy masturbates. I spanked him for it—do you think I did wrong? I think our older girl does, too. Is there any harm in it? What should I do?"

I spoke to her about handling such problems with youngsters, and impressed on her the importance of doing nothing to inculcate fear and worry on their part as to any possible consequences, and to accept such behavior as a normal part of their development. I gave her the pamphlets, *When Children Ask About Sex*[1] and *Growing Up in the World Today*.[2]

Third Interview: When the client was seated, she seemed to be quite tense. I asked her how things were going. She said that things were much better than they had been, but she had been assailed by more doubts and wondered if she was sliding back. Though she had tolerated her husband's approaches two or three times, she hadn't been as co-operative as she had been immedi-

[1] Child Study Association of America, New York, 1943.
[2] By Emily Clapp (Boston: Massachusetts Society for Social Hygiene, 1938).

ately following our first conference. She seemed to have something on her mind, started two or three times to say something,
then said, "Do you mind if I smoke?"

I said, "Certainly not." I arranged an ashtray conveniently for
her. She said, "Will you have a cigarette? I said, "Perhaps I will."
Took one, lighted her cigarette and my own.

Mrs. N—"Something has come to my mind but I don't know how
   to tell it."

I didn't press the matter for a moment—then she continued,
"Well, it's about my husband. You know I love him, but he did
something once that I never have forgiven him for." She proceeded to tell of an incident when she suspected her husband of
trying to fondle a young girl in whose room they were sleeping.

C—"Did the child report it to you in the morning?"

Mrs. N—"No, she never said anything about it, and that is something I can't understand. But I didn't want to speak to her, because I didn't want to let her know that I thought my husband
   would do such a thing."

The client said that this episode frightened her and she was
very resentful toward her husband—that she had often thought
of it when he had tried to have intercourse with her. She then
started weeping and burst out, "Why *will* men do such things?"

C—"*Men?* Would you care to tell me now about any similar incident in your own childhood?"

She wept for a moment and then got control of herself and said,
"Well, when I was 14, I was sleeping with a woman whose
husband was in the next room. In the middle of the night, I was
awakened by the husband who was standing over me and I was
frightened. In my struggles, I kicked the woman and she woke
up. The husband immediately withdrew. The wife said, 'What's
the matter?' and I said, 'Nothing.' "

Tears started again, and she said, "Suppose this happened to my own little girl who is only 8?" She quickly followed this with the statement, "I might as well tell you. It has already happened." She went on to tell how this youngster had been sleeping at the house of a little girl her own age, and a man in the house had exposed himself. The child had told her mother and she was very much shocked by it.

(In these experiences, the basis for a psychosexual trauma can be early seen.) Counselor told her that she would feel much better, having gotten all this off her mind. "I feel things are going to work out all right."

Fourth Interview: Upon entering the office, Mrs. N seemed in high spirits. Reported that she had been completely happy and said, "I never thought that such happiness could exist! My husband is very happy; I can't believe it is true."

She then reported that there had been considerable improvement on her part, both in the matter of allowing him to fondle her when he desired to, and in her response to his caresses. She said, "You know, this whole business had had a terrible effect on my husband. I am sure now that there will be no other woman in the picture. And not only are we getting along better, but he is doing much better in his work. He said he never talked about his affairs while on the job, but the boss seemed to know something about it because recently he had said, "I am glad you are making up with your wife. You don't know how near we came to firing you, but you are doing all right now!" She reported that her husband got a promotion a few days later.

The client went on to say that her husband had once wanted mouth-genital contact. She rather indignantly said, "Of course I wouldn't do such an abnormal thing!"

C—Why, *is* it abnormal?"
Mrs. N—"Sure—isn't it?"

I then talked with her at some length about the many variations in sexual foreplay which are not only normal in themselves but tend to enhance the satisfaction to be obtained from inter-course. She wanted to know more about the variety of positions in intercourse. At this point, I introduced Dickinson's *Human Sex Anatomy* [3] and discussed with her the various positions which he had so graphically portrayed. We then talked about the ways in which a woman may herself initiate actions and manually and visually stimulate her husband to a point where his own aggressive tendencies become released resulting in a complete and satisfactory sexual experience.

Fifth Interview: Mrs. N reported that since seeing the counselor last, she had had a "down phase," but had quickly recovered. Here, we talked about the normality of moods; that we all go up and down; that when we recover quite quickly from feelings of depression it is pretty good evidence that we are becoming adjusted.

Interview with Mr. N: There was no difficulty getting Mr. N to talk. From the very first, he wanted to tell how happy he was in his home life at present. He talked about the change that had taken place in his wife.

He also talked about the children and the fact that he was buying them all bicycles, one by one. The youngest now wanted one, but would have to wait for it. Because of the way things were going, it didn't seem necessary to go into any deep exploration with him. Counselor took a sexual inventory and there was disclosed boyhood masturbation with worry. He said he did this quite often up to the time he was married and had done it several times since. "The only reason I thought of another woman was that when my wife wouldn't have me often enough, I would have to masturbate and thought that this might drive me crazy, so I went out with a woman, but while she let me fondle her, I didn't get any further. I really didn't want to, because I love my wife."

[3] By Robert L. Dickinson, M.D. (Baltimore: Williams and Wilkins, 1931).

He had intercourse with three or four women before he met his wife and he reported sexual relations with her before marriage. He knew she felt guilty about this. The rest of his story confirmed what she had already told.

Sixth Interview: Wife came in again, and there was some recapitulation of what had already been talked about. Nothing new was reported. Things seemed to be going along well. This was noted as a report of progress.

Seventh Interview: Mrs. N told how much better adjusted she was and how happy she was. Her family relations had so greatly improved she said she could hardly believe it. Even their relations with the children have improved. She now encourages her husband to be interested in their training and discipline—something which she had resisted before. She said, "Though we have our ups and downs, things are much better and we are both very happy."

C then told her that she must not expect perfection but that she could anticipate the continuation of the kind of happiness which she has now, if they both continued to be as co-operative as they are now being.

No further appointment was made at this time, but C suggested that she get in touch with him should she feel the need of further counseling, and hoped that she would let him know later how things were going with her.

Nothing was heard from the client until about eight years later when the counselor received a letter from Mrs. N in which she apologized for not having written before. She wanted C to know how much good counseling had done her marriage. "We are getting along fine with an understanding of each other we never had before." She had gained weight "on nothing but contentment" and again expressed her thanks.

About six months later she wrote again saying that her re-education had been not only helpful in her relationships with her husband but extremely helpful in her relationships with her children; however, more recently she had had some problems with the children she wanted to talk over. In a follow-up conference, she said that she was aware that her daughter had been masturbating and her son also. She talked with the father and he talked with the son and she with the daughter. This was done in a friendly tone and nothing was said to frighten the children or to make them feel that there was anything wrong with this. She said she didn't want them to feel abnormal so told them that most boys and girls did masturbate occasionally and that her only caution was a casual "Try not to do it too often." She felt that she was responsible for seeing to it that the children got proper sex education.

Summary: This is a case in which *catharsis* and *reassurance* were seemingly immediately effective. It seems to show what the process of re-education can do under certain conditions.

The latter part of this report shows clearly that what counseling may accomplish is not only to help the couple to a better personal adjustment but pave the way for avoidance of similar difficulties in the lives of the children.

6. The Triangle in Marriage

Case 11. *Divorce and Remarriage*
Case 12. *The "Other Woman"; Divorce Avoided*
Case 13. *Pastoral Counseling in a Triangle Situation*

These cases are variously concerned with divorce and "the other woman." Case 13 illustrates how the unique position of already established rapport which a minister may possess furnishes the springboard for pastoral counseling in a crisis situation.

CASE 11

Problem: Divorce and remarriage
Presented by: Marriage counselor (Ph.D.; graduate work in Sociology and Psychology) in a counseling center in a large Midwestern city

Introduction: This case extended over a period of approximately one year and consisted of 25 interviews with the husband, 20 interviews with the wife, and one interview with the woman who precipitated the husband's separation from his wife. For brevity in reporting, the husband will be referred to as Ed, the wife as Ann, the other woman as Sue, and the counselor as C.

163

The Situation

After almost sixteen years of marriage, Ed, age 38, had left Ann, age 40, two months prior to his first coming to C. He saw Ann about twice per week to give her money and to leave and pick up the automobile. He had become emotionally involved several months prior to the separation with a woman who worked at the same establishment as he and rode with him in a car pool. The first indicated bond between Ed and Sue was their expression to one another of dissatisfaction with their respective marriages.

Sue, fifteen years Ed's junior, had been married five years and had a two-year-old child; Ann and Ed had no children: gonorrhea had rendered Ed sterile prior to his marriage. Ed's presumably cured gonorrhea flared up early in his marriage, and Ann became infected. It was at that time they discovered Ed's sterility through a medical examination.

Ed said that he had been dissatisfied with his marriage for about ten years, had had three affairs during this ten-year period, had almost broken up his marriage four years previous to the present separation in order to marry another woman (but had at that time lacked the courage). He showed strong guilt feelings about having "wasted" sixteen years of Ann's life, felt guilty about having infected her with gonorrhea, and felt "pity for her" because he thought she would be incapable of successfully leading an independent life.

Since separation from Ann, Ed had been eating all breakfasts and dinners at Sue's house and having lunch with her every day at work. Sue's husband, described by both Ed and Ann as a very confused person who had had one year of psychoanalysis but had broken off treatment, apparently accepted Sue's definition of her relationship with Ed (good friend). Ed felt himself definitely in love with Sue and seemed happy to receive any "crumbs" of her affection. Sue had told him that she wanted to make her marriage work and that she could never be anything more than a friend to him. Sue had, however, definitely supported Ed in his break with Ann because she felt Ann was "bad" for him.

Ann admitted that she had become careless in her relationship with Ed during the last year or so, but contended that they had a "better than average" marriage. She accused Sue of having "broken up" the marriage and felt Ed would "come to his senses" if he could be persuaded to get away from the "bewitching influence of that woman." Ann thought Ed was weak and immature, but was still in love with her (Ann) and needed her. Sue, according to Ann, would never leave her present marriage because of lack of courage to face adverse social judgments and would make Ed "a horrible wife" even if she did. It was at Ann's urging that Ed came to see C. Although she was sure that "there was nothing wrong with her" she agreed to consult with C regularly, providing Ed did so.

Personalities and Backgrounds

The Nature of Ed: Ed was born in a small Midwestern town where he spent the first sixteen years of his life. He left to join the Merchant Marine, in which he served until the age of 22. At the latter age he quit to marry Ann, two years his senior, who convinced him he should finish high school and get a college education. This he did, with her support and coaching in his studies. He graduated as a mechanical engineer and obtained a position with a large automobile manufacturer where he is still employed.

Ed's father had been an ineffectual person who drifted from job to job and inadequately supported his five children of whom Ed was the oldest. The mother was a strong and capable woman who supplemented the father's shaky income by laundry and dressmaking work and who brought up her children in a strict, Puritanical fashion. Ed was very fond of his mother during childhood, he said, but found her "impossible to live with" from the age of about fourteen onward. It was to get away from her domination that he left home at sixteen to join the Merchant Marine.

His earliest memory about sex was being caught by his mother in the act of fondling his genitals around the age of eight. His mother delivered a stern talk about the (alleged) evils and dire consequences of masturbation. He did not remember masturbating again until after the onset of puberty. He said that he always felt guilty after masturbation, but that he was never again caught in the act by his mother. His first heterosexual experience was at the age of 15 with a married neighbor about twice his age, who, he said "taught him a lot." After several weeks of successful coital experience with her, however, he began to feel increasingly guilty and to worry about discovery by her husband or his mother. This anxiety led him to premature ejaculation and then to complete impotency in the relationship. After two or three unsatisfactory experiences he stopped visiting the neighbor and resumed masturbation. He did not undertake coitus again until, at the age of about 16½ years, he had successful sexual relations with a prostitute. From that point on, with guilt apparently reduced, he had no potency difficulties with a series of prostitutes and pickups. He had "never really known a respectable woman" before he met Ann.

Ed never had premarital sexual intercourse with Ann. Marital coitus with her, Ed said, "was just so-so, never really hot." He felt inferior to Ann for most of the time of the marriage, he said, and she made him feel part of the time as if he were "a kind of feeble-minded child."

He loved Sue, Ed said, because she not only let him be himself, but "inspired me to start and carry out things that I would otherwise never do." He tended to be quite general and vague regarding these inspired accomplishments, but made clear that he had a greater feeling of worth and self-respect when in the presence of Sue.

In some of his early counseling sessions, Ed showed optimism about his separation and about the possibilities of future marriage with Sue. In other sessions, he indicated pessimistic and guilty reactions. Whether depressed or elated, his thinking about the present and the future was confused and unrealistic in these early sessions. He was completely ignorant, for instance, of his state divorce laws and felt he had grounds for divorce (which he did not). He also somehow believed (despite much evidence to the contrary) that Ann would not be vindictive, that Sue would get a divorce and marry him, and that many other things would, by some childish pattern of magic, fall into line with his dreams.

The Nature of Ann: Ann was a woman of lean, hard attractiveness. Unlike Ed, she showed no confusion in her thinking, knew that she wanted her husband back "at practically any price," understood fairly well that she had been "careless and pushed him too hard," thought she had learned her lesson and could make him happy if he returned. Ann's attitude toward Ed seemed, in general, like that of a dominating mother who wanted to create the impression of being patient, tolerant, understanding, and forgiving about a wayward son.

During the first several interviews, Ann constantly avoided C's attempts to get her to talk about herself. She wanted to talk about Ed and to get C's judgments about how he was "coming along." Outside C's office, Ann's behavior apparently alternated between long hours of brokenhearted weeping and the pursuance of various strategies to "force him to his senses and to return." She used friends, relatives, and business associates to attempt to effect this end, as well as direct techniques of assumed gaiety, expressed sorrow, and hostile attacks in her semiweekly encounters with Ed. Although these varied strategies were sometimes successful in arousing guilt feelings in Ed, they seemed to increase, rather than decrease, his determination to "stay away from that woman."

At the fourth session, C was able to persuade Ann that whether Ed came back or not, she needed to face squarely some things about herself. Although her motivation to do so seemed to stem entirely from the hope that changes in her personality might prove to be the long-hoped-for technique of getting Ed back, Ann began to talk about herself.

Ann was the eldest of seven children and was born on a large Midwestern farm, where she spent the first twelve years of her life. Her father, a successful farmer, suddenly sold his farm when Ann was twelve and moved his family South, where he entered the real estate business. The reason given for the move was the ill health of Ann's mother, who died of intestinal cancer three years later. Almost simultaneously with the death of the mother, Ann's father went bankrupt in his real estate business. The family moved back North, and the father was able to obtain a home as a tenant farmer.

Even prior to their first move, most of the burdens of child care and household maintenance had fallen to Ann because of her mother's increasing ill health. Thus, quite early in life she took on the role of managerial mother and carried these responsibilities until about the age of 17.

About the time Ann graduated from high school her father remarried. Ann was "crushed" by this marriage and immediately came into conflict with her stepmother. The father convinced Ann of the desirability of her going to college. Although she felt rejected by the marriage, she was glad to go to college both because of her interest in education and because of her desire to get away from the stepmother.

Ann enrolled at the State University in the School of Home Economics, soon entirely supported herself through work on and off the campus, and had an outstanding academic record. Upon graduation, she obtained employment as a food manager in a large restaurant.

Ann's premarital sex history was largely one of inhibition. She claimed never to have masturbated and said she "didn't even have time to think about boys" until her senior year of college. Farm living and the care of five younger brothers had taught her "the facts of life," but in cold, unerotic terms. In her senior year, however, she "really fell" for a college athlete who reminded her of her father. Because the athlete moved too fast and far in love-making for inexperienced Ann, however, she soon broke off with him. The incident left her heartbroken and embittered, and she left college determined not to "have anything to do with men."

Ann held to this resolution for three years after leaving college. Through a girl friend, however, she met Ed. Her reactions to him were mixed; she thought him a little coarse and her intellectual inferior, but thought he had a "good heart" and fine potentialities. She thought she was just the sort of person to help him "make something of himself." During the brief courtship period, love play did not go beyond kissing and light petting. Ann said she felt real fear and disgust about sexual intercourse during the first few months of marriage, but later came to adjust to it as "her duty." She had never experienced orgasm.

Her only complaint about Ed in marriage was that he was irresponsible—"just like a big kid." She "had to manage all the money, see that bills were paid, and keep him from buying foolish things." "I may have been a little careless about showing him love during the last year or so, but I realize my mistake and will change if he'll only come back."

The Nature of Sue: C had, of course, obtained two quite incompatible pictures of Sue from Ed and from Ann. To Ed she was loving, gentle, unselfish, and beautiful. To Ann she was "not much to look at," scheming, selfish, immature, and "unfit to be a wife and mother."

Three months after Ed had first come to C, he called to make an appointment with C for Sue. Sue appeared in this interview as a relatively unattractive and carelessly groomed young woman of a degree of plumpness not generally regarded as pleasant. She stated that she had decided to get counseling help because the pressure for a decision had become unbearable from her husband on one side and Ed on the other.

Her husband had reached a point where he no longer accepted the presence of Ed on a friendship basis and had issued an ultimatum for her to choose between Ed and himself. Ed, too, had become restive, and had attempted to convince her that her future happiness lay with him rather than with her husband.

She said that what had started out with Ed as a "fine friendship" had grown into what she thought was deep love. She felt that she had never really loved her husband, that he didn't understand her, that she was not given freedom of action and expression with him, that he brought out the worst in her. She thought divorce would be a horrible thing, however, and still wanted to "make her marriage work." She felt that she could not at this point, however, give up Ed, for life at present seemed impossible to her with just her husband's companionship alone. The child was not a planned one, she said, and offered her no compensating happiness.

In the course of the interview, Sue not only indicated nervous symptoms that might be presumed to be situational (tears, wringing of hands, tense voice, and expression, and fiddling with hair and ears), but a frequent and inappropriately timed nervous laugh and a slight tic in the cheek that was apparently chronic.

She spoke of a very unhappy childhood, of parents that were "no good," of the unfairness of people and life in general, and of "just not knowing what to do or where to turn." She said that she had not had coitus with her husband for six months, had had no premarital affairs, still masturbated (but less frequently than prior to marriage), and felt that having sexual relations with Ed or anyone else to whom she was not married was "unthinkable." She admitted, however, that she fantasied coitus with Ed while masturbating.

Developments, Therapy, and Conclusion

No therapy was undertaken with Sue. In the one interview, C was successful in convincing her of the desirability of her undertaking psychotherapy with a psychiatrist. The referral was worked out, and a telephone report to C from the psychiatrist six weeks later revealed a little progress on Sue's part in facing and handling her own problems.

Two weeks after Sue undertook psychotherapy, she told Ed that he could no longer visit her home, that her seeing him at work must be of only the casual greeting variety, and that their relationship had "been a mistake for which I am sorry." Ed called for an emergency appointment with C when he heard this news. He at first contended that "life has lost its meaning," but soon quieted down and agreed that he was actually relieved that "the whole deal's finished." He was all the more determined, however, not to return to his wife.

Ann's response to the news was first one of elation, but, after two weeks had passed in which her efforts at reconciliation were rebuffed by Ed, she became very depressed. It was at this point that she began to make considerable strides forward in understanding her own difficulties, the role she had played in the marriage, and the need to become emotionally independent of Ed. She launched divorce proceedings and began to build up her circle of friends, to entertain, and to accept invitations. C helped her to work through the relationship between her childhood conditioning and early assumption of the mother role and her adult emotions and marital functioning. Her earlier resistance to the need to develop her own interests and friends, to clarify her own life values, and to understand her own deeper feelings tended to melt away. She achieved an almost childlike delight from her recounting of new "insights" into how she felt and of various social successes.

About three months after filing divorce papers, she had a date with a widower five years her senior and "had a wonderful evening." This date was rapidly followed by many others with the same man. He fortunately seemed to have no need to be mothered and thus helped Ann to avoid patterns of "maternal domination." Her last interview with C, two months after meeting the widower, revealed a happier, femininely softer woman, who was becoming quite impatient with the divorce courts. Four months after this last interview, C received a letter that read in part as follows: "The State finally broke down and released me from 'my son' as you would probably put it, several weeks ago. John and I got married as fast as we could arrange it, and we're now away on a three-week honeymoon—I'm very happy and will always . . ."

Ed's climb toward a happier life situation was less rapid and less dramatic. He saw C twice a week for three weeks following the "news" from Sue and once a week for several weeks thereafter. Most of this time was spent in giving him continuing support in his efforts to achieve emotional independence. He had transferred his need to be mothered from Ann to Sue. Sue also aroused him sexually to a much higher degree than Ann, and she also apparently stirred in him all kinds of dreams of future accomplishments.

He suddenly found that his world of fantasy had evaporated and that he had no "mother" to comfort him. If he had not had the help of C at this time, he might either have returned to Ann or have turned to alcoholism (toward which he had shown some earlier tendencies).

If he had returned to Ann, it is C's judgment that the growth away from immaturity and neurosis on both Ann's and Ed's part would have been prevented. Their disturbed conditions had been reciprocally reinforcing for sixteen years; it is unlikely that either of them could have risen above such long-established habits while still associating with the other.

Without a "mother," however, Ed gradually came to see the kinds of things that he needed to undertake in the long-delayed growth toward emotional maturity, stability, and independence. He began to re-establish friendships that he had neglected and to make new friends. He started a serious program of investigating possibilities for further college training. He talked with his supervisor, made appointments at near-by universities, and wrote to others. The quality of his work increased on the job he held. He used his vacation to travel for personal interviews to places he had written. He finally worked out a deal with an Eastern concern where he had superior opportunities for advancement and a chance to take graduate courses at the company's expense.

Approximately one year after C's last interview with Ed, C received a phone call from him that things were going well. "What about your love life?" C asked. "I stayed away from women for about six months," Ed responded, "both because I was afraid I'd start leaning on another one and because I was knocking myself out on the new job and the engineering courses. After dating around a little, though, I did run into a girl that I think I'll probably marry. She's divorced and has had some psychotherapy, too. She's a nurse in one of the hospitals, and I think she's the gal for me. I'm not rushing this time, though. But whether I marry or not, I'm not getting mothered by her." They were married two or three months later.

Conclusion: Healthy, happy marriage in modern society calls for adult love, respect, and companionship. In the Ann-Ed marriage the love was largely of the mother-son, not the husband-wife, variety. From the very beginning there was no real passion of one for the other. Ann and Ed likewise did not respect each other as adult equals.

Was it the marriage counselor's responsibility, then, to "heal this sick marriage"? There are those who would contend that C was negligent in his duty in not constantly urging reconciliation upon Ed. Others, like C, hold that the primary responsibility of the marriage counselor is not to "save marriages," but to help people with problems which center around marriage. Sometimes both ends are accomplished and lead to a "new" relationship in the "old" marriage. Such help in this instance leads not to reconciliation but to divorce and another marriage.

C's role with Ed was largely one of providing acceptance, understanding, general support, and at times direct guidance in his process of maturing emotionally. C probably helped Ed enough during the Sue episode to get him soundly started in the process of growing up and facing his own problem. Ed was thus able to carry through the painful situation of his rejection by Sue into an adult and emotionally independent life.

C's role with Ann was at first one of getting to know her and being ready to help when the crisis of Ed's permanent departure finally struck home. Once she had emotionally accepted this disagreeable fact, she found it rather quickly possible to give up her maternal hold on Ed and to move out into adult relationships. When the mothering tendency was broken (with the fortunate cooperation of the widower), her high intelligence and capability enabled her to adapt herself promptly to a more adult type of relationship with another man.

CASE 12

Problem: The "other woman"—divorce avoided
Presented by: Marriage counselor (Ph.D. in Sociology; in-service training in marriage counseling) in a marriage counseling service located in a large industrial city

Statement of Problem by Clients: Al and Sandra Stein had been married nearly ten years when they came separately to the Marriage Counseling Service on referral from the County Medical Society.

Mrs. Stein, a slightly built, sallow-complexioned, plain-looking woman, reported grimly that her husband wanted to divorce her in order to be able to marry "the other woman"—a Gentile girl who was then in the midst of divorce proceedings with *her* husband. Asked by the counselor what she knew about the other woman, she answered, "It's no cheap affair—maybe that's fortunate. I really believe that he's in love with her." Sandra, herself, had practically "gone haywire" when Al first told her he didn't love her any more and wanted to marry Marge instead. However, with the help of her doctor, Sandra had been able to pull herself together and was now determined not to give Al the divorce he wanted because he's "a good father and a good husband." However, she added, "My faith in him has been completely blasted. I feel sorry for him, but there isn't a doggone thing I can do to help him. It's a situation he's going to have to work out for himself."

Summary of Interviews with Wife: Hers was the first appointment, at which time she made a tentative appointment for Mr. Stein (which he subsequently kept). But neither this counselor nor a colleague to whom Sandra was experimentally referred was able to break down her resistance to examining her own role in the marriage. Throughout a total of nearly twenty interviews, Mrs. Stein continued to place the entire blame for the marriage difficulties on her husband and the other girl. Her chief motive in seeking counseling seemed to be the hope that the counselor would be able to manipulate her husband into seeing the light. In fact, just before Al's first interview, Sandra came in for an "emergency" appointment in which she urged the counselor to take a directive role with Al, since "he usually follows what doctors tell him whether he believes it or not." The counselor explained to Sandra that marriage counseling does not involve writing prescriptions for unwilling clients but helping them to clarify their feelings, to understand their behavior, and to make their own decisions.

Interviews with Husband: When Mr. Stein arrived for his *first interview,* his resistance to counseling seemed just as high as his wife's. The only difference was that he blamed his "affair" all on her. There had been a short but intensive wartime courtship followed by the birth of their baby while he was overseas. Everything about the present situation seemed to him to go back to the days when he had just returned to civilian life after World War II to find Sandra and his three-year-old son entrenched with his in-laws. Moreover, he felt Sandra let him down by not helping him out in the store while he was struggling (unsuccessfully) to get started in the clothing business. She claimed she didn't feel well, but he thinks she was using her pregnancy as just an excuse. One evening after he came home from a long day at work to find she'd been to the movies, he told her off. It was the only time that she struck him and she told him that she hated him. He took her at her word and "from then on I realized that everything was up to me. For the sake of my children I would stick the thing out, but I would have to adjust myself to living without the love, the companionship, the affection that I thought were there."

As his first interview continued, Mr. Stein told how he had sold the store and taken a minor executive position with a local auto company. Disappointed in his marriage, he had thrown himself into his work. His efforts had been rewarded by several promotions. Gradually his casual acquaintance with the office receptionist ripened into friendship until one day during a coffee break Marge confided that she, too, was unhappily married. After that it seemed as though they were made for each other. In cocktail lounges and out driving in his automobile they shared their troubles until he came to feel that here at last was someone who understood him. "Marge and I have found true happiness together. I've never been more happy or contented with anyone else." The only fly in the ointment was his wife's refusal to give him a divorce. Because of her refusal he even threatened to elope with Marge—"I know what I want and I know it's right—even if I end up with nothing!"

His first melodramatic interview had not disclosed any eagerness for counseling on the husband's part. However, when the counselor initiated the *second interview* by asking Mr. Stein about his family background he readily launched into a report of his father's divorce and strictness in raising his children. His father was a self-made man who had worked hard all his life and was very strict with his sons. Al clashed with his father his senior year in college and they didn't see each other for a whole year. During the war, he finally made up his mind to break with his father's church because it no longer met his needs.

Mr. Stein didn't take his first drink until he was 27 and still hasn't told his father of his departure from the paternal code. "At first the mere fact that I differed with him bothered me. But I think you have to make your own decisions." He disciplines his own children the same way his father did, expecting prompt obedience. He also grew up expecting the man to be the head of the house.

The counselor inquired how his wife fitted into this picture. "She grew up under the opposite circumstances. Her father is a mild man, dominated by his wife." He thinks his own background of male dominance and his wife's of female dominance has caused much of the trouble in their marriage. His wife tends to take after her mother, although "she has tried to get along with my opinions." He also felt he might be just following in his father's footsteps if he, too, got a divorce. In view of his ambivalent feelings toward his father, he felt a bit challenged to see if he couldn't make something of this marriage before giving it up for lost.

The counselor encouraged this kind of introspection and this resolution as a wise investment for the future, no matter whether Mr. Stein decided to reconstruct his first marriage or establish a new one. Al confided that his feelings toward both his parents were very mixed, that he had never been able to talk to anyone about them before, and that he wondered if his strained relations with his parents affected not only his marriage but his work as a businessman, too. He also wondered whether he was "stable" because other girls had previously attracted him romantically, though to a lesser degree. He certainly didn't want his children to grow up to go through the kind of emotional turmoil he had. The counselor suggested that counseling was the client's best hope for clarification of such questions and for ending the unhappy sequence of events which could be traced as far back as his grandparents' divorce. However, such a process would take considerable time.

In his *third interview,* Mr. Stein indicated his readiness to undertake such long-range counseling. An eight-week break ensued, during which the counselor and client took their summer vacations. At the end of that time, Mr. Stein reported that he had already come to the conclusion things would never work out with

Marge. He had heard from another man in the office of her esca-
pades during his absence. Despite his disillusionment with Marge,
he still had considerable feeling toward her and none at all for
Sandra. Hence he felt torn between what his intelligence dictated
and what his heart commanded and had not yet found it possible
to let go of Marge completely. Even his usually even-tempered
aunt has been quite upset by the situation and has expressed the
fear that he might commit suicide. His wife, too, had another attack of "the shakes" a few nights before after they had had a rare
discussion about the triangle.

In regard to Mr. Stein's expressed sense of obligation to be
loyal to his wife and children, and his puzzlement that he should
be so strongly tempted to leave them, the counselor suggested
that like his father, the client had treated his wife's independence
of thought and action as disloyalty, had felt let down and be-
trayed and therefore psychologically justified in seeking security
elsewhere. Much of the subsequent counseling was designed to
help Al see why he responded so positively to Marge. He came
to recognize that his feeling toward her closely resembled the way
he had felt toward his wife until she "let him down" after marriage. Her non-co-operation he interpreted as intolerable "disloyalty" in the same way his stern father would have. But this
was not merely an acquired belief in the importance of loyalty.
He drops disloyal friends because they threaten his precarious
sense of security. Actually he has had few lasting friendships
because he'd rather take over a responsibility himself than trust
someone else with it. One of his limitations in the firm has been
his inability to delegate as much responsibility as he should to his
subordinates. Similarly he has drawn away from his wife ever
since he concluded she was undependable, too. This leaves him a
very lonely man, Al confessed, and this is probably the motive
which has driven him frantically into the arms of a whole series
of women, only to be disappointed with each of them in turn.

By the *tenth interview* this outwardly successful businessman
was confessing to a deep sense of inferiority which had been en-

gendered by his domineering father's humiliating criticism. As a boy he had come to hate his father, though he had successfully controlled his desires to rebel because his father's punishments were too severe. Now he had transferred some of these hostile feelings to his wife and his extramarital affair had been at least partly a delayed adolescent rebellion against his wife and against society.

In the *twelfth interview,* Al blamed his own unresponsiveness to his wife's affectional overtures on his childhood resentment of the way his father would punish him severely and then an hour later try to kiss him goodnight. By now rapport was so strong that the counselor could ask embarrassing questions pointblank but with a twinkle in his eye and have Al accept them in good humor. When Al confessed that he had never forgiven his father for being so punitive, the counselor asked whether he had ever forgiven anyone for anything. Al winced good-humoredly and suggested that to forgive would be too much like admitting he was wrong—something he was too insecure to admit even to himself outside the counseling situation. At the same time he had been extremely critical of his wife, expecting from her complete devotion and complete submission to his will.

Mr. Stein began to see that despite his resentment of his father, his own authoritarian behavior was repeating his father's faults "all over again." This disturbing similarity led him to seek to establish a "more up-to-date pattern of divided authority in marriage." As a boy he had always been "afraid to give up any authority for fear of being a weakling" and he had brought this fear of making concessions into his marriage.

In the *following interview,* Al reported that he had become more tolerant of Sandra's foibles. He decided to quit "chewing her out" for leaving the lights on (one of his many forms of "nagging")—after all, it only wasted a few pennies a month. Subsequent weeks focused on Al's attempts to learn how to cope with disappointment and anger as his marriage went through occasional reverses on the path to reconstruction. He had resumed wearing his wedding ring after a lapse of many years. "Now I have just one interest—to patch up the old wall of my marriage. Now in my own mind I'm not going to carry a torch for that girl. But it's going to take a long time to convince my wife. I still don't respond to her, but she has more support from me than she realizes."

When he remarked that he still hadn't found out why he got into all the trouble in the first place, the counselor inquired whether he didn't have some clues. He was reminded of the way in high school, as soon as he found someone who liked him, he'd rush her off her feet. "I must have been seeking something awfully bad."

Counselor—"What?"

Client—"Was I looking for a mother, for something I never had?"

Counselor—"What do mothers give their children that you feel you never got?"

Client—"A child can go to its parents and be mostly right in their eyes. It's like if my boy had done something wrong, I'd still want to support him and not disown him. So maybe in these girls I've sought someone I can count on for support. This girl respected my judgment, was interested in my progress, never criticized me or ridiculed me, so I felt she was behind me."

Counselor—"How come you never found anyone who satisfied you permanently?"

Client—"It sounds like I'm not as right as I think I am. First, I'm tentative with a girl, then there's a honeymoon period of intense activity, followed by a falling-off at about 90 degrees when she disagrees with me. My wife says a person can't live up to what I expect of them because I expect too much. I want her to do so many things and it's a terrific job for her to fulfill. Anyway, as soon as somebody falls short, it's too bad for them as far as I'm concerned."

Mr. Stein added, "The example I saw in my family was of women giving in constantly to men. My wife saw the opposite extreme. I've got to accept a more up-to-date pattern, one of divided authority, realizing that doesn't challenge my authority. As a kid I was always afraid to give up any authority for fear of being a weakling." The counselor asked for clarification of the concept of divided authority. "That means I'm not right all the time, that my wife may have the better approach . . . more of a partnership. Actually in my marriage, I'm setting up a line of authority just like my Dad did. But I really want my kids to have a more normal family than I did. Originally my wife and I started out talking things over. But I think we both brought to marriage something of the same attitude of rebellion, but mine was the more extreme and unbending. I really feel that my wife wants to get this thing solved. At first, I was afraid that as I came around, she'd go the other way, but she hasn't." The counselor interpreted this fear that he would be taken advantage of as related to his earlier efforts to hold the line against his father's encroachment on his independence. The counselor also pointed out that the client interprets every disagreement as a struggle where either the husband or the wife must lose, rather than recognizing the possibility of compromise decisions.

The materials above have been quoted extensively from the written records because this interview was unusually productive of insight into the client's past behavior toward women and into the implications this insight had for his subsequent treatment of his wife.

By the *seventeenth interview,* he reported triumphantly that he had succeeded in taking the initiative in patching things up after Sandra and he had had a tiff. Although the couple had continued to have sexual relations all through their months of trouble, Sandra's orgasm capacity only now returned to normal. He went on to say that he felt his wife's worry about him the other night when he came home late was a sign that she "wanted to fix things up."

Counselor asked, "Did you tell her this?" Client ducked behind his coat sleeve, sheepishly, and joked, "That would be too hard!" Since he's never sure what her reaction would be, he doesn't dare express such feelings. Counselor interpreted this as a lack of communication. Client agreed: "Neither of us has known what the other was really thinking. I've always had a strong reluctance to show my hand. No wonder she doesn't know what to expect from me."

The counselor applauded Al's successful ventures in problem solving and encouraged him to attempt to communicate even more of his feelings to her toward the goal of increased empathy between the partners. When Sandra occasionally failed to reciprocate his conversational overtures, Al now tended to press her too hard to talk and had to be cautioned to respect her moods. At other times, however, the two of them found it possible to have some lively discussions of religion without losing their tempers—in fact, they could even enjoy matching wits.

By the *twenty-third interview,* Al had become aware that his wife was basically insecure just like himself. As a result of this discovery, he began being more diplomatic and more protective with her. When he complimented her on the way she entertained recent guests, she remarked that this was "the nicest thing he had ever said."

At about this time, the counselor felt that Al's progress was becoming so rapid that Sandra should be reinvolved in the counseling process. Although she dutifully kept a number of counseling appointments, she continued to feel disillusioned about her husband and unable to make any move toward reconstruction. It became apparent that she needed an opportunity to hear her husband make the kind of positive remarks about her and the future of their marriage which he had been privately telling the counselor.

Joint Interview: Therefore, after thirty-two interviews with Mr. Stein alone, the first joint interview was held. In order to begin the communication on a positive note, the counselor asked each partner to mention the things the other had done recently which he had appreciated. When Mr. Stein told how his wife had helped him to get ready when he was late for a trip, she expressed surprise because she hadn't realized how much this had meant to him. Each reported other such favors and considerations, including such romantic touches as a box of candy and a walk in the moonlight. The couple were in a good mood and could laugh when (after she reported that she had written him that he was "the captain of the ship") he rejoined, "But I didn't know I was going to be vetoed so often by the first mate!"

The counselor felt that this joint interview set a useful pattern for the couple by helping them to reveal to each other reactions toward the other. Both partners were pleasantly surprised to discover their efforts had been appreciated more than they had realized.

Unfortunately, this was the last interview with either partner since Mr. Stein's firm suddenly transferred him to a new branch plant in the East, and his family followed him as soon as housing could be arranged.

Follow-Up: Seven months later the counselor received the following letter:

Dear Dr. ——:

Progress is being made by Sandra and me, although for a while it seemed painfully slow. It took us a week after she and the kids arrived here for us to knuckle down to a good talk, and even then it seemed that more damage than good was being accomplished for the first half. By the time we finished, however, we both felt we were on the right track.

Sandra and I are very much thrilled over the prospect of a new little Stein whose arrival is scheduled for October or November.

With best regards,
Al.

Conclusions: The counseling was effective in helping an intelligent client achieve a high degree of insight into his motivation for seeking extramarital partners. When he discovered how immature his motives were, he decided to turn his efforts to rebuilding his marriage. Despite initially strong defenses, he came to recognize the many ways in which he was making life difficult for his wife, and to be willing to experiment with more appropriate ways of acting toward her. Although space has prohibited giving details, he also moved toward more sympathetic treatment of his children and of his subordinates at work. Aided by counseling sessions which spanned a whole year, this couple survived the severe crisis which first led them to seek professional help, and began rebuilding their marriage on a sounder basis than it had ever been before.

CASE 13

Problem: Pastoral counseling in a triangle situation
Presented by: Minister (B.D.; in-service training in marriage counseling) in suburban church

Introduction: The Q family moved to our community four years ago. After a year of "shopping" they decided to visit our church. I greeted them as a family following the church service and they invited me to visit them in their new home. I made a routine pastoral call as an expression of friendship and good will. They were very cordial and inquired concerning our total church program. I told them of a variety of activities which might be of interest to them as a family group, and of other activities they could participate in as a married couple. Then I visited with their four daughters aged 4, 6, 8, 10 and explained activities that might be interesting to each of them. The following Sunday the Q's told me that they would like to join the church together as a family. They requested a private service of membership that might have meaning to the children. I made three visits in the home to deal with some questions about a variety of our particular denominational beliefs that they wished explained. These were discussed with the entire family. Our relationship was warm and spontaneous, and Mr. Q requested a "prayer of blessing for their home." I offered this spontaneously, and the following Sunday received the family as members into the church. Together before the altar, the six Q's presented an ideal picture as a "happy," healthy family.

During the following year the Q's became active in many phases of the church life and volunteered for several responsible jobs in various church organizations. I made two home visits to consolidate my relationship with the Q's. In every respect they were accepted and admired as an exceptionally well-adjusted and intelligent family.

I mention many of these details because they are integral to the understanding of the "setting" in which the counseling was done. The counseling relationship I later had with the Q's was based on the total relationship that developed in all my associations with them. During their first year as church members, they attended a sermon series that I delivered on home and family relations. In an informal way after the services, they often discussed briefly some things that I had mentioned. Thereby the content of my relationship with the Q's before they sought counseling was focused upon our mutual interest in marriage and family relationships.

One morning two years after the Q's had become church members I was awakened by a phone call from Mrs. Q. She was tearful and unable to talk. I sensed that she was acutely disturbed. She was able to communicate to me only that she wanted me to see her as soon as possible. I decided to call on her in the home since she was too disturbed to come to my study. As I approached her home I experienced great anxiety and concern, for I had developed a close, warm relationship with the Q's and could share in their feelings of distress. Mrs. Q opened the door before I had a chance to ring the bell. Her eyes were red and she burst into tears when she saw me. I entered and we sat in the living room for fifteen minutes before she was able to stop crying. Mrs. Q said that she did not know how to tell me what had happened. I told her that I could see she was feeling very upset and that perhaps she wanted to sit for a few moments, until she might feel more able to tell me what had happened. Mrs. Q cried for a while and then "blurted out" that last night her husband had asked her for a divorce. He told her that he was in love with someone else and that he had been having sex relations with the other woman for over a year. Mr. Q had said that he no longer loved Mrs. Q and there was nothing she could do to change his mind. After telling these few details, Mrs. Q began to tremble and repeated over and over, "What shall I do? I love him. I cannot leave him." We talked calmly for a while and I told Mrs. Q that I could understand in part the great shock and loss which she was feeling. I then suggested that she consider marriage counseling. I told her that it would be better if Mr. Q would participate too. I then suggested several persons that the Q's might see, including myself in the list. Mrs. Q made an appointment with me and declined to ask her husband to come. All further interviews with the Q's were conducted in my office at the church.

The Problem as Presented by the Clients: Mrs. Q is in her late thirties. She is tall, attractive in a sensual, maternal way. She comes from a strict "middle class" family and is an only child. She is intelligent and quite talented as a "homemaker." She relates to people with deep feeling, but is rather compliant and tries to please everyone. She did not present any marriage problem, stating that she was always very happy with her husband. There were no conflicts or major differences. As she presented the difficulty she said, "I only want to know what I can do to win my husband back. I feel that what has happened is all my fault. I have failed as a wife. . . . I don't know how, or why. This would never have happened if I had been a good wife."

Mrs. Q could see no possible cause for her husband's "affair" and it came as a complete shock. Mrs. Q said her love for Mr. Q is much stronger as the years go by. She presented a picture of perfect harmony, sharing, and happiness prior to the difficulty. She was able only to admit cautiously that her husband was "very good in working around the house, but not always ready to help her with the heavy workload that she carried." She blamed herself completely for the difficulty but initially had no insight as to what way this might be possible. Mrs. Q wondered if her own "lack of energy and drive" was partly responsible for the trouble. Beyond this, she would admit no problem and could not face the reality of her own and her husband's deep dissatisfaction with their relationship.

Mr. Q is tall, large-boned, and handsome. He is in his early thirties, an only child, and comes from a rigidly severe family. He is of very superior intelligence and holds two postgraduate college degrees in unrelated fields. He works in a third field as a highly skilled specialist. He also relates to people with a superabundance of feeling. He is aggressive without being hostile, defensive, and vacillating from overtalkativeness to morose quietness. The main difficulty as he saw it was his wife's "jealousy and domination." He stated that he has always been unhappy with his marriage. Since marriage, his love for Mrs. Q has gradually weakened. He said that there had been disagreement over household management, friends, sexual adjustment, children, and sharing of household chores. He felt that all differences and disagreements ended with his giving in. Mr. Q felt that he had some part in the difficulty because of his unwillingness to take responsibility. During counseling Mr. Q said, "I really feel that I cannot forgive myself for what I have done. It went against all my principles." Mr. Q confided that marriage had become dull and uninteresting. He complained of his wife's lack of enthusiasm for sex relations. Often she went to sleep and seemed to avoid relations whenever possible. She did not seem to be interested in him. The other woman was very attentive, complimentary, and stimulating. She was "passionately excited by him sexually and seemed to desire him constantly." In contrast, his relationship with his wife had been a disappointment. Most of all, he was disappointed with himself for going against his own moral code.

First Counseling Interview: See Introduction.

Second Interview: Mrs. Q came to my office alone. As soon as she sat down, she began to cry. She acted as though she were in mourning, and went through extreme grief. She expressed the feeling that what had happened was quite unreal to her. She recounted all the details of the way her husband told her of his affair. She recounted all the happy years they had shared together, and said that she could not believe that "it was all over." She was very defensive about the relationship, and tried to picture her marriage as an "ideal" one in every respect. She was not able to admit any hostility toward her husband for what he had done. She reiterated her deep love for him. I wondered if it would help to ask him to come in and share in the counseling. Mrs. Q was sure that he would not consent, but she agreed to ask him to come see me if he wished to. As the interview ended, Mrs. Q confessed that she was quite hopeless, but also anxious to hold Mr. Q and feared that if he came to see me he would become more determined to leave her. I pointed out that it would more likely improve his feelings for her if they could each talk of their concerns and feelings with a "neutral" person, and then share these same feelings with each other.

Third Interview: Mrs. Q brought Mr. Q with her to my office. She entered first, and he followed, looking rather "sheepish." He sat tensely on the edge of a chair in one corner of my office and seemed ill at ease. Mrs. Q was very anxious as she sat in a chair in the opposite corner of the office. She fingered her handkerchief throughout the hour. Mrs. Q began talking, and said that her husband was now "very sorry for what he had done, and that it hurt him more than it hurt her." Mrs. Q then spoke of her love for Mr. Q and her unwillingness to leave him. I suggested that perhaps Mr. Q might want to tell himself of the way he felt about the marriage relationship. He agreed, and as he began to speak, Mrs. Q interrupted and said, "Mr. Q feels that we have been very happy for many years, and that this was all a mistake. He does not know why it happened, but it won't happen again." Mr. Q looked rather hostile, and I asked him if he would like to have the chance to explain how he felt in his own words rather than in Mrs. Q's words. Mr. Q said that this illustrated their relationship quite well. He said his wife usually had the "last word." Mrs. Q began to cry, and while she did, Mr. Q had a chance to speak. He said that this was not something that had happened on the "spur of the moment." He had been discontented for many years, and this was the culmination of accumulated unhappiness. Mrs. Q interrupted and began to argue with Mr. Q, saying that he had never told her he was unhappy before. She wondered why he had to tell her the way he did, instead of years ago. I suggested that it might be easier for both Mr. and Mrs. Q if they could have some time to talk with me alone, rather than together. I felt that it had been helpful for me to see them together for a few minutes, so that I could have the opportunity to observe how they related to each other, and how they handled problems with each other, but perhaps they could talk more freely alone. Mrs. Q said there was "nothing that she had to say or her husband had to say that they could not say in the open while together." In light of Mrs. Q's fear and anxiety about letting Mr. Q talk alone, I decided to finish the interview with them together.

Mr. Q then insisted to his wife that she give him a chance to speak. He then said that he was in love with Mrs. Z whom he had met at an office party a couple of years ago. He said that

Mrs. Z also loved him, and they were planning to elope, but now he felt differently. He said that he could not run away from the children because he felt responsible to them. He told Mrs. Q that he was no longer sure whether he loved her, or even liked her, but he was willing to try staying with her, if she would consent to stay in marriage counseling and face her part in the problem. Mrs. Q burst into tears and wailed loudly for several minutes. She said, "I realize that I am largely at fault. Tell me what I can do to make you love me again." Mr. Q said he was not sure if he would ever love her as he once did because he now loved Mrs. Z. He said that by giving Mrs. Z up he was making a "great sacrifice" because he loved her dearly. Mrs. Q cried uncontrollably, and because she was losing control and Mr. Q was becoming quite punitive, I decided to terminate the hour. I asked the Q's if they wished to continue in counseling, stating that I felt they would do much better seeing me separately. Both Mr. and Mrs. Q then agreed to continue and see me alone. Mr. Q asked me if I would offer a prayer for them. I did so, asking God to grant them strength, insight, and understanding to cope with their problem, and guidance for all of us as we sought to work on their relationship together.

Fourth Interview: Mr. Q came first to see me alone. We spent an hour during which I encouraged him to vent his hostility toward his wife. He complained that she was unduly jealous of him. She always suspected that he was in love with other women, and finally after years of this suspicion he really acted out her fears and had an affair. He spoke of her extreme domination. Everything had to be done her way. The things he wanted came last, and all his time and money went into the things she desired. If he objected, she accused him of depriving her of what any woman has a right to have. In addition, he blames her for interrupting the promising career that he had begun. Before marriage, she "seduced" him and became pregnant. He had to leave his graduate work and seek a job. They were married, and shortly later, Mrs. Q became pregnant again. She had told him that she was practicing birth control, but she deceived him. In fact, all four of their daughters were not planned, and because of financial responsibilities, Mr. Q abandoned all hope of a career in his chosen field and entered a more lucrative but less satisfying career. Mr. Q then complained that his wife had lost all interest in him and in sex relations. She did everything she could to "avoid" relations, and always went to bed at ten o'clock while he watched television. When he came to bed, he was never able to arouse her in order to have sex relations. I inquired whether Mr. Q helped around the house, realizing that Mrs. Q probably had considerable work, caring for a large new home and four children. Mr. Q was very angry and said that it was her job and not his. He works eight hours a day, and when he comes home, he likes to read the paper and relax. I suggested that they both might have a chance to "relax and do the things they both wanted to" if there were more sharing in the home care and child rearing. Mr. Q was "insulted" and left my office without speaking, slamming the door as he left.

During the fourth interview with Mrs. Q, I encouraged her to express some of her own resentments toward Mr. Q. Quickly, she told of his "selfishness and neglect." He did not share in the work, and he expected her to be a "sex machine" or act "alive." "How could he expect this when he sits around all evening while I work until I am ready to drop?" Mrs. Q then told of some unwise financial investments that her husband had made. She felt that in order to protect the budget she needed to insist that they buy only the necessities. Mrs. Q said that she had not gotten any new clothes for herself in over a year, and felt somewhat deprived.

I then explored with Mrs. Q her need to "hold her husband so tightly." Mrs. Q soon brought out that she had lost her father when she was young. In her teens, she married a man whom she loved very dearly. Just after the honeymoon, he was killed in an accident. She was heartbroken. She hardly dared let herself care for another man again, but when she finally risked having feelings for Mr. Q, she became so anxious and desperate lest she lose him, that she was always fearful that this would happen. I could see how upsetting these past losses had been, and could understand her need to "hold her husband closely."

We looked together at the sex relationship, and Mrs. Q brought out that she was always tired after a long hard day, and felt that sex was a "luxury one enjoyed when not tired." I suggested that perhaps it felt to Mr. Q as though she no longer was interested in him sexually, or as a husband. Mrs. Q was angry and left my office saying that I was not "fair" to suggest that.

Fifth Interview: Mr. Q came in with elation. He told me that he had done some "soul searching" after our last interview, and now realized how much he expected of his wife, and how little he had given of himself. He surprised his wife and himself by "pitching in" with the housework. Then he talked out all his resentments about sex with Mrs. Q. As a result, they had a "sex orgy" where his wife would not let him out of bed for twenty-four hours. The children were away, and it was a week end. He was exhausted, but both felt that the "air was cleared." They were even making plans for a vacation together, and then had decided on some projects at home that they could work on together.

Mrs. Q came to my office saying that she could not understand what had "come over her." After she talked with me, she had felt strong sex desire for her husband and had not been able to leave him alone for the past week. She was enjoying sex with him, surprisingly. She then said that she had told him of all her resentments about his unwillingness to share, and about his selfishness. She never dared say this before because she feared she might lose him. Now, for some reason, they seemed to feel closer than before Mrs. Z entered the picture. I gave Mrs.

Q *Marriage: The Art of Lasting Love,*[1] by David R. Mace, and suggested that she read Chapter 14, "Enter the Other Woman," together with her husband. I felt that this might help each of them to gain some understanding and acceptance of the significance of Mr. Q's affair with Mrs. Z.

Sixth Interview: Mr. and Mrs. Q came together to this interview. They brought the book with them, and said that it had helped them greatly. They now saw that an "affair" need not mean that a marriage had ended, but could mean "danger . . . your marriage needs repair." They both felt that this crisis had actually drawn them closer together as they tried to cope with it. They felt that there were many problems to be worked out, but they were encouraged that they had made a beginning. They felt that now they wanted to try to work on their problems together, because they had learned for the first time that they could share feelings with each other and thus work on their own relationship. Mr. Q discovered to his embarrassment that Mrs. Z was a "professional marriage breaker," for he learned that he was number six in a series of affairs that Mrs. Z had had. Mr. Q was somewhat bitter that he had been "used" but was more confident that his relationship with Mrs. Q was now growing, and that the affair with Mrs. Z was a symptom, perhaps a necessary development that had motivated them to improve their relationship. The Q's requested that I offer a prayer, and I prayed in thanksgiving to God, that we had received guidance and skill in dealing with their relationship . . . that Mr. and Mrs. Q be granted continuing insight and awareness to handle their feelings day by day in all kinds of situations, to their mutual satisfaction.

The Q's ended counseling stating that they realized it had been incomplete, and that later, each wished to come in separately for extended pastoral counseling to gain greater under-

[1] Doubleday & Co., Inc., New York, 1952.

standing of themselves individually and in their relationship to each other and to their children.

Follow-Up: I had an opportunity to see the Q's informally several times over the period of one year. On many occasions, they told me personally that they felt closer than ever before, and that they had more "warmth and love" for each other than they had experienced in years. I have received a few letters from the Q's since I left that church in which they stated that they were happy and still working on their differences. I received a token gift from the Q's and a note saying that they were very grateful for the help that they received. This came over a year after counseling was terminated. In all outer respects, the marriage and the family seem to be functioning well, and Mr. and Mrs. Q seem reasonably content with each other.

Conclusions: This was a case of pastoral counseling which I call "brief counseling." Mrs. Q had four single interviews, and Mr. Q had two single interviews. There were two joint interviews, making a total of six contacts for Mrs. Q, who initiated counseling, and four contacts for Mr. Q, who participated willingly and co-operatively. Mrs. Q was anxious and fearful, and had many doubts about herself as a woman. Mr. Q was angry and resentful, and had some anxiety about his "maleness." In brief counseling, I worked with Mrs. Q around her anxiety and fear, but did not touch her doubt about herself. With Mr. Q, I encouraged the expression of his anger and resentment but did not handle the more basic feelings about his masculinity. Interpersonally, the "lines of communication were down," and through ventilation with me, Mr. and Mrs. Q were able to reestablish feeling contact with each other. I believe that the "affair" was actually helpful in Mr. and Mrs. Q's relationship in that it dramatically confronted them with the illness of their relationship. Counseling with Mr. and Mrs. Q, done in a religious setting which used the resources of religion and marriage counseling, appeared to be effective in helping Mr. and Mrs. Q cope with their immediate problem.

The main weakness of counseling, as I see it, was my failure to motivate Mr. and Mrs. Q toward seeking more permanent help on a deeper level. I believe they are both capable of using psychotherapy or even psychoanalysis, and feel that in the future they may need further counseling or therapy of some kind. If the Q's come to me for further assistance, I plan to help motivate them for therapy, and will refer them to a qualified psychiatrist.

7. Psychotherapy in Marriage Counseling

In each of these situations, although the clients presented themselves for marriage counseling, psychotherapy seems to have
been the major technique employed by the counselor—in one
case, a clinical psychologist; in another, a psychiatrist and his
wife (psychologist); in the third, a psychiatric social worker,
working in close and constant consultation with her staff psychiatrist; and in Case 17, a psychiatrist, using psychotherapy
with one partner only as his approach to the presenting marital
problem.

Perhaps it is pertinent to point out that use of psychotherapy
by these marriage counselors is in line with established AAMC
policy: ". . . in no sense are psychotherapy and marriage counseling to be considered synonymous. Members of the AAMC
may do psychotherapy—many of them do, but not by virtue of
their work in marriage counseling. This activity derives from
their individual basic training and unless they are so trained and

qualified, marriage counselors per se are not considered to be psychotherapists." [1]

CASE 14

Problem: A marriage of two neurotics
Presented by: Clinical psychologist (Ph.D.) in private practice in a large Eastern city

Introduction: The initial contact was with Mrs. M, a 48-year-old woman of American-Jewish background, who came to complain that she did not see how she could "take it any longer" after twenty-five years of marriage to an impossible husband. Her husband, 49 years old, did not want to come for counseling, but was seen at his wife's insistence.

The Problem as Presented by the Client: Mrs. M stated that her husband gave her no affection; neglected his business; talked incessantly of his problems in front of their children; spent as much as four hours at a time eating heavy meals; ran continually to the bathroom to urinate; was greatly upset by sex relations and refused to sleep in the same room with her; and generally acted in a selfish and inconsiderate manner. Their oldest child, a girl of fifteen, was ashamed to bring her friends to the house because of her father's odd behavior; and the other children were also seriously disturbed because of Mr. M's behavior. Mr. M, when first seen, complained bitterly that since he had seen a psychiatrist a year ago his wife, on the psychiatrist's advice, no longer allowed him to come home all afternoon to rest and eat, but insisted on his keeping regular hours at his business. What he needed, he said, was plenty of food, rest, sunshine, and strenuous gymnastics and going away to health re-

[1] Minutes of Executive Committee, May 19, 1955.

sorts every few weeks. Sex relations, on the other hand, gave him a pain in the right side of his penis and made him feel weak for a day or two after he had them. The psychiatrist and several physicians had told him he was sexually normal; but he still thought that there was something wrong with his urethral tract and also felt that sex relations would bring on a heart attack, although he had often been medically assured that there was nothing wrong with his heart.

The Counseling: Mrs. M was seen once a week for twelve sessions; Mr. M was seen twice a week for a total of thirty sessions. Mrs. M was tentatively diagnosed by the counselor as a distinctly neurotic woman who outwardly conformed to family and social pressures but who seethed with underlying, unacknowledged hostility. Because of severe feelings of inadequacy, which largely arose from gross neglect by her father, and the favoring by her mother of a chronically invalided sister, she adopted an extremely ingratiating attitude toward almost everyone; and she hated herself for not standing up for her own rights. In compensation, and under the guise of love and solicitude, she ruthlessly dominated her three children and supervised the most minute aspects of their lives.

Mr. M was tentatively diagnosed as having a long-standing, deep-seated anxiety neurosis with conversion symptoms. Ignored by his father, he had been exceptionally overprotected by his mother, and had been encouraged by her to remain weak and unathletic. He had also been continually warned by her that sexual intercourse was weakening and that food was strengthening. He claimed that he loved his children dearly, but actually neglected them completely and was, instead, immoderately attached to his mother, although she had been dead for several years. He literally talked about himself incessantly, to any stranger he might encounter, and made endless written notes about himself and how unhappy he was. His stream of words would go something like this: "I don't know what's the matter with me. I just can't seem to get hold of myself. If I could only get more sunshine and air. I must attend to my business more. I know I shouldn't eat so much, but I feel weak without food. If only we didn't live too far from the business and I could go home to rest in the afternoon. Maybe I ought to go away to a health resort for two weeks. I don't know what's wrong with me: as soon as I have sex, I get pains in my sex parts. I really should have another physical examination. . . ."

With Mrs. M the following counseling and psychotherapy techniques were employed:

Clarification and insight. Mrs. M was helped to see, through the counselor's interpretations, that she was only self-sacrificing and passive on the surface, but that underneath she was quite controlling and hostile. Particularly in relation to her children, she was shown that she continually pressured them, and that much of their disturbance resulted from this pressure. In relation to her daughter, she was able to see that she was underlyingly jealous and feared being replaced by her daughter in her husband's affection. In relation to her own son, she was shown that her rigid methods of controlling him were unconsciously influenced by her hostility against, first, her father and, second, her husband. In relation to herself, she was enabled to see, through the counselor's interpretations of her past and present history, that her main problem was not, as she had thought at first, her husband, but herself; that she had the lowest possible estimation of herself, and hence masochistically encouraged exploitation by her husband. She was led to see that nothing short of a drastic change in her attitude toward herself, with consequent stiffening in her behavior toward her husband, would induce important behavior changes in her husband.

Support. While interpreting Mrs. M's underlying patterns of behavior to her, the counselor offered her considerable support. He emphasized how capable she was, and how she had the ability to handle her problems if she changed her attitudes. He encouraged her to lose weight, which enhanced her estimation of herself considerably. He went over with her, in minute detail, some of the problems she had with her children, and helped her find solutions for them.

Commands to action. The counselor insisted, at first with considerable resistance on Mrs. M's part, that she put into action some of her new attitudes toward her husband.

Thus, at the counselor's insistence, Mrs. M began, for the first time in twenty-five years of marriage, to serve meals at a regular time, to cook only a reasonable amount of food, and to limit the mealtimes to a half hour, instead of allowing her husband, as he had done for all the previous years of their marriage, to prolong his huge meals for several hours at a time. She also, at the counselor's urging, began to develop her first outside interest. At the beginning, Mr. M fought bitterly against these changes in his wife's behavior; but as, with the counselor's firm backing, she maintained them, he gradually became inured and began to exploit her less. This sticking to her guns and doing some of the things she had wanted to do, but had not the courage to do, for many years, enormously increased Mrs. M's estimation of herself and did more to help both her and her husband than any other aspect of the marriage counseling in this case.

Information giving. Like most women of her generation, Mrs. M came to the counseling process with a good many sexual misconceptions. She was a highly sexed woman, but was quite guilty about her own sex inclinations and loath to do much about them. The counselor showed her that she was not a "nymphomaniac," but that her sex proclivities were completely normal and harmless. He also disabused her of the notion that certain of Mr. M's and her sex activities were "unnatural" or "abnormal," and she soon lost her guilt concerning such activities. Oral-genital relations were particularly satisfying to her and her husband; but only after several weeks of counseling were they able to have such relations without feeling an enormous sense of guilt. The decrease in Mrs. M's sense of guilt which accompanied the sex information given to her by the counselor also served to enhance her general sense of self-esteem and to make her better able to meet many of the difficulties of her marriage.

The main techniques of counseling and psychotherapy employed with Mr. M were as follows:

Clarification and insight. With Mr. M, clarification and insight produced minimal results. In many instances, particularly in regard to interpretation about his attachment to his mother, he simply refused to accept the counselor's interpretations, or else blandly accepted them but made no attempt to use them to change his behavior. He would continually ask the counselor why he acted this way or that way; but when the cause was explained to him, he would disregard the explanation. In fact, the truer the counselor's explanations seemed to be, the more Mr. M would tend to disregard them. He would also, when he did understand and accept an interpretation, tend to use it negatively, to destroy further his own sense of self-esteem. Thus, he would accept the fact that his sexual inhibitions were related to his mother's direct anti-sexual teachings; but he would then say: "What an idiot I am to be taken in like this! Why can't I act more intelligently? What a dope I am!" All told, Mr. M obtained, at best, verbal but not behavioral insight. It was quite a while before the counselor fully realized that Mr. M simply did not want real insight; he wanted to remain the way he was, and would continue to resist acquiring insight to the bitter end.

Support. One of the counseling techniques that worked best with Mr. M was that of support. When the counselor showed him how he *could* do things, how he was intelligent and strong enough to do whatever he wanted to do, Mr M sometimes reacted quite favorably. In regard to his business, for example, considerable success was achieved. Mr. M insisted, at first, that he had lost his grip as far as business was concerned, and could no longer manage his business properly. The counselor insisted that this was not true, but that he was fully capable of taking up the managerial reins again and doing an excellent job. Partly through showing consistent faith in Mr. M in this connection, and partly through getting Mrs. M to do likewise, Mr. M was induced to expand his business considerably and to do fairly good work in it. Also, in relation to Mr. M's sex ability, the counselor was continually encouraging and supportive; and, quick to respond, Mr. M suddenly gave up most of his sexual complaints, and much to his own surprise began having sex relations four or five times a week, and often two or three times a night, in place of the once a week regularly to which he had forcibly and fearfully held himself for the previous twenty-five years of marriage.

Commands to action. Except in the area of sexual behavior, the counselor at first had very little success with Mr. M as far as urging him to action was concerned. He still insisted on overeating, on incessantly seeking sunshine, on fetishistically going to the gymnasium, and so on. He would ask the counselor exactly what to do in these connections; and, in no uncertain terms, the counselor would tell him. But then he would almost completely disregard the counselor's urgings. After a while, however, the counselor's persistence began to pay off in some respects. Mr. M did give up lying in the sun and running to gymnasiums and health resorts; and he also dieted a little. As soon as he carried out these demands of the counselor, he felt much better and was able to do some things, such as taking care of his business, that he had not been able to do for years before. He had a tendency, however, to backslide. Finally, the counselor realized that Mr. M was childishly resisting all demands, by both the counselor and his wife, that were not backed by some kind of penalty. Since the counselor could not too easily penalize Mr. M, he induced Mrs. M to do so at times. When, for example, Mr. M was late for meals—which he often deliberately was, in order to annoy his wife—Mrs. M was induced to refuse to feed him entirely. When he talked incessantly to strangers about his troubles—which he also partly did to annoy his wife—she was induced to go home without him. To the extent that Mrs. M

quietly and non-angrily penalized Mr. M for his childish behavior—and it was exceptionally difficult to get her to do so
in a consistent fashion—he improved enormously. To the extent
that she failed to penalize him or angrily punished him, he soon
returned to his old ways. It was only after some time, and considerable work with Mrs. M, that the counselor was able to get
her consistently and unvindictively to penalize him in certain
essential regards. It was this kind of consistent penalization
which finally helped Mr. M more than any other counseling
procedure employed. He never became thoroughly mature in any
area, and to the end fought against both his wife and the counselor. But he at least improved considerably, and the one thing
that made the marriage of Mr. and Mrs. M tolerable was Mrs.
M's unwaveringly insisting, at the counselor's continued urging,
on Mr. M's toeing certain essential lines.

Information giving. If anything, Mr. M came to the counseling
situation with more serious sexual inhibitions than Mrs. M.
He had been an exceptionally high-sexed individual from the
age of ten, but had rigorously squelched most of his sex desires
throughout his life. At his insistence, he and the counselor had
many talks about sex; and, repeatedly, the counselor had to go
over much scientific information in this connection. As a result
of these talks, Mr. M's sexual prowess improved enormously;
he entirely overcame his tendencies toward premature ejaculation which he had had for many years; and his pains in the
penis disappeared whenever he permitted himself to have steady
sex relations. His guilt about sex decreased considerably, and he
became much better adjusted in this area.

Follow-Up: Mr. M prematurely discontinued counseling because
he felt he had obtained all he wanted to obtain through it. Mrs.
M sporadically saw the counselor from time to time after her
husband's counseling ended. Immediately after the counseling
was discontinued, their marriage was much better though far
from perfect. Mr. M was considerably improved in business and

in his sex life with his wife; and he lost many of the fears with which he came to counseling. He was still, however, overeating, paying relatively little attention to his children, and acting in a generally neurotic manner. Mrs. M was much more improved, was doing many things on her own, and was much less irritated by her husband, to whose behavior she had become somewhat resigned as a result of the counseling process. She was also acting in a less pressurizing manner toward her children, all of whom had benefited considerably from her changed behavior. Two years after the counseling process had ended, Mr. M had kept most of his gains but had not augmented them and was still a seriously neurotic individual. Mrs. M had not only retained her gains but had somewhat surpassed them and was leading a much calmer, more contented existence.

Conclusions: The case of Mr. and Mrs. M shows, among other things, that marriage counseling and psychotherapy can be somewhat effective with seriously neurotic clients even where one of them is being counseled against his will. It also shows, however, that under these circumstances only limited gains may usually be made. The counseling strengths, in this case, would chiefly seem to lie in the fact that the counselor was able to do as well as he did with Mr. M in spite of his steady resistance to therapy. This was probably because the counselor used Mrs. M as a sort of auxiliary therapist, and through strengthening her could enable her to do certain things which helped to strengthen her husband. The counseling weaknesses lie largely in the fact that the counselor was never able to win Mr. M's complete co-operation. This was perhaps because, at first, he relied too much on giving Mr. M insight, and perhaps not enough on giving him support, encouragement, and approval. If, from the start, the counselor had clearly seen through Mr. M's resistances and had induced Mrs. M to be more firm, while he, the counselor, was more accepting and lenient, more movement by Mr. M might have been effected. At the same time, it is also possible that

under the circumstances almost no other counseling procedure
would have been more effective with Mr. M than was the one
employed. His exceptionally deep-seated neurosis and his unwillingness to face intensive psychotherapy presented a real
problem; and the counselor is content with even the moderate
results achieved in this case.

EDITOR'S NOTE: This case is interesting, because of its
somewhat unusual procedures. It is a clear example of
directive counseling. The use of the partners as "auxiliary
therapists," as in this case, was seldom undertaken in other
cases submitted for this manuscript.

CASE 15

**Problem: An immature and dependent woman (15 A) married
to an immature and hostile partner (15 B)**
**Presented by: (a) Psychologist (M.A.) in private practice
(b) Psychiatrist (M.D.) in private practice
sharing offices in a large metropolitan city**

15 A

Introduction: Mrs. B, 26 years old, married six years, first consulted the psychologist because her husband wanted a divorce—he
expressed a strong desire to "have his freedom." She complained
of headaches, loss of appetite, vomiting, inability to carry on
any conversations except by telephone, and difficulty in handling
her children. She did not wish to undergo therapy, but felt that
if she got a larger home she would have less difficulties with the
children and be free of all her other complaints. Therapist advised her to try this course and to return if she changed her
ideas about the need for therapy.

One and one-half years later, Mrs. B came for a second interview. She had the same symptoms and difficulties, but now ex-

pressed a desire to improve her marital relationship. This, she said, had become worse. Her husband had been drinking excessively, had lost interest in the home, and did not come home until the early mornings.

Family History: *Her father.* Foreign born, came to the United States at the age of 18; little education; a self-employed housepainter, making a moderate income. He has no interest in his home, wife, or children; spends his evenings watching TV, avoids conversation and prefers to be alone. Has bitter feelings toward people who are more successful financially, but makes little attempt to improve his own business.

Her mother. American born, grammar school education; meticulous housekeeper, strict disciplinarian, overpossessive, frugal to the point of miserliness. Has suffered from migraine for the past thirty-five years, which completely disabled her and made her demand care and attention from her daughter. She was much concerned with maintaining an attractive figure, hence followed popular reducing diets and resorted to self-induced vomiting after meals. There were no visitors, no interest in current events, no reading.

Her brother. Five years her junior, was an unplanned "beautiful baby" and her parents' favorite.

Personal History: Patient is an attractively dressed bleached blonde, who usually looks very depressed and withdrawn. She has a trim figure, but appears hard and unfeminine. She has average intelligence.

Patient was told by her family that she was an ugly baby. As a child, she was very obese, and was not permitted to play with other children. She barely "passed" through grammar school; had very few friends—children were not permitted to visit in the home.

In early adolescence, patient found excuses to sleep at home of friends. Her clothes were last year's styles; she was ashamed of her mother's bargaining tactics. Her few friends were girls of better economic status who had prettier clothes. She felt frustrated, but she feared her mother and never dared express her anger and irritation.

When she was 12, she began to go with a group of boys and girls who met in a near-by candy store. Although she dated early, she never permitted any sexual play. Courtship with her future husband began when she was 13½. Although he had a bad reputation for drinking and sexual urges, he came from the wealthiest family in town and was considered a "good catch."

Patient's physical health was good, with no known systemic disorders. She was shamed into losing weight, developed much concern with diets, and weighed herself after each meal. She became thinner than her build required.

After graduation from high school, where she was "forced" to take a commercial course, she worked for six months as a comptometer operator. She did not enjoy her work—married to abandon boresome work and to escape from an unhappy home.

Patient reported little masturbation and no overt homosexuality. She usually developed a relationship to one girl at a time. During late adolescence, she had only an occasional date; she refused to pet, and never had a second date with the same boy. The exception to this situation was her future husband, but she refused intercourse with him until they got married.

Although he wanted to get engaged prior to his military service, his parents opposed this plan but gave their consent to his marriage after completion of military service. Her parents, however, announced the engagement before he left for the service, to the annoyance of his parents. But shortly after his departure, his parents indulged her with many expensive clothes, lavish entertainment, etc. However, on their son's return, three years later, they again balked at the marriage. It was only after many emotional scenes that they agreed; and then arranged and paid for a costly wedding.

Background Data on Married Life: A small house was bought by the in-laws for which the couple had to pay a nominal rent. No furnishings were provided; the husband's parents suggested that the couple furnish the house out of income, "even if it takes many years." The young wife expected the husband to take all the bills to the "business" for payment, but he feared his father's reactions; he developed severe headaches. She continued to buy lavishly, fully believing that this was what her "in-laws" wanted her to do. Finally when the bills piled up, her husband disclosed the situation to his father, and there was an explosive episode. The father-in-law paid the bills, but the wife was admonished to discontinue her extravagant ways.

Since the business had "charge accounts" for theater tickets and restaurants, the couple went out continuously. The husband drank excessively and he taught her "how to drink." She enjoyed drinking because it helped her to avoid food, made her more talkative, and less inhibited, socially and sexually. When sober, she participated willingly in the sex act but never enjoyed it. She was frigid. Under the influence of liquor, she indulged in fellatio, permitted cunnilingus, and then, continuing the sex act in the usual relationship, went on to orgasm.

Two months after marriage, she became pregnant because "all her friends were pregnant." Her husband objected to the pregnancy and insistently suggested an abortion. She refused. She vomited throughout the pregnancy, spontaneously the first four months; during the last five months induced vomiting by tickling her soft palate with her finger. She developed a severe secondary anemia and remained in bed for two months following delivery.

She gave birth to a son whom everyone considered an "ugly baby." She cared for the child herself and felt "shut in" since her husband continued his round of "nightly entertainment." She had no strong love for the baby, but carried out the routine duties.

Two years later she became pregnant again—with the same

repetition of spontaneous and induced vomiting, secondary anemia and postpartum weakness. She again gave birth to a son. This time she had a nurse-governess who took complete charge for 2½ years. This child was "beautiful" and she could "show" him to people. However, her husband continued to go out several nights a week without her.

During this period, patient spent most of her time playing golf, painting, or doing hospital work. In the evening she visited her neighbors or remained at home alone except occasionally, when her husband took her out.

She never expressed her anger toward her husband directly, but turned her aggression toward her children. Both were toilet trained before they were one year old. The children expressed their opposition to her demands for cleanliness and orderliness by soiling in bed and smearing their bowel contents on the walls.

Patient was further irritated by her in-laws who compared her children to other children in the family and derided her ability as a mother and housekeeper. She received these criticisms without protest, but became even more assaultive to her children—making more demands and increasing punishments.

Treatment: Patient came for treatment three times weekly for about four years. At the first interview she appeared depressed, hopeless, with little interest in herself, the environment, or any activity. She had lost all initiative. She accepted her husband's occasional invitations to go out, submitted to all his wishes, but with complete indifference. She repeated her complaints about her physical condition and about her inability to function as mother and housewife. She admitted that her husband was justified in his criticisms of her inadequacy as a homemaker and her inability to discipline the children. She agreed that he had good reason to stay away from home or even seek a divorce. She had difficulty in expressing her hostility to her husband or his family.

In the subsequent interviews, as her history unfolded, she began to realize that because she came from a family of low economic status, she had feelings of inferiority. To keep the marriage, she readily agreed to any demands her husband made, permitting him to spend money as he wished, to come home drunk in the early morning with a minimum of complaint on her part, and attempting to woo him by allowing any form of sex play.

There was little communication between them. She showed an ambivalent attitude toward her house—it was her one possession, hence she was eager to beautify it, but recognized that her husband used it merely for room and board—hence she rejected it because it was not a "love nest." Her hostility toward the husband was displaced onto the children. They in turn took on the attitudes of their father and showed no respect.

She dared not confide her marital difficulties to her parents or his.

Gradually she became aware that her need for her husband's approval was self-debasing. By encouragement and realistic evaluation of her mental capacity, she was able to develop a sense of self-esteem. She changed her approach to her husband and suggested that his lack of participation in the home had had a deteriorating effect. Instead of making daily complaints she sought his "advice" in handling situations. Instead of showing tremendous emotional upheaval, she remained calm, engaging him in discussions and even suggesting that he could perform many of her tasks much more efficiently. She particularly stressed his effectiveness in disciplining the children. She arranged for him to spend his Saturday afternoons with the boys. And, following many discussions with the therapist about the need to build a family life, she arranged activities for them all.

The husband continued his night life. But when he came home in the early morning hours in a drunken state, she took him to task, pointing out that she would not permit this sort of life to go on. She demanded that he, too, receive marriage counseling. He agreed to go to the psychiatrist for help.

(The case record for 15A, Mrs. B, is resumed on page 217.)

15 B

Introduction: Mr. B, 28 years old, married eight years, reported the following: marriage incompatibility—wife poorly organized —too emotional, constantly yelling at the children—shows little interest in improving herself, is poorly informed, is a poor sexual partner. Patient wants his freedom—does not wish to continue the responsibility of a home and family. His marriage was a big mistake.

He has had recurrent attacks of stomach trouble—X rays of stomach suggested an ulcer. He admitted imbibing 20-30 ounces of liquor each day "but never appeared drunk"—his business was so hectic and exciting that unless he took a drink he would "explode" emotionally.

First Interview: Mr. B presented himself at the appointed time. He greeted the therapist with an attitude of distance and coldness. He questioned the value of marriage counseling. He came because he wanted a divorce. He recognized the futility and hopelessness of continuing his marriage. His wife was stupid. They had nothing in common. During the evenings, usually while watching TV, she insisted upon sitting on his lap, hugging and kissing him. Always it was "Where did you go today?" "What did you do?" "Whom did you see?" He is sick and tired of her questions and fondling annoyances. He loathes going home. The children are completely unruly, undisciplined, destructive. His only source of satisfaction is liquor. Toward the close of the session, the psychiatrist suggested that at this time it would be difficult to determine whether or not divorce would be the most desirable course to follow. Patient was advised to postpone any action until the entire story was unfolded. The

patient agreed to continue three times weekly. The therapist
noted patient's hostility toward his wife and children. He gave
him no encouragement or reassurance, but followed a course of
strict objectivity.

First Month of Treatment: Initially the patient was unfriendly,
resistive. His general demeanor was one of continuous disgust.
The therapist, in order to direct him away from his extreme
antagonism toward his wife and home environment, suggested
that he talk about other possible sources of irritation. He accordingly related with equal bitterness his feelings concerning
his father and brother. He described his father as a very forceful,
aggressive organizer, although of short stature. His father, aged
60, born abroad, had migrated to the United States during childhood—worked as a stockboy, later salesman of textiles—worked
long hours—had little education. He had no time for family—
never home for dinner—slept most of Sunday afternoon on a
couch in the living room with his face covered by a newspaper.
Later, he entered his own business, became fabulously wealthy.
Although his two sons are in business with him, he actually is
the "brains."

Patient continued with a description of his brother—four
years older than patient. He had had a half year of college, is
in his father's business as an executive. He is an obstinate,
stubborn, "know-it-all," impulsive person. He is unhappily married; remains entirely away from home at least one night each
week, "entertaining buyers."

Patient was placed in charge of sales and production, yet all
decisions were made by others. But when things went wrong,
patient was blamed. Under stress he resorted to whiskey, usually
beginning about 10 A.M., continuing throughout the day and
after closing. His attitude toward his employees was one of
domineering aggression with an uncontrolled flow of vulgar,
obscene invectives. He admitted that his interest was in neither

business nor selling, but in writing. Yet he feared his father and had to attend to business, although he loathed it.

Gradually, the patient became more friendly and began to look forward to the opportunity to vent his feelings. By the end of the fourth week, there was no further mention of divorce, nor did he ask whether there was any hope of salvaging his marriage. He accepted his need to come to the therapist; he needed a listening ear.

Further treatment revealed his strong attachment to his mother, but his inability to gain her attention. He described her as a meticulous housekeeper and a strict disciplinarian—aged 56—born in U.S.A.—high school education. The children were not permitted to enter living room—ate in kitchen. With advent of wealth she devoted much time to her personal care, her clothes. His mother was always praising his older brother and made patient feel inferior in intellect, manual skills, and physical appearance.

Third Month of Treatment: At this point patient began to disclose his personal history. He had been much concerned with playing baseball during childhood and adolescence. Of average intelligence, he had passing interest in school work. The family had been in moderate circumstances until he was 12 years old. At 15, he had had a sports car of his own. Also, at 16, began drinking and experimenting with sex. He enjoyed the reputation of being "fast." He developed an irregular courtship at age 15; became engaged at 19. Went into military service—three years abroad—always had difficulty with his superiors. Had advanced to rank of sergeant but subsequently had been demoted to private. On discharge from the service, he began work in his father's business. He insisted on getting married, over his parents' protest. The wedding was held in a prominent hotel at tremendous cost—his parents paid all expenses.

Patient and his wife enjoyed a harmonious relationship with a minimum of friction during the first two months of marriage.

They had an expensive honeymoon and were a very happy couple. His interest was centered on developing a home life. Two months after marriage, his wife became pregnant. He insisted that wife be aborted. She refused. He preferred to remain in the city at least three nights each week, arriving home in early morning hours, usually under the influence of liquor. He shared the "hide-away" apartment with his brother. During wife's sixth month of pregnancy, husband, working at his father's mill, crushed his left arm and hand in a machine and was disabled for eight months. Until wife's pregnancy, patient had had no extramarital experiences. However, during this period, he participated with other women. He then became attached to one woman of foreign extraction. He thought seriously of divorcing his wife and marrying this woman. Although he retained a relationship with this woman for five and one-half years, he had lesser affairs as well.

Although his wife was under the impression that his salary was $75 weekly he was actually drawing $250. While constantly scolding his wife for her inability to economize, he used the difference for "sporting" purposes.

When, two years later, his wife again became pregnant, he again demanded that she be aborted. She refused. He became abusive, assaultive, drank excessively, came home late at night. He showed no positive interest, despite her numerous physical complaints. He threatened to leave her; called her "ugly, dumb, stupid"—admitted he had no love for her.

Social Life: His friends were those he met at various bars, and also one salesman (married) who worked for him, but was his companion and confidant in his extramarital affairs. He resented his wife's social evenings at home. He joined the local country club but played no golf. His interests there were the Saturday night parties.

Sexual Life: He participated in sexual intercourse at 14; no homosexual activity. After marriage, he preferred fellatio and cunnilingus to genital intercourse. He blamed his wife, claiming that she was unskilled. His extramarital partners were much better.

Interpretation of First Six Months of Treatment: During the first six months of treatment, there was a definite reduction of hostility. The therapist had established excellent rapport, and the patient unhesitatingly disclosed information. The therapist avoided comments. During the following year, most of the sessions were concerned with repetition and elaboration of the material, for the purpose of giving the patient some insight into his personality, and how it affected his marriage.

Through psychoanalytically oriented psychotherapy, the material presented was interpreted. He began to understand that his inability to displace his brother or father during his childhood caused him to develop hostility toward them, together with strong feelings of rivalry—but they were so much stronger and more powerful that they created in him feelings of inadequacy, inferiority, and inability to cope with them. Hence he displaced his aggression from them onto the environment. To keep peace with them, and to avoid further frustration, he relinquished his mother, by selecting his own wife. His brother had married shortly before entering military service. Patient was eager to do likewise, but his parents objected and would permit only a betrothal. Soon after return from service, he, too, had to marry. The girl he chose has the same height, coloring, and physical measurements of his mother. His attitudes of spontaneity, carefreeness, irresponsibility, were the result of his protest against earlier, rigid childhood training. His lack of love satisfaction during childhood, caused him to seek out "any woman" who paid attention to him and showed some feeling for him. His feelings of inferiority were reduced when under the influence of liquor, but gradually the latter became a habit.

His wife's pregnancy revived and increased his feelings of

rivalry, with his father and brother. He reacted by his assaultive behavior to his wife, his need to drink more than ever, and his need for extramarital sex relationships. His reason for his rejection of both his sons became apparent to him. He further recognized his fear of his father's authority as a carry-over from childhood, so that he basically possessed a rigid, disciplined make-up although outwardly he appeared undisciplined.

Patient also became aware of his ability as a salesman and manager. He was able to assert himself and demand recognition by his father and brother. He was placed in charge of the sales-force and permitted to make all decisions referable to his department. He proved himself to be forceful at weekly business conferences where he contributed creative ideas that were adopted.

Many of the sessions were devoted to redirection of his interests and the establishment of new satisfactions. He recognized the importance of the development of a family life. He cut down his drinking, came home regularly for dinner, had his sons join him at table, played and studied with them. Together with his wife and children, there were Monday evening "art" activities at home, Saturday afternoon visits to museums, and Sunday afternoon attendance at baseball or football games. He developed an interest in the local community, instituted a newspaper for his concern. He has abandoned his "night life," given up all extramarital affairs, finds his wife to be an excellent sexual partner. He enjoys spending much time with his third child, a daughter, for whom he has developed strong attachments.

He has learned to understand the psychology of his father and brother and the role he plays in relation to them. His somatic complaints are gone. He takes pride in showing his family's pictures to all who will look.

Treatment was terminated after three years and two months.

There was contact with Mr. B six months later. He reported a happy, satisfying home life and finds his wife a comforting person whenever he has a difficult business situation with his father and brother.

15 A (continued)

Follow-Up: The encouragement that Mrs. B had obtained through marriage counseling had given her a sense of self-esteem and an ability to express her hostility and independence. Her husband, although at first protesting her "new personality," came to admire her assertiveness, especially when she would not become embroiled in arguments but insisted upon a wholesome discussion. This resulted in more communication, and greater co-operation on his part. His "night life" changed. No longer needing to bolster his ego by playing host, they often go out alone, or join others, sharing the bill.

While under treatment and during the period of improved marital relationship, she had a desire for another child. Her husband opposed this and had to be won over. Her third pregnancy was free of nausea or vomiting, though she had much concern for her shape and weight. She accordingly restricted her diet, developed a secondary anemia and required regular medical care. The baby, a daughter, brought much joy to her parents and her husband's parents. She was the first granddaughter.

In her sexual life, patient made known to her husband her dislike of fellatio and cunnilingus. There is now much fondling in foreplay, followed by sexual congress that is satisfying to them both.

During the course of treatment, patient became aware of her personality make-up. Her identification with her mother became clear to her, in her need to escape from conflicts by creating conversion symptoms, using them to avoid undesirable chores and as a means of gaining sympathy from her husband. Her harsh, domineering, scolding attitudes toward her children were recognized as the methods used by her mother. Her mother's concerns with diets, need to be shapely and attractive, were recognized as a carry-over. Patient also recognized her rejection of her children throughout her first two pregnancies. Her physical debility served as a means to stay in bed, be waited on, and take a completely passive role. Thus, by regression, there was identification with a baby. She recognized that her personality was that of a dependent child who had a feeling of abandonment and rejection.

Because she was made to feel inadequate and not as intelligent as her brother, she was unable to compete with others, and withdrew readily in every situation; she was deserving of nothing. She understood how this pattern of behavior caused her to accept a minimum of worldly goods from her husband.

Since she had little perseverance, she had no skills or accomplishments. During treatment she turned her interests in many directions—golf, dancing, art—graduated as a Nurse's Aide and now gives two full days of volunteer service.

Her somatic complaints disappeared. She developed the ability to express herself with confidence and without anxiety. Careful budgeting won the admiration of her husband and family. She enjoys her husband, family, and home.

The prognosis is good. Patient and husband are showing such mutual understanding that the need for further therapy is slight.

Summary Note by Dr. J (Mr. B's Therapist)

The case of Mr. B illustrates that the therapist served as a listener, establishing rapport and thus reducing patient's hostility; as an interpreter, helping patient to develop insight into his personality and to understand how it affected his marriage. The therapist also helped the patient to understand his frustrations and thus redirect his energies. His behavior patterns changed; the patient had esteem and confidence in himself as a personality. His competence increased; he was able to utilize his skills satisfactorily. All told, he became a good husband and father.

Additional Data from Mrs. B's Therapist

When patient returned for therapy, the therapist recognized that Mrs. B was much depressed and in need of support. As her history unfolded, the positive transference to the therapist made it possible for her to express hostility. It took a long time for the patient to express anger, disappointment, and hostility directly to her parents or husband.

Much time was devoted to educating patient in positive aspects of child development. During this period there were episodes of negative transference when patient feared that she was unable to participate actively in a situation. Possible failure meant, to her, loss of esteem in the eyes of the therapist.

Patient was given information regarding the psychosexual development of children. This was effective in increasing her self-esteem, proving that she had adequate intelligence to meet most situations, provided her emotions did not get in the way.

Once patient had acquired sufficient awareness of her capabilities, it was possible for the therapist to interpret some of her behavior, such as her identification with her mother and escape into illness (conversion symptoms). She also was helped to recognize her need for power to cover a long-standing dependency. She was shown that her aggression was directed at her children without regard for their activities or feelings.

During her third pregnancy, patient continued her regular treatments. There were frequent communications between the therapist and obstetrician.

Collaboration of Therapists

Once each week, both therapists conferred and discussed their respective material. Rarely did the two clients present similar material at the same time. Each seemed to think about personal activities and problems as though each had an independent sphere of activity. It was only when a definite "explosive scene" occurred that both referred to the episode. Neither therapist used the material given by one patient for or against the other. Whenever it was important to bring some material directly to the attention of the other patient, permission was requested. This occurred particularly in the situations referring to family life experiences. By agreement of the two spouses, the family life situations were first worked through by the wife and her therapist. Both therapists were careful to emphasize the positive aspects of their separate patients and to avoid any debasement of the spouse.

CASE 16

Problem: Homosexuality in marriage
Presented by: Psychiatric social worker (graduate degree in Social Work) in the marriage counseling service of a Maternal Health Association

Introduction: Patient's wife came to the Planned Parenthood Center referred by the family physician. Her husband had not been able to have an erection, or, if achieved momentarily, during three and one-half years of marriage had not been able to maintain it. As a result, they had never had intercourse. Reading material suggested by the physician made him worse; the whole business "disgusted him a little bit."

The background material the wife gave the (woman) counselor is as follows: The marriage to "prove" himself is now a failure. At the age of 5, his mother caught him playing with boys and spanked him. He had a well-adjusted five-year-older brother. His father was domineering and aggressive. Further history which husband had revealed to her was to the effect that his friends thought him a homosexual. The only thing which stimulates him is getting a haircut. After an attempted seduction by the wife of an older friend and benefactor he had wanted to take a bath.

Counselor's Conference with Psychiatrist: A consulting psychiatrist is on the staff of this center, available for weekly conferences and, in the counselor's preliminary conference with the psychiatrist before seeing the patient, it was pointed out that it appears to the patient that women are untouchable, and he equates body contact with dirty things (example: bath after attempted seduction). Obviously he has not made the transition to "clean" sexuality. With a man as sick as this man appears to be, the only hope would be to make a drastic clinical lead, saying flatly that anyone who has so much fear of women must have had an enormous urge to be close to a woman. One would then move directly into childhood feelings regarding women.

First Interview: Patient is attractive and well educated. He seemed to have a tendency to intellectualize. I did not learn much about his childhood feelings in relation to women. He told of his mother discovering him and two other boys in the outhouse, experimenting. Sex was taboo in his family. As a boy, he "kind of worshiped" his mother. However, he felt it was a relief to get away from his mother and her rigidity. He added that perhaps marriage threatens this feeling of independence. Weekly interviews were set up.

Second Interview: In the second interview patient brought out his fear, since adolescence, of the sex act, a fear which has extended to other aspects of his life. He brought out clearly his fear of homosexuality. He told of a homosexual approach in the army which was not repulsed. Also a ten-year-old cousin fondled his penis when he was between 6 and 9. He had an attraction to and jealousy of certain boys in college. The traumatic experience with the wife of his benefactor intensified his fear of homosexual tendencies. There was no masturbation in adolescence. The first time he tried masturbation was at the age of 19 after he had read about it in a book.

The patient talked about his erotic pleasure in having a haircut, or even in watching someone else having a haircut and commented that the barber was a male.

Between the ages of 6 and 9 he also discovered his mother

in the act of urinating and was aware of a great curiosity about his mother's genitals.

Counselor's Conference with Psychiatrist: In a treatment conference with the psychiatrist about the man's clear presentation of homosexuality, the suggestion was made that the counselor point out the obvious—that in fighting against homosexuality he has negated all sex.

Third Interview: Patient talked about being intrigued by the idea of his hair representing the genitals. He thought I had made this interpretation, though I did not recall having done so.

He went on to say that he was always very anxious. He thinks now that since the matter has been brought out into the open his feeling about homosexuality needs to be explored further. He told of having an erection while observing other men's curly hair. He talked further about what he might have seen in relation to his mother, whether he had observed the genitalia or just the pubic hair. He now thinks he must have been 6 or 7 years of age at the time.

He also thinks that he reacts to his wife as if she were his mother. Her advances rob him of initiative.

Counselor's Short Conference with Psychiatrist: The suggestion was made that the parents' responsibility to protect children from this experience should be pointed out in order to relieve the patient of too great a feeling of guilt. It might also be suggested that had such an experience occurred later, it would not have had as deep a traumatic effect.

Fourth Interview: Patient talked of a tonsillectomy which had been performed sometime between the ages of 6 and 9. He felt he had been prepared for the tonsillectomy but not the circumcision which was done at the same time. He did not "swallow" any of the explanations they tried to give him. He remembers that when he saw another circumcised adolescent, he thought, "That poor fellow is in the same boat as I am."

Immediately after marriage he had an ejaculation while having his hair cut. The association of hair with pubic hair was again brought out.

Following this, the patient talked of what amounted to a textbook presentation of the mother with a penis which had been cut off. He toyed with the idea of whether or not his mother had been menstruating at the time and correlated this with his fear of loss through circumcision. The *psychiatrist,* commenting on this interview, thought that patient might be saying all this in an effort to avoid something else.

Fifth Interview: The man talked about his distaste in touching the female genitalia. To him, it was "a wound and slime." His boy cousin used a flashlight to locate his penis; he thought those things should be kept in the dark. He also brought out his avoidance of observing his wife in the nude, or her genitalia. He had never looked at them: he had fantasies of the female genitalia being a devouring hole and became anxious at such fantasies and talked of his fear of looking. He was given assurance that it was all right to look.

In conference with the consulting psychiatrist, held by the counselor, the discussion centered around the man's continuing fixation and sexual stimulation over having his hair cut. He is, in effect, presenting the barber with his hair as a female genital, and then identifies with the barber. The problem is to continue to show him that he obliterates the memory of his mother's pubic hair and moves it to a situation where he dares look at it. He was undoubtedly horrified about his excitement over his mother's genitals. Counselor should continue to give him the assurance that it was a traumatic experience he should have been spared and for which he was not responsible. It seems clear he is very deeply afraid of looking at the female genitals.

Positive assurance should be continued that if it happened later, it would not have caused the same trauma.

Sixth Interview: Patient reports that he feels a little nearer success. He still recoils from his wife's sexually stimulating him. He feels safe if he doesn't have to try—safe from having to make an effort he doesn't want to make.

Also, he is not ready to give up the only stimulation he has known—having his hair cut. He feels that if he loses that experience he loses everything; the stimulation from his haircuts has become more intense. Again, the interpretation suggested above is given. He accepts it intellectually; it makes sense and besides he says he cannot think of a better one.

He then talks about his strong desire to please. When he thinks of disapproval he always thinks of his mother.

Seventh Interview: The patient relates that he has had the courage to examine his wife's genitals. The distaste at touching remains. He feels he might do harm with his hands.

Eighth Interview: He talks about intercourse being associated in his mind with hurting and being hurt. He complains that he does not want to get emotionally involved with another. Also he expresses anxiety that he might hate himself if he sees himself too clearly. Reassurance was given at this point and praise at the way he has worked at getting a better understanding of his problem. He also announced that he could see how his obsession with hair and haircuts took the place of masturbation for him.

Ninth Interview: Following the counselor's vacation of six weeks for which patient had been prepared, he talked of his weaknesses in social adjustments and lack of self-confidence. However, he feels he is getting a better opinion of himself and thinks he's beginning to do something about himself, though he still tends to back up when he feels he's becoming emotionally involved.

The erotic stimulation in relation to haircuts continues, much to his disappointment, though he thinks it is lessening. He brought out that the more hair the barber cuts off, even as he sits watching, the greater his stimulation. I suggested that if he were the barber the more he would be able to see. Again there was intellectual acceptance, though I sensed a deeper struggle against it.

Tenth Interview: However, in this following interview he reported that he's doing better. He now allows his wife to stimulate him manually, and he stimulates her. He feels there's a beginning of a closer relationship. He thinks some of the preoccupation with haircuts is fading.

He then talked of his father. The patient was always afraid of him and he felt like a nonentity in his sight. The father would always let his older brother do the "man things" but would not let him. The patient guessed he was more like his mother.

Eleventh Interview: He tells that he now helps his wife to orgasm manually. Socially, they've become more active and he finds it good.

He then talked of his rejection by his father. Almost everything that he wanted to do that was masculine his father put off—he was not big enough and not strong enough. The patient announced that his preoccupation with hair was receding.

He then brought out the fear that has been with him for so long, that his homosexuality might be "inherited" when he had children. This was relieved.

Next Interview: Very little new revelation was brought out, though he called my attention to the fact that he had said "when we have children," not "if."

Following Interview: Patient expressed the fear that he "won't be able to complete the act"—he "doesn't deserve children"—"there's something dirty about the whole thing" to him. A certain amount of repulsion remains.

He talked about his great anxiety as an adolescent over nocturnal emissions, which always were associated with dreams of haircuts. He had a morbid fear of losing his mind, and great distaste over the semen.

Fourteenth Interview: He reported complete intromission though no ejaculation. The realization he can achieve an erection is "wonderful."

He then talked about the remaining fear and anxiety and revulsion at his wife's genitals. Again, the interpretation of the great trauma of seeing the mother's genitals at too early an age was given, obviously a trauma so great that he had to transfer all erotic feeings to his hair where he could feel safe from discovery. Again I sensed polite agreement and sliding away. He told of great resistance to Freudian psychology in college and a tendency to reject it. He thought probably this was because he was fighting the idea he might be homosexual.

Then he confessed to "strong narcissistic elements" in himself, and I agreed, using the example of a displacement of strong sexual feeling from the genitals where they belong, to his hair, so it was shared by no one but himself. I agreed that this complicated his shift to sharing.

He complained of difficulty in personal relationships and has worried about his "narcissism" for a long time. However, this is the first time he named it here. He said, "I feel that I am committing myself to something from which there is no escape if I really give myself to another."

He says he is now anticipating love-making with "the curiosity of puberty."

I recapitulated what he already knew intellectually, the strong sexual urges toward the parent of the opposite sex, the obvious great sexual trauma that must have occurred, his retreat to homosexuality, inability to accept this, and finally the solution in narcissism in keeping the erotic satisfactions entirely in himself through his hair fantasy. He says that these things make more emotional sense to him now as he is beginning to catch glimpses of the satisfaction possible in sharing. He added that these are not shocking new discoveries to him. He has thought of them all himself; I have just rephrased them. If they were entirely new, he could see how he might "react with panic."

Counselor's Conference(s) with Psychiatrist: It was suggested that undoubtedly what the patient rejected was the Freudian theory of defenses. In other words, he had to find a thing repulsive in order to protect himself from becoming too fascinated by it. For instance, if he became too fascinated by his own feelings he would not be able to stop masturbating and ejaculating; then he has to find himself repulsive. Also, it was pointed out that the relationship between the counselor and client is now strong enough and the progress so clear that this counselor can interpret the client's dislike of Freudian theory as probably based on the fact that it is too upsetting to find things opposite to what they seem; they have to be revolting to keep them from becoming too fascinating.

Following Interview: This interpretation was given to the patient at an appropriate spot in the following interview. Patient quite readily brought out fascination with fantasies about being a homosexual in adolescence, and being caught; of running away and changing his identity, and so on. Also his fascination with the semen and pride in his penis which he has brought out before, as well as his fear that a woman would scorn or ridicule it.

Counselor's Conference with Psychiatrist: Regarding the material above, the psychiatrist suggested the possibility that the patient was bringing up fascinating material to please me. We might suggest at this point, "We have gotten you to think very deeply about these things. The danger now is you will 'talk a good game' but our real purpose will not be achieved." The psychiatrist thought it was time to take it out of the organic sexual, stating our fear now is that he won't be a sincere, confident, generous man in love with a woman. Thereby we spoil his fun in talking about these things with me.

Next Interview: Patient announces that he has had an ejaculation during intercourse and is very proud.

I then suggested that now that he has achieved success in the physical act, the problem of next concern is his ability to be a warm, sincere, loving husband.

He sees what I mean. He thinks his success in intercourse is just one more step in a long series of things giving him more confidence.

Interview a Week Later: He reported that his success continued. He said that now both he and his wife are fully sold on this process and his wife would like an interview because she feels he has learned so much that she thinks there might be something I can tell her that would be helpful. An appointment was given for his wife for the following week.

Interview with Wife: When the patient's wife came to the office she told me they are having successful intercourse about twice a week, which seems to be a satisfying frequency for them. She senses his self-confidence and considers him cured. She has a private physician and is beginning to take temperatures to establish her fertile period. Her husband has become involved in a number of activities this fall along with his work, which makes it difficult for him to get away, and the appointment for him the following week was cancelled for this reason.

Wind-Up Interview with Husband: In this interview a month later he reported that all is well.

They hope for a pregnancy and feel they can hold up their heads "with the neighbors." He says this is a "new beginning in marriage, a new beginning in life." He feels that "this step like many others has increased my self-confidence in many other ways." He feels it's another step in a long series of things that have given him more confidence. He does find himself thinking less of himself and more about others.

He knows people working with youth groups and wanted some of our educational material so that others might be saved the anguish which he had gone through because of lack of knowledge of the facts involved in growing up.

Conclusion: There were actually three initial interviews with patient's wife during the time patient was making arrangement in his work to be available for interviews. She talked of her frustrations and fantasies of another man potentially available to marry her, should patient not be able to function normally. When patient began regular interviews, it was fully explained to her why I would not continue to see her during the time I was working with her husband. She was assured that another counselor would be available at any time if she wished further help.

The counseling appears to have been successful, primarily because of the intelligence and intrinsic strength of the two persons involved in the marriage. Patient was respected in his chosen profession, enjoyed it, and in fact was well on his way to excluding any other satisfactions not involved in his work.

Treatment covered a period of six months of weekly interviews. It should be noted that the confidence of the counselor during the treatment process stemmed directly from the continued direction by the psychiatrist. Treatment would not have been attempted on the same level or at the same speed by the counselor, if close psychiatric consultation had not been available.

Follow-Up: One year later the couple indicated that satisfactory sexual relations have continued. They are feeling happier and more relaxed. Their social contacts have broadened. The hoped-for pregnancy did not materialize, but this did not cause a set-back. They are now making application for study in the fertility clinic.

CASE 17

Problem: A wife's neurosis and her marriage
Presented by: Psychiatrist (M.D.)—private practice in large city

Introduction: Mrs. B was sent to me because she was undecided about her marriage. She had previously gone to another doctor because of nervousness, irritability, frequent and uncontrollable periods of crying, and a feeling as though something were about to burst within her head. At work she had noted an increasing inability to write. This was most marked when in the presence of someone.

Mrs. B was an unusually intelligent woman and a highly competent secretary (until the writing defect developed) and was highly thought of by those with whom she worked. Because of her competency she had been offered the opportunity of working for another agency of the governmental bureau in the same community, but because her present boss was understanding of her writing difficulties, she could not bring herself to leave.

Mr. B as Described by Wife: Her husband (according to Mrs. B) was a quiet, shy individual, who was very tolerant of his wife's irritability and periods of ranting at home. He was quite respectful of her ability and at times was rather awed by her. He was a rather schizoid person, who was well adjusted in his own work and reasonably satisfied to live a somewhat lonely life. He found great solace in books and tinkering with his tools in his workshop. Although he was a steady and constant person and a good provider, he offered little of himself in an interpersonal way. He described himself as a "plodder" and a "wallflower," who liked to see the other fellow having fun in an "active way"—a way that was foreign to himself. He wanted to be more talkative, but felt he probably would never change much. He was frequently distressed when his wife demanded so much reassurance because he couldn't give it as often as she seemed to require it, although he admired her a great deal. He felt that if she became a little more satisfied with "the little things in life" she would feel better, and was quite willing to give her the opportunity to come to this conclusion if and when she saw fit. One got the feeling that he was a rather desperate person but one who tolerated it well.

Mrs. B: Mrs. B was a very talkative person, highly skilled in social situations, had an unusual ability to carry on a rather empty conversation of "the socially required kind." She appeared tireless and energetic but she felt tired and without energy most of the time. She smiled a great deal, but her eyes were tired and easily conveyed tension and depression, both of which she denied at first. She was anxious, tremulous, hyperactive and driven by a back-breaking desire to please. She was sensitive to the slightest criticism and took it as though she had been "damned." She was frequently depressed but never actively or directly hostile. She was suspicious of everyone and, at one time in her late adolescence, may have been actively psychotic and perhaps had hallucinations (auditory) but, if so, had made an excellent social recovery. She felt that she was a failure and spent a great deal of her time in self-condemnation. Suicidal ideas were fleeting and frequent, but she felt that the possibility was practically nil. She had a good number of gastrointestinal complaints and obviously boiled with hostility and tension which found no outlet.

Mrs. B was 35, quite attractive, and excessively meticulous, and quite concerned with her personal appearance. Her clothes were in perfect taste, but she picked flaws in her dress constantly. A physical examination revealed that she was in good condition.

From the First Interview: At the age of four, she was in an automobile accident with her mother. Her mother was killed, and the little girl was raised by an aunt who was rigid, compulsive, stern, and who resented the obligation of having to raise her sister's daughter. A strange sense of right and wrong ruled her life and those around her, and she imbued the little girl with the idea that she was doing her a favor by raising her and that she should appreciate it all. The aunt was apparently a lonely person and upon occasion stated that perhaps she was a little strict. At these times, she would be rather tender only to withdraw quickly and crush the little girl's request for more. A feeling of inconsistency had built up in Mrs. B at an early age and she learned that it was unsafe to trust anyone for fear of rebuff. The aunt, for the most part, lived an "honor and obey" sort of parental role, and would tolerate no impudence from her niece. She held the idea that sensual and sexual things were wicked and permitted no conversations about it. She also taught the little girl never to speak of it to anyone and as a result, the patient had practically no idea of sexual things except that sexual relations did occur but that they were degrading and disgusting. In five years of married life she had had intercourse no oftener than once a month and then at her husband's request. It was distasteful to her although secretly she had a strong longing and desire for it. Thoughts of masturbation had occurred to her, but the practice of it had not.

Although Mrs. B slowly told more and more about the very unpleasant relationship with her aunt she steadfastly maintained that she loved her. Over the course of years, Mrs. B developed a rigid although intuitive personality, dedicated to pleasing others and seeking what praise she could from them in order to soothe a deep sense of shame because of the hostility that she felt. She was ingenuous in her concern over what others thought of her and constantly felt a gnawing sense of not "belonging." A great deal of her life had been based upon the principle that people "should" or "must" do things. Thus she finished school, learned to be a secretary, and had married because it was "what girls do." Because she had set for herself an unattainable goal of "goodness" she was constantly disappointed and frustrated, and felt herself to be a failure. To be fallible and human, to her, was to be slovenly and worthless. As a result of her desire to be perfect and her sense of failure because she was not, she was not aware of her actual as well as potential capabilities. She had no friends with whom she could talk comfortably although she had a great many fleeting acquaintances. These she secretly resented because "they took what they could get" and then left her. She felt that she would inevitably be taken for a "sucker" and as a result allowed no one to get very close to her.

In her marriage she had little fun for *herself* because she once again was constantly on the search for approval. She got little because she had married a rather uncommunicative husband, although nonetheless an admiring one. She was offensively on the defense and could not stand to be dependent upon her husband although she longed for it. Rather, she ran the family affairs and appeared to be independent. She was not independent, however, but was more of a lonely tyrant to whom sharing and collaboration was foreign. Because of the love and affection which her lonely and false self-sufficiency prevented from occurring she had recently decided to get a divorce; and yet because of her realization that her husband was steady, tolerant, and reasonable, even though uncolorful, she was not sure that divorce was a solution. Six months before coming for therapy she had had an affair with her boss. He had been lovable to her for a while, but this had broken up without a word and had never been spoken of between them since. He, apparently, was a good deal like her and could "give" for a while only, or perhaps he resented the load that she placed upon him. His own marriage was rocky and apparently based upon a tolerant, although seething uncommunicative attitude. It was after this affair had broken up that Mrs. B noted the difficulty in writing. It happened mainly when she had to countersign her boss's name on checks or interdepartmental orders, but eventually happened under any circumstance where she was asked to write or sign something.

This patient had a childlike personality in which growth had been fostered by a resentful and domineering aunt whose own living code was a rigid moralistic one and who knew little of tenderness herself and as a result could not dispense it. Adherence to the word "must" held sway over a gradual development of an attitude of "wanting to." As a result the patient suffered from very low self-esteem because of striving to be a perfect organism rather than a simple fallible human being. Her self-esteem was a hostile one but indirectly so because to be directly hostile meant to her to anticipate horrifying self-censure and an invitation for others to despise her more than ever. The hatred that she felt had no outlet except in physical symptoms as a result of the tension that she felt. To maintain her head above water, so to speak, she was compelled to function at a back-breaking speed in order to get the approval that she needed, and yet she hated people who fell for her supposed benevolence and seeming co-operation. Collaborative friendship was unknown to her and in its place were more or less vertical scales—that is, who is best. She had no confidence in her husband and assumed the role of the organizer of the home although she longed for someone to do it for her. Her quiet husband was bait for this lonely activity of hers. In recent months she had dared to get some satisfaction in an extramarital affair but this had fallen through for reasons unknown. She sought medical care for her marriage difficulties and for her writing handicap. Fortunately she was feeling desperate about herself and wanted help and entered into therapy with a certain vigor.

Therapy: In the beginning, therapy was directed toward offering the patient an opportunity to feel comfortable to complain, and to realize that she was not a "bad girl" because she did so. When her problems were viewed as a difficulty in living rather than an example of her "innate badness," as she put it, her self-esteem was raised. She began to look upon her difficulties as an illness that could be helped much as the orthopedic patient views a broken bone as one that will heal. When she had sufficient increase in self-esteem and began to see some hope it was possible for her to look at her supposed benevolent activity (such as *running* the home to *save* her husband the trouble) as a cover for more hostile feelings. It was very necessary to view her past (with her aunt) frequently so that she could realize that with "that degree of rigidity" of rearing it was no wonder that she "felt as she did" today. In other words, through no fault of her own, she had learned to act in such and such a way and therefore she was not to blame for what she did today. It just did not lead to comfortable living. Slowly she learned to hate what had happened to her at the hands of her aunt and yet at the same time got on more peaceful terms with the past; that is, she began to realize that her aunt was a sick but decent human being, too—not bad and deplorable. She learned to like and dislike things at the same time. In other words, living became less black or white and took on some of the degrees of gray in between.

Slowly she learned to work her way through the day as best she could and bring her problems to the therapeutic sessions where she could give vent to stored-up feelings and then learn to understand them. Surprisingly, quickly she stopped acting out her problems and learned to talk them out. I believe that it was only her desperateness about herself that made it possible to move as quickly as she did. She was not playing at therapy, but working at it.

Insight into her writing difficulty occurred one day when she had become fed up with therapy and in a rage wrote out a check to me and announced that she was never coming back. I noted the ease of her writing when she was wholeheartedly angry at me and pointed it out to her. She stopped short and said, "Do you suppose that the reason I have trouble writing my boss's name is that I feel the same way toward him, but can't bring myself to say it to him?" We entertained the possibility and discovered together that she never knew why he had broken off their affair of six months ago. She had felt rebuffed and yet felt that if she talked to him about it she would lose him altogether. She decided, however, that if he was that indirect she was not in love with him as she had thought, and furthermore would not collapse if she did lose him or her job. Subsequently they had a talk, and decided that although their affair had been somewhat of a mistake, both had gained, but that from then on they would go on separately. They felt that it would be better if she took a job in another governmental department, and he got one of his associates to help her get placed. This was handled by her in a surprisingly mature fashion and with such relief that her self-esteem grew in leaps and bounds from this point on. Her writing difficulty subsided quickly and has not returned, although she noticed a tendency to shake a little when she felt caught in a situation that was beyond her temporarily. As she grew, this, too, subsided.

Slowly her self-requirements became less and she found some fun in sharing her feelings with a few well-chosen people. She was gratified to find that she was not the only one who had problems. As she put it, "I feel more at home when I see that I am not so different from other people." She frequently asked me if I had any problems. My "of course" was relieving to her.

She stated, "I guess most people have some sort of problems—just a matter of degree." We agreed that this was probably true.

Education: I spent some time educating her about anatomy and sexual matters, and encouraged her toward a freedom of investigation of herself. This led to a period of masturbation about which she felt guilty. Slowly, however, she developed an attitude toward masturbation and all sexual contact in terms of "fun." This period of turmoil started to subside when she said to me, "It's fun to masturbate when I feel like it, just as it's fun to eat when I am hungry."

Summary of Changes: Over the course of a year rather surprising changes occurred with her. She became less suspicious, more direct, she "smiled" less and when she did it had a true ring to it, she found herself less required to please others, and as a result found that she actually pleased others more. Her somatic symptoms disappeared and her psychomotor hyperactivity decreased. She found a few people with whom she could talk and her interpersonal relationships became more and more cemented in terms of "together," "we two," and "with." Less and less the term "they" was heard in her conversation.

Her spontaneity registered with her husband and she noted that he had a "color" that she had missed before. In addition to this I believe that her husband actually came out of his shell and was a more active participant in the marriage. He learned to dance, and his frequent fishing trips (alone) gave way to picnics together. Mrs. B became less demanding and sought "fun" in the marriage for herself; one day she told me she noted that the more fun she had for herself the more he joined in. They established a common bank account and for the first time experienced "the fun" of working out and adhering to a family budget.

Sexually there was an increase in frequency of intercourse

and although at first she did not experience an orgasm, one of the two of them would stimulate her until she was relieved. She became more patient toward herself as she built for herself a new way of looking at life as well as sex, and slowly orgasms made their appearance.

It was necessary to stop therapy because I left the city in which she was located. By this time, however, she had enough tools with which to work so that she felt that she could carry on.

Follow-Up: We corresponded frequently throughout the next eighteen months, and about six months ago I saw her when I visited her home town. She was quite relaxed in both attitude and dress. Her hair which had always been pulled tightly over her head had been cut, and she had had a permanent so that rather soft waves fell to her shoulder. Beyond doubt she had continued to progress and said that she felt better each day. She feels hopeful about her marriage and is glad that she picked a man with whom she could work things out. She had learned to admire his readiness to find solace in books, at times, while at others he can find solace in doing things with her. She says that she found great comfort in these activities as well.

I believe that the outstanding example of her progress was the last statement she made to me during my visit. She sincerely thanked me for the relationship that we had had but went on to describe several relationships that she had developed since I last saw her. They obviously were more complete than the one that the two of us had had. She said, "Dealing with you was the first real relationship that I ever had, but it was just a beginning."

EDITOR'S NOTE: The philosophy expressed in a covering letter from the psychiatrist to the Committee is significant far beyond this single case. ". . . I don't feel that we *do* psychotherapy or counseling on our patients. . . . I do feel that we work *with* our patients and after accepting them as they are we attempt to understand what they are trying to tell us. This very investigative process is the kernel of psychotherapy itself. . . . I also feel that the psychiatrist needs a great deal of humility before either he or his patients will benefit. . . . The psychiatrist and his patient, whether they know it or not, are working toward a more fluid giving and receiving of interpersonal tenderness."

8. Marital Conflict and Family Problems

Case 18. *A Small Boy—His Family, His Play, His School*
Case 19. *Stepchildren and Marital Conflict*

The presenting problems in these two cases focus on parents' difficulty in relationship to children. To be sure, in each case a direct approach is made to the child's problem—in one instance, by referral for examination to a child guidance clinic, in the other by definitely scheduled sessions with a therapist. However, as revealed by the counseling, much of the strain and tension is resolved only as the adults are able to gain insight into themselves and each other. The counseling was directed to the marital as well as the parental relationship.

CASE 18

Problem: A small boy—his family, his play, his school
Presented by: Two counselors and a therapist (one counselor, Ph.D. in Psychology and Child Development; the other counselor and the child therapist, doctoral candidates in Psychology and Child Development) working in a state university clinic

Introduction: Mr. Bert Spencer, an investment broker, and his wife were referred to the University Clinic by their family friend
240

and physician because of the recent trouble they were having with their nine-year-old son, Archie. He was doing poorly in school and recently he had been taking rather large sums of money from his father's billfold, twice treating his class at school rather lavishly and once paying a friend a fabulous sum for a model airplane. Archie was punished on these occasions by a paddling by his mother and again later by his father who used his belt on him because Archie had upset his mother.

In the intake interview, which was joint, the Spencers expressed deep concern over Archie's unhappiness and lack of enthusiasm and of his great jealousy of his younger brother, John, who according to the parents, was a model child of six and one-half years. The Spencers have two younger daughters, three years and eighteen months of age. On leaving the clinic after the intake interview, Mrs. Spencer implied that Mr. Spencer had come along merely to state the case, but that he probably would not continue coming as he was a very busy businessman. Whereupon, Mr. S took the clinic appointment letter from his pocket and said, "But, dear, this is addressed to both of us."

It was decided that it would be best for Archie, the son, to have a male play therapist. Mr. S was assigned to work with a woman as counselor, and Mrs. S to work with a man.

It is the policy of the clinic whenever possible to work with both parents as well as the child as it has been proved by experience that greater progress is achieved and in less time.

The Problem as Presented by the Clients: The Spencers displayed much knowledge of psychiatric services. The intake counselor was told that the mothers on both sides of the family had received psychiatric treatment. They joked during the interview about whose mother was the "worst off." At the same time this background of need for psychiatric help in both parental families gave them a sense of great anxiety regarding Archie and his future. "We want to do preventive work on both ourselves and Archie. That's why we are here."

Mrs. S described herself as "very strict and old-fashioned" in the matter of training. She said she had her children "potty trained" when they were four months old. They were drinking out of a glass at seven months.

Archie has nightmares, bad dreams, and covers his face with his hands when looking at certain television programs. When the children lie to Mrs. S, she washes their mouths out with soap. There is a colored servant in the home, a "mammy" whom the children love. "She spoils them."

Archie is in Cub Scouts, and Mrs. S is an active den mother. The couple are very active in civic and social affairs. They met and married during World War II, and Mr. S is ten years older than Mrs. S.

The Counseling: To date the three Spencers have had from twenty-one to twenty-three weekly individual sessions with their counselors. They kept their appointments regularly.

After about ten separate sessions with the three counselors, Mr. and Mrs. S had an evening joint session with the three therapists. From the therapists' point of view, this session seemed necessary in order for the parents to be more willing to accept themselves and to accept Archie as he was and, in addition, for the parents to begin working together as a team with all the children. The parents were eager to know what "changes" were taking place in the playroom with Archie.

Short descriptions will be given of the work with each counselee, later giving growth patterns of interaction in the family as a whole.

Archie: Archie, when seen for the initial session, appeared to be a very well-mannered child who was unusually at ease among adults. During the first session, Archie talked a great deal concerning his and his parents' achievements and material possessions. In this session, play was of an exploratory nature with short attention given to specific activities and objects. During the first session, it was also discovered that the child was completely unable to make any decisions for himself, always wanting the therapist to "say" what objects would be used.

The child did not, at any time, attempt consciously to "test" the limits and was always overly polite. A pattern of behavior soon crystallized which suggested that Archie was attempting to ensure the friendship of the therapist by bringing gifts and acting in a manner he thought the therapist would approve, as seemed to be his mode of behavior with all adults. As the sessions progressed, Archie's type of play changed, and he participated in activities which were more likely to mirror his feelings and attitudes. During these play sessions, Archie exhibited extreme compulsivity concerning cleanliness and orderliness.

The majority of the play therapy sessions with Archie consisted of activities which included building or construction with objects such as model airplane kits. Although at first no tasks were completed, Archie soon was able to participate in activities which he could complete and in which he could succeed, thereby gaining personal satisfaction along with praise from the adults around him.

Although much of the benefit from the therapy was of a cathartic nature, it is felt that the principal value was in the building-up of a relationship with an adult which did not depend on the child's "good" behavior for its continuing existence. Archie, at the conclusion of the therapy sessions, had learned that he was loved and respected for his worth as an individual and for his ability to give of himself rather than giving of his material possessions. Not only was a breakdown in the compulsive behavior effected, as was shown by his enjoyment of finger painting, but further progress was evidenced in his initiation of a small business venture independent of his parents.

Mrs. Spencer: When the therapist first met Mrs. S, she appeared somewhat apprehensive about being separated from her husband for counseling, but was responsible from the beginning.

Rapport was quickly established, and she began to relate the incidents with her son which stimulated the parents to seek help. She said that "somewhere I've failed as a parent although I've tried to do my best." Mrs. S even reported that they had considered the possibility of sending Archie to a military school.

Mrs. S was greatly concerned as to how the counselor viewed her and she spoke of how important it was to her to have others think well of her. She discussed her strong need for having her children meet her expectations for their behavior. She said, "I can feel myself tensing up when Archie misbehaves, as I want to spare my husband from getting upset." One area that greatly concerned her was the fear of the son's possible inheritance of some of her tendencies. These tendencies included a poor self-concept, severe headaches, tenseness, strivings for perfection, and general impatience.

Mrs. S spoke frequently of her role in "raising" the children and assuming the major responsibility for their actions. She mentioned an occasion in which her husband interfered with her discipline, and an argument ensued.

On one occasion she brought along a report card; and, even though the grades were above average, she disclosed signs of dissatisfaction as she compared Archie's marks with those of a younger son. Considerable family emphasis had been placed on reading, and this was met with resistance by Archie.

When the therapist began to discuss the needs of Archie, Mrs. S seemed quite resistive and said that "if the children had their way, the clothes wouldn't be picked up, beds left unmade, water left in the bathtub, and in general the mother would be only a servant to her children."

As the sessions progressed, Mrs. S began to talk about her feelings of inferiority. She also superficially discussed her relations with her mother-in-law and sister-in-law, indicating a lack of acceptance by them. She also questioned the possibility of her son not loving her but did not dwell on these points.

After a conference with the other counselors, the idea was presented to Mrs. S that in order to deal more effectively with Archie, it would be helpful to try to deal more fully with many of her underlying feelings.

At first there was considerable resistance to this idea as Mrs. S feared that disclosing her inner, mixed-up feelings would possibly disturb the relationship between her and the therapist. After considerable reassurance, Mrs. S began to discuss her poor self-concept and wondered what her "real self was like." As well as evidencing other indications of positive transference, she evidenced her dependence on the therapist.

Mrs. S had previously briefly mentioned her dominating foster mother, but now delved far more deeply into her childhood relationships. She described her true father as a man of little account and explained that after her mother's death, she was adopted by an aunt who "expected me to be an angel, but never loved me." She pictured the foster mother as strict, demanding, and as one who had punished her most constantly. She told of being afraid to bring friends to her home, of constantly being accused of lying, and of being accused of having a love affair with her foster father. She felt that the foster father sympathized with her but feared to exert any influence. She had desires to escape from the home, but feared being unable to survive in the world around her. Gradually she submitted more and more to the foster mother's wishes, and partially repressed any desire to assert herself.

Some areas in which progress was noticeable were as follows: Mrs. S verbalized her feelings indicating a refusal to let her foster mother control her. She began to see that she was far more capable of dealing with the mother although she had never felt that she could do so prior to this time. She asked her sister-in-law to accompany her on a shopping tour; and even though there was a difference in taste, she enjoyed the experience. Mrs. S also began to see the relationship between the way she was dealing with her children and the way she had been reared.

In spite of several backslidings, progress was apparent as the sessions continued. However, about a month prior to the end of the university year, there was a sudden reversal. Around this time a brother visited Mrs. S and there was also an argument with the mother-in-law. Shortly thereafter, she was plagued with severe headaches. When the therapist again saw her, she talked at length about her recent illness and partly connected this with the incidents surrounding it. She could now verbalize very real hostility toward her mother-in-law, which heretofore had been repressed; but she still possessed some guilt about the argument.

Evidence of considerable insight was shown during the last session in which Mrs. S disclosed that she has become more sensitive to the feelings of the children. She also told about her early dating prior to the meeting of her husband, and about the mental breakdown of a suitor after telling him of her plans to marry Mr. S. As she relived some of these experiences, many of the guilt feelings in this area seemed greatly relieved as though a burden had been lifted.

Plans for a summer vacation with her husband were discussed. She possessed a warm feeling toward the family, and expressed her ideas in a far more mature and self-satisfying manner.

Mr. Spencer: For the first three interviews, Mr. S was very uncommunicative. The counselor was not sure whether it was due to his general inability to communicate or his identification of the middle-aged counselor with his mother. He was encouraged to talk about his early family life, and great bitterness was reflected toward his mother. Said he, "She is and always has been a selfish-selfish woman. Oh, she will write a check. That causes her little discomfort. But, as for sharing of herself, she just doesn't do it." He told of her favoritism for his younger brother and how lonely and unloved it had made him feel as a boy, even though he loved his father who is not now living. He looked the counselor straight in the eye and said, "Archie is so much like me that it is pitiful. We'll come here as long as all of you think we should, if only you can help Archie to be happy and radiant like his mother. I guess all of us need help."

In sharing his past experiences, Mr. S had told how his family had shown a lack of acceptance of his wife. He told with emotion how this had hurt Mrs. S and how he sided with her. Said he, "We have decided we can't lick the problem; but my wife and I understand each other, and we have got it in check. We go through the motions of being on good terms with my mother and my brother's family for the sake of the community, but we do not have real respect for them." One could see from this that Mrs. S held a very real and significant place in Mr. S's life, even if they were unable to communicate as they should if they were to be partners in the rearing of a family. Because of his own unhappy childhood, the happiness of his wife and children was of great significance.

The three counselors had joint sessions to talk over their findings each week before the S family came for conferences. Mrs. S felt that Mr. S was "no good" in managing the children; that he left it all to her, but found fault with the way she was doing it. Mr. S did have high standards for the behavior of his children, both at home and in the public eye. He praised their remarkable table manners and gave his wife credit for this accomplishment. Mr. S delighted in comparing the behavior of his children with that of his brother's children.

The counselor, knowing that Mrs. S felt very much alone in the rearing of the children, praised Mr. S for how he stood by his wife when his family was attacking her and said, "Do you think it would give her more confidence and security in dealing with the children if she felt this same sort of support from you in bringing up the children?" Mr. S said, "Do you want me to get right in there and pitch, or is it enough to pat the little woman on the back and tell her that she is doing a good job?" The counselor asked him to think it over until the following session.

When Mr. S returned, he thought it over and "felt that he was too old to play ball with the children, too tired to read stories to them, and also a fellow had to have a little time for golf over the week ends." Yet, he wanted to do more than make a good living for them. He had already tried a fishing trip that failed, but he decided to try another. Before termination of the case, Mr. S said, "Believe it or not, I would rather fish with Archie and John than with my contemporaries. It is hard to believe, but it is true."

The counselor and Mr. S worked on his frequent statement, "I didn't approve of what my wife did, but I didn't say anything." The basis seemed to be the inability of Mrs. S to accept criticism. As a result of the unbelievably high standards and critical attitude of her foster mother, Mrs. S seemed to connect criticism with withdrawal of love. The counselor and Mr. S worked on how he could let her know the many ways he loved her, but at the same time be frank in talking all things over together, one of which was management of money which he thought she did very poorly.

In the last session, Mr. S reported that he thought the family was at last working as a team. "We have really come a long way. Why, I can even, with a twinkle in my eye, say to my wife things I would not have dreamed of saying six months ago."

Progress of Family as a Whole: Regarding progress or growth patterns of the S family as a whole, one was very conscious, at the beginning, of their rigidity in dealing with Archie; they demanded perfection even in his play. No wonder the boy never finished anything he attempted, fearing dissatisfaction on the part of the parents. Archie's therapist could get him to make no decisions for himself at first. He sought approval in doing what adults wanted him to do. In spite of Mrs. S's resistance to the high standards that had been set for her as she was growing up, she was unconsciously repeating the pattern with Archie. Both parents were favoring the younger son as well, which experience had previously caused so much unhappiness to Mr. S.

As insight and understanding grew on the part of the parents, they were able to accept and appreciate Archie for what he was. As this was shown in countless ways, Archie began to "blossom." Along with the parents' insight, however, must be evaluated the great help from Archie's therapist. Here was an adult who gave him acceptance, freedom, and the opportunity to be himself.

Also, came the growing ability of Mr. and Mrs. S to operate as a "team" in the rearing of their children and in their appreciation of each other. They gradually developed better "self-concepts" and countless new ways of real communication.

As Archie ran and folded himself in his father's arms when they were leaving one day, one would know progress had been made in their relationship.

Follow-Up: In order to provide a more meaningful follow-up, a longer period of time should elapse. However, upon seeing the S family approximately five weeks since the previous visit, various changes appear significant enough to point to a satisfactory prognosis.

During the interval that had elapsed, Mrs. S's foster father passed away, and both parents left town for the funeral. As this could have been a great shock to Mrs. S, it was of great interest to learn that the relationship with the foster mother was unlike anything of the past. Both Mrs. S and her mother were able to discuss sensitive areas without domination by the mother or friction.

Upon returning to their home town, Mrs. S feels that she can relax by spending her time leisurely and no longer feels it necessary to impress others. She said, "I can even take a daytime nap without feeling guilty about it."

Mrs. S also reported being able to see into the relationship that many of her friends have with their children and has observed some old patterns previously shown by her.

The ability of the parents to communicate with each other and to value each other's opinions has been an important change.

The barriers formerly restricting communication seem to have been removed, resulting in a closer and warmer relationship between them.

The experiences that the sons are having at camp have been favorable as well as the interest that Mr. S demonstrated by talking to the counselor and looking forward to the return of the children.

With regard to Mr. S, another important insight indicated by him is his ability "to see life through the eyes of the children." He remarked that he previously "had the children in a showcase for people to see." And now both parents not only are sensitive to their children's feelings but tend to accept them as they actually are.

The rigidity has been replaced by flexibility, the strictness by understanding, and the barriers and obstacles by new hope for the future.

Senior Counselor's Notes on Interchange Between the Therapists

It is the practice in this particular clinic for the therapists responsible for a case to read the reports of the other counselors on the case as well as to have weekly conferences together before meeting the counselees.

In the case the three therapists were helped greatly by their weekly conference. For example, the therapists, working with the parents, found that neither parent really accepted Archie. They wanted him to be completely transformed into the likeness of his young brother—then they could give him warm acceptance. This helped Archie's therapists to try to meet this need in Archie's life in the play therapy situation until the parents could grow to accept him for what he was.

The parents complained that Archie never finished anything which he began. The three therapists, working together, found that perhaps the reason for this behavior on Archie's part was due to the critical attitude of the parents toward Archie's efforts

and the impossibly high standards which they set for his achievements. He could avoid this painful situation by stopping short
of the finished product. These insights were helpful to all three
therapists and probably shortened the total process of counseling.

It was found by Mr. S's therapist that he was critical of many
things which Mrs. S did, in managing (or not managing) the
family budget and in dealing with the children, but that he found
he could not talk these things over with his wife; he bottled
them up inside himself. In the weekly conference period of the
therapists, Mrs. S's therapist suggested that since the foster
mother (the aunt) of Mrs. S had been so very critical of her all
during her growing up period, perhaps criticism had come to
mean, "withdrawal of love," or fear of it, in Mrs. S's life. This
helped Mr. S's therapist. Mr. S had himself told her of his wife's
girlhood troubles with her foster mother. And it was easy and
natural for her to ask Mr. S whether or not he thought his wife
might be associating criticism with "withdrawal of affection and
love" because of her childhood experiences. He felt sure that this
could be so, and together Mr. S and his therapist planned for
ways in which he could assure his wife of his love, and yet treat
her as an adult partner in their relationship.

Perhaps the greatest benefit came from the interchange of insights, as well as doubts and misgivings, as the therapists prepared for their meeting of all three therapists with the parents.
All the therapists had reread and summarized for their own benefit
the reports to date. In general, it was agreed that Archie's therapist would lead off, describing Archie's compulsive behavior and
his inability to make decisions, giving examples as he talked.
It was the plan, that as A's therapist, he could also tell of A's
beginning progress. Next, it was agreed that all three therapists
would seek to help the parents see, for themselves, what might
be some of the reasons back of A's behavior and that all five
persons would work together toward solutions. This was an
entirely different process, and much more rewarding for all, than

had each therapist worked alone or had Archie been referred, alone, to a Child Guidance Clinic.

> EDITOR'S NOTE: The important contribution of this case to professional thinking—namely the training and co-operative experience for the counseling staff—cannot be discounted (perhaps envied?). It is highly expensive, however, and in the majority of installations would be impossible because of lack of specialists and heavy demands on staff time. The contributors of the case suggest, however, that research is in order to determine whether *results* would warrant this co-operation on the part of staff members even if *training* were not one of the prime functions of the clinic.

CASE 19

Problem: Stepchildren and marital conflict
Presented by: Counselor (M.A. in Education) on teaching faculty of Southern medical school

Introduction: This is a second marriage for both Mr. and Mrs. Jackson. Mr. Jackson is a 46-year-old business executive, whose gray hair and heavily built figure at first give the impression of a man in his fifties. He looks weary. Mrs. Jackson is 40, and slimly built. Each have two children by a previous spouse. Mr. Jackson was happily married for twenty years to his first wife, and remarried ten months after her death. Now, six months later, he sees divorce as the only solution for his unhappiness with the present Mrs. Jackson. Mrs. Jackson was unhappily married to an alcoholic who was killed in World War II. Prior to his death they were planning on a divorce. Before her first marriage she had worked as a saleswoman, but had not been gainfully employed in the years following her husband's death, preferring to live carefully on the small income from his estate. Mr. Jackson's children are: Dick, aged 19, and Mary, aged 6. Mrs. Jackson's children are Betty, aged 13, and Nancy, aged 10. On the morning that Mrs. Jackson called for an appointment Mr. Jackson had informed her that he was going to send her and her children back to "the little house," as Betty irritated him so much that he could not continue to live under the same roof with her. Mrs. Jackson had persuaded him to come with her to a marriage counselor before taking such a step. However, she had achieved this only by telling him that she would go to court if necessary to ensure an adequate standard of living, equivalent to the one in the present marriage.

Referral: Through an article describing a Marriage Counseling Course held for ministers.

The Problem as Presented by the Clients: Both Mr. and Mrs. Jackson believe that a major cause of their marital unhappiness stems from their disagreement over Mrs. Jackson's 13-year-old Betty. Mr. Jackson says that his younger stepdaughter is easily lovable, but that Betty is a persistent whiner who ignores him. Her silences irritate him to such a degree that he can no longer stand to have her around. If her mother would send her to boarding school this would help solve their problem, but Mrs. Jackson will not even consider this idea. She says that Betty is a normal thirteen-year-old who gets good grades in school, is helpful to her around the house, and who is generally well-liked. She believes that her husband is jealous because his own 19-year-old son is getting too many failing grades in college and is running through too much money. She dislikes him, but keeps quiet about it. Mr. Jackson adds that his wife's persistent complaints are driving him mad. She says that her husband is unpunctual, temperamental, and that he believes the schedule of the entire household should revolve around him. However, she is strongly against the proposed divorce.

The Counseling: There were two interviews with Mr. Jackson, four with Mrs. Jackson, and one meeting of the director of the Child Guidance Clinic, whose help was utilized in this case with Mr. and Mrs. Jackson, and the marriage counselor.

First Interview with Mrs. Jackson: Mrs. Jackson smokes throughout the interview. She maintains her composure, speaking in strident tones. She is very dissatisfied with her husband and with the fact that his father lives with them, making up a household of seven persons, including three males. Mrs. Jackson has never lived for any lengthy period with a man in the house. Her father deserted her mother shortly after her birth. Her first husband and she lived together only briefly, and always unhappily. Her present husband, she claims, is unpleasable. He grumbles that they have no friends and never entertain, but when she prepares a party list he refuses to let her send out the invitations. When they are invited out, he comes home from the office too tired and she has to ring up with last-minute excuses. Yet he moans that they no longer have friends. He demands that all meals be served the moment of his return, but he never comes in twice at the same time and never lets her know when to expect him. If she asks for a time, he says, "Mabel always had a meal ready when I came in, she didn't have to know." Says Mrs. Jackson, "Maybe Mabel could predict him after twenty years, but from all I hear she didn't put up with this kind of nonsense." He ruins the children by his quixotic generosity, and ridicules her idea that they should be given an allowance and made to stay within it. He complains that she gets tired from working too hard, but still insists that everything be in perfect order, despite his own inability ever to pick up a shirt or to wipe out the bathtub. In his previous household two servants were employed. This she considered an unnecessary expense and cut down to one. Actually, she explains, servants never work well enough to suit her and she prefers to cook, clean, launder, and chauffeur rather than be constantly frustrated by their inefficiency or nonappearance. Her husband, she feels, should be grateful to her for working so hard. Not him: he says, "You should never have let Nettie go." She dislikes his 19-year-old son, whom she sees as stubborn, self-willed, spoilt and a spendthrift. Her husband acts as though the boy could do no wrong. Her husband's 85-year-old father is unobtrusive, but in view of his increasing helplessness, an added source of strain to the household.

All these difficulties would be minor if her husband did not treat Betty so badly. He makes plain his dislike of the child, who can do nothing right for him. Only last week all three of the children brought report cards home from school. The husband gave a dollar to the two younger ones, but he read Betty's report, which was much the best, and handed it back without comment or reward. Betty cried and asked, "Why can't Daddy like me too?" Mrs. Jackson has developed an aching back, a spastic colon and has difficulty in sleeping; all ailments characteristic of the periods of both her marriages. Before her first marriage and even after her first husband's death she never knew what it was to feel ill. Mrs. Jackson hopes that the counselor will be able to change Mr. Jackson's ways.

First Interview with Mr. Jackson: Mr. Jackson is adamant, the marriage cannot continue. He can stand it no longer. The difficulties center around Betty, who whines through every meal, ignores him at breakfast by taking hers onto the porch, and who generally is unresponsive; and his wife's overactivity and persistent complaining. After twenty years of happiness in his first marriage this one has made him a nervous wreck in six months. He cries for several minutes. His wife, he says, has never known happiness, in her own family or with her first husband. He thinks that she feels inferior because her education terminated at high school level. His conscience tells him that he should try and make this marriage work; his common sense tells him that it never will. Counselor and Mr. Jackson discuss Betty, as he relates incidents that annoy him. She spends hours on the telephone, studies till midnight, seldom says "Good morning," never can make up her mind, complains when any new suggestion is offered. The counselor comments that many of the incidents, for example, the telephone conversations, are typical of her age. Others, such as her withdrawal at breakfast, are typical of many thirteen-year-olds, but there is enough in the picture he paints to indicate that specialized help of a limited nature would be useful, especially help of a diagnostic type which would give both parents a better understanding of Betty. Counselor's suggestion of taking Betty to a Child Guidance Clinic is eagerly accepted by Mr. Jackson.

Second Interview with Mr. J: This concentrated on Mr. Jackson's feelings about his wife. Here his inability to think in any terms except those of punishment and reward is demonstrated. He "carries" his wife on trips but leaves her behind if she has not been "good." He resents her threat to go to court for a settlement; she will do better to rely on his generosity as he hates to be forced in any way. He loves to buy surprise presents. He wants the children, all of them, to have "glossier" clothes than his wife buys. He likes to surprise them with extra money and bitterly resents his wife's pleas for budgeting. He is sick of her aches and pains. "Mabel" never acted ill. Counselor talks of the difficulties that all families have to face just because they are made up of different ages and sexes. The three-generation family has more gaps to bridge. When two ready-made families are brought together, stresses have to be expected and worked through, since each already has its own inner loyalties, habits, and rituals. In these two families each is still more conscious of its own rather than of a joint entity. Even steps like both attending the same church might help. A family discussion council could air tensions and look for ways of agreement. Mr. Jackson does not pick up these ideas, but reverts to the Clinic visit, to which Mrs. Jackson had agreed reluctantly. She is certain that it is a waste of money. To agree seems to indicate victory for her husband.

Child Guidance Clinic Visit: Parents and counselor are behind the one-way vision screen as Betty is tested. On every test her responses improve dramatically on repeat trials, true of personality tests, general intelligence, and tests of manual dexterity. She includes no people in her responses. Certain eye difficulties are also revealed.

Mrs. Jackson resents the findings. Mr. Jackson is delighted to find out that it was not only prejudice which made it difficult for him to reach this stepdaughter. He realizes he has to work with Betty, rather than demand immediate response from her. The director tells him that he has the kind of personality which can make him a "warm father figure."

During the next months his wife reports a change in his relationship with Betty. He now gives her time to respond, and does not feel slighted by her silences. He does not like her in the way he likes the three other children, and still wishes that she could be sent away to school. Nevertheless, he often refers to himself as her father, likes to hear repeated the phrase "warm father figure."

Second Interview with Mrs. Jackson: Mrs. Jackson expressed bitterness re the Clinic's findings about Betty. However, she is relieved that Betty and her husband now get along fairly well and that her husband no longer tells Betty that she will cause the marriage to break up. Betty's confidence in herself is increasing and she has received more invitations to go out than ever before. Her homework is taking less time and the general strain is less. Mrs. J pours out her anger against the stepson, who gets more money than his "fair" share, drops his laundry on the floor and wants it ready that day. *He* needs psychological testing, not Betty. This interview centers around Mrs. Jackson's hostility to Dick and her determination that all the children be reared her way with regular allowances, chore responsibilities, and budgeted time. Incident after incident pours out about Dick's rudeness, her husband's upsetting of her training of the other children with extra money, special treats, and so on. Only after this outburst is she able to recognize that her attempts to get her husband to act in her way are doomed to defeat. She begins to see that the cost of a happy family will be a willingness to try and mesh their ideas about training into a joint pattern. Dick must be thought of not as a maddening intruder but as an adult who can receive services in so far as they are compatible with the general running of the household and in proportion as he assumes his share of responsibility. But he is a member of the family too, with his own special troubles, a boy who is not sure of his way, still grieving for his mother and resenting his father's immediate remarriage.

Third Interview with Mrs. Jackson: Betty and her stepfather are improving in their relationship. Mr. Jackson has learned to accept sudden silences. And Dick even confided some of his college troubles to her (Mrs. J). Although miffed at first about his laundry, he now gets it into the hamper in time. This next week end he is bringing friends home, and she does not feel imposed upon. She has employed an extra servant to do the heavy cleaning and is herself physically less fatigued and is keeping backaches to herself. She has taken to listing jobs to be done while she is out, and she has started to praise rather than complain. She remarks: "It must be hard to work for a perfectionist like me." Counselor suggested that in the parental family Mrs. J had been the picker-upper, the tidy and responsible one. This set counselee off into a description of a demanding mother, a sister who dreamed and read her way through the teens and went to college as a result, and a brother who lived on his charm;

of her resentment of her father's desertion, and of her first husband's drinking. "Guess Norman (Mr. J) thinks I nag and complain. I don't want to. I don't want to be like my mother. Norman isn't so bad when I do not nag him to live my way. He's generous and he's fun, but he's maddening too. He told me yesterday that I had not mentioned that I was feeling ill for two weeks—and he asked me would I like to go to Europe with him this summer. I'm doing more community work and my section was top in the Community Chest drive. Norman liked that and I did too. My brother and sister have always been given all the recognition in our family. I sent them my picture and the story in the paper about the Community Chest."

Fourth Interview: Mrs. Jackson makes it clear that she wants to discontinue visits to the counselor, although her husband wants her to continue as he thinks she improves with every visit. She wants him to come and he says he will, but never gets around to it. However, life is easier as he now phones from the office when he is leaving to come home. He and Betty started to argue because he objected when she didn't respond to his morning greeting. Dick jumped into the fray with: "Dad, people don't always feel pleasant before breakfast. Remember how I wanted to eat by myself when I was thirteen. Just because you bounce out of bed and feel it is a wonderful day doesn't mean that we all do. We don't jump on you if you come home from the office looking like thunder. We steer clear until the fatherly brow unfurrows." It all ended up in a laugh. For the first time she feels they are becoming one family and not two. "I certainly never thought Dick would help in this. Don't misunderstand. We still have a lot of rough spots." She referred to the Diagnostic Clinic's suggestion to Mr. Jackson that he slow down. His answer was to buy two more businesses. But they are going to Europe next month. Her father-in-law will stay with another brother while they are gone, and she hopes on their return they can arrange to share him more.

Follow-Up: Eighteen months later the family is still progressing. Mr. Jackson calls up when a problem disturbs him, but the calls are now infrequent. Mrs. Jackson writes occasionally. She usually begins with a complaint, but ends up with a reasonably good analysis of the situation and a plan for working at it.

Conclusions: This case leaves dormant many personality problems, but in view of the age of the counselees and the long distance which they have to travel for counseling, it seemed best to accept their desire to terminate regular sessions. Subsequently Mrs. Jackson has demonstrated her ability to use the insight she gained as she encounters new problems. Mr. Jackson regained his ebullience through encouragement. He accepts the need for some household routines. The family is considerably better united as a group. The two younger children are devoted to each other. There is no longer any suggestion of divorce by either Mr. or Mrs. Jackson.

PREMARITAL COUNSELING

Introduction

Premarital counseling differs from marriage counseling principally in terms of timing, as it focuses on an earlier stage of individual or "couple" development and interaction. As in marriage counseling the emphasis is on developing skill in handling the interpersonal relationship of the two partners. The counselor assists the person or persons to discuss pertinent questions and anxieties and to resolve some of the problems or conflicts that arise before marriage and to attain a more flexible perspective. But, although by definition this type of counseling focuses at the premarital level, it is also anticipatory of later marital adjustment.

There is, too, a strong educational emphasis in premarital counseling. It may well be considered as preventive in character. It is believed on the basis of experience to date that careful examination and discussion of the suitability of the personalities to each other, of personal and cultural attitudes and differences, of the impact of parental relationships, of the influence of sexual concepts, information and experiences, facilitates the process of later adjustment. Premarital counseling aims not only to prepare a couple to avoid serious problems but helps them to recognize conflict at an incipient level and, when indicated, to seek professional assistance.

9. General Premarital Counseling

Case 20. *Counseling on Important Areas of Early Marital Adjustment*

Case 21. *Premarital Medical Consultation*

These two cases are illustrations of general premarital consultation, where there is no overtly expressed presenting problem.

Case 20 gives a good idea of the kind of subjects brought up and discussed in a "normal" premarital consultation—such as finances, sex and contraception, friends, family, wife's job as it affects marital roles. Case 21 demonstrates the strategic position of the doctor who in the course of medical consultation can do much to alleviate anxieties surrounding the sexual relationship.

CASE 20

Problem: Counseling on important areas of early marital adjustment

Presented by: Counselor (Ed.D. in Marriage and Family Life Education; in-service training in marriage counseling) in a marriage counseling agency located in a large metropolitan city

Introduction: Miss X wrote our agency asking for the appointment. She had heard one of our staff members speak on marriage counseling two years ago. She is 23 years old, a college graduate, and currently employed as a dental technician. She is a nice-looking young woman, of medium size; had on a tailored suit, but looked very feminine. She was quiet in her manner. Mr. Y is a tall, good-looking fellow, with quite black hair and brows, somewhat on the slender side. He was dressed in ordinary, neat-appearing business suit. He is 24, Jewish as is she, and still going to college.

Counseling: They were invited into the counseling rooms together, seemed friendly and at ease. C commented that they were right on time. Miss X began by saying that they weren't sure whether they were coming to the right place or not. C replied that he understood she had heard one of their staff speak. She said yes, and she thought this agency could help them, or tell them where to go for help. C then explained that the agency does help people with general premarital discussion and that he would be glad to have them use the time in any way they wished, to their fullest advantage. He explained that they could all talk together, or after a few minutes together, if they wanted to have separate time, C would be glad to see each of them separately for a short period and then have them come back together again for the rest of the time. Mr. Y said that he had nothing "that he wouldn't want her to hear." Miss X said that was true of her, too, but she thought if the agency usually worked separately and then together, they might try it that way—so it was agreed. Before separating, however, C asked if they wanted to discuss the amount of time, or the fee for the interview. (They had been advised by the secretary that there would be a fee, established on a sliding scale to conform to their income, and that premaritals usually took two hours, or a little more.) They understood this and had all the time necessary, but Mr. Y said he would like to know what the fee would be. The fee schedule was given to them, and discussed. They chose a figure based on his income for one hour, and hers for the other. They then decided she would be first.

Interview, Miss X: Mr. Y left the room, and took with him two of the research schedules routinely used by the agency to fill out. Miss X came to the point readily and without embarrassment by saying it was birth control information she wanted. (Apparently, this is why she wondered if this were the right place to come.) She explained that Mr. Y was a student but she would continue to work. C noted two aspects of the problem: the medical and the psychological, and suggested that he could discuss the latter with her, and refer her to a doctor for the former. This was just what she wanted. C asked about her own family doctor to which she replied that she did not wish to see him because he "wouldn't be a good counselor." C explained the referral system, and she chose three names and addresses from the agency's list.

Then she seemed not to want anything else. That was why she had come and that would give her all she wanted to know. C inquired about reading. She had read *When You Marry,*[1] and taken a course at the university.

C asked several questions, and the exchange of conversation indicated assurance, stability, and favorable conditions. She had dated Y four years, but had had many other friends. Her parents, themselves happily married, had provided her sex education. She had had petting experience but not intercourse, and on the whole had had a happy life. When C asked about personality factors she said, "Well, it will be a change, and I will have to give up a little of my independence which I have had for two years." This was discussed in relation to finances, to the routine of meals and housework, and to giving up her dates. She seemed to have good insight on these points.

Interview, Mr. Y: Mr. Y came in, said that the schedules had

[1] By Evelyn Millis Duvall and Reuben Hill (New York: Association Press, 1953, rev. ed.).

made him think of "a couple of things." He then said: "One thing worries me, on which we do not have complete agreement." It was the fact that he had "to live off his wife" for the next two years. C discussed this with him at some length along two main lines: his feelings about marriage, whether it was a joint venture, in finances as well as in other things; and his feelings about how his wife viewed it. The latter led him to say: "She doesn't mind doing it; her only worry is what I will think about it." He was very thoughtful about this and finally said that he could see that his thinking about it as a co-operative job would "probably be much better." He said to C: "I like what you said about both of us working for both. I'll quit using singular pronouns."

Counselor waited, and Mr. Y then brought up the subject of birth control. He was troubled because he had got the idea that women have a "maternal instinct" and unconsciously want a child, and therefore could not really be happy using contraceptives. Counselor said that he understood that it would be a troubling idea, and encouraged him to talk further about it. It appears to be only "an idea" he has, without any basis in his own experience with Miss X. She has never given him any reason to suspect this conflict. So Counselor said that it was his experience that young women of Miss X's age, education, and apparent maturity, usually mean what they say when they decide to plan their family. He was much interested in our discussion, said that he felt he had been somewhat misguided, and that he felt reassured.

Mr. Y showed interest in how to assume his sex role in marriage. He had not had intercourse, but has read a good deal. C asked if he felt at any disadvantage in not having had experience. He did not. The importance of psychological as well as purely physical factors in the sexual act was briefly discussed but C decided to leave most of it until the joint interview. Glancing at the completed schedules which had been filled out, C noted that he had checked a "little disagreement" on matters of friends, health, and personal habits. Mr. Y insisted that these were minor matters. His girl didn't like his playing poker with his gang, and she also complained a little because he smokes so much, purely on a health basis. C asked how he felt about these points and he said he thought they would iron out all right. This led to the question of his getting a physical examination before marriage. It was agreed that he would talk that over with her, and would get it if she wanted him to. He had no objection to it.

C's questions brought out that his parents have been happily married and his relation to them seemed very good. C then had a chance to check over the schedules with them both and note important points of variations.

Interview with Miss X, Mr. Y: The schedules showed that they both wanted more information about birth control, and the "psychological aspects" of sex. C discussed nonmedical aspects of birth control with them: the comfortable, nonharmful, and relatively safe features of the diaphragm. (They had no moral or religious ideas that would create problems about it.) C then discussed with them sex relations in marriage especially in the matter of timing, questions of modesty, and the importance of the passage of time. C stressed that sex adjustment often took time. He warned against impatience and perfectionism. Also, they decided to buy the Butterfield booklet, and took a reference to *A Marriage Manual* [2] (by Drs. Hannah and Abraham Stone) which they said they would buy. They both seemed very appreciative of this phase of the interview.

C raised the question of their disagreement over friends. Mr. Y mentioned his crowd at the service station, and she said they could be his friends, that she "would never close the door on them" and that she would have her friends, too. C noticed some tension here. He listened, and then suggested gently that he was concerned about the matter of friends, because it sometimes can have importance. He repeated the emphasis made earlier of "our" instead of "my" and "your." It was suggested that this

[2] New York: Simon & Schuster, 1953, rev. ed.

was another area to explore, and their reaction was to be thoughtful and agree that they ought to think about it some more.

C asked if they had had any breaks in their engagement. They had split up once for six months, but both felt this improved their situation. But they did not elaborate the point. Then Miss X said that they had broken up several times. This was discussed, and C felt that the main point they presented was that she felt "above him intellectually" because she had finished college when he was just starting (because of his service). He remarked that now he had caught up, and furthermore she was not so much above him "as she thought she was." Miss X agreed to this very good-naturedly.

Miss X had checked that she doesn't like domestic activities. C raised this matter and it was discussed around the point of roles of the husband and wife. C asked about the mother of each of them, and discussed it in the light of what image each had built up. Mr. Y's mother, was "95 per cent a housewife." Miss X said her mother had "chosen business and always taken the initiative." They saw the importance of this background and agreed to discuss it more deeply.

Then there was a pause and the couple said they were thinking of whether there was anything else to discuss. Apparently not. C then observed that they checked their willingness to fill out some postmarital schedules in three months. These were explained and arrangements made to write them about it.

As they paid their fee, Miss X said that it was "well worth it," and Mr. Y agreed. As they left they thanked C, said it was very helpful, and they appreciated his taking time in the evening for them. C offered them his best wishes, and they departed quite happily.

Follow-Up—Postmarital Schedules: Marriage adjustment schedules were checked five months after the wedding of this couple, and mailed to the agency. They indicated that the husband was in school and the wife still working. He was receiving G.I. funds and veterans' pension, however. Both checked that they were somewhat dissatisfied with this arrangement. They were living in their own quarters, and indicated very good relations with in-laws on both sides. They reported little disagreement on twenty-three items tested. Both indicated that the working out of disagreements was by mutual give-and-take. They share responsibility for daily household tasks and indicated five or six outside activities in which they participate together. Neither checked any trait of himself or spouse which caused any difficulty. Both rated their marriage as very happy, and each believed that the marriage was very happy for the other.

Two specific points raised by them in counseling, or on premarital schedules, were sexual adjustment and friends. On the postmarital schedule both checked a little disagreement on the former. The husband, only, checked a little disagreement on the latter.

Note by Counselor: The evidence suggests some positive benefits from the premarital counseling session. Miss X received psychological support in her feelings about the importance for her of using contraceptives immediately in her marriage and concrete assurance through referral to a reliable physician, both of which were her felt needs. Also, her realistic attitude about trying to adjust to a job and settling down, rather than holding out for "independence," seems to have found support, for their postmarital schedules indicated a togetherness in accepting the work role and student role. The counselor felt there was some tension between them on the point of friends, when seen premaritally, yet after marriage this did not appear as a problem.

It is apparent that Mr. Y gained in being able to understand and accept equality as a marriage partner. His sensitivity about her higher education and her bread-winning role seems not to have caused trouble. Presumably this problem which was major in his mind at the time of counseling, is being faced and resolved.

The counselor (and the schedules) threw out feelers in connection with a variety of possible adjustment problems, but when nothing obvious arose, he (the counselor) was quite comfortable and willing to focus on the specifics raised by the two counselees.

CASE 21

Problem: Premarital medical consultation
Presented by: Gynecologist (M.D.) in private practice in large metropolitan city

Some years ago, a young woman came from New England to consult me in my private office. I saw at once that she was on the defensive and ill at ease in her surroundings. When I asked her what I could do for her, she said she'd come for premarital advice. With this statement she sat up stiffly and drew her mouth into a tight line.

I began by asking her simple questions about her general health, past illnesses or surgery, but I soon concluded from her monosyllabic answers that she resented finding herself in such a situation. "You don't want to be here, do you?" I said. "No, I don't," she replied. I explained that this was not a police station and that she didn't have to remain. I suggested that she go and said that I had many things I could do in what remained of the hour I'd reserved for her. I busied myself with something else and completely ignored her until she said, "I promised my friends I'd see this through," with which she sat up still straighter and drew her mouth into a still tighter line. I took up the threads where they had been dropped and obtained the basic information necessary to proceed. She was 26, an only child in a conservative New England home, her family was in comfortable circumstances financially, she was a college graduate and a Protestant. Her fiancé was a couple of months older than she and in business in a Midwestern state. They were to be married in two months.

On that first visit I went no further with my questioning but took her to the examining room for a pelvic examination. She was resigned and co-operative about this but entirely uncommunicative. I found her hymen to be intact, fairly elastic, and relatively insensitive. After a little gentle massage it admitted my index finger. I explained and instructed her in the use of a small vaginal dilator and asked her to return in a week.

The second and third calls were almost identical. I talked to her and showed her various models of the genital organs, gradually leading up to a discussion of intercourse. During all this time she was polite, unresponsive, but co-operative in following directions in the use of the dilators. These were producing painless and progressive dilations of the vaginal orifice. On the day of her fourth visit I started talking to her about coitus. This was an entirely one-sided conversation because she took no part in it. Finally, I made some statement which unfortunately became lost in the subsequent turn of events. She drew herself up and with a look of disgust which I shall never forget, said *"Doctor, you sound as though you thought that intercourse should be fun."* My immediate and not too adequate reply was, "I think that you and your husband should get pleasure from it. What do you think?" Then, as Dr. Dickinson[1] would have said, "the flood gates opened." She suddenly became vocal and poured out the story of her mother who had told her that no "lady" ever enjoyed intercourse, that it was "something that a woman had to put up with for the first year of marriage; then her husband wouldn't bother her any longer," and so on.

I found myself in a difficult spot because, on the one hand, I wanted to change her attitude and persuade her that it was quite proper for a lady to enjoy intercourse but, on the other, it was necessary that she retain her respect for me else all would be lost. One of the discouraging features of the situation was that her fiancé was going to fly from the Midwest directly to New

[1] Robert Latou Dickinson, M.D., 1861-1950. See footnote 4, Appendix.

England for the wedding and there would be no opportunity for me to talk with him.

She returned twice after that for further talks, and for instruction in the use of a contraceptive diaphragm. In my talks she was again uncommunicative but it was apparent that she was very much interested. I had no inkling as to how she was reacting to all this until the day of her last call. When she left she shook hands with me, thanked me, and smiled for the first time. I asked her to return in not more than two months and much sooner if she could plan a trip to the city.

I heard nothing more from her until about six weeks later, when my secretary told me that this patient and her husband were in the waiting room and wanted to speak to me. Because there was no one else in the room at that time, I went there to greet them. As I entered they both stood up and my patient, with a broad and happy smile, said, "We wanted to come in together to tell you that it *is* fun."

EDITORIAL COMMENT: The gynecological examination and the factual information imparted are basic medical ingredients of premarital counseling. However, the relationship with an attractive woman (the physician) whom she could respect and whose attitude toward sex was so obviously different from her mother's, gave the client new identification. The giving of information together with the subtle reduction of hostility and the use of therapeutic release to build a positive attitude toward the whole sexual relationship also claim attention. The professional marriage counselor will be interested in how an apparently negative and unresponsive counseling relationship yielded such positive results.

10. To Marry or Not to Marry

The common element in the following group of cases which deal with one or another or both of the engaged partners' serious doubts concerning marriage is the consistent refusal of any one of the counselors to be directly (or indirectly) pressured into persuading a client in one direction or another. Even when on the surface the situation seems to be moving along fairly smoothly (Case 22) it might have dangerous implications. Cases such as these require a high degree of technical skill and professional integrity.

It is interesting to note that in Case 25 apparently quite early in the counseling relationship the counselor consciously decided not to involve the partner—"the problem was with Mr. B, not his girl friend."

Case 27 is an interesting report of a problem of indecision regarding marriage handled in a group counseling situation. The reader's attention is directed to the introductory remarks concerning group counseling which precede the case.

CASE 22

Problem: A fiancé's withdrawal from plans for marriage
Presented by: Counselor (graduate degree in Psychiatric Social Work) in a marriage counseling agency located in a large city

Introduction: Miss X was referred to the agency by her father, to discuss her fiancé's uncertainty and conflict about going through with marriage, a marriage scheduled to take place within three months. Both Miss X and Mr. Y are college graduates; both Protestant; both employed, he as chemist and she a settlement worker. She is 25 years old, he twelve years older. This was a first engagement for both (it had once before been broken) and was approved by both sets of parents.

Impression of Clients: Miss X was a fine-looking, genuine, warm, stable type of person. She was friendly, frank, and co-operative in her manner, and was also obviously disturbed by the situation. She was extremely anxious for help and put everything she had into getting it.

Mr. Y was a tall, blonde, well-built, healthy-appearing man. His manner was extremely disturbed, at times making it impossible for him to talk at all. He sat for moments with his head in his hands, contracting his eyes and forehead into an acute squint. Leaning forward uncomfortably in the chair, he only very occasionally looked at Counselor. Was too ill at ease and withdrawn to make much out of the (first) interview. In addition, there was a fair amount of resentment evident at being in a marriage counseling office.

Counselor asked the couple whether they wished to be seen together or separately. Miss X elected to have the first individual interview. With tears in her eyes, she said, "It looks as if our engagement plans have blown up . . . every time a definite date limit comes, announcing engagement, wedding invitations, and so on, he goes into a tail spin; consequently, our engagement has been a series of crises."

Counselor asked Miss X a bit about how long she had known Mr. Y and how well. For over a year, they had had a wonderful time together at a summer resort where both families have a cottage. Felt they both had a lot in common, although he is 11 years older. She did not feel this a barrier, but he did. He had never been engaged or married before. "I have always been able to help him through these muddles. He has been upset ever since our engagement, is worried over his job, feeling that business is falling off acutely. He has a hard time making up his mind over everything."

Counselor commented that this must be a very difficult situation for Miss X to find herself in. Miss X answered, "You have to make plans. I wonder now, if I should call things off. Maybe I have pushed him all along. I wonder if he is getting married because he thinks he ought to. This last week end I raised the question of children. To me they are part of marriage. He feels he is not sure that he wants children. This was what precipitated the immediate difficulty. Whenever he is upset, he doesn't write or call. When he feels all right he gets in touch with me all the time. This week end he said he was not sure he loved me. (Again Miss X's eyes filled with tears.) She continued, "He is so fine and sensitive, I hate to throw it over on account of his fear of marriage."

Counselor asked about the expression of affection. Miss X stated that the sexual side is perfect and both enjoy heavy petting, but no intercourse nor mutual orgasm. She did not know if he had ejaculation.

Counselor asked Miss X directly if she felt she could stand trying to work this thing through for a few weeks, since there was some leeway before the invitations would actually have to go out. She (the counselor) spoke of a certain type of personality which reacted as did Mr. Y to the finality of marriage. Explained that she had seen other men and women reacting in an extremely upset way when the date was set. Often this was something that a person could not help, but if they were willing to work on it they could sometimes be helped to come to a decision. Whether this meant marriage or breaking up, the decision would inevitably be more valid to both partners because it had been thought and felt through.

Counselor then asked whether Mr. Y would be willing to come to the agency or to go to a psychiatrist, which could be arranged. Miss X was not sure whether Mr. Y would come in. She felt he would be very upset if the suggestion of psychiatric help was made. She would be willing to urge him to come. "You have helped me to get perspective; I am anxious for him to come in."

First Interview with Mr. Y: Mr. Y was obviously uneasy; asked (and was given) an explanation of kind of service offered; pressed for clarification of Miss X's father's relation to the service, commenting cryptically that there was a personal connection between the counselor and Miss X's family. Counselor agreed that there was a connection which was, however, professional rather than personal. She knew it must be very difficult for Mr. Y to find himself in such a place. Mr. Y said, it certainly was; in fact, "I hardly know how I got here." Counselor wondered if he felt so uncomfortable that he would rather not be here, adding that she thought he should feel quite free to terminate the interview now, or at any time. The agency was here only to try to be of service to those who wished help. It could be of little help to a person unless he really wanted to work on his or her problem. Mr. Y commented, "I do not feel free to talk to you, because you know the family."

Counselor then explained the availability of other counselors or psychiatrists, the way records were kept by numbers with no names, her conception of a confidential service stressing the fact that no material or report would be given to family or any other person without permission. At this point, client looked directly at Counselor for the first time, a penetrating, sizing-up sort of glance. Counselor had the feeling of an extremely intelligent man rather desperately caught and very unhappy. He sat with his head sunk in his hands and Counselor simply waited. Finally, Mr. Y said he should be able to work this thing out himself or with Miss X. It had gotten to be more and more of a problem. After another long pause, he said, "It is my way to try to work at things from all sides and try to get an answer." Again, there was a very long pause. Counselor finally commented how hard it was for Mr. Y to feel comfortable about talking, explaining that usually the Counselor might ask some questions which would be helpful in pointing up the interview, but because Mr. Y felt so uncertain of being here Counselor in turn did not feel free to ask questions, which he might not want to answer.

Another painful pause during which Counselor decided that in her ten years of experience in marriage counseling, this was the most difficult interview she had ever had. Finally, Mr. Y, with breaks here and there said, haughtily, he thought he had been quite cool to Miss X. When he began to talk of his job, he was more free. Two years ago, he felt he was unequivocally needed, but no longer feels so. He explained at length the hazards of a man nearing 40 attempting a new type of work. He felt he might have to start over and it made him wonder if he should change jobs before the wedding and marry on a shoestring or should he take a chance on all this working out later. Mr. Y then shut his eyes, sighed deeply and sank in misery on the edge of the chair. Counselor commented that this must add greatly to his general feeling of uncertainty about his attitude toward marriage.

After more moments of silence, this time not quite so painful, Mr. Y with a desperate effort, again darting a glance at Counselor, said, "Getting engaged was quite a step for me; I wondered then where I was going and have ever since." Another pause and gulp, and he remarked that he had abhorrence of publicity of any kind. Reading of his own engagement in the paper, "certainly got me down."

After another long pause, Mr. Y looked at Counselor pathetically, saying, "I feel as if I am growing up at a very fast rate and I should be grown up at my age." He added that when at Miss X's home, he usually brightened up and that at their vacation place, everyone thought they were having the time of their lives. "What did you think?" Counselor asked. "I guess I thought so too, then," was his reply. He worried over the difference in age. Miss X didn't see his job difficulty as serious. Was this related to their differences in age and experience? "This job uncertainty and the whole state of the world makes me wonder if I want to raise a family. I would be 65 when my children were grown up. Miss X wants a family. I am awfully cool about it. This could have an awfully cooling-off effect after marriage."

Counselor then asked Mr. Y directly, "How do you feel about the sexual side of marriage?" Mr. Y answered directly with a tiny semblance of relief: "I imagine that that drive is what takes most fellows over the hard spots. This has changed with me in the last two years. I don't have much feeling of sex urge. I don't suppose a medical examination would do any good." Counselor commented that there seemed to be a good many things about marriage which didn't offer very much advantage to Mr. Y. She wondered what he felt he would lose if he didn't continue with his plans? Again, Mr. Y looked directly at Counselor and stated without much hesitation and more forcefully, "I feel I would hurt her irreparably, and I would lose my self-respect." He then asked his first question, "What do you think, would I be doing a good thing by marrying?"

At this point, Counselor again spoke of the agency and how through its service people had an opportunity to find suitable answers for themselves. He might prefer to think this whole thing over and let her know later whether he wished to continue counseling. Mr. Y said he knew Counselor wanted to be helpful, but he thought that he would not decide on any more appointments. He would get in touch with Miss X and just see.

The following morning, Miss X phoned saying Mr. Y wished an appointment the next day.

Second Interview with Mr. Y: Mr. Y seemed more comfortable although still tense. He had called Miss X on the phone and told her everything he had talked about with Counselor. Mr. Y again looked haunted and very worried, asked, "Is the material here confidential?" Counselor repeated the agency's philosophy in regard to confidential material. Mr. Y then said, "Well, maybe talking will help me get perspective." There was a long pause; Mr. Y looked directly at Counselor, and stated, "I think I can trust you implicitly." With a sort of gulp, he said, "Maybe I should not have these questionings; maybe they are not so serious." Counselor commented that things were serious if they seemed so to the particular person. With another gulp, Mr. Y commented he was interested in heredity. He spoke of Daltonism, and finally that he had learned that Miss X's father was color-blind. He had read that color blindness was related to poor eyesight. Miss X had poor eyesight which admittedly made her self-conscious about being dependent on strong glasses. He visualized a family of children all with poor eyesight and glasses. Counselor recognized Mr. X's feeling in this matter making a few simple comments to the effect that modern science had been able to contribute a great deal to control poor eyesight.

Mr. Y then spoke of his great admiration for Miss X's father and mother as persons. He switched to his own family; his father had had a stroke when he was over 70. His father's older brother was in a private sanitarium with what sounded like the onset of senility. Both men had been very successful in business, but now got pretty much confused and mixed up. This might indicate weakness in his own heredity. Counselor commented, if everyone could make their place in the world without breaking down physically or mentally until after 70, there would be comparatively little trouble in the world! Mr. Y was able to smile rather wanly at this, saying he supposed that after all it wasn't too bad. He added that he had told Miss X about his worries about his family a year ago and they had decided to break off at that time. Then, they had gone to the same summer resort and things had really moved. He supposed people would say he had had a lot of fun that summer. He then continued, but this time with comparative ease and the assumption that Counselor was listening interestedly. "I had a Phi Beta Kappa Key at ————. Have always worried over slight imperfections, want anything I do to be as near perfect as possible, so I keep asking questions. Do I want children who may have poor eyesight? Yet I cannot tell Miss X I worry about her poor eyesight; that would be cruel."

Mr. Y repeated something of last week's discussion, how he had stalled making any public announcement.

Mr. Y was then able to say that sexually Miss X was not so attractive to him as some. "I have never found a person who was sexually attractive, and also appealed to me otherwise." Here Mr. Y squinted, hunching his shoulders and said, "I never 'got the bug' (fell in love) so it interfered with my work; blonds seem to appeal to me. I have known one for ten years, taken her out a few times, but haven't seemed to get very interested." There was some discussion here of Moss Hart's point of view on American fantasy goals, and marriage as status. Mr. Y then commented, that he and X had many congenial interests. "Why do I keep thinking of ways of getting out of it? I might do much worse."

Third Interview with Mr. Y: Mr. Y looked much more cheerful, seemed quite comfortable saying there was probably nothing much more, but he found it helpful to talk. He had enjoyed his week end. They hadn't talked over any decisions. "I still can't make up my mind completely. Miss X's father and mother are wonderful, they bring no pressure. Miss X is just completely

in love." Here, Mr. Y said rather surprisingly, "I guess it will
hurt her now, and perhaps me more, if I keep looking for perfection."

Mr. Y then commented that the wedding date was set for
three months hence, and he realized that something would have
to be decided. "I am learning through you that sharing with
another human being can help. That is a milestone for me. Know
I will be a bigger person because of that no matter what happens." Counselor said, "It is like swimming, isn't it? Once you
learn how, it will always be with you." Mr. Y continued, "The
fact that I have been to see you *three times in a week* is amazing to me. I hand it to the X's for suggesting it. I wouldn't have
thought such a thing would be possible."

The interview then swung into a discussion of imperfection as
part of life and living. Mr. Y raised the question, How could
he be sure of having healthy and normal children? Counselor
spoke of the work in eugenics going on at the Cold Spring Har-
bor laboratories. Spoke of the possibility of getting an expert's
opinion on heredity in connection with color blindness or the
general family situation. Mr. Y listened attentively and was able
to comment on the relative unimportance of this imperfection.
Counselor drew a little diagram of a circle which she labeled
the ideal and then put little notches around this circle, which
were the dents of the imperfection of life. Mr. Y looked pleased
at the little drawing, "That is a scientist's way of talking, I can
understand that." He launched into a discussion of pain and
frustration as part of life.

Mr. Y now got up and walked comfortably around the room
smoking, and offering Counselor a cigarette. He had been reading the books on marriage which Counselor had loaned him.
He had no idea there were such books. If he had only had something like this twenty years ago it would have made a difference.

Second Interview with Miss X, Three Days Later: With a beam-
ing smile, Miss X said, "Have you heard what happened to Mr.

Y? I just got a special delivery letter. When he returned to work Monday morning, he had been chosen to go on a special trip to work on a big deal. He left by air in a few hours and will be back by next week end." Counselor and Miss X agreed together that this was the most marvelous thing that could have happened at the moment. Surely, it would give Mr. Y the feeling of being wanted and important in his job and should help in his feeling of security.

Miss X looked attractive. Her manner was calmer, no tears, but quite often a rather lonely look. She reported that Mr. Y had spent the week end at their house, coming out Friday after seeing Counselor. "He seemed so different, so much more relaxed as if the worst tension had gone. I just felt as if there was no problem after he was here. Don't know what you did, but it seemed just like magic." Quite a discussion followed in which Counselor raised the question as to how long Miss X thought such a change in Mr. Y might last? Personality growth and the varying speeds in which this might take place were discussed.

Miss X seemed to get a great deal from this discussion and was able to raise real questions as to the kind of person Mr. Y was and might be expected to be in a marriage relationship. Would decisions always be difficult, would he always worry, would he get around to be willing or to really want to have children, and would he enjoy them? She was able to express something of her feelings about his attitudes in these matters and to have more realistic appreciation that marriage might not change him completely.

After this, Miss X wished to discuss where they went from here. The wedding invitations had to be ordered. Rather sadly, she added, "It isn't as if I would mind waiting if I thought it would be any different, but plans have already been postponed two times before this. I feel if it is put off now, I have no guarantee that it won't happen again."

There was discussion of personal integrity, and how much anyone could give in to another person without harming his own fundamental feelings for the other person. Counselor then questioned whether Miss X could drift along this week end without pressing question for decisions. Perhaps, if Mr. Y was left the responsibility, he might relate to the situation differently than if Miss X were the initiator as she had been in the past. Miss X got the implications of this and thought she could handle it. She added that Mr. Y was the one who had always taken responsibility for his own family. Counselor commented that if she became one of his family, might he more naturally take responsibility? Miss X nodded.

The question of premarital physical examination then came up. Miss X felt that if her plans materialized she would like to be referred to a physician for instruction in contraception, so that she might take responsibility for this. There was some discussion of sexual adjustment, as this might be affected by Mr. Y's age and his rather unusual amount of anxiety.

Third Interview with Miss X (Ten Days Later): Miss X looked extremely pretty and well to all outside appearances. Her manner throughout the interview was bright, responsive, and only occasionally sad. For the most part Counselor felt that this was natural and not too much assumed. She asked Counselor if she knew how things had turned out. Counselor had had no word. Miss X then said, "I finally broke the engagement last Sunday. When Y came back from his trip, he did not get in touch with me until Sunday afternoon, which is in itself unusual, as he almost always gets over for dinner. When he did come he seemed very depressed, appeared no more certain of wanting to go on than he had before and was so upset that I felt the only thing to do was to break the engagement. He was terribly upset when he left and I have not heard from him since." Counselor expressed her sympathy and her regret that there had to be so much suffering for Miss X and Mr. Y.

Miss X then said that she was here because she was so worried about Mr. Y who she hoped might feel like continuing to get help for himself. She believed he would have great difficulty in doing this. She wondered whether she should write him and suggest this. She went on to say that she felt as if there had been a death. For weeks and months she had been thinking one way (toward marriage and that kind of future); now, this was gone, and Y with it. Counselor agreed with her that it was like a death from her point of view. Miss X commented that in a way it was a relief to know that it was settled. The uncertainty of last week had been pretty awful. Spoke of how wonderful her family had been in backing her up and in understanding.

Counselor then said that she would be glad to write Mr. Y stating that Miss X had told her of the present situation and indicating Counselor's interest in talking with Mr. Y further if he felt it might be of any help. Miss X seemed very appreciative. She discussed her plans for the summer. Should she or should she not return to the resort where both her family and Mr. Y's have outings, where they had had such a good time last summer? She thought she should not run away from this. Counselor agreed that she wouldn't want to run away, but raised the question as to whether such associations at the present time might not simply reopen old wounds, and if Mr. Y had not made any more moves by that time, it might interject something quite artificial to be there together. They perhaps would drift back into the same feelings without any more possibility of resolution than at present.

Counselor asked about her plans for next winter, and raised the question of undertaking something quite new and different in which she could lose herself and which had a future to relate to. Miss X responded to this understandingly and enthusiastically. She was thinking of graduate work and not living at home and she felt she would definitely want to develop new activities. She thanked Counselor for all her help and again expressed the strong hope that Mr. Y might return; asking Counselor, "Please let me know if you hear from Y." Counselor said that she would unless Mr. Y objected.

A letter subsequently written to Mr. Y telling of Miss X's last visit and suggesting he come for another conference was not answered. A second letter (two weeks later) was written in regard to the two books which he had borrowed. These were subsequently returned, with no comment.

A letter from Miss X's father expressing great appreciation was received a few days later.

Conclusion: This case illustrates a type of premarital counseling where one partner is unsure of his willingness to enter marriage. Through the permissiveness, and the neutrality of the counselor, Mr. Y was able to see his own feelings more clearly and to realize that marriage per se was not for him at this point. Miss X, a mature, sensitive, and highly intelligent person was aided through counseling, to accept and understand Mr. Y's attitudes and limitations, and thus was spared the bitterness such an unhappy experience might entail. She also came to realize the validity of her own needs.

Follow-Up: *Three months* later, Miss X saw Mr. Y at the summer resort. Her father reported to C that he felt Mr. Y was much the same as before, looking well and apparently doing very well in his work. He was accompanied by his mother. Nothing evolved from the meeting and Miss X realized that nothing ever would.

Six months later, Miss X wrote that she had a very interesting new job.

Three years later, Miss X wrote of her engagement to a "brilliant man," two years older than herself and currently holding an excellent position in another city in a field congenial to Miss X. They were completely sure of their feelings and "looking forward to marriage early." They both wanted literature which would be helpful in terms of the physical adjustment and wished referral for reliable child-spacing information. Miss X ended her letter as follows:

I have been continually grateful to you for helping me through my former "crisis." Because of your help, I feel that I came out of it with greater understanding of why people react as they do and with more rather than less confidence in myself. All this in turn has undoubtedly helped me to understand what values are important in life. . . . Thank you for your part in this.

Another six months later, a wedding invitation was received.

Two years later, an announcement of the first baby and a letter from Miss (now Mrs.) X's father following a visit to his daughter and son-in-law. He described them as "radiantly happy," having "a lovely home" and being "extraordinarily congenial."

EDITOR'S NOTE: Over and beyond general interest in the case, from a technical point of view, two points will be of special interest to professional workers in the field: the counselor's accepting, unpressuring, sympathetic role in dealing with Mr. Y's initial reluctance to participate in counseling; and the follow-up, spanning five years. It tempts one to quote directly from the last letter of appreciation received from Miss X's father:

I suppose you marriage counselors cannot keep in touch with your boys and girls the way a minister who marries them does, but there must be many all over the country who feel as my daughter does.

CASE 23

Problem: A fiancée's uncertainty and conflict about going through with marriage

Presented by: Clinical psychologist (Ph.D.) in private practice in large city

Subjects: Miss Winston, age 25, and Mr. Evans, age 30, are attractive, intelligent, but rather inarticulate and indwelling persons who came to the "Big City" from a small town four months ago. They became informally engaged just before leaving home, after having gone together for about a year.

Referral: By former clients of the counselor. Mr. Evans had told these friends only that he was "perplexed about what is happening—or what is not happening" to their engagement and that he felt they needed some professional advice.

Background: Both are only children of conservative, moderately religious parents, from comfortable, economically secure, rather sheltering homes. Although the families have known each other for years, the young people did not have an opportunity to become well acquainted until after the completion of their education. Each has attended select, noncoeducational preparatory schools, she as a day student in her home town; he in a large New England boarding school. Each had also made an excellent record at college. She studied creative writing and contemporary literature at a small woman's college near home and then secured a job as assistant editor of the women's page on a local newspaper. He completed a university engineering course with a record which won him a promising job with a large construction firm. After service as an ROTC lieutenant with the Corps of Engineers, he was assigned by his firm to a construction project near home.

In exploring this background, it became evident that Mr. Evans' social experience has been more limited than that of the young lady. He states that he knows nothing about women; Miss Winston is the only person in whom he has been seriously interested. There were opportunities for only casual dating during his army service, and academic requirements and sports consumed all his time and interest during college and prep school. Throughout his boyhood and during his vacations he enjoyed a close relationship with his father, a successful building contractor, and they spent their time together on fishing, hunting, and camping expeditions, in which the mother often joined. The family did little entertaining, and he believes that the satisfying, close-knit family life diminshed the need for outside social experience. Just since his attachment to Miss Winston—"or rather since these perplexities have developed"—has he become concerned over his limited experience with the opposite sex and his need "to learn to understand women." A careful review of his background, however, reveals nothing to raise doubts as to the normality of his psychosexual development or the wholesomeness of his heterosexual attitudes.

Miss Winston, the daughter of a prominent lawyer, comes from a family which has led a more active social life. During her school years she had dated "every nice young man in the small community except Mr. Evans." She denies any prior emotional attachments, however, and states that she was always able to keep her relations with boys "under control" in order not to interfere with her greater interests in her studies, her family, and her plans to become a writer. Soon after she began dating with Mr. Evans, however, she became aware that she "was more interested in him and marriage than in a professional career." She blames herself, in his presence, for their many misunderstandings; she "went into her shell" often because he did not seem to show the intense interest in her that other boys had, nor did he insist that she date him exclusively. It hurt her pride that for almost a year she never felt sure where she stood with him, whereas with other boys she had to develop considerable skill in restraining their advances and putting aside their proposals. When Mr. Evans' firm gave him a promotion and decided to transfer him, he abruptly proposed, and urged her to come East with him. She accepted and quit her job without hesitation, although she recalls that the idea of leaving home and coming to the city frightened her considerably. Fortunately, she found a nice place to live with a girl she had known casually at home, and during her first week found "a very interesting but not important job with a magazine."

Immediate Problem: In the initial interview (both present), Mr. Evans stated bluntly that he hoped the counselor could clear up his fiancée's doubts and fears about marriage, which he had failed to do despite the fact that both feel they are very much in love. He would like to get married as soon as she is ready, but because her "vague uncertainties" have been increasing ever since they came East, they have not been able to start making the necessary arrangements for the wedding, such as setting dates, looking for an apartment, or selecting essential furniture. Miss Winston interjected that she had come for help willingly —in fact, although Mr. Evans had initiated the consultation, she was just as eager as he because she had read magazine articles on marriage counseling, and it seemed intelligent to get help. She hoped the counselor could tell them if they were "incompatible and should not marry." She also hoped the counselor could tell them "what to do about setting the date for announcing the engagement and how long after that to set the wedding date." When asked why she felt the counselor could help on that, she said, "Well, I hope you can find out what is the matter with me—how long it will take—how long we should delay the marriage because of it."

Exploration of the Problem: In the first interview with Miss Winston alone, she said she was aware that she might have given the impression during the joint conference that she was hoping the counselor would advise postponing or even calling off the marriage. She is not sure that this was not her hope, but she is sure that she loves her fiancé and that he loves her. When he proposed, however, and wanted to get married at once, their relationship changed: she became frightened at the idea of setting even a tentative date for their marriage, and even of announcing their engagement. She has become "moody and difficult" and is full of worries and doubts about herself which she finds hard to explain.

At first she thought they must not do anything definite until they knew each other better, but they have not been making any progress toward better understanding. He is confused because there is nothing he is worried about and would be willing to get married tomorrow. Because of "this thing, these fear states" which bother her—something which she cannot define or expect him to understand—she even wonders if she should marry anyone.

After good rapport had been established, she brought up three things which worry her:

1. General fatigue which has persisted since a severe attack of virus pneumonia two months before leaving home. She had always enjoyed good health and energy, and was annoyed that she could not return to work as quickly as she had expected. She was in especially poor health during the period of uncertainty over whether Mr. Evans was going to propose before leaving for New York.

2. A tactless remark made by a nurse during her illness, to the effect that there was nothing wrong with her and that what she needed was a psychiatrist, not medicine.

3. A brief homosexual episode in early adolescence. She has mentioned all these things but not her feelings about them to Mr. Evans and he seems to dismiss them as unimportant. At least they have not changed his evident willingness to get married at once.

Added to these specific worries are some rather vague insecurities; she and her fiancé do not seem to communicate effectively; they can now be together only on week ends since he has to live on a construction project; she finds it hard to adjust to living away from home for the first time, particularly in a large city; she misses the emotional support of her family, particularly the father with whom she has always been very close; and lastly, "with no actual experience" she wonders if either of them knows enough about sex relations.

Diagnosis: The first problem was to decide whether there is evidence of a chronic neurosis in which intensive psychotherapy is indicated to uncover deeply repressed materials; or whether the difficulty, however acute, is one that is temporary and situational, and therefore suitable for treatment on a conscious, marriage counseling level. Evaluation of the background materials and further exploration of the current worries, appeared to justify the latter conclusion. The three principal worries are clearly interrelated. The nurse's remark that she needed psychiatric treatment was a great shock to her, and has caused her to worry about her continuing "tired feelings." She went to her roommate's physician just before coming to the counselor. This general practitioner gave her a thorough examination and assured her that her condition was a normal one after such a severe illness. After she became engaged "so suddenly" and decided to leave home for the first time, her recall of the nurse's remark precipitated her anxiety over the homosexual relationship ten years before. This was a not unusual episode in which a girl of thirteen found herself the passive participant in an affair with a greatly admired seventeen-year-old who was staying with her over a week end during an absence of the parents. She thinks it is peculiar that she knew nothing of sex until this occurrence. Whatever her parents had tried to teach her, or she had heard at school, had made no impression on her. Because she had never heard of such things before, and was sworn to secrecy by the older girl, she assumed at once that it was wrong. She suffered intense guilt feelings, probably because the experience was pleasurable.

After several days of silent concern, she was asked by her father what was wrong and she told him all about it. He must have handled it constructively, since she recalls that he did not reprimand her and relieved her guilty feelings by indicating that her reactions were natural since she was "not a little girl any longer" and that she must talk to her mother about her physical development. She recalls also that she resolved she would never get involved in another affair like this, and was careful to avoid the other girl from then on. After the discussions with her parents she believes she seldom thought about this episode again. Her manner of handling this material during the interview, and the fact that she had already told Mr. Evans about it, indicate that it had not been repressed. During her casual attachments to many boys, there have been mild intimacies, but her straightforward discussion of her subjective reactions to these, and to her present feelings for Mr. Evans indicates that there is no reason to doubt the adequacy of her sexual development and heterosexual attitudes.

Although her recent concern made it seem advisable to deal with this adolescent episode first, her developmental history was thoroughly explored. At no point was there any emotional blockage or resistance. In the past there have been no psychosomatic symptoms nor psychoneurotic traits. She has had no serious frustrations or deprivations and no periods of moodiness or anxiety. Although she has always had a steady flow of love and affection from her parents, she believes when she thinks about them now that their relationship with each other always came first. She is sure that it never occurred to her to try to play one against the other; although they always had many independent interests and activities, and even were active in opposition political parties, they appeared always to be in agreement in their reactions to her. She never doubted that they were happy together, nor that they were greatly in love. She realizes that hers was a fortunate upbringing, in a sheltering home, but she does not believe she was ever spoiled. Nor does she recall ever feeling that she was not living up to her parents' expectations. She knows that they were proud of her consistently successful school work and glad that she was fairly popular with both boys and girls.

During this discussion, she began to wonder if the realization of what a wonderful home life she had enjoyed—about which she thought little before leaving home—had not made her worry over the fear that she and Mr. Evans might not be able to do as well in building their relationship as her own parents had done.

From the beginning, her parents have accepted Mr. Evans wholeheartedly. Whenever she has thought about how much she would like to have her father to turn to with her present problems, she realizes she would be embarrassed because her parents would be so surprised that there have been any difficulties.

Treatment: As usual, the separation of diagnosis and treatment, which makes for clarity in the presentation of case materials, was not possible nor desirable in the counseling relationship. Several interrelated treatment objectives were formulated in the initial interviews and utilized whenever the emotional climate of the counseling relationship seemed appropriate. Four of these objectives were as follows:

1. To encourage each to face the rather enigmatic and inarticulate personality he presented to the other, and to help both to understand the influence in the development of their indwelling and somewhat inhibited natures of their unusually satisfying and definitely sheltering homes. Miss Winston was already aware that she was overly dependent on her family. Mr. Evans said he had been somewhat concerned about his inflexibility and social exclusiveness. He had long felt that although socially acceptable and respected by his associates, he had had few warm relationships with contemporaries. He had tried to rationalize his peripheral social status by assuring himself that by nature he did not need a lot of friends; but he at once admitted that he had always hoped that no one would realize what a "lone wolf" he really was. Because of their mutual regard, intelligence, good taste, and similar backgrounds, marriage could in time become a solacing refuge and develop great mutual dependence. Being perceptive, however, and not without humor, they agreed that they wanted their marriage not to provide a refuge, but to further the extension and enrichment of their personalities not only for their own sakes but in the interests of the children they looked forward to having.

2. To give Miss Winston opportunity to verbalize and objectively face all her recent fears and insecurities, and assess them against the many constructive factors in her background. She was encouraged to relive in the interview situation her anxieties during the weeks when she felt that the desired proposal was not coming, her exhilaration and the romantic hopes that soared when he did propose just before his date of departure, and then the self-doubts that assailed her during her initial loneliness in the big city as she brooded upon the nurse's remarks and her continuing fatigue. She was induced to face realistically the marked contrasts between her home life in a small town and her first experience away from home in the noisy bustle and impersonal atmosphere of a great city. It was not surprising that Mr. Evans was unable to reassure her, since they could not see a great deal of each other, and their past relationship now seemed inadequate. When she recalled in the interview the misunderstandings before their engagement, they all appeared to be minor, specific, and understandable. Both he and she had been obviously defensive in the fear that the other might not care enough. They actually knew little of each other. Although they had gone to parties, shows, dances and athletic events together, there had been no sharing of significant activities or personal problems through which to build understanding. Each had been extremely inarticulate and had kept his insecurities largely to himself. Nor was it surprising that she could not utilize constructively the favorable report by the doctor to whom she went for a general check-up. She told him nothing about her emotional states, and when he told her that the continuing fatigue was natural after her illness and that there was nothing wrong with her physically, this increased the fears precipitated by the nurse that there might be something wrong with her.

During the second interview, she admitted that the fatigue had diminished, and when it was brought up again at the end of the counseling relationship she realized that she had "rather suddenly ceased to think about it." It was possible to date this change as having occurred immediately after the attempt to relieve her resurrected guilt over the homosexual episode in adolescence.

In the permissive atmosphere of the discussion of the sex problem, she raised several questions about this aspect of marriage. Her meager information in this area, and her lack of experience suggest that she has had less preoccupation with sex than most girls. This is not unusual in the light of her upbringing and the superficial inhibitions of her ever "proper" fiancé. As indicated above, however, nothing was revealed to cast doubt on the normality of her sex needs, reactions, or heterosexual attitudes. This was later confirmed by a gynecologist to whom she was referred just before marriage, because she felt it was intelligent to have a pelvic examination and to secure instruction on birth control.

3. To develop Miss Winston's insight about her dependency on the home, and particularly her strong attachment to her father, in the hope of preventing interference with the marriage adjustment.

She was able to agree readily that her warm, confiding relationship with her father had much to do with her ability to handle her dating relationships with boys during school years. Though she always hoped for marriage, she began during her college years to doubt if she would ever meet a young man as attractive as her father. She had a brief "crush" on one middle-aged professor of journalism, but her parents laughed at her for picking someone so safely unavailable.

She was less able to accept, however, the suggestion that her emotional dependency on her father may have been a factor that interfered with the progress of her relationship with Mr. Evans and made their marriage something of a threat to her. This resistance appeared to dissolve somewhat when she was led to relive their early misunderstandings and her recent conflicts. She conceded that she had been silently making unjustifiable comparisons of him with her father at some points.

This insight on an intellectual level began to be converted into emotional change when several instances were pointed out in which she had sought to use the middle-aged counselor as a father substitute. One such instance was her initial expectation that the counselor should set the date for the announcement of the engagement and the wedding, matters which she agreed she would have left to the father had he been available or had she not come to the counselor. Throughout the first interview her participation took the form of asking for information and direct advice. In the conferences alone, she realized that she talked more freely than she did when Mr. Evans was present or they were alone together. She recalled also that she had always talked more freely to older men.

4. To foster improvement in these young persons' techniques of interpersonal relations and mutual understanding. Such improvement seemed essential to the accomplishment of smooth adjustment to the demands of marriage for shared living, since their self-contained attitudes toward each other threatened continued ego-clashes in spite of—or perhaps because of—their superior intelligence and past achievements. Although perceptive and sensitive individually, when seen together they were not only somewhat inarticulate but decidedly lacking in empathy.

It was hoped that progress toward this treatment objective might be achieved incidental to the discussion of a number of engagement and marriage problems. For this purpose the last four conferences were conducted with both present. Since each has been successful in school and never ill at ease in class, these conferences in the beginning were conducted somewhat like class discussions with the counselor serving as discussion leader or moderator. The problems on which their views were drawn out were in the area of homemaking, decoration, family financing, social activities, child care, and of course sex relations—problems on which, excepting the last, one or the other had definite views, but on which there had been little sharing of subjective reactions. Only on religion and recreations—reading, music, and sports—had they arrived at prior understanding and acceptance of each other's preferences.

In the beginning of this experiment, each tended to "recite" his views independently, politely ignore any differences and expect the counselor to express expert judgments or fatherly authority. Of course the counselor resisted the attempts to put him in these roles, which seemed more obvious in these joint sessions than in the individual conferences. By the counselor's questions as to their feelings and frequent restatements, he confirmed his conviction that many seeming disagreements were essentially failures to understand due to differences in points of reference. As they became more interested in the discussion, rapport improved; and warm deference and even some gayety took the place of reserve and mild ego-sensitivity on the part of each. It was clear that this progress continued outside the counseling sessions, when they agreed that they felt much better about their relationship, although they were not sure what was helping.

In the final conference the counselor assumed a definitely directive role. He pointed out that as was to be expected from their similar backgrounds, temperaments, and standards of value, there were no serious disagreements even on many matters they had previously not felt free to discuss. Furthermore, they had each begun to look at the matters under discussion first from the viewpoint of the other; they were learning to be empathetic. They obviously enjoyed the process and sensed the keener satisfaction of emotional sharing in contrast to mere intellectual reaction. They came to agree that with understanding based upon empathy and mutual respect, agreement or disagreement was relatively less important. As a parting thrust, they stated that they had announced their engagement and ordered the wedding invitations without the aid of the counselor. They also hoped that he would not develop an anxiety state if his bill for the eight conferences was not paid until the first pay day after the honeymoon. This was gratifyingly empathetic.

Follow-Up Contacts: In addition to the favorable report from the gynecologist, noted above, a telephone call from Miss Winston, just after this examination, expressed relief that no new problems had been encountered. She said that the arrangements for the wedding were progressing smoothly and that they are now enjoying their engagement.

A short letter from them on their wedding trip sounded carefree and cordial. After their return Mr. Evans made a promised call. He is confident that the marriage is a success and that they are extremely happy. He attributes this mainly to their care in always taking each other's feelings into account. This, together with their need of affection which he now feels is greater than that of most people, has resulted in satisfactory sex adjustment despite their lack of previous experience. They feel that this phase of their relationship developed more smoothly because they did not need to utilize contraceptive precautions, having decided that they would just as soon have their first child early in marriage. His wife has decided to continue at her magazine job as long as it doesn't interfere with home life, but that she really has no ambition for a professional career. He hopes however that she will want to maintain her interest in writing, even after she quits her job.

He states that he is glad that through the counseling conferences he learned to express his feelings. He also said one thing that had not been mentioned before, that he had been somewhat jealous of the young lady's father. Most important of all, however, was his growing understanding of his wife's nature.

CASE 24

Problem: Postponement of marriage because of fiancé's job
     uncertainty
Presented by: Counselor (M.A. in Social Work) in a marriage
     counseling agency located in a large city

Introduction: Miss X was referred by the head of a social
agency, her personal friend. The latter described Miss X as very
uneasy about coming to the agency because of her previous
unhappy marriage and her mother's pushing her to get counseling. The problem apparently consisted mainly of her mother's
concern over certain aspects of the engagement, rather than any
concern Miss X herself recognized, and her friend felt it would
take skill to help her see she could get something out of counseling.

The Problem as Presented by the Client: Miss X and her fiancé
in their late 30's had been engaged a year. They had called off
their wedding plans at the last minute several times because of
uncertainty in Mr. Z's job situation. Miss X was a successful
free-lance writer and teacher, while Mr. Z was trying, in the
face of considerable difficulty due to postwar shortage, to establish his own business. At each change in plans, Miss X's mother
became very disturbed and raised questions about the relationship, which in turn upset Miss X. Miss X understood her fiancé's
fear of unemployment and of her having to support both, though
she was willing to take this chance and wanted to go ahead with
marriage in spite of it. She felt she had made this amply clear
and was trying to avoid putting any pressure on him. She had
confidence in his abilities, was sure he could get a job elsewhere
but sympathized with his reluctance to give up his line of work,
in which he had already achieved a good deal of status over a
period of years.

Miss X's mother had other objections to Mr. Z, especially that he wasn't a professional man. Her mother was also concerned over her remarrying because of the unhappy first marriage. Though Miss X admitted there had been serious sex difficulties in the first marriage and she was still uneasy about sex, she was evidently reluctant to pursue the subject. She insisted she was completely satisfied with all aspects of her relationship to her fiancé and concerned only about whether they should marry soon in spite of the financial circumstances and, if so, how to reach a decision. With a little help, though, she realized that her most acute problem was with her mother, and she discussed her resentment of her mother's domination and yet her need to maintain a close relationship.

The Counseling: Before seeing Miss X for her first interview I had some picture of her and her fiancé through the questionnaire she was asked to fill out in the waiting room prior to counseling (a routine agency procedure). These showed she was an only child, her father a professional man. She was a college graduate, an active Protestant, participated in all types of social activities, especially artistic and professional. She described herself as very happy during her teens with many friends of both sexes, her parents as very happily married, warmly affectionate and demonstrative with each other. She had been divorced after four years of marriage, the divorce occurring several years prior to the start of this counseling contact. Mr. Z had a number of brothers and sisters, and his father owned a small business. In the interview Miss X described her fiancé's family as having little money but considerable social status. Mr. Z was also Protestant, but not active, and had had the same amount of education as Miss X. They had known each other two years before engagement, confided in each other about most things, were each satisfied with their frequent demonstration of affection, shared most of their interests and activities together and had no disagreements. They agreed by mutual give-and-take, and she was very confident their marriage would be happy.

First Interview—Premarital: Miss X, very attractive and well-dressed in a simple sporty style, was poised and friendly from the outset of the interview. She admitted immediately her doubt about needing help and said she was here mainly to placate her mother. I accepted this feeling and encouraged her to tell me how she felt about her engagement. She easily launched into describing her fiancé's business difficulties, on which she blamed her mother's concern. I reacted mainly with interest and recognition of how difficult the situation was for both Miss X and her fiancé.

Miss X said that marriage now would not change things too much for them, except that she "could sleep with him in ———" (about 100 miles away, where he was living and working). At present he visits her week ends. Mr. Z stays at her apartment, which she feels quite guilty about as it is entirely contrary to her upbringing; however, it seems foolish for him to spend his money to stay at a hotel, and she feels that how she conducts herself is her own business. Again I did little in this part of the interview except to accept Miss X's feelings. (Although she said nothing indicating they were having sex relations, she spoke so feelingly about her guilt, that I got the impression this was what she meant. This proved not to be the case.)

She went on to tell of her mother's other objections to Mr. Z, but throughout contrasted her own feelings with her mother's and maintained how sure she felt of her love for him and of their future happiness. Her mother stresses the difference in their backgrounds and the fact that Mr. Z has no profession. For the first time Miss X mentioned her first husband, whom her mother liked only because of his profession. Miss X described her fiancé's family very appreciatively, saying how well she gets along with them and their easygoing way of life.

One reason Miss X's mother is so concerned about her remarrying is that her first marriage broke up over a sex problem. Quite calmly, but with obvious feeling, Miss X told me how painful the experience of her first marriage was. She described her husband as "frigid," but throughout the marriage and until she got help later she felt she was at fault and was abnormal. She lived with him only a year, as he was overseas for three years. His letters grew colder and eventually he wrote he did not love her and never had. This hurt tremendously, and she began divorce proceedings. He left her with no money at all, which she still feels bitter about, although not so much as her mother, who uses this in arguing about Mr. Z's financial status.

During the divorce Miss X had helpful discussions with her doctor and her minister, which convinced her the sex problem was her husband's. She feels she has worked this through. Miss X said this with so much finality that I hesitated to pursue the subject further. I tried to keep it open by referring to her indication on the engagement questionnaire that she anticipates sex relations in marriage with mixed feelings. I asked if this is related to her experience in her first marriage. She supposed it is and said she has "butterflies" when looking forward to married sex life. Because I had the impression that she and her fiancé were having sex relations, and in hopes of getting her to discuss her present sex behavior without asking about it directly, I asked whether or not she had had enough experience with her fiancé to give her some feeling about how sex would work out. She very definitely said they had not and quickly went on to state that all in all she feels very satisfied about her relationship with her fiancé, that she is ready for marriage, and has conquered the problems of the past.

She and her fiancé talk everything over with complete freedom, which she feels is very important and a complete contrast with her first marriage. Her fiancé knows all about her first experience and has been considerate in not pressing for sex relations. They have discussed sex and he knows how she feels. I agreed that being able to talk things over so comfortably is one of the basic essentials in marriage. (At this point it seemed evident that Miss X didn't want to discuss her feelings about sex further and would resent any more exploration. There was obviously a problem in this area, but since she didn't seem to want help with it I felt it best to support her feeling that they would be able to work things out.) I asked if she would be interested in a pamphlet on sex, showed her *Marriage and Sexual Harmony*,[1] which she hadn't seen before. She bought it.

I commented that she did seem sure of her feelings and it seemed what she needed most was some moral support in working things out with her mother. Although Miss X loves and respects her mother, their relationship has always been stormy and they "pick at each other." Her minister advised her to leave home and completely sever the bond. However, she feels there must be some way she can be more independent and yet preserve their relationship and the fun they have together. I supported this and suggested she might confide less in her mother. She thought this a very good point, has already made some gain in avoiding discussion of her finances. She admitted that she tends to share everything with her mother and that this naturally leads her mother to express her opinion. Her fiancé helps her to hold her own and in some ways she feels almost as if she is marrying him for this support. She has thought of marrying secretly but this would disappoint her as well as her parents.

In ending the interview Miss X asked if I felt the financial difficulties were important. I felt they were only if they seemed so to either her or her fiancé. Since she feels sure that he can get a good job, I wondered if she could help bolster his confidence in that, rather than stress her willingness to marry him in spite of the uncertainty. She felt this was a helpful suggestion.

We discussed fees and on the scale she chose one slightly more than the minimum for her salary. I hoped she would feel

[1] By Oliver M. Butterfield (New York: Emerson Books, Inc., 1950, rev. ed.).

free to get in touch with me if she felt it might help to talk things over further. She replied, "If I have any more trouble with mother, I'll come screaming here so fast." She did not plan to tell her fiancé about coming to the agency, for fear it would upset him.

Follow-Up: Four months later, I wrote Miss X asking how things were going and saying I had neglected to mention our premarital service as a possibility for both her and her fiancé. She answered in a long letter thanking me for my interest and telling of her marriage plans. The problem of her parents' attitude had been overcome and they all had paid a very successful visit to her fiancé and his family. Everyone had gotten along very well, and as a result Miss X felt like "an entirely different person." She had received a promotion which made it possible for her to live in ———, after marriage, and commute.

I wrote thanking Miss X for her letter and expressing my pleasure at her news. I hoped she would let me know her new address after marriage so I could send her the marriage adjustment questionnaire which I had previously explained was part of the agency's usual procedure in premarital counseling and which helped in evaluating the service.

A few months later, Miss X, now Mrs. Z, wrote about how happy her marriage was and that her parents were pleased too. She still had a problem with her mother, but her husband was helping her with it. She would be glad to fill out any questionnaires. The doctor I had referred her to was "excellent . . . thorough, very explicit, and easy to understand."

Later, I sent Mrs. Z the marriage adjustment questionnaire, mentioning another one on sex adjustment which she could go over with me in a personal interview in our office. I said this would be free of charge as a regular part of our counseling service and would give her the opportunity to bring up any questions she might want to discuss.

Second Interview—Postmarital: Mrs. Z came in by appointment, friendly, immediately making it clear that she was very happy and satisfied with her marriage. Her completed questionnaire described the marriage as very happy for both with mutual give-and-take and no disagreements. She had checked positive answers on all aspects of the marriage.

She had finally decided not to ask her husband to fill out questionnaires, which I had enclosed in case he might be interested. Although she wanted to co-operate in every way possible with the agency, she had never told him of her premarital visit, feeling it might disturb him to realize she had had doubts before marriage. I accepted this, agreeing it might not be wise to tell him since everything now was working out so well.

Mr. Z's business had not worked out well and he had a low-paying temporary job. She had been doing very well and getting public recognition for her work. In spite of the contrast she felt her husband was very proud of her and not resentful of her job. The financial difficulties seemed unimportant as their marriage had been so happy.

Mrs. Z remarked on my (the counselor's) pregnancy and said they would like to start a family next fall. She wondered if she is getting too old. We discussed the matter of decreasing fertility especially after thirty-five, and older parents in relation to bringing up of their children. I felt the success of this depended on the individual couple and their flexibility.

Mrs. Z was enthusiastic about her wedding, which her parents attended, having accepted the marriage completely. She described how her husband is helping her with the continuing problem of her mother's domination. He doesn't get mad, but takes a firm stand when her mother tries to interfere with their plans. She wondered how things would work out on a contemplated visit to her family. Her husband wants to keep it short, but she wants to stay longer and is thinking of going ahead of him. We discussed briefly some of the problems involved in going home, especially where one's parents have been dominating. I felt one inevitably falls back into some of the old patterns.

Mrs. Z suggested doing the sex adjustment questionnaire. I encouraged her questions. Mrs. Z had stated that she had orgasm about half the time and the definiteness with which she said "orgasm always by penetration," made me wonder whether she felt rather rigid about any other means. I commented on the fact that orgasm by other means is quite common, explaining to her question what was meant by this and stressing that manual stimulation is frequently a very natural way for the woman to obtain orgasm where timing has not worked out so that she can have orgasm at the same time as her husband. Mrs. Z seemed interested in my remarks and said she and her husband do have discussions about what is right and wrong in sex behavior. When we got to questions about what their sex activity includes, Mrs. Z admitted her mixed feelings about sex play.

When I wondered why she felt this way, she did not know, said her upbringing was not particularly puritanical on this point. The only thing she could think of was that during high school sex scarcely entered her mind as she was occupied with other activities, and even in college she was very little interested in necking or petting. Her sex interest was aroused all at once in her first marriage and then completely rebuffed by her husband, which she feels got her pretty mixed up. It is about sex play that she and Mr. Z have discussed rightness and wrongness, and she feels that she is gradually changing. She asked some questions about oral contact and in this connection I commented that although fewer couples do this than have other types of sex activity, it is not unusual for educated people as a part of human sex behavior, provided it is desired by both partners and not enjoyed to the exclusion of intercourse.

Mrs. Z reported no difficulties in their sex adjustment except a slight problem in early marriage of her husband having orgasm too quickly. As their adjustment has become more established he has gained better control. I stressed the fact that almost every sex adjustment takes time to establish, that flexibility is important, and that frequent simultaneous orgasm is rare. Mrs. Z seemed very relieved, had wondered about this and also whether it is natural for her to feel sometimes that she doesn't want any more sex play even though she has not had orgasm. It disturbs her husband, who feels he is not being fair to her. I said if she is no longer desirous, it is perfectly natural, and that sometimes orgasm may be less definite and exciting than at other times and still release the tension. She is sure this applies to her, and was pleased to feel that she is quite normal. At this point she decided she wanted to talk all this over with her husband and began to think of how she might tell him she had been for counseling. We discussed this briefly, with my suggesting that she could stress the premarital preparation aspects of her first interview, since she did get a referral to a doctor and bought the pamphlet, which her husband has read too. I felt she could discuss it with him without going into the doubts she had had. She felt quite excited about telling him of this discussion.

She talked briefly about how helpful her experience with the doctor was, her satisfaction with the diaphragm, about using it during menstruation.

Evaluation: In the premarital interview I felt I had to move very slowly because of Miss X's initial resistance. It was clear she had a good many problems but I felt I had to let her use the interview entirely in her own way. Therefore, I was more passive than I might otherwise have been in exploring her situation and bringing out the problem areas. I hoped to gain her confidence so that she would return for further discussion if she wanted it. She began with a polite sort of friendliness and a somewhat superficial and defensive discussion of her problems, ended by being able to express her hostility against her mother. I believe the discussion helped her to accept these negative feelings and contributed to her plans for working out a more independent relationship. Although there were potential marriage problems—sex, finances, and careers, and feelings carried over from her first marriage, I felt the problem with her mother was uppermost and all she was ready to use help with at the time. It was hard to evaluate her relationship with her fiancé because of her defensiveness against her mother's criticism. On the surface it appeared as if they had the ingredients for a happy marriage, but the issue was clouded.

In her second interview, after marriage, Miss X had none of the earlier resistance, although she seemed a little shy in discussing sex. This time I was much more active in initiating discussion and attempting to bring out her feelings. She seemed quite uninformed about sex, in spite of the counseling she had had at the time of her divorce, and now apparently welcomed the opportunity to discuss the subject. The discussion seemed reassuring and resolved some of her more inhibiting attitudes.

CASE 25

Problem: A (not so) young man's indecision regarding marriage

Presented by: Counselor (Ph.D. in Sociology) in the marriage counseling service of an educational institution located in a large Midwestern city

Introduction: In a college evening course in Family Relations, Mr. B heard about the school's marriage counseling service and called for an appointment.

At the in-take interview, at which he arrived ten minutes early, Mr. B was extremely tense. He raised questions about the items on the routine questionnaire he was asked to fill out. He wanted to know if he could read the case write-ups before they went into the files; he was told that no write-ups would be made until he felt ready to permit them. (At the third interview he joked about this hesitancy and said he didn't care if notes or even tape recordings were made.) He discussed the fee at some length with the counselor (it was a very small one and his income was quite adequate). This was the last time he ever mentioned the fee, and his bill was always paid promptly.

Mr. B dressed very well and very conservatively for his interviews. He was a man in his late thirties, not handsome, but pleasant-looking; due to his curly hair and round face he seemed slightly feminine in appearance. He had a full-time job as a minor executive with a small business firm; he took an occasional college evening course.

The counselee said that his problem was whether or not to marry his girl friend. He did not care to elaborate on this during the first interview, but used his time (other than for the items mentioned above) to question the counselor about the nature of premarital counseling. He seemed to the counselor to be asking for assurance that he could use the counseling only for what he wanted it used. He seemed assured by the end of the hour, and raised some question concerning whether he should wait a full week before returning. (It was necessary from the counselor's standpoint, however, to wait a week for the next meeting.)

The Problem: During the eight following interviews, Mr. B elaborated on his simple statement of his problem: to marry or not to marry. At the end of the second interview he took a big breath and said the problem was raised because he had been enjoying sexual relations with his girl friend and that should mean that he should marry her—but still he didn't want to marry her. In the next interview he said that he didn't want to marry her because she was such a different kind of person from what he had always wanted to marry: by this he meant that she was from a working-class family, Catholic, and a rather leftish Democrat. This all produced a kind of behavior which was in conflict with the conservative, elegant wife-as-hostess-to-business-associates role he looked for in a future spouse. To complicate matters, he said that he felt guilty about having such snobbish ideas, and also that he *did* want to marry the girl but felt he *shouldn't* want to marry her.

Also in the third interview, Mr. B first struck a theme which he repeated many other times thereafter: *Why* wasn't he married at his age? Was there something wrong with him? Was he normal?

In the fourth interview Mr. B told about some symptoms he had recently acquired: inability to sleep, headaches, lack of appetite, "wild" sexual dreams, and lack of interest in the one thing which had never before failed to interest him—his job.

The Counseling: Six of the post-intake interviews with Mr. B were set up for an hour and a half each; this was longer than the usual interview in this counseling setting, but fitted the counselee's method of operation well (he was slow in starting each interview, but worked very hard and wanted to accomplish a lot once he got going.) The other two sessions dealt with tests administered by a clinical psychologist (see below).

The counselee structured the first interviews himself—elaborating his statement of the problem(s), supplying what he felt to be pertinent material about himself, asking the counselor questions, trying to see if the counselor would decide whether the marriage should take place or not. At about the fourth interview, the counselor assumed a more directive role. The counselor asked for information *he* felt might help him understand Mr. B. Also, he made some tentative interpretations of the behavior Mr. B had related. Further, he encouraged Mr. B not only to discuss what he felt like discussing, but to describe the *feelings* he associated with these events, because by then it was obvious that Mr. B, a person who was filled with strong feelings about his behavior chose to discuss problems in a "factual," intellectual manner which implied that if all the facts were seen, rational decisions could be made and the mere logic of these decisions would make them acceptable to everyone.

The counselor, however, never became directive about the problem of to marry or not to marry, and Mr. B accepted the counselor's explanation that *no one* could decide that matter except the counselee himself.

As the interviews progressed, Mr. B became comfortable in them and lost his need to continually test the counselor and the counseling situation. He allowed his feelings more room in his decision making (and, as seen by his evaluation, below, *he* felt he was taking them into account *very much*), but he never really left the rational, logical plane of analysis. The counselor concluded that a dispassionate description of himself-as-object was so necessary to the counselee, that to work against this further would be either futile or dangerous. At the same time, this limited the counselor's objectives in this counseling situation.

It soon became clear that Mr. B was in many ways a "mama's boy." His strong need to be a social conformer, to take (at least openly) a conservative stand on public matters, and to "get ahead" were all traced to his close relationship with his mother. He rationalized these ideas by saying they were part of the role of a young executive in his occupation. He had been raised with the ideal of being "mature," and maturity meant acting older than one's age. He was extremely ambitious as far as his job was concerned. He saw his future as president of a company such as the one for which he worked. But he had discovered that he was unable to move ahead in this small company; and yet a jump to a large corporation—where there would be more opportunity—entailed the risk of a loss of security and status. More and more in the counseling, he discussed his job indecision rather than his marital indecision.

Catholics, liberal Democrats, and people who chewed gum

and used slang were, he felt, out of place in his business and in his middle-class community. His girl tied back to his childhood, where his father had been an unambitious workingman and his mother had used the father as an example of what the boy should not be. (Both mother and father were dead at the time of the counseling, but the mother's "presence" was still felt.) The girl, then, represented both the life he was most habituated to and the life he had rejected but was still fighting against in himself. She obviously also represented the kind of partner with whom one could enjoy sexual relations but whom one did not marry. The girl, Mr. B felt, wanted to get married; if he didn't marry her, shouldn't he break their relationship so that she could marry someone else?

Rather direct interpretation helped the counselee see the familial roots of his feelings about such seemingly isolated traits as gum chewing and voting for Democrats. He said he could understand why his own workingclass background made him reject factors in his girl and in his own background. From what followed, it would seem that understanding this helped him feel less repulsed by these factors (see "Follow-Up" below). As he told about his sexual relationship and as the counselor, again rather directly, pointed out that he would not necessarily be doing the girl a big favor either by marrying or not marrying her, he seemed far less upset by what he had termed his illicit relationship. The counselor could not personally view this relationship as any more exploitative of the girl than it was of the man; neither one could guess at this stage whether or not it would lead to marriage, and both, according to Mr. B, found the sexual behavior and the rest of the dating very satisfying.

In general, in regard to his social class snobbery, inability to make up his mind whether to marry or not, enjoyment of nonmarital sex and great occupational drive, the counselee seemed to come by the last interview to the point of saying, ". . . well, this may not be good, but it is how I am and if the world doesn't like it, that's too bad." The counselor felt surprised at the extent to which the guilt seemed, if not to dissolve, at least not to consume so much and to which the counselee could accept himself. One other thing, perhaps the most important single item, helped the counselee:

In an effort to understand the counselee better, to evaluate certain neurotic tendencies, and at the same time, if possible, to offer his assurance in the matter of the counselee's underlying fear about his normality (the exact nature of this fear never came out in the interviews, although the most obvious guess is that it was related to homosexual thoughts or actions), the counselor arranged for Mr. B to meet for two sessions with a clinical psychologist who administered the TAT and Rorschach tests. The clinician's interpretation of the tests was that although they showed considerable evidence of repression, sexual immaturity if not actual fixation, and some hint of homosexual fears, there was no concrete evidence to lead to the belief that the counselee was suffering to the point of being unable to operate effectively in a kind of life he had planned for himself. This material was interpreted for the counselee and seemed to relieve him very much.

Although no decision was made by Mr. B at the time of the last interview as to whether he should or should not marry his girl friend, he was very happy about the course the counseling had taken. He reported a loss of his physical symptoms—lack of sleep and appetite—and he reported his decision to quit his job and try for another one which had more promise. He said he thought he would marry some day, and he joked that the counselor might be surprised when and with whom.

Follow-Up: In the years following the conclusion of this case, the counselor had three chances for communication with the counselee. An appreciative Christmas card and a routine short evaluation follow-up within a few months after the case was closed merely showed that Mr. B thought the counseling had done him a lot of good; but the nature of the "good" and the sincerity of the statement were more fully understood in a more extensive follow-up four years later.

By that time, Mr. B had moved to another community, taken a better job, married (the same girl), and had a child. He reported that he was very glad he had made these major changes in his life, and he said that "the counseling was one of the important factors which equipped me to make the decisions resulting in these events."

Mr. B felt the counseling had helped because of these things: (1) It gave him the chance to discuss his problems with "an objective specialist." The counselor "listened understandingly —and I needed someone to talk with." (2) It helped him reason things through and "re-establish perspective." (3) The counselor did not "diagnose my case and present me with a solution." (4) But the counselor did ask "penetrating questions which forced my thinking into areas I had slighted." (5) The counseling "formed a sort of mirror in which I saw myself in certain particulars in a completely new way," and by knowing more about himself he felt more confident to make a move (he particularly appreciated seeing the link between present behavior and childhood home). (6) The counselor gave "straightforward answers to questions when answers were available." (7) The counseling showed that "emotions were inherent in the problems, not just intellect." (8) And it relieved his mind regarding his "normalcy."

As seen in retrospect by Mr. B, the keystone problem was the job dissatisfaction. Once he had made the decision to change jobs, he felt he could make the decision to marry. This is difficult for the counselor fully to understand, but the events were actually in that order. That is, the job-change decision *was* reached first; the change meant leaving the community and the various social pressures which worked against marriage to the girl; it included leaving the realm of his mother. The counselee also remarked that when he could accept the fact that he had to keep moving ahead on the job and could still accept the fact that he would never find the *perfect* job, he could then see the good qualities in his girl and not expect the perfect *spouse*. Later, he said, he felt *lucky* to have such a woman for a wife; he particularly appreciated her ability to enjoy life fully, something he realized he was less capable of doing.

Conclusions: No counselor should hope to accomplish major personality changes in the relatively few interviews included in the present case. From this counselor's point of view, the accomplishments of the counseling as seen by Mr. B far exceed the expectations of this type of short-term counseling. Perhaps they boil down to one accomplishment: A relatively isolated urban man found someone with whom he could discuss his problems without fear of punishment and he was able to reach decisions based on factors and forces which never became fully obvious either to him or to the counselor. In Mr. B's words: "I felt bewildered. I wondered if I could ever return to normalcy. You let me see the problems but left the solution to me. I was relieved to see myself as a normal person but one who had problems."

Therefore, if the counselee had major personality problems which evaded the personality tests he took, they were not solved by this counseling. Neither was his seemingly lifetime habit of viewing phenomena in a textbook manner (omitting the emotional dimension) really changed. And, of course, the whole matter of the girl herself remains a mystery which was not even examined. The counselor took the view of the girl as presented to him by the counselee; that view changed from the time of the interviews (and even *in* the various interviews) to the time of the postmarriage evaluation of the counseling. This certainly does not make this marriage unique. But it does mean that the counselor had to keep reminding himself that whatever the girl was like, the presenting problem in terms of marriage was with Mr. B, not with her.

EDITOR'S NOTE: One of the interesting features of this case presentation is the client's own detailed summary-in-retrospect of the effectiveness of counseling.

CASE 26

Problem: Termination of an engagement
Presented by: Psychiatric social worker (B.S.; M.A. equiv. in Social Work) in small counseling service in urban area

Description of Situation: Miss G is a very attractive, highly intelligent young woman of 23, who was referred to me by a professional colleague. The referral was precipitated by her inability to set a date for her marriage although she had known her fiancé for five years and they had been engaged for several months. Her fiancé had originally suggested that she seek counseling and she had grasped at this (although aware that in part she was using it as a delaying tactic). She was both ambivalent and anxious about really looking at own self.

She indicated that although her fiancé was a very nice person in every way and she had never met anyone who compared with him, and she did want to get married and have children, still she felt quite uncertain. It was her fiancé's pressure which resulted in the engagement at Christmas. She thinks of the many things she still wants to do and couldn't if she were married, but if her fiancé, in recognition of her feelings, suggests that they sever the relationship she becomes still more anxious and rejects this. My relationship to the fiancé's brother (he was a colleague) was clarified and discussed but she did not feel it would interfere with our working together.

The Counseling: Miss G was seen for a series of seventeen weekly sessions until her summer plans necessitated terminating the counseling. She was so caught up in the anxieties and pressures of the present situation that she found it hard to take time to fill in past relevant background material.

Family Background: *Her father,* age 56, was one of a large family. He received parochial rearing which Miss G felt tended to make him somewhat rigid. She did not feel close to him because he was never overtly demonstrative except in material ways. She would not go to him with her problems as she felt he would not be understanding. She saw him as a rather isolated person with very few friends and no hobbies. Most of his life has been centered about his work as an accountant. She had little memory of him as a child except that he frequently worked late, and constantly argued with her mother, mainly about her mother's mother who had lived with them from the time Miss G was 6. (She died two years ago.) Miss G also was aware that he usually went along with what her mother wanted till he got very mad. Then they would fight, and her mother would win out. Her basic feeling toward her father was one of feeling sorry for him. She definitely would not want his type of man for a husband.

Miss G's mother, 57, is healthy but a nervous, tense, person "who is a worrier and an arguer." She sees her as a very intelligent person who has been quite independent the past ten years by virtue of her job as an office manager. Miss G always went to her mother for advice as she knew she would be understanding and open-minded, and there could be a free emotional exchange. She saw her mother as definitely the more intelligent and more dominant of her parents. Miss G's relationship with her grandmother who her mother had insisted should live with them was a good one, and she did not feel that her presence in the home had any special effects on her except for her parents' conflicts. She was aware that her mother did not marry until after 30 and that she chose her father rather deliberately. She felt they were never really close or affectionate and that her mother's intellectual interests were not matched by her father, but by and large they got along well.

Her brother, 22, had been in the Navy four years and returned during the course of counseling. They had been close companions, with her the leader. She adored him and saw him as the ideal American male, tall, broad-shouldered, and masculine. Following his return home and their talks together she was able to recognize that he really felt quite anxious and insecure about himself and his future and she was able to help him seek counseling through the Veterans Administration. An incident which revealed his strong hostility to dominant women helped her to begin to understand the effect of their family constellation on his personality structure and to examine more closely its possible effects on her, especially in relation to her choice of husband.

Her Attitudes and Feelings Toward Marriage: Miss G took to the counseling process well and made good use of it, not only in the sessions themselves but as a stimulant for further thinking on her own during the week. She agreed that it would be valid to find out if she were basically resistant to the idea of marriage per se. Periodic explorations in this area did not seem to substantiate this. She seemed eager for marriage and children (perhaps a little anxious as she moved toward her 24th birthday). Her problem seemed to center about her conscious and, even more important, her unconscious standards and concepts of what a husband, her husband, should be; and she measured her fiancé against these. The problem was initially made more complicated, but later helped, by the return from California, after three years' absence, of a former ardent suitor. She was able to bring out that she turned him down because she saw him as not sensitive and altogether too masculine. This enabled her to question if she saw her fiancé as too much of the opposite, using as examples of her reactions, his use of make-up in connection with his acting and TV work.

She felt that she ought to feel very selfish about keeping her fiancé waiting while she used counseling to make up her mind. She asked for twice-a-week appointments, but exploration of this revealed that the request was based on her fiancé's suggestion and not her own needs. They were not scheduled. In relation to the above she was helped to recognize that she did not let her feelings come through to her until she had screened them intellectually and decided how she *should* feel or until it was *safe* to feel. She was then able to demonstrate this with examples in her relationship with her fiancé and she became more aware of negative feelings which she repressed and suppressed and rationalized away. This also helped her to account for not having the strong emotional feeling of love toward her fiancé which she felt she should have.

Separation from Fiancé: Midway in the counseling process her fiancé again indicated that he could not continue to accept her ambivalence and again requested that they call off the engagement until she was ready to make a decision. This time she was able to accept the separation and was more directly aware of her feelings. She was able to bring out the feeling of pain caused by the separation and she was able to cry. (In the past she had always felt this was a sign of weakness and she would not let herself do it.) Yet underneath, she felt she was really glad.

The separation seemed to enable her to look at herself and her relationship to her former fiancé with less unconscious resistance. She spoke of his patience and tolerant understanding of her in the past five years and wondered if it had not been too much so. She recognized her passivity and her need for others to take the active responsibility. She wondered if anyone else would be able to love her as much as he had, and then brought out her doubts about her own capacity to give, in return. She was then able to bring out her over-all doubts of her capacities as a woman and to question her readiness to assume the re-

sponsibilities of a wife and mother. She was aware that she had
learned to cover these feelings up well by an outward poise and
that this was related to her need for a very strong male. She
was able to tie this in with her strong dislike of anything non-
masculine and her negative reaction to her ex-fiancé's fondness
for cooking. An incident in the family helped her to become
aware that she had a strong fear of marrying a man who was
weak like her father, and recognized what that had done to her
as a child.

She started to date other men and this helped to bring out
other feelings. She frequently wondered if men dated her because she was so pretty or for herself alone. This was a doubt
she did not have with her ex-fiancé. She became aware of how
meaningful it had been to her to have someone she could really
count on emotionally. She compared her feelings for her fiancé
with those she experienced on a date with a man whom she thought
of as being very masculine and secure. (She recognized her
own need to see him this way and later realized his behavior
was something of a façade.) She was able to be comfortable and
secure with him and really be herself whereas with her fiancé
she became aware of the feelings of "always needing to wear
white gloves." She expressed her feeling that her ex-fiancé did
not have "not nice things in him whereas I have, but he doesn't
like it when I express them. I can hate and he can't." She
brought out her recognition that she had actually felt his all-
giving as very demanding upon her as she would feel selfish if
she didn't meet his implied demands.

Concurrent with our exploration of the feelings which kept
her from moving closer to or away from her ex-fiancé we also
explored the meaningful positives which she would want in any
relationship. She recognized that she had built up a fantasy
ideal which no man could live up to in all respects and that she
would have to make some compromises but now she had a
better perspective of some of the important values. She was

also aware that her beauty made more men available from whom to choose but would add to her anxiety about being sure of her choice.

Review of Counseling: As the planned period of counseling drew toward an end it was agreed that a brief period of review might be helpful. Miss G indicated that she had found the counseling extremely helpful and meaningful especially as it enabled her to go through with the decision to terminate the engagement, and to withstand the pain of separation. She felt she had begun to become aware of some important emotional needs and problems within herself, especially as they existed in her relationship to men. She was aware that she did not understand the dynamics of these nor how to handle them but felt that being aware of them, and perhaps being able to recognize their operation in the future, was an important step. She felt that most meaningful to her in her awareness was her pattern of intellectually screening her feelings. She recognized her need to examine the source of her inner doubts about herself and her own adequacy.

Her Future Plans: Her summer plans would take her West for the first time, and not having anything in the East to hold her she thought she might decide to stay out there for a while. She was planning to move into many relationships to test out her newfound feelings and awareness. She was aware of her anxiety and fear of the potential pain of new relationships but was able to recognize that all relationships carried this possibility and that most people felt the rewards worth the risk. She recognized that it would be helpful to obtain further counseling were she to stay West for any extended time but was not sure if she would do so. She would definitely continue our contacts on her return. She felt she would like to write and let me know her plans.

Conclusion: It is felt that this relatively brief period of counseling with Miss G was helpful to her in enabling her to move out of a relationship to which she was emotionally tied, and indeed felt considerable anxiety about terminating but was not one which she really wanted to carry through to marriage. She was helped to develop beginning awareness and insight into some of her problems, mechanisms and patterns especially as they related to her relationships with men. She was able to recognize that she had certain emotional problems that interfered with her making as meaningful an emotional relationship with a man as she would like to; that probably she would need help in working some of these through.

I saw her as basically an emotionally healthy person who was able to make good use of the brief period of counseling toward working through a specific problem and obtaining a greater understanding of herself. I feel she will move into new relationships with a greater freedom and better awareness. Her reactions to this brief period of counseling would seem to imply that she would readily seek further counseling help should she feel the need for it.

CASE 27

Problem: "All's well that ends . . ."
Presented by: Counselor (Ed.D. in Marriage and Family Life Education) in a marriage counseling agency, located in a large urban area

Introduction to Group Counseling

Group counseling is the counseling process in a group setting which facilitates the development of effective interpersonal relationships through conscious modification of attitudes and behavior. The aims, content, and focus of group marriage counseling are the same as those of individual marriage counseling. As in individual counseling, counseling in a group setting focuses on feelings, a major goal being the development of insight. Implicit in this goal and focus there is a marked difference between group counseling and social group work, family life education and other discussion groups whose purpose is primarily educational.

To date there has been little published on group marriage counseling per se. However, those who are familiar with literature on group psychotherapy will be aware of the therapeutic implications of group counseling. With selected cases it has therapeutic advantages to offer which may not be present in individual counseling. Patterns of behavior as they emerge within the group are typical of the patterns of behavior group members exhibit outside of the group. External reality and limits are readily perceived in a group setting as they constantly impinge upon individual group members. Through assuming a role of responsibility toward others, egos become strengthened. Because of the support given each other by group members, resistances are frequently worked through more quickly than in individual counseling. The support which is given and received and the strengthened ego both motivate and facilitate modification of behavior. Briefly, the group approximates a real-life situation where clients can immediately reality-test the emotional reactions involved in their interpersonal relations.

Inherent in a counseling setting which approximates a "real-life situation" are disadvantages which may be briefly mentioned. Counseling in a group obviously makes greater demands upon the abilities of the counselor. Instead of an awareness of the meanings behind the actions and reactions of one client, the counselor must strive to develop awareness simultaneously for several people. He must be alert to multiple transference and countertransference possibilities. In group counseling, case selection becomes a significant aspect of the counseling because of the interaction among group members. Related to this potential difficulty is the frequently encountered tendency on the part of a group member to attempt to dominate the group, thus inhibiting the spontaneity of other group members.

In spite of these drawbacks, group counseling conceivably has a valuable contribution to make in the area of marriage counseling. Marital problems usually are the responsibility of both partners. When partners are working together in a group, by having the feelings about each other's verbalization brought into focus, the mutual acceptance of responsibility for the relationship is enhanced. The following case particularly illustrates this point. The case is presented as an illustration of the counseling process and ensuing progress of one particular couple. It is not the purpose of this presentation to consider the over-all group interactive process.[1]

Introduction to Case: Mr. X, having heard of the marriage counseling activities in this agency, telephoned the office for an appointment for his fiancée and himself. At the time of his call a group had just been set up for premarital group counseling. Since his presenting problem revolved around his indecision about moving into marriage generally and, specifically, his feelings about his fiancée, the application was given to the counselor for the premarital group. Although most couples for group counseling have at least one individual interview with the group counselor prior to being accepted into the group, the procedure was waived in this instance. The rationale behind this move was: (1) the concept of group counseling which these young professional people had was sound enough to warrant their inclusion into the group

[1] Suggested references:

Hinckley and Hermann, *Group Treatment in Psychotherapy* (Minneapolis: University of Minnesota Press, 1951).

Lena Levine and Jeanne Brodsky, "Group Premarital Counseling," *Mental Hygiene,* Vol. XXXIII, No. 4, Oct., 1949.

Gerhard Newbeck, "Factors Affecting Group Psychotherapy with Married Couples," *Marriage and Family Living,* Aug., 1954.

Abraham Stone, M.D., and Lena Levine, M.D., "Group Therapy in Sexual Maladjustment," *American Journal of Psychiatry,* Vol. 107, No. 3, Sept., 1950.

without detailed interpretation; (2) they were interested in the possibility of group counseling; (3) their problems, involving nothing bizarre or pathological, were apparently of a nature which made them accessible to group counseling; (4) they wanted immediate help, there was an opening in the group, and individual counseling would have entailed a delay. However, the couple did have a half-hour interview with the group counselor immediately prior to their first group attendance. At this time the counselor arrived at the same conclusions she had drawn following the telephone conversation with Mr. X.

Description of Clients: *Mr. X* was of average height, but painfully thin. His intellectual superiority was apparent, but he had very little practical sense in the area of human or interpersonal relations. Of serious demeanor and lacking ego strength he had a rather aesthetic quality, a quality of religious mysticism. There was nothing prepossessing about him, either physically or in personality. Nor did he possess any of the qualities which would stimulate confidence in him as a professional person.

Miss Y was tall, slim, fair, rather attractive in a very passive, unresponsive way. There were times when she had a petulant expression around her mouth. She gave the impression of a person who had set up a defense against the exploration or penetration of her own feelings of insecurity by maintaining an exterior air of complacent competence. Of the two, Mr. X had the more acute problems. Although he was not aware of their nature, he recognized their existence to the point of seeking both individual psychotherapy and marriage counseling. (This search for help from these two sources was concurrent.)

Problem as Presented by the Clients: Mr. X and Miss Y had "gone together" for a period of fifteen months. By the time they came for counseling not only had an implicit agreement to marry been reached, but on two occasions tentative dates had been established. These dates were postponed by Mr. X, the second time indefinitely. Although professing love for Miss Y he could not with conviction move into marriage. She was sure of her love for Mr. X and was soon to be graduated from a professional school when she would be able to help financially while he continued to obtain more advanced professional training. Mr. X specifically sought help in clarifying his feelings about whether or not to marry Miss Y. Miss Y's desire for counseling help was, initially, focused on supporting her fiancé as he attempted to work his way through his indecision.

The Counseling Process: Mr. X and Miss Y attended regularly the weekly group counseling sessions for a total of sixteen weeks. The sessions were an hour and a half in length. The recognized basis for Mr. X's indecision was the difference in their religious backgrounds. Mr. X's background was that of Orthodox Judaism; Miss Y was an inactive member of one of the Protestant denominations.

Unrecognized by Mr. X at the beginning of counseling were strong family ties with strong undercurrents of resentment, and an unconscious desire to rebel, exemplified largely by his choice of a Gentile girl. His vacillation in his relationship with her was the overt expression of his conflict between family and independence. His conflict was evidenced by the fact that even though Miss Y wanted to embrace Judaism, Mr. X made this very difficult in various subtle ways. Counselor's efforts in working with him were directed toward the goal of helping him to see his problem as the all-encompassing problem it actually was rather than the relatively narrow problem of a decision to marry or not.

The dynamics behind Miss Y's behavior were equally significant. On the surface she gave the impression of being a very levelheaded, stable person with few problems. Actually, she too harbored a considerable amount of resentment against her parents, the result of strong feelings of rejection. Her interest in Mr. X had its roots partly in her desire to strike back at her parents, both active church members, and partly in a satisfaction of her status needs, since Mr. X was preparing for a profession notably high in prestige.

During the early group sessions Miss Y frequently withdrew in a rather deliberate way, figuratively turning her back on the group. In essence she was saying what she felt at that time. She was there because of Mr. X's problem, not because of a relationship problem. Her attitude was unrealistically optimistic and at the same time detached. It was almost as though she were saying, "This is his problem. I shall support him as he works it through, and after that we shall be problem free."

As time went on and she felt the support of other group members she became a more active participant. Counselor's work with Miss Y was primarily to help her become involved in the counseling process so that she would be able to face her own involvement in Mr. X's problem.

In contrast to Miss Y, Mr. X was a highly verbal member of the group from the beginning. Because of his tendency to intellectualize and to make dogmatic statements, he was a ready target for the comments of other group members. Occasionally he would respond with a pseudohumorous self-derogation; rarely he would withdraw; but most frequently he would argue defensively, or use evasive tactics. These were picked up and reflected back in such a way that Mr. X, midway in counseling, was becoming aware of this pattern of behavior and would frequently catch himself up in his own defenses. Mr. X was helped by the group to recognize his struggle with family loyalty versus independence needs, and to accept the underlying hostility toward his family.

As Mr. X talked about his indecision, Counselor, through reflecting back some of the things he brought out, helped him to recognize that conflict between his choice of a Gentile girl and his wishes to please his Jewish family. Whenever given the opportunity Counselor pulled Miss Y into the discussion by encouraging her verbalization of the feelings of rejection she had from his family. With Counselor's help Miss Y was able to verbalize Mr. X's conflict fairly clearly, but she still did not allow it to touch her. She pointed out her willingness to convert to Judaism, but at that point in counseling was not able to accept the conflict inherent in her conversion. When other group members frankly faced Miss Y with the fact that she had a conflict similar in many ways to that of Mr. X, Counselor was supportive. In effect she (Counselor) gave tacit permission to Miss Y to have negative feelings toward her parents. As Miss Y brought out the feelings of resentment toward parental control, implicit in their rejection of Mr. X, Counselor offered her limited interpretation of her rebellion. Miss Y was then able to accept her choice of someone so different for a mate as defiance against the subtle control of her parents.

Mr. X obviously had strong needs for acceptance. He wanted desperately to be liked but with masochistic comments rejected the efforts of others to accept him. Occasionally he would refer to his individual psychotherapy saying the psychiatrist thought he was a "jerk" to let himself be "pushed around" by the members of the group. In spite of this, Counselor's support of him and the efforts of Counselor and group members to bring Miss Y into his problems resulted in Mr. X's feeling of acceptance.

Undoubtedly the most important factor in the counseling process in this case was utilizing the responses of each of them to bring out the feelings of the other. For example, Mr. X spoke frequently of his family's rejection of Miss Y. This was picked up directly with him and indirectly with her by eliciting her feeling response to what Mr. X said. Both of them were able to see this as a projection onto his family of his own feelings of doubt. As the counselor picked up other statements either of them made, and elicited a feeling response from the partner, their relationship and the interweaving of their problems came into much clearer focus.

Counselor's Role: Counselor's role with this couple varied depending upon the activity of the group as a whole. Frequently Counselor was passive because of the very active interaction between group members. To Mr. X, Counselor was undoubtedly a mother figure to whom Mr. X turned frequently for support and approval. Usually this was dealt with by turning Mr. X's questions and comments back to the group; occasionally it was handled directly by helping Mr. X to understand what he was doing in seeking Counselor's support. On a few occasions when Mr. X seemed to be particularly threatened, Counselor gave him the support and approval he sought. More than any other of the group members Mr. X had outstanding dependency needs which he attempted to meet through Counselor. At first he was completely unconscious of this; later he began to recognize this tendency, although Counselor doubts if, during the group counseling, he completely accepted it.

Miss Y's relationship with Counselor was a relatively realistic one. While she did eventually become really engaged in counseling, she never established a close or dependent relationship with the counselor. The interaction between Miss Y and Counselor was the rather objective one of two adults working mutually on a problem. Miss Y's defenses against establishing a warm relationship with a mature woman were quite high, probably because of her poor relationship with her own mother. This was apparent in her constant efforts to focus on Mr. X's problems, not encouraging any attempt to focus on her own. Counselor did not attempt to remove these defenses because Miss Y was apparently making a satisfactory adjustment in most of the areas of her life. Toward the end of the counseling experience Miss Y had reached a point of recognizing her situation and the steps she needed to take without having explored the dynamics behind her behavior. Help in looking at the potential results of both sides of her decision was undoubtedly Counselor's greatest contribution. Miss Y seemed to be quite prepared to face the possibility of giving up her relationship with Mr. X. She also was consciously aware of the sacrifices she would need to make if their relationship were to continue. She accepted the fact that the decision was hers to make. The group experience as a whole enabled her to understand better Mr. X's conflict and what it would eventually mean to their relationship, as she gained insight into the severity of the problems facing him if they moved into marriage. Further, she understood that her own solutions of "conversion" and simply ignoring his family's opposition were unrealistic.

Follow-Up: Three months following the termination of this particular group counseling series, Counselor received a long letter from Mr. X. The last time he had seen Miss Y (about a month after counseling ended) she told him that she was planning to marry someone else in the near future. (During their relationship Miss Y had occasionally dated other men.) Mr. X had gone through a period of depression and emotional upset between the time this happened and the time of his letter to Counselor. By the time he wrote, he had begun to accept the termination of their relationship as a healthy move for both of them. His ability to do this was undoubtedly enhanced by his continuing psychotherapy. In his letter Mr. X also verbalized his gains from the group experience, saying he felt that it had been of value in the opportunity it gave him to relate to others to a more meaningful degree than had heretofore been possible for him.

Conclusions: From the beginning it seemed to Counselor and to Group Observer that this was a fairly unhealthy relationship which had been held together by mutually satisfying sex relations. Each of these two young persons was unconsciously using the relationship as a means of retribution against his parents, Miss Y punishing her parents (particularly her mother) for their rejection of her, and Mr. X rebelling against parental control. One of the factors which did not have a wholesome foundation was Miss Y's enthusiastic determination to convert to Judaism without ever really recognizing that this could not make her a full-fledged member of Mr. X's Jewish community. This probably was an indication of her need for "belonging" which she did not receive from her own family. Mr. X went along with her plans only in a very superficial way. Fundamentally he did not want to accept her into the Jewish faith. This was shown in several ways: for example, the unsatisfactory arrangements he made for her religious instruction, including several avoidable postponements. Both Miss Y and Mr. X were moving in a positive direction at the termination of group counseling. By positive movement here is meant: their increasing ability to recognize and accept the problems inherent in their relationship, increased understanding and acceptance of the feelings of each other, and increased insight into their own neurotic motivation in their efforts to perpetuate a relationship already beset with unsurmountable obstacles.

Even though Miss Y never conclusively verbalized her own need for help, she gained some insight. By the time the group sessions ended Miss Y was beginning to recognize her unwholesome relation with her own family and the probability that her interest in Mr. X was a retributive rejection of her parents. As Miss Y's own feelings, as well as those of Mr. X, were explored, she became better able to verbalize her negative feelings and to express some of the anxiety she felt about their relationship.

Mr. X's major improvement lay in his ability to recognize feelings, and to accept them as a part of himself. As the group progressed he frequently showed feelings of hurt and anger; initially he had tended to deny completely the existence of these feelings. Through the acceptance of the group he was able to look at them with much greater honesty. He began to accept himself as a worthwhile member of the Jewish community, which was an indirect gain.

11. Sex Problems at an Engagement Level

Each of these cases specifically presented a so-called "sex problem." It is thought provoking and significant also that presentation here of educational factual material was at best only incidental to developing a healthy attitude and emotional acceptance of sex.

From the point of view of agency structure, the interrelationship of the medical, psychiatric, and counseling services of a Planned Parenthood Center are most interesting (see Case 28).

CASE 28

Problem: A fiancée's difficulty in facing sex, complicated by her fiancé's weak sex drive

Presented by: Counselor (graduate study in Social Work) in a marriage counseling service of a Planned Parenthood Center in an urban community

Introduction: Miss A, who was having difficulty facing the sexual relationship in marriage was referred to the Counseling Service by her private physician. Both patient and doctor questioned whether she should go ahead with the marriage which was scheduled for the next month. On the other hand, her fiancé (Mr. D) was eager for the marriage, thought she was more ready than ever before (she had previously at college sought counseling in regard to her mixed feeling about marrying Mr. D) and hoped the marriage counselor would think marriage advisable.

Miss A had requested a pelvic examination in preparation for contraceptive advice but had not been able to accept a complete examination.

She is 24, a college graduate, a Protestant, and doing general clerical work in the same organization where Mr. D is employed. He has a B.S. degree, is 28 years old, and is Jewish.

The Counseling: They chose to be seen together at first and later were seen individually. They corroborated each other's story. Miss A's father is a manufacturer in a large Western city. She was graduated from an Eastern college and met Mr. D while taking graduate work at a Western university. Her parents are strict in their religion. Her maternal grandmother was in the home during her childhood. She has a young sister at college. Miss A is an attractive person and intelligent, but she has not had satisfying relationships with her family. She broke an engagement when she was nineteen years of age because the man had not been to college and she felt she could not continue her intellectual pursuits. She has dated a number of men but has not been seriously interested in any except Mr. D.

Mr. D's family live in New England. They are at present in good financial circumstances, although it was later revealed there were deprivations during the depression years. Mr. D was an adolescent at the time and evidently this left emotional scars. His family is of the Jewish faith. Neither he nor his fiancée attend any religious services and do not seem to feel the need of such contacts. Both have visited in the other's home, and the relationships have been pleasant. They both feel, however, their families would not be accepting of their plans to be married quietly. Mr. D is the oldest son. He has one brother. He thinks that traditionally his family would expect him to have an elaborate wedding.

While doing graduate work last year, Miss A had some counseling from a psychologist. She felt her uncertainty in regard to marrying Mr. D had to do mostly with breaking away from her family and that she had accomplished this. Both were glad when the opportunity presented itself for them to secure work with the same organization. She has been living in a rooming house and Mr. D located an apartment with the thought that they would eventually marry and have this place to live in.

They said they came to see me to discuss the physical relationship in marriage. They have a good intellectual background in anatomy and physiology and seemed at ease discussing this together. However, I felt they both approached it from an intellectual viewpoint. They asked questions that were practically impossible to answer, for example, what exactly would happen between them when intercourse occurred. Miss A discussed her difficulty in having the pelvic examination. She was very accepting of her physician and was annoyed with herself for having so much difficulty in her readiness to place the diaphragm pessary. As far as I could determine, she had had no unpleasant experiences of a sexual nature. Mr. D did not commit himself at this time, but neither showed any warmth about the subject. He stated they had talked it over and decided they would be married, undress in front of each other and sleep together, but would make no effort to have intercourse in early marriage. His point was that Miss A makes changes very slowly and it had taken her a long time to make up her mind to marry him. He would be quite willing to wait for the sexual relationship until she was ready for it. Miss A agreed with this. He was so calm in discussing this that I felt his sexual drives were not strong and that problems might be presented later. We talked together about the frequency of coitus and the part sex plays in relation to the total marriage but emphasized that it would be important for them to change their attitude in the direction of a more normal relationship in early marriage. They felt the interview had been helpful. They purchased a pamphlet and made an appointment to talk with me again.

Prior to their next interview, I discussed the situation with the consulting psychiatrist. Because of their aloof, intellectual approach to marriage, I wondered whether they could be reassured. It was suggested that I share with the couple my admiration and acceptance of them and that they be reassured about the sexual relationship; but that too much pressure should not be put on Mr. D. Interpretation regarding sex should be aesthetic and the couple should be helped to see that such experiences would not detract from their personalities.

Again they came together for the next interview. Their attitudes seemed to have improved through their discussions together. It developed they have never really been very frank with each other about sex until after their interview with me. They had gleaned considerable from reading the pamphlet and believe they are closer to making a decision about setting a date for marriage. The discussion centered around suggestions given by the psychiatrist who they knew had been consulted. Miss A was interested in further interpretation of the female pelvis as she is finding it necessary to make a number of visits to the doctor's office in order to be fitted with a diaphragm. She was determined to conquer the technique and recognized that she blocks emotionally. Both want to have children but after marriage Mr. D plans to continue graduate work. They have not told their families they are thinking of marriage at an early date. We discussed marriage laws in this state. They would like to be married by a Justice of the Peace but feel this would be very hard for Miss A's family to accept. We had considerable discussion about how their families would feel if they were not told ahead of time about the marriage. Miss A writes her family about once a week and Mr. D talks with his parents on the phone periodically. He told me his parents, his father especially, would have a great deal of feeling about his marriage. He told me his parents are not happily married. Miss A stated that individually they are very nice people, but together they are not a happy couple. In her family, her mother played the dominant role for many years, but in the past five or six years, since her grandmother's death, "my father has blossomed and become an individual rather than being enmeshed." Both want to do the right thing by their parents but they are confident that if the parents are notified in advance of the wedding date, they will "descend on us and insist on a great ado."

When they left the office they were in an amiable mood about marriage and agreed to let me hear from them.

About *two weeks later,* Miss A telephoned for an appointment which was set for the same day. She reported that until the past couple of days, she had been eating and sleeping well and seemed quite happy about her decision but did not sleep the previous night. She felt she and Mr. D were a perfect, intellectual match and their social interests were similar. But in addition to her general reluctance regarding sex, she wondered why Mr. D did not have stronger physical attraction for her. I thought it possible it was because they had built up a barrier about it. She wanted me to tell her whether to go ahead with the marriage. They had seen the minister and planned to be married three days later. They both wrote their parents but had postponed mailing the letters until that day (of the interview). Miss A talked with her sister at college and she was coming to be her attendant. She was sure her sister had kept her confidence. (Her sister had always gotten along better with the family than she had, although Miss A is the one who had been pushed regarding studies.) We talked together about the meaning of marriage, what she expected to get from it. I told her I could not make the decision for her, but she kept coming back to the point of wanting to be reassured about it. I then asked how sincere an effort she had made to break away from Mr. D during the past two years. She had never seemed to want to break away from him because of the emotional support he had given her and she thought he felt the same way. I asked if she thought it would be possible for her to break away without regret. She did not think she could do so. Together we came to the conclusion that since her desire for marriage at this time is stronger than her desire to break away, it would be advisable for her to go ahead, but I frankly stated it was her prerogative, up to the moment of her marriage, to change her mind if she wished. She is paying no attention to a trousseau or wedding dress and when I asked what she was going to be married in, she calmly stated she had not thought about it. She evidently has a nice wardrobe and always looks attractive when she comes in. Mr. D is also an attractive person, but when finances in marriage had been brought up in the previous joint discussion, it was indicated they would have to manage carefully.

Mr. D telephoned *a few days later* to tell me they were married. He seemed quite happy and stated everything was going along "remarkably well, better than we ever expected, except I am having problems in carrying out my part of the sex act." He was calling from home where Mrs. D was present and where she could hear the conversation. He was quite frank in discussing his difficulty of impotency. I tried to be reassuring and suggested it might work out but that he could call again if the problem persisted. He called *three days later* and was given an appointment a few days hence. He was not distressed and found it easy to talk with me. We first discussed the wedding. As soon as Mrs. D's family heard about their plans, they came here and were present for the service and took them to dinner later. They were very accepting and Mr. D feels there will be no further difficulty with them. His family telephoned them and were also accepting. I got the feeling from him he thought his wife's family had been more generous in attitude and in a material way than his family. They do not want to be dependent on either family, but it seems to me Mr. D carries over some feelings against his parents for some of the deprivations he suffered at various times in his life.

Mr. D talked about his impotency. It was quite a surprise to him, for he had had successful relations a few years ago on one occasion when he dated a girl. He had had considerable guilt about this. We talked together about his protectiveness of Mrs. D prior to marriage and felt perhaps this was a part of the present difficulty. I mentioned that this is not an unusual problem in early marriage. I asked him about masturbation and at this point, Mr. D who has a delicate coloring, flushed and said he had masturbated excessively throughout his teens, but as he became more adult, it was practiced less. He seemed to have considerable guilt about this and I dismissed it as something he should not feel uncomfortable about. He was inclined to think he had resorted to masturbation as a result of love deprivations in his home. I asked if he felt any conflict about the interfaith marriage. This had been discussed somewhat in the first interview, but both had been inclined to by-pass it at that time. He said he had not been conscious of it but perhaps there was more basis for conflict than he was aware of, not particularly the interfaith marriage—but the fact that he had pretty completely broken away from his faith. We discussed some of the fine qualities of the Jewish culture and I tried to relieve some of the feelings about the unpleasant things that had happened in his early life, particularly the relationship between his parents.

We talked further about their sexual relationship. I had earlier made a point of their not procrastinating but suggested they proceed with coitus in early marriage and I thought perhaps they had made too great an effort of it. I suggested they forget about it for the moment and refrain from any attempt for a few days, unless there was a spontaneous urge in which event they should then feel free to develop it. He then told me he had greater sexual excitement when he and Mrs. D were together at the office. I said this was interesting because it occurred at a time when he knew they could not have intercourse and that it indicated he had some fears. We talked more about this and he thought perhaps he had been afraid as he would not want to do anything that would hurt Mrs. D. I told him that there are times when men take this attitude and their wives are really disappointed. He asked several times if I wanted to talk with Mrs. D and I said it was not necessary at this time unless she wanted to see me. He said he felt better after talking with me about the situation and he seemed confident he would be able to work out his problem, emphasizing he would be willing to resort to any means necessary as time went on. I got no indication that Mrs. D was reacting unfavorably toward the particular problem. They had both been extremely busy in their work and he spoke of a party that had been given for them.

Three weeks later, Mr. D telephoned, stating that the situation was "just the same" and that he wanted to come in. Mr. D was prompt for his appointment but obviously had hurried and was tense as a result of pressures at work. He gradually relaxed and while willing to talk about his sexual difficulty, he was discouraged. He believed that other areas of their marriage are more than satisfactory. Their hours have continued to be irregular. Mrs. D had less experience in cooking and housework than he, so he seemingly had done a great deal of the homemaking, but they are gradually doing things about the house together. I wanted Mr. D to have some positive attitudes toward his problem and tried to be reassuring, mentioning that many couples in early marriage have similar difficulties. I mentioned that one's earlier attitude toward sex was quite likely to be reflected in the adjustment in early marriage and asked him to think about his earlier experiences.

He again spoke of his parents' unhappiness. I learned he had two brothers instead of one. Both are younger and married, and he has an affectionate feeling for both of them. At this point, he injected that both his and Mrs. D's parents were writing and they were glad that their families had accepted their marriage. I told him this should be gratifying. He said they hoped to visit his family later but they do not want to go until after they have worked through their present sexual difficulty. Then they would visit Mrs. D's family. I felt Mr. D was not complying with my request to talk about his earlier sexual experiences, and again focused the discussion in that direction. He told me that when he was fifteen years of age, he learned that coitus could occur for pleasure. He had some knowledge of sex prior to this but his conception of coitus was that it was only for procreation. This new idea made him feel that sex was vulgar. He shied away from girls, but before he was seventeen he began seeing quite a bit of an older girl who was an artist. They spent considerable time at night clubs. He did not drink much but seemed intrigued with the atmosphere. At the same time he felt guilty about it and the breach was wider with his parents. He seemed to have liked this girl but I could detect no fantasy of her in relation to his marriage. We talked further about the girl to whom he had been engaged and with whom he had had intercourse. He realized that it had not been a serious engagement. The girl had married and he seemed to have no ties to her. He felt he had had interest in sex but he had endeavored to refrain from intercourse as it had not fitted in with his ideals.

We then discussed sex as being a normal part of marriage, talked about conception control and he seemed to have no conflict. He also seemed more comfortable about his masturbation, which I gathered had not continued. The only erections he had had since the last interview, occurred when he was in deep sleep and this awakened him. On one occasion he approached Mrs. D who was not interested because of her drowsiness. Throughout, Mrs. D had been encouraging to him, for which he was grateful. When he first came in he seemed full of horror and feared this might be a problem that "I couldn't lick." As the interview progressed he seemed able to see that his earlier attitudes were possibly the cause of the problem. He wanted to know if he could return for further interviews and I told him he could, that I had anticipated he was going to be able to work this out, but to alleviate his fears, he could remember that other help would be available. I told him I was not surprised that this had happened as he earlier had conveyed to me, through his willingness to get married and not have intercourse, that he might encounter some difficulties. I commended him for having an intelligent approach and told him I felt he could deal with his attitudes. He planned to see me again in two weeks and would call. He also was assured Mrs. D could come in if she wished.

When he telephoned, there was a cheery note in his voice. He said he would be glad to come in if I thought it necessary but he was happy to report that successful intercourse had occurred on several occasions. He wanted me to know that the last interview had been "particularly helpful" to him. I responded that I thought they were getting along fine and that I did not think it necessary for him to come in.

Almost *four months later,* Mrs. D wrote a letter which stated, "The D's are getting along fine." I replied congratulating them and reminding them that Mr. D had not sent check for last interview. Mr. D telephoned. He had forgotten that he owed a balance. He and his wife were getting along "very, very well."

A *couple of years later*, I learned indirectly, in conversation with an acquaintance of Mr. and Mrs. D, that they are living in a Western city, that both have responsible positions and that they are thoroughly enjoying themselves in a new home, which they have recently purchased.

Some years later the physician who made the original referral reported that Mr. and Mrs. D seem well established in marriage and have three children including a set of twins.

EDITOR'S NOTE: This case is of particular interest because of the counselor's ability to treat the problem of impotence with delicacy and lightness and not induce anxiety. Many counselors would have attempted to suggest psychiatric referral by the time of Mr. D's second postmarital appointment and in so doing impress on him the basic gravity of his problem instead of emphasizing the naturalness of experiencing difficulty in early marital sex. The counselor gave him confidence by her discussion of his past experiences in an accepting, noncondemning manner and by her expressed belief that he would be able to work out this aspect of their marriage.

It is also of interest that the counselor did not offer to

see Mrs. D when Mr. D reopened contact after marriage. Ordinarily it might be surmised that Mrs. D would have been reassured by direct exposure to the counselor's conviction of ultimate success. However, this situation responded successfully without this, so it would seem the counselor's judgment was subtly correct.

CASE 29

Problem: Premarital sex with other than fiancé
Presented by: Clinical psychologist (Ph.D.) in private practice in large city

Subjects: Jane, 25, competent, calm, good-looking girl; a social worker in a child care agency.

Fred, 26, to whom Jane had been engaged for years; a soldier on his way home from Europe, soon to be discharged after three years' service.

Referral: Jane had heard of the counselor from Fred who had taken an introductory psychology course from him at college six years before. The counselor remembered him only vaguely, if at all.

Jane did not "come to get psychoanalyzed." She has a problem she cannot handle, and doubts if anyone could, but she wants to talk it over with someone. She would not take a personal problem to any of her professional associates, although some of them are very good, because she does not want them to think *she* is a problem. She has always handled her work successfully and has been happy enough until the present situation developed.

Problem: Fred wants to marry her as soon as he is discharged. She loves him very much, but she cannot bear to tell him that she "stupidly" had an affair recently with another man. It was her "own doing"; she was not seduced. She thinks she knows why she did it, "and it is not pretty." She is ashamed to tell Fred because she refused to go to bed with him before he shipped overseas, and had previously refused to marry him although they had been engaged for years. She feels that unless she tells him, she could not pick up their old relationship again as she would like to. Nor does she want to hurt him. She is sure he could not understand any of this. She wonders if she has gotten herself "boxed-in as an escape." She has been growing more and more skeptical of marriage recently, as she has taken a more realistic view of her own home.

Asked what she hoped the counselor could do, she said, "Nothing. I don't see what anyone could do, but I feel I ought to talk to someone about it to be sure I am thinking straight before I put on a hero's welcome at the boat."

Treatment: Jane took charge of the counseling situation from the beginning. She had the materials well in hand and revealed considerable insight. She talked rapidly and well, without emotional tension and blocking. She paused only when the counselor asked questions for clarification.

Jane and Fred seem to have known each other all their lives. They grew up in the same crowded neighborhood; went to the same church, same schools; played in the same block. When very small he treated her with the usual contempt little boys show girls, but she hung around him, held his bat, ran for his ball. He grew large for his age; she remained "tiny." During grade school he treated her like a big brother although they were about the same age, helped her in street games, and protected her in kid gang fights. She can't remember when she first got to be regarded as "his girl," but he could risk this earlier than most boys because he was large and strong, and therefore never an object of ridicule.

When it was rainy or cold, they spent lots of time together at her house because her mother was out working late every afternoon.

They first learned about sex together. She recalls no sense of guilt about it because most kids learned early in their congested neighborhood and learned "everything Kinsey checks up on." They started "going steady" in high school and were soon secretly engaged. She recalls with pride that they were different from the rest of their gang because they petted only with each other and never in public. In their intimacies they always stopped short of intercourse because "he was determined they should go to college and therefore must not get into any jam that might interfere."

Jane was never very clear about what she wanted of the future except him, so when they were together she let him make the plans and the decisions. Although engaged through college, they did not plan to marry soon because he was set on taking a graduate course in business management and did not know how long that might take. When he knew that he would have to enter the service, he changed his mind and wanted to marry at once. Because of her home situation she felt she could not agree. Now he writes that there is no reason why they cannot marry as soon as he is discharged, because he can complete his education on the GI bill and the money he has saved from his overseas pay.

From early childhood Jane adored her mother, but has felt that she scarcely knew her father, who was a traveling salesman. She cannot recall that he played a significant part in her early life. Feelings of hostility, she thinks, were caused not only by his being away on business so much, but also because her mother did everything for her and went out to work for the family as well. During Jane's sophomore year in high school, her mother developed cancer. Because of this the father took a job in the city and Jane took over most of the housework.

When the mother died after a year of illness, it was a great shock to the girl. She was in utter despair and doubts that she could have stood it had she not had her "work cut out for her." Her mother had taught her to run the house competently; her last words to her were that she knew that she would always look after her father. In addition to keeping up with her studies, she managed to do the housecleaning, shopping, and cooking, and now realizes that she also hoped for a time to take the mother's place in the father's affections as well. It was a good thing that she had Fred, for the father never seemed to realize her need for affection after the loss of the mother. He always praised her efforts and bragged about her to friends, but in the manner one praises a child for washing behind the ears, or a puppy for sitting up. These feelings she had never put into words before the interview.

Although he was making more money now, she continued to be an economical housekeeper as her mother had taught her to be. The father brought her presents on occasions and provided money whenever it was needed, but she could not bring herself to ask for anything until it was absolutely necessary. He often urged her to go out more and have a good time, but it never occurred to him to hire someone to do the work which was so difficult to get done with her heavy school program. She does not recall that he ever offered to take her to a movie. Often he stayed away from home at night, and she silently resented it when he did not turn up for dinner after she had hurried home from school to shop and cook for him.

"Perhaps all this was good for me," she decided in the interview, "for if he had not been too immature and selfish to show me consideration and affection, I could have developed an Oedipus complex that would really have been a 'beaut.' "

All this, she realized, affected her relations with Fred. After her mother's death she became more constrained in sharing affection with Fred because she felt that since it was uncertain that she would ever be able to marry they should not become too dependent on each other. She told him that she did not want to think about marriage because it was her duty to look after father. To this, he said: "Nertz, let him look after himself."

When a move by Fred's family made it impossible to attend the same college as they had planned, she felt she had to suggest to him that they break off their engagement so that he could be free to find someone who had no family obligations. She was not yet ready to reassess her "duty" to the father. Fred's reaction again was "Nertz!" and he became more possessive and outspoken in his antagonism toward her father. He dated her as often as their work would permit throughout college, and she agrees that it is remarkable that they were able to achieve excellent records.

After graduation he wanted to get married before induction in the army, and since she refused, he urged that they have intercourse. He urged this again on leave after basic training and before embarkation for overseas duty, but she again refused. Although she thinks he was deeply hurt by this, his letters have been frequent and always affectionate. Now on the way home he is all set to marry at once.

Through this much of the story, she feels she understands her reactions clearly. "But now comes the climax of this soap opera," she said, "and I am not sure I understand it at all."

The father had a long week end coming up and said that he was looking forward to a good rest at home. Jane cleaned the house throughout, planned attractive meals and got the shopping done. This took every minute before and after work, and all her energy. She recalls having vague plans to take this opportunity to discuss her future with her father. She knows that she was getting pretty tired of combining housework with her interesting job, but she says she is sure she had not yet reached the point of making any definite demands. Certainly, she had not thought of pulling out, she is "sorry to admit." She feels that she probably just intended to sound him out. "Chump that I am, I probably would have been satisfied to discover that he had a little appreciation of all I did for him," she said.

That night he came home and announced that his holiday was off. He had to make a business trip, and since he would be away, he had decided that she should find a girl friend and go to Atlantic City for the week end. He would foot the bills.

"I should have been suspicious, but being a sucker I was delighted, phoned a friend, and got ready to leave early next morning. When I called to pick up my friend, she had just learned that she could not leave town because of the arrival of relatives that evening. So we went to a movie and returned in the late afternoon.

"When I let myself into our supposedly empty house, I found father with a woman in mother's bed. I stormed out of there so fast that I did not see who she was, but I am glad I got out of there before I blurted out something I would have been ashamed of.

"In the room I found at the YW, I swore I would never go home again. I was so angry I had to talk to someone, so I called up a favorite 'prof' I had taken a number of courses with at college and went to cry on his shoulder at his apartment. What happened was not his fault, although he probably does not know that and feels very guilty. I practically threw myself at him, in a modest way, although I did not know why I did at the time, and feel like an awful fool now. Under the circumstances, it was not very satisfactory, and I am sure we shall avoid each other in the future.

"A most contrite letter from father awaited me at the office Monday and I decided to return home. I realized that I had little reason for anger at him. He is over 21 and has a right to do as he pleases, and it really doesn't matter whose bed they were in. Somehow I had come to realize over the week end that my rage had really been at myself for all I had given up for him; that is, for letting my little girl's need for approval from daddy prevent my marriage to Fred.

"At home I immediately made it clear that I held no blame against him, but that the time had come for us to plan our lives independently. He readily agreed. So we are closing out the home and hunting separate apartments. I think we are both greatly relieved. We can still be friends, but now I am on my own at last."

The narration of all this appeared to relieve her guilt. Her use of the counselor to clarify her feelings, formulate her ideas, and confirm her insights, restored much of her self-confidence.

It is interesting that she did not ask for an interpretation of the episode with the professor, but by her manner indicated that she could now look at it objectively and that it no longer baffled her.

The pessimistic attitude with which she initially stated her problem as one about which nothing could be done, and no one could help, had now disappeared. The frank recital with no attempt to spare herself, had relieved her need for self-punishment, and she clearly expressed this relief. She ended the interview with the statement that she felt much better; that there must be something she could do; and that she would do anything to save her relationship with Fred. It was because she had just heard that he was on the way home that she decided to see the counselor, and she wanted to come back next week to plan "the next moves."

The second interview did not prove to be very much of a strategy-planning session. She used most of the time to try to predict what her reactions would be to a variety of things that might happen. She insisted that this was very helpful, because she said, "This kind of thinking I cannot do alone; I just go around in circles." To her, her sexual intimacies with Fred were respectable and honest because they were nonpromiscuous, private, and based on mutual affection. She was convinced that she was not herself in the episode with the professor, but because of her relationship with Fred she could not consider not telling him about it. The problem was how it was to be done. The counselor thought her frank story should put itself across, but not knowing Fred, he could not predict his reactions of course. She was certain she could not tell it to Fred as rationally as she had to a disinterested person. She had been calm and unemotional in the interview situation, but she felt sure that if she talked about this to Fred she would break down at the first sign that he was hurt or angry at her. In the past they have talked about everything and there have never been any serious misunderstandings, but she feels now that he has been away so long and she has been so worried for fear she might lose him that she could not control herself. He has always been so considerate that if she cries he will forgive her anything and she doesn't want that. Perhaps if the discussion took place here with the counselor and Fred together the same emotional climate would enable her to keep control of the situation. She wanted the counselor's help in telling and interpreting the "critical incident."

Her decision was this: When she first saw him, she would tell Fred that she was ready to marry him just as soon as they were both sure that that was the thing to do. To give him a decent warning of a possible shock she would remind him that he had been away a long time and many things had happened, and one of them might raise real doubts as to whether their marriage would succeed. Because of this she had been to a marriage counselor whom she knew he respected, and before anything definite could be decided she wanted them to go together to discuss the whole problem.

About a week later, Fred phoned to make the appointment. He was carefree and happy to be home, but said, "Hey, Doc, I wish you would tell me what this is all about." The counselor said he had agreed with Jane that it would be best if they discussed it all together.

The sturdy, mature, pleasant young sergeant who arrived with Jane the next day was hard to identify with the vaguely remembered student of six years before. After cordial greetings and a brief exchange of views about the military service, the question of the marriage was raised at once. Fred volunteered that there were no doubts on his part and never had been, but he was willing to discuss anything because he knew Jane had had doubts; otherwise they would have been married long ago.

The counselor briefly worked through some of the material of the previous interviews to indicate his familiarity with their relationship. He also indicated that Jane had definitely grown up while Fred was away, mentioned the respect she had won as a professional worker, and emphasized that she had now matured beyond the dependency on her father that had caused her to defer marriage in the past.

Jane then elaborated her reasons for feeling she couldn't marry after her mother's death, her role in the home, and her father's exploitation of her in that role. She indicated how her feelings toward the "duty" her mother imposed had undergone a change; then related briefly her father's week-end affair which brought the mobilization she needed to finally break away. The counselor then again took up the story as Jane had asked him to do. He related and interpreted her emotional state over this incident and then described the episode with the professor as an understandable attempt at compensation for her frustration and emotional deprivation and a gesture of hostility toward the father.

After a pause during which Jane was very tense, Fred said: "Oh, boy! So that is it. You are worried about something you have done, and I was afraid all along that it was something you had heard about me. I did not see how you could have, but I was sure worried because it was something I would rather have told you myself sometime."

There was silence.

Then the counselor lamely began a sentence: "Well now, most of us have. . . ."

Fred broke in, looking at the counselor, not Jane: "Well, I might as well get out with it. I had an affair with a beautiful WAC in Berlin, but she did not mean a thing to me and I meant nothing to her."

Jane caught her breath, grew pale, then looked angry until she caught the eye of the counselor, and burst into laughter as if greatly relieved.

The counselor started talking to relieve the tension, said such things as they had revealed happened in many love relationships and often caused a lot of trouble, but that he thought the courageous honesty on the part of each was the encouraging aspect of this situation. Since he was sure they deeply loved each other he was confident that they could accept these things as having happened under rather extraordinary circumstances.

Fred said he could accept it all right, meaning Jane's affair.

Jane, still a bit jolted by the "beautiful WAC," said she did not want acceptance if it meant that he forgave her, because she did not feel guilty; she had made a fool of herself, but she did not want forgiveness. The counselor pointed out that unless they were able to accept the reality of the two experiences, the professor and the WAC might move in with them as unseen saboteurs of their ego security.

FRED: "I see what you mean. But speaking of egos, why did Jane have to pick that professor? I am sorry I know who it was. It is not flattering to me that she sent me off so virtuously and then finally turned to an old fuddy-dud."

JANE: "Sure, he is an old man, but when I had to break away from my father, this silly affair at least proved to me that I did not need a father substitute. But how about that *beautiful* WAC?"

COUNSELOR: "The WAC raises a question. Do you think you would feel better about Jane's affair if instead of the professor she had selected a handsome young athlete with a Cadillac convertible?"

FRED: "Well, I guess I can't really be jealous of that professor."

The counselor suggested that perhaps the choice of the professor indicated that the meaning of the affair was symbolic, not real; that he understood it, first, as a gesture of protest over having let her fancied obligations to her unappreciative father block her marriage to Fred. Second, it seemed a demonstration of her ability to break completely her dependency on the father and her adolescent need to try to fill her mother's role for him.

FRED: "OK, I can buy that. Let's forget it. I hope I can make all the adjustments to civilian life this easily."

Follow-Up: They have been married eight years, have two children, and are buying a home. Fred is personnel manager of a good firm. Jane expects to return to professional work when the two children are older, to help pay for their home. They indicate they are happy.

CASE 30

Problem: Twice-postponed marriage due to "vague fears" of fiancée

Presented by: Marriage counselor (Ph.D. in Education) in private practice in small city

Presenting Problem: The young man, a student at the college, was extremely disturbed about vague fears shown by his fiancée. Marriage had been postponed twice before. The man indicated that both he and his fiancée earnestly desired some help in tackling the problem.

Some Aspects of Personal History

Male	Female
Age: 26	Age: 24
Occupation: Auto Mechanic	Occupation: Office Secretary
Health Status: Sound	Health Status: Sound
Interests: Music, radio, engineering	Interests: Not developed in any area, but interested in continuing education
Educational Background: High school—at present enrolled at college under G.I. Bill as engineering student	Educational Background: High school graduate

Development: At the initial interview both persons were seen to-gether. The woman spoke well, used good speech patterns, and in general created the impression of being a moderately intelli-gent person. The young man, who is an excellent student, ap-peared to be somewhat tense; however, the information he pre-sented was concise and helpful.

The woman indicated that she was in love with her fiancé, that she wanted marriage, but that the question of living with him created some deep emotional feelings that she could not describe. She revealed that previously, as the date for the wed-ding ceremony had come closer, she had reacted with severe nausea, stomach pains, and headaches. When asked as to how she saw the problem she replied, "Actually, there's no problem. I've just got to decide what I want to do—and do it!"

The young man saw the problem as one which involved the attitudes and opinions of her family, a point to which the young woman objected strenuously.

The following two sessions were held with the woman. Dur-ing these two meetings she spoke freely and with a great deal of emotional undertone.

Her family history showed an extremely rigid training, with emphasis upon "good" and "bad" actions. "There never seemed to be anything in between good or bad. I always had the feeling that my world was either, 'You're a good girl,' or 'You're a bad girl.' "

Her father had watched her every action, at times going to the extent of making her report minutely her experiences and conversations of an entire day. The mother's religious training and practice did not extend overly toward the young woman, but there was always the feeling that "if I did not do as mother did something would happen to me." Though she defended the actions of her parents as being kind and thoughtful, but strict, other material she verbalized carried with it her feelings of re-sentment and her sense of never being loved and accepted. Her constant references to a lack of training and preparation for marriage revealed a fear of sexual intimacy. Additional material also indicated an amazing distortion in knowledge of sex hygiene and its practice.

A third and fourth session continued to bring out further her fears and distortions. She was afraid that she could not conceive because of what she felt was excessive masturbation, a practice that she started when she was eleven years of age. "When I would go to school I thought that every boy and every teacher could tell what I was doing and I had the feeling that mother knew but wouldn't want to say anything to me."

The following sessions brought out her fear of being punished by God, of being rejected by her father and mother for falling in love, of not being able to bear children, of being physically incapable of sexual relations.

At this point the counselor carefully began to point out connections between her childhood experiences and her present actions. These she accepted with great interest and willingness, at times interrupting by stating, "I can see how Mother and Dad squeezed me emotionally." "They really had their own problems and they were pushing them on to me." "There must have been something in the way I reacted to their tensions."

The appearance of her physical complaints—namely nausea, stomach pains, and headaches—she began to view as symptoms associated with her many fears. Her physical reactions as the time for marriage came closer were also viewed as protests against facing these fears (1) of being punished (2) of indulging in physical intimacies (3) of exposing her resentments toward her parents. There were her childhood grievances; these were followed by feelings of self-indulgence, self-pity, and self-punishment; slowly the physical symptoms were brought into existence with the concomitant complaints that were utilized for sympathy and as an excuse for not entering into a mature relationship, since this very act of marriage now reinforced all the old fears. Fortunately, this process was not too far removed from consciousness. The client was able to comprehend rather quickly and with a noticeable decrease in tension.

Two interviews held with the young man revealed a great deal of understanding on his part. He indicated that he had had a year of intensive psychotherapy. He had recognized that much of her difficulty lay in her previous poor education and family attachments. Having attempted sexual relationships with her at the beginning of their courtship, he had come to sense her difficulty and had no desire to further increase her tension and anxiety. Though he felt that he loved her, he was also aware that unless she obtained some insight and understanding the situation would become destructive to himself. It was then that he had suggested counseling as a possible solution to the situation.

During the eighteenth session, the woman spoke in a somewhat excited tone for the first few minutes and then stated, "I've made an appointment for a medical examination—I want to clear up this business about children and aches and pains."

At this point it was felt that interviews with both people were practical. Three such sessions were held and consisted primarily of exploring changes that had taken place in the relationship. The man expressed the viewpoint that it was easier for both of them to communicate feelings and although he thought her family still threatened her, he also sensed an increased willingness and ability on her part to handle this area in a realistic manner. He also felt more secure in his role as her fiancé.

At the last session both persons presented a rather sound and concrete plan of action; the young woman had decided to enroll at college as a nonmatriculated student for purposes of increasing her knowledge and efficiency as a legal stenographer and in addition had registered for an adult extension course on Marriage and the Family. She had visited her family physician, a warm, sympathetic person, who had allayed her fears as far as sexual intimacies and child bearing were concerned. They had decided to postpone the marriage for an additional six months for the very practical purpose of permitting the young woman to gain more insight.

A follow-up four months later revealed that the relationship had ripened considerably; that the young woman looked forward toward marriage and that her feelings of respect and affection for her fiancé in view of his wholesome treatment of her had acted as a tremendous source of security. The young man stated, "I now feel that we can concentrate on our real struggles, a job, finding a house, enjoying ourselves; and she acts and lives like somebody you really feel is here."

Two years after this they report they are married, have one child; and a substantial payment has been made on their own home.

Counselor's Comments: This case represents a situation that benefited from the experience and attitudes of the man. In discussing the presenting material with the supervising psychiatrist, it was felt that the counseling relationship might best be maintained by offering supportive therapy and utilizing educational factors in order to neutralize some of the effects of lack of sound information on the part of the woman. A complete psychological report was submitted by the clinical psychologist and indicated among other factors a marked passive-aggressive character structure; impairment of independent fantasy; anxiety easily aroused and related to difficulty in establishing wholesome relationships; in connection with sex, markedly passive with extreme fear in conceptualization of sex.

The resistance shown by this client initially against becoming emotionally involved in a prolonged counseling relationship gave evidence of the wisdom of a treatment plan of supportive and educational goals.

It might appear that substantial progress was achieved, but

the counselor is of the opinion that there will be difficulty in the future. The counseling relationship did achieve this point, however: namely, that the woman obtained enough understanding of the nature of the process so that should problems arise, there would be less hesitancy in seeking help.

12. Problems of Mate Selection

These three cases (Problems of Mate Selection) are quite typical of the sort of problems found on any college campus today, as young people strive to break their dependency ties to their parents and venture into love-relationships at a (not always) adult level, on their own.

CASE 31

**Problem: Effect of premarital sex relations on mate selection
Presented by: Teacher-counselor (Ph.D. in Educational Psychology) in a small state university**

Problem as Presented by Client: Helen came to me about a month before the close of college. She was in my class in Marriage and the Family. Her opening question was "What do you do when you are engaged to one boy, but have come to like another better?"

First Conference: Questions brought out the fact that although she was engaged to Bud, she did not like him as well as she had when they became engaged. During the last month she had gotten to know Tom who was chairman of a student committee on which she served. They had gone for coffee a few times recently but he had not asked to date her, because he was a friend of Bud's and knew of their engagement. She felt sure he liked her.

A further attempt was made to find out why her feelings for Bud had changed and why, if she no longer "loved him," she did not break the engagement. This approach brought on a rush of tears and the confession that about a month after her engagement, Bud had persuaded her that since they would be getting married in about a year and a half, there was no reason to forego having intercourse all that time, that it was normal for engaged couples to have intercourse. She did not feel that way, but he had been persistent, evidencing more and more irritation at her refusal, and she had finally given in.

This had not solved the problem, however, which changed from "whether to have intercourse" to "when to have intercourse." More and more he expected it on every date. She resisted, giving in only when he became really demanding. After about a month of this she missed her period. She was terribly frightened and after few days told Bud about it. He did not show too much concern, saying that his uncle was a young doctor, and he would be able to tell them of an abortionist. Fortunately, her period had apparently been only delayed by emotional factors, for at the crucial stage, the flow came. But her feelings were now clearer. She realized she no longer loved Bud. She began to be more and more irritated by his selfish—and even rude—behavior. She had gone to his home for a week end to get to know his parents. She had been depressed by the atmosphere in his home. His parents were quiet and lacking in any show of warmth or cordiality. Bud's relations with his mother and sister were that of a demanding spoiled child, and she remonstrated with him on their return trip for the way in which he treated them. They had gone riding together, and he had been very harsh in his treatment of a horse. All in all she had begun to see him more and more as a selfish and rather cruel and demanding person—and she became more and more fearful that a marriage with him would not be a happy one.

Helen had by this time soaked up all her tissue, so I dug out a box that I keep handy. Why, I asked, if she felt this way about Bud, did she not break her engagement? A torrent of self-depreciation followed. She was just as bad as he was. She had been as responsible for giving in as he had been for demanding intercourse. It appeared to her almost a case of marrying him—or no one. "If any nice boy ever asked me to marry him—the only kind I would want to marry—I would have to tell him about my affair with Bud—and then he would never marry me." Tears flowed freely.

Questions established her feeling that she was "damaged goods." She would feel guilty in marrying "a really fine person," but "Bud is as much responsible for this as I am and he could never look down on me." This assertion was challenged, and she was helped to face the question as to whether she was planning to marry Bud to punish him—or to punish herself for having been a "bad girl." Could such a marriage be a happy one for either? She seemed gradually to be more understanding of her own feelings, how she had really come to hate Bud, and how unwise it would be to think of marriage with him under such conditions.

For the last few minutes, an attempt was made to reassure her that her alternative was not marriage to Bud or no marriage. She was told that once she was clear about her own feelings, she would probably feel differently. She was also assured that the damage had probably been to her feelings about herself, and that if a boy really grew to love her he would probably be understanding and forgiving of her "mistake." She agreed to return in a few days. In the meantime, she was to write her autobiography, using the outline suggested to the class. (The conference had lasted over two hours; Helen seemed greatly relieved as she left.)

Second Conference: She returned five days later with her autobiography written out. She opened the conference by announcing decisively that she had broken her engagement to Bud. She expressed a great feeling of relief that it had been accomplished and said she had been very much more at peace with herself since she had made the break. How had Bud taken it? Rather casually—convincing her further that she had been wise. Did she feel that he had really loved her—or she him? She said she was not sure either of them knew what love was—and that she wondered if he could ever really care about and be devoted to anyone except himself. Did she feel she could? Yes, she was positive about that. She had told Tom about her break with Bud the night before, and he had been very sympathetic—said he hadn't been able to understand how a girl like her could marry a guy like Bud—that although he was a fraternity brother, he did not really like him. She was sure she could adore a person like Tom, and would be quite happy spending her life making him happy. We discussed the danger of rebound affairs and she agreed that no hasty decisions should be made.

"What do you think you learned from writing your autobiography?" She plunged into her personality and background. She loved her mother, but felt she had always played second fiddle to her father's every wish. He was a very successful businessman with a huge corporation. He was known as a sort of "trouble shooter," and when one of the company projects seemed to be lagging behind the others, or internal conflicts were hurting the business, he was sent there for a year or two to get things running smoothly again. This had meant a series of changes all during her school years. She had seldom attended a school for more than a year or two. They had always lived in apartments until recent years when they rented furnished houses.

But there had been no sense of any place being home—or permanent. In her earlier years it had not been so bad to be uprooted just about the time she had developed strong friendships and come to feel at home. But during adolescence she had been more and more upset by each move. In one place she had deliberately decided not to try to make friends or to adjust. She had moped around home, read "scads of romantic novels," refused to join a church group or any other. She said she hated this place and told her parents she could never be happy there. Her father had asked for transfer and got it after one year. Her parents had done everything possible to consider her wishes in the place to which she transferred, and she saw "how foolish I had been to punish myself and them when Daddy couldn't help moving." (I assured her that ninth grade would have been the most difficult time to move—especially when it meant entering the last year of a junior high school.)

She made a good adjustment in high school. She became active in many things and had a wonderful group of friends. She dated a number of different boys, going steady with some for a few months. During her second year there she had started dating a boy she was very fond of, and they had gone steady the rest of the year. During that summer, her father had been compelled to make another move. She had rebelled, wanting to stay behind with Bob. But nothing was worked out, so she found herself entering her senior year in a new school. Her first impulse had been to withdraw again, but she decided that would be foolish, and she might as well "get it over with." She and Bob continued to write for most of her senior year and hinted at love and marriage, but after Bob graduated from high school he went into service, and his letters became less frequent and finally stopped.

Her first two years of college were characterized by confusion of goals. She changed majors several times, did very mediocre work, and never seemed to care about more than getting by. She dated frequently, but did not care for any of the boys particularly, and since the man ratio was high and she could get all the dates she wanted, she enjoyed "playing the field." She had not formed any attachments until during her junior year when she and Bud, both members of the riding club, had started running around together.

We discussed the unusual problems brought on by her frequent moves, particularly during adolescence, and the danger that this might result in an abnormally strong desire to marry and "settle down," or to revert now to the ego-satisfying pattern of playing the field. We agreed on one final conference before school closed.

Third and Final Conference the Following Week: Helen arrived happy—quite in contrast to the "down in the dumps" attitude of her first conference. She hastened to tell me that she had been out with Tom and in a very nice way he had indicated that he was definitely interested in her. They had agreed to correspond during the summer which would see them separated by several hundred miles, and she felt certain and happy that they would be going steady in the fall. She said she admired Tom more than she had ever known.

We discussed again her feelings about Bud, and the effect of her relationship with him. She still felt very hostile toward him, and wondered how she could ever have thought she loved him. She agreed that it might have been largely physical attraction resulting from necking, and her growing desire to form a permanent attachment. She remembered definitely feeling that she ought to at least "get pinned," because of the social pressure to do so—that there was a growing feeling among the girls that if you graduated from college without being engaged you were sunk. A few statistics seemed somewhat reassuring.

We discussed the danger of carrying too many guilt feelings —or hate feelings for Bud. She said she felt much better about the whole affair, now that she had a definite feeling Tom knew about it—and that apparently he still liked her. She realized that the important thing was how she felt—and whether her experience had seriously damaged her feelings about herself as a person. She felt it would not prevent her from being a good wife and mother. She thanked me for the help I had given. This was my last contact with Helen, as school closed the following week and she did not return in the fall.

CASE 32

Problem: Indecisiveness regarding marriage—overprotective parents

Presented by: Teacher-counselor (Ph.D. in Sociology) working in a college setting

Introduction: Marshall B and Jane M were brilliant students and well known at the university where the counselor was a teacher-counselor in marriage. Both were known for their leadership in student activities. Jane had taken courses with the counselor during which she had had several vocationally oriented conferences. She was a quiet, personable young woman who elicited protective impulses from her teachers. She found it productive to "sweat blood" before making any major decision.

The Problem as Presented to the Counselor: Jane's initial visit was a rehearsal of why she thought Marshall would make a good husband. She was vague about when she expected to marry, had a year to go before graduating, and was primarily concerned with testing the hypothesis that they would be good for one another. Marshall postponed seeing the counselor until he had a clear-cut problem, that is, when it was clear to him that he was losing the battle with Jane's parents concerning the date for their marriage.

Counseling: Jane made an appointment in great distress early in February. Marshall had won a fellowship to another university and wanted to get married in June. Decisive, methodical, aggressive, and versatile, he was pushing for an immediate decision. Jane tearfully reported that her father, a prominent business man, was dead set against her marrying at all, felt Marshall wasn't good enough for her, thought Jane too young (22 years) and felt she should work a year or two. Jane's mother broke into tears every time the subject came up. Since she had never crossed her parents before, she told them they were probably right. In a flare-up with Marshall after reporting her parent's refusal, she gave back his ring.

The counselor asked Jane to explain why the parents felt the way they did. She thought they wanted to shelter her from failure, that they had been slower than most parents to allow her to date, to take the car, and to take summer jobs. The counselor asked if this might not be another instance of refusal to be followed by consent. Jane had no such hopes.

The counselor told of other couples whose parents, more rigid than her own, had been won to the couple's plans when the couple had presented a *solid front*. Jane stiffened and guessed that she had let Marshall down.

A week later Marshall dropped by to say Jane had accepted the ring back and was prepared to face her parents with him on the issue. He is hurt that the parents don't approve of him, had always hoped his in-laws would like him.

Counselor asked Marshall to analyze the father's reactions in the light of his protective feelings for Jane. Marshall did an able job and concluded it was probably just a tug-of-war between father and fiancé over who would protect her. Any boy who got serious would arouse the father. Marshall's plans were to fight through Jane, weak reed though she might be.

The following month, Jane reported a stormy session in which the parents refused to give an inch. Jane wants a fancy wedding and Marshall's family can't afford to contribute. Jane knows her parents have $2,000 set aside for her wedding and she is determined to tap it. Marshall is willing to marry with a simple campus wedding, and is irked at her indecisiveness.

Counselor asked Jane to outline her strategy for resolving the dilemma. Jane had none. Counselor asked if she still wanted to get married. Jane opined if she had known how much disagreeable messiness would develop she would never have got involved. Why did parents have to be such stubborn souls? Counselor asked if stubbornness didn't serve some function. It didn't register with Jane who left shortly for class.

A few weeks later, Marshall and Jane postponed their plans for a June wedding in favor of a June announcement of their engagement and August wedding date. The announcement will be from the campus and without the approval of the parents. Jane is afraid and fidgety, and Marshall is triumphant. At this time, Counselor asked Jane how the parents would be notified and she cried a bit and said, "I don't know. Oh, why do I have to be such a baby?" Marshall showed embarrassment, and the counselor reminded Jane that crying was an acceptable release, to go ahead and howl. She glared, and began to laugh between tears.

The June announcement parties went off successfully and as the counselor had predicted (privately) the parents capitulated; excerpts from Jane's letter reveal the ambivalence with which she reacted:

> Thought you would be interested in knowing that my folks have completely capitulated and while not enthusiastic are accepting the idea of my getting married on August 31 and here at home. Only drawback now is me. Before, the battle spirit spurred me on, but now that it's settled I find that I not only don't want to get married but the more I try to talk myself into thinking that I do the more convinced I get that I don't. In fact I have moments when I'd like to dig my way to China like I used to try to do or get lost or something. The funny thing is, what I think of Marshall is just

the same. I'm sure I like him much better than I've ever liked any of the others—although I've certainly been fascinated by some of them. And we get along perfectly and seem to think the same things but it doesn't seem that it could be just right when I get so convinced that I don't want to marry him or anybody else. Would merely like to go out into the world and seek my fortune and see what there is to be seen.

But if I break things off, I want it to be the right thing and for good—hate wavering back and forth. I did try to give Marshall back his ring once, but just couldn't quite do it and neither could he—so he gave it back again. We're both going to be hurt by it—probably he more than me 'cause he takes things much more seriously than I do—but if it isn't the right match it's better to break it now than later.

Reading this letter it's beginning to sound like something Dorothy Dix might have to answer in her lovelorn column, and if anybody else wrote it I'd think they were sillier than anything. But it doesn't seem so trivial to me—naturally. I realize brides are supposed to have butterflies, but are they supposed to be such persistent ones and arrive a month early?

Counselor had expected this ambivalence to appear if the parents withdrew their objections but felt he should not play too heavy a hand at such a critical stage of indecision. He consulted with another counselor and wrote a supportive letter, explaining the ubiquity of doubts and mixed feelings as engaged couples have as the date approaches, and asked how Marshall was taking the parents' capitulation. Did he have doubts, too?

The answer was a personally penned invitation to the wedding.

Follow-Up: Two letters written during the following year indicate general satisfaction with the marriage. The most recent gives evidence of losing themselves in studies and jobs, taking for granted their marriage. See excerpts below:

From Jane:

We're still holding down our third of the apartment and figure that it's a pretty good arrangement for right now (sharing with two other couples). I just started a new job. After working two months and being bored, I quit the office job and went out searching greener pastures. Got a job as a counselor in a school of maladjusted children placed there by courts to be treated until their personalities are normal enough to be placed in foster homes. The kids are awful unattractive things who spent their first day or rather *my* first day testing me out to see how much they could get by with and then called me every name in their vocabulary (which is quite a lengthy one) when they found that it wasn't very much. They spent most of their time threatening to throw rotten eggs or tomatoes or anything that happens to be handy but because this is the psychological approach, all counselors are supposed to act as though they liked rotten tomatoes best of all. It may be dangerous but at least not boring. Marshall is so intrigued he has decided he wants to work there too since there is always a fellow on duty to handle the older boys.

Again—a Merry Christmas, and Marshall wants to add a note.

From Marshall:

My work in public administration is very interesting here. They have an approach that is sound, I think. We're having a good time and will have lots to tell you when we visit you again.

Conclusion: This is a sample of one of the most frequent problems faced by young couples as they break the ties with parents and launch marriages of their own. In this case a not-yet-quite-adult young woman was aided in asserting herself with her parents more effectively through a pair relationship than she had been able to do alone. Her fiancé was supported in his course of winning the battle with her parents through a common front attained in prolonged discussion and planning.

At no time was the problem out of the hands of the two counselees. The proof of the success of the methods of counseling used is in the excellent adjustment reported in the first year of marriage.

CASE 33

**Problem: Premarital counseling at a pre-engagement level
Presented by: Marriage counselor (M.A. in Sociology) in private practice and college teacher**

Introduction: Bob and Betty, college seniors preparing for identical careers, took the marriage course taught by this counselor. They came for premarital counseling at the close of the semester.

Betty, 21, was attractive and intelligent but quite immature. Throughout the term she had shown very naïve ideas and warped attitudes about sex. She expressed fear of pain, not only in childbirth but also in sexual intercourse.

Bob, 23, was debonair and charming but with a strong need to be the center of attention. Although Betty had initiated counseling, Bob came in for a brief interview the day before Betty's first appointment.

Interview with Bob: After mentioning Betty's need for help in straightening out her ideas about sex, Bob asked for help in deciding whether he was sufficiently in love to marry her. I was surprised to learn they were not engaged since they had been inseparable throughout the term and their relationship had in it the "belongingness" of an engaged couple. Bob felt that he was not quite ready to settle down, that he would like to get some of the things he had always wanted for himself before he took on the responsibility of supporting a wife. He thought that once established in a job he would probably begin to feel the need for marriage.

He was further troubled because their relationship had grown less exciting than it was in the beginning. He wondered if this indicated a loss of love. Physical expression had never gone beyond warm kissing which at times led to an ejaculation. Since they had shared twenty hours of class work and had dated about three nights a week, I pointed out that they had about as much of each other's companionship as most married couples have, with the exception of sexual union. It wasn't surprising that after a separation they were always highly responsive to each other. Also, he had no interest in anyone else. He had a very protective attitude toward Betty and deep concern for her welfare.

Counseling sought to help Bob evaluate his feeling for Betty and to lead him to postpone definite plans for marriage until he felt more sure that he was ready for it.

Interview with Betty: Betty had no doubt about her love for Bob but doubted that she was ready for marriage because of her attitudes toward sex. She feared she would be frigid and wished to correct that. The sincerity of her desire was unmistakable.

Betty's mother, probably a frigid woman, spurns all demonstration of affection from the father, waving it off as silly. In preparing Betty for dating she had given her some sex instruction and, among other things, said to Betty with a wry face, "Even in marriage, sex is bad enough!"

Betty feels very close to her father who seems to turn to her for some of the affection he does not receive from his wife. Betty sits on his lap and he talks over problems with her that he cannot discuss with his wife.

It seemed in this interview, however, that Betty's relationship to her older brother created the greatest handicap to normal sexual development. He has taken the lead in trying to keep her a virgin. When she began dating he told her she could become pregnant from kissing a boy. He also pictured to her the "unpleasantness" of intercourse.

The brother has broken up every dating relationship of hers that promised to become serious. The only reason he has done nothing about Bob is that she has kept the family from knowing how deep her feeling for him is. The brother has no interest in any girl and is not considering marriage. He has gone so far as to say to Betty, "If you just won't marry, I will set you up in your profession and we can live together and you can be my hostess."

We looked at this relationship with her brother as the core of her problem. I suggested that only if she broke free of this close tie could either of them marry happily. She agreed, saying, "I couldn't marry Bob now because if I went home and faced my brother I would feel so guilty about having had sexual intercourse."

Also I tried to help her see the need to make her own decisions and live her own life even though her parents and brother might object. I encouraged her to think in the direction of a job away from home after graduation.

She decided that her next step would be to encourage her brother to date more, to talk with him about the need for them both to grow up and look toward marriage. She still felt, though, that she could not reveal her feeling for Bob lest the brother interfere.

Betty expressed a feeling of guilt over the petting she was doing with Bob and I reassured her on this point, saying that she was behaving in a normal way. I tried to guide her toward a more wholesome attitude toward the whole matter of sex, emphasizing what had been said in class about the positive value of a happy sex life in marriage. I explained the possible cause of pain during intercourse at the beginning of marriage and the way in which this could be eliminated through adequate premarital medical examination and instruction.

Consultation with Social Worker: Following this interview I discussed the case with a worker at the Mental Hygiene Clinic. Her first reaction was that Betty needed complete analytic treatment but, as we thought through the case together, it seemed that Betty's development during the past semester, her strong wish to change, and the constant pull toward normality of her love for Bob were such positive factors that it might be possible through counseling to help her achieve independence from her family, and from the brother in particular. I planned to continue as a parent substitute, encouraging independence of thought and action and providing an attitude of permissiveness toward sex, hoping that psychiatric treatment could be arranged later if indicated.

Second Interview with Betty: Three weeks elapsed before Betty's second appointment because of her heavy examination schedule and registration for the next term. She was much less tense and troubled than on her first visit and reported that she felt relaxed with her family as she never had before. In reporting our first interview to them, she had emphasized the emotional-immaturity aspect of our discussion, telling them that she had resolved to "grow up and be an adult." They were all highly pleased. Since then she and her brother have talked more as equals than they ever had before. She had informed them that she was seriously considering marriage to Bob.

Betty was exceedingly proud of a change in her relationship to her mother. Customarily her mother pouted when things didn't go her way, and this so upset Betty that she would shut herself away in her room. After the previous interview she had laughed off her mother's pouting, and her mother had not repeated it.

Betty insisted her fear of sex was completely gone. She didn't know how it happened and realized how impossible it sounded. She thought it had come about because of the insight and encouragement she had received in her first interview, and also as a result of the new freedom she experienced with her family.

Most of this interview was spent talking about her relationship to Bob. During the holidays, after a separation, he became very ardent and began for the first time to talk definitely of marriage. After a week, however, they were back in the same old rut; he seemed to take her very much for granted and tried to avoid any talk about their future. Betty had reacted to his uncertainty by withdrawing and by taking his offers of love rather lightly. She wondered just what her attitude ought to be.

Together we thought of this in the light of Bob's personality, which seems deeply affected by his insecurity and his need for recognition. I tried to help her see that Bob apparently needed the security of her love, since he became upset when anything threatened their relationship, and he seems to be genuinely torn between his wish to get married and his fear that marriage would endanger his professional progress. I suggested that she try to give him a feeling of security, to accept as a fact his love for her and to try to make him less fearful of marriage. Let her assume they will be married but not until they are both established job-wise, and let her also assure him on the point of her sharing in the earning during the early years of marriage. This seemed to be acceptable to her and she decided to work along this line.

I told Betty I would like to talk to Bob again to see if we could think through some of his personality needs. At her request he called for an appointment.

Second Interview with Bob: When Bob came in he seemed on the defensive, as if he expected me to scold him for keeping Betty so unsettled. I quickly directed the interview, however, to his own uncertainty about marriage about which he had first consulted me.

According to Bob, his hesitancy about marriage grew out of a love affair back in his teens. At 17 he had met a girl about his age. Friendship had ripened into love but while he was away in the service she had thrown him over for another man. He resolved never to trust another woman, became suspicious of everyone and hesitated to commit himself wholeheartedly to any person or activity for fear of being disappointed or let down. He found it hard to admit the girl episode to me, believing it a reflection on him as a person for anyone to treat him that way.

Through discussion Bob came to realize that his reaction to this teen-age experience was out of proportion to its importance. I suggested that we look back still further for some other causes of his present feelings. He revealed a good deal of hostility toward his brother Jim. Although Jim is three years older he had enrolled in the same college a year after Bob. At first they got along well because Bob was in the position of "showing Jim the ropes," but as soon as Jim found himself Bob began to be envious. He described Jim as the "black sheep," feared he would ruin the family reputation. (Actually Jim was a very mature and stable person who became a much more prominent student than Bob had been.) Since time was up I suggested that we talk further about his family ties next time.

Third Interview with Betty: Betty came in next day looking very pleased; she didn't have a single problem to talk about. I expressed surprise at this—and wondered why such a serious problem had disappeared so suddenly. She felt she had been much too sensitive to her brother's criticism. Also she had been getting on better with Bob because she hadn't felt so uncertain of him when he wasn't showing her his love. She felt secure and, not being as demanding of him, he was not putting up a defense of being indifferent.

She spoke of Bob's jealousy and his need to be the center of everything. I wondered if she were prepared to live with that sort of person for the rest of her life.

The rest of the interview was spent in considering some job openings that interested her.

Third Interview with Bob: A few days later Bob came in with an attitude of having resolved to "tell all." Significant facts that came to light were a history of enuresis and a feeling of parental rejection.

At the age of five or six, after having been trained, Bob had begun to wet the bed again. This continued until he was nine or ten, with a great deal of teasing from his father and his two older brothers but with a more sympathetic attitude from his mother and sister. His parents took him to several doctors who all agreed that there was nothing physically wrong with him. His father seemed to think it was deliberate.

Bob is the youngest of four children, having an older sister and two brothers. He supposed he was "one of those unwanted children." It seemed to him that all family activities were set up for the older children. When his father played ball with his brothers Bob had to watch from the sidelines. When his father read stories they were chosen for the older children. He had only one recollection of his father doing something for him alone—he took Bob to see the launching of a ship.

Bob's father was a domineering person, "always right." He was quite rigid in control of his children and of his wife.

Bob found it hard to describe his mother. An efficient house-keeper, she kept the children clean, took care of Bob when he hurt himself, but did not "baby" him.

Bob has few close friends. In spite of his man-about-town air, he had dated very little. Although friendly to everyone, he did not make close friends.

We tried to evaluate his personality in terms of a job and in marriage. He admitted that he resented criticism even from his instructors but he seemed not to realize what that would mean in a job where one must please a critical public. Although possessive and jealous of Betty, he thought that after marriage he would be so sure of her that he would never have such feelings.

At the end of the hour I made some suggestions for modifying these attitudes and threw the ball to him for the next move.

He showed extreme unwillingness to accept the challenge, however, saying, "Now that *we* have established that I am insecure and passive and can't take criticism, what are *we* going to do about it?"

An appointment was made for two weeks ahead to give an opportunity for psychiatric consultation on the case.

Consultation with Psychiatrist: The psychiatrist termed Betty's improvement a "flight into health"—one means of escaping the anxiety of unresolved illness—unless she had been exaggerating her problem in the first place. He approved my approach (of assuming that there were no problems).

He felt that Bob was much in need of psychiatric treatment. His real hostility was not toward his brother but his father. Due to an unresolved Oedipus complex he wants to remain a child and is unwilling to assume the responsibility of marriage. The psychiatrist recommended that I lay the foundation for psychiatric referral when Bob is established in his job. He also suggested that I urge caution and patience about marriage on the part of both Betty and Bob since neither seems ready for it yet.

Developments: Bob did not keep his scheduled appointment and after waiting several weeks (apparently too long) I wrote him. He called to say he was just leaving town and would call me when he returned. Nothing further was heard from either of them. The following October I ran into Betty on the street and she told me they were going to be married in the spring. Bob is happily established in a job in a small town. She, too, is happy in her work here but is looking forward to marriage and feels that everything is going to work out. I invited them for further counseling if they felt I could help.

Six Months Later: In March, about six weeks before the wedding date, Betty came to see me. I thought she had matured a good deal, had developed poise and self-assurance. She was upset, though, by the attitude of her parents and friends. They seemed to think she didn't know what she was doing. Still strongly influenced by other people's attitudes, this had caused her to question the marriage plan. Questions revealed that she was going ahead with the marriage and was merely seeking reassurance for it. I tried to be as positive and constructive as I could.

One question had to do with giving up her job. Bob expected it—there was no opening where he was and besides he did not want her competing with him. She knew she would have to put up with that attitude until he found security in his work. We talked of ways in which she could keep her hand in so that she would not get too rusty and also ways in which she might tactfully help Bob.

Betty asked for information about family planning. They must not have any children for a while. She had recently visited a newly married friend who was using such an array of equipment that it rather frightened Betty. Betty was greatly relieved at my description of the minimum essentials for careful protection, and the general importance of a premarital physical examination. Like her mother, Betty was acutely embarrassed about going to a doctor but after a good deal of discussion she decided she would go.

She had no fears about sex relations with Bob; in fact she was looking forward to that part of marriage and trusted him implicitly.

She concluded the interview by saying that it was her nature to be indecisive and to weigh all factors before making a decision. Now she felt encouraged about going ahead with wedding plans.

Follow-Up: Four years later, a follow-up report indicated that Bob and Betty had achieved a balance in their marriage which was satisfying to them during these early years. He is making quite a name for himself in his work and Betty helps him out at times, although she enjoys her role of homemaker. She is not by nature competitive and appears to find dependence on her husband highly satisfying. She thinks he is wonderful and is enjoying his success as much as he is. There are still no children and no plans for any.

Neither had taken any psychiatric treatment. Although help was given in counseling there were still many unresolved problems. Whether the marriage would stand up under adversity or the accidental birth of a child is somewhat questionable.

13. Cultural Differences and the Choice of a Marriage Partner

---

These three cases deal with contemplated marriage between persons of vastly different cultural backgrounds. In spite of the dramatic quality of these differences, the reader will note that counseling in each case is concerned with the development of the psychological competence of the persons involved to deal with these differences on a reality basis. One's interest is particularly arrested by the "experiment" in interracial living described in Case 36.

CASE 34

Problem: Contemplated interfaith marriage
Presented by: Family consultant (Ph.D. in Psychology; graduate degree in Social Work) in private practice in a Western city

The Problem: The case came to my attention through Mr. C, the girl's father, a wealthy manufacturer, whom I had known for some time. He was fairly prominent in his community; the president of his synagogue, of middle-class attitudes and convictions, self-made, and inordinately proud of his status in the community. A, aged 22, the third of his four children, was doing some graduate work in American History in a local university. An older sister and brother were married in the family tradition; a younger brother was still in college, preparing to enter medical school. The problem arose when A announced that she was engaged to B, a non-Jewish fellow graduate student in the same department. Her father was shocked beyond words. He did not know very much about the boy's parents except that they had a fruit market and were of very modest means with a very large family. His principal worry was that the young man was non-Jewish. Mr. C was only vaguely aware of the fact that B was Catholic; he had given no thought to the significance that might attach to the religion of the boy except that he was not Jewish. He was mostly concerned about the problem his daughter would face in making a happy home life for herself with a non-Jew. In addition, there was the economic problem the young people would face; and Mr. C was unwilling to help the young people to a start as he had done for his other married children. Mr. C had broached the question of conversion to Judaism, but his daughter would not bring any pressure to bear upon the young man in this regard, saying that she would no more insist on this than she would want B to insist on her conversion to Catholicism.

The mother was rather indifferent to the situation. The youngest son insisted that religion, religious practices, proscriptions, and differences are of the past and have little place in American life. The other two children sided with the father, although they were not very emphatic in their opposition to the intermarriage. The father pleaded for my help in bringing his daughter "to her senses." In addition to the personal problem, he felt his daughter had become lukewarm or indifferent to the cause of Jewish nationalism and seemed convinced that the best interests of American democracy lay in the direction of social and biological intermingling of peoples and cultures. All this he considered highly romantic, immature, and impractical.

When I asked how I could help, he replied that he would like me to tell the girl how impossible and unwise her program is and that she should abandon it. When he was told that this was out of the question, that if I entered into the situation it would have to be on a completely objective and impartial basis and only on his daughter's request, he replied that on the basis of his previous experience with me, he had feared that this would be my attitude. He admitted that he had already seen his rabbi, who agreed with him but had not the slightest influence on his daughter. He further admitted that he came to me at his daughter's suggestion, as a last resort, hoping against hope that I would help him.

The Counseling—First Interview: A came in as per arrangement. I remembered her as an attractive, pleasant, and rather bright girl. In the two years or more since I had last seen her she had matured considerably. Still somewhat voluble, she articulated well and easily, and seemed to take considerable pleasure in formulating her ideas. She seemed prepared for a debate and launched out by saying that she supposed her father had filled me with all kinds of reasons why this marriage could not take place for her sake, and she was prepared to defend her position, although she hoped that it would not be necessary. She was told quite frankly that her father sought my help in persuading her to abandon her marriage plans with the young man in question, but that I had told him that I could not and would not enter the situation on such terms.

She expressed appreciation of this point of view and then asked what I would like to know.

My reply was, "I want to know what you want to tell me. Since you have come prepared to defend your proposed marriage, you might as well begin with that, although you should bear in mind that no defense is needed." That seemed to me as good a way as any of starting.

She began by saying that she had known the young man a little over two years; that they are both interested in American history and have other interests in common such as music, literature, art, and participation in liberal movements on and off the campus; that they have been seeing a good deal of each other for over a year, during which time they had come to know each other pretty well; that he had asked her to marry him a number of times in the last six months, but she had refused to commit herself until she was sure of her own mind, that she had given him an affirmative answer about three months ago and had no reason to regret it; that except for her father's attitude she would be very happy. She declared that she will go through with the marriage whether her father finally agrees to it or not. She felt that his objections were due to prejudice and outworn racial and nationalistic pride which had no place in twentieth-century America.

I reminded her that not so long ago she had sought to awaken in her younger brother a deeper interest in his people and their suffering; that then she seemed convinced that as long as the Christian world discriminates against and persecutes the Jew it is cowardly and disloyal to turn one's back on one's own people. Had she changed her mind about that? If so, what was the basis of the change? If not, how does she reconcile this intermarriage with her previous attitude and interest? She replied that she had given the matter a good deal of thought, had discussed it many times with her fiancé, and had come to the conclusion, on the basis of their discussion, that there isn't much sense in maintaining Jewish separatism, especially on a nationalistic basis, for American Jews. Since neither she nor her fiancé is very religiously inclined, their religious differences would have little influence on their happiness together.

I suggested to her that her present attitude may be a convenient and order-made rationalization. Though she had every right to whatever point of view she wished to adopt, and whatever basis she wished to utilize, it would be rather foolish to deceive herself. Hence it was very important for her to face the matter frankly with herself. It was also important for her to ask herself how much of her present attitude was due to her fiancé's influence.

She seemed somewhat embarrassed by this, but said that although she was considerably influenced by her discussions with B, she accepted this point of view not as a matter of convenience, but conviction. This, however, seemed to be said without real conviction on her part; at least it did not carry conviction to her auditor. Nothing further was said on that score at this time.

The question as to when the marriage would take place, she answered with the statement that they had not yet made definite plans because B had a somewhat similar problem with his parents, who are devout Catholics and do not look with favor upon his marrying a non-Catholic, especially a Jewess. She explained the last part by adding that although his parents are good Americans, they had been influenced by the Fascist attitude and Nazi propaganda against Jews. She said, also, that she had not yet met her future in-laws because she and B had thought it best to wait until his parents and siblings became more accustomed to the idea of his marrying a non-Catholic. She added that he is a very devoted son and brother and did not wish to hurt his people any more than absolutely necessary. She was apparently completely unaware of the implications of this statement for her own attitude and its reflection on her as a dutiful and loving daughter as evidenced by her readiness to inflict a deep hurt on her father. This, too, was left unexplored for the time being.

She said further that she had taken happiness for granted where the marriage partners loved each other and were free from religious observances. However, further discussion revealed that she did not really know how free she and B were. She did not know whether he would want to be married by a priest or would be satisfied with a civil marriage. She thought, or rather guessed, that he would prefer a church wedding because of his parents. Nor did she know anything about the requirements of the Catholic Church in the case of an intermarriage before it would permit it to take place. To the question whether she would be converted to Catholicism if that were required of her, she replied with a shocked "No," and added that she would not desert her people or her religion. This spontaneous reply seemed more like her former position and was considerably at variance with her more recently professed attitude. But again this was dropped without further discussion. The question apparently set her thinking, and she inquired what the requirements would be of her by the Catholic Church. I expressed surprise that she did not know the actual conditions either from B or the rabbi who had discussed the matter with her. She replied that B seemed to avoid the subject, and the rabbi mainly sought to persuade her on the basis of her duty to her people and her family, neither of which considerations she thought very compelling.

Again she asked what the requirements would be and was told that she would have to get them from B, his parents, or their priest. She wondered also where she could get some information on intermarriage in general and asked whether she could have another appointment to discuss the matter further. She appeared much more thoughtful and much less certain and aggressive when she left than when she came.

Second Interview: A appeared even less sure of herself. She said that the reading she had done on cultural and religious factors in marriage left her very much confused and uneasy. Her efforts at getting a clear and unequivocal statement from B as to his position on religious matters, to what extent he would adhere to his parents' demands, and what precisely are the requirements of the Church and to what extent he would abide by them, were more or less fruitless. He assured her that he did not hold very much to religious observance, but he insisted that he could

not ignore altogether his parents' sensibilities in the matter and
would have to conform, although he could not or would not say
to what extent. Nor would he commit himself with respect to
the church requirements. He said that his parents had sought a
statement from their priest, who had refused to give it to them
and asked to see him and the girl. The young man confessed
that he did not have the courage to see his priest because of his
awareness of the seriousness with which the Church looked
upon such deviation.

She said that a situation which had seemed to her very simple
had suddenly become very complex and involved and was much
beyond her capacity to deal with unless she received some help.
She could not expect such help from her folks and she now
knows that she can't expect any real help from B or his people.
She pleaded rather piteously for help from me.

When asked what kind of help she wanted, she replied, "I
want to know what to do." She was told that she must reach her
own decision on that question, that no one could or should assume the responsibility for that decision for her, that at most
one could only direct her to the sources of information which
might help her in reaching a decision. She accepted this reluctantly.

She then asked for information on the problems and results
of intermarriage and for an authoritative statement on the attitude of the Catholic Church. I promised to try to help her in
both items and suggested that in the meantime she do as much
reading as possible in the literature. She asked for the privilege
of discussing the results of her reading until the other information was secured.

Third, Fourth, and Fifth Interviews: During the next three weeks
A discussed her readings. In the meantime I obtained the type-
script of a study on intermarriage from the head of the department of sociology in a Midwestern university, and secured an
authoritative statement in the form of a letter from another

friend, a priest, as to the requirements of the Catholic Church. These two documents she studied carefully and discussed with me. She came to the conclusion that she was facing three alternatives: (1) decide to accept Catholicism; (2) give a binding pledge to rear her children in a religious belief which was not hers; or (3) abandon the idea of marrying a Catholic who was loyal to his parents and his church. She felt reasonably certain that B would not break with his parents and began seriously to doubt whether he would abandon his church.

At first she felt let down and outraged by what she thought was the lack of frankness and courage of B. She felt that she had met him halfway in being willing to turn from the traditions of her family and her people, but that he failed to meet her halfway.

When it was suggested to her that it might be better for her to give him an opportunity to decide for himself rather than decide for him, and that the counselor have an opportunity to discuss the situation with him, she said with considerable bitterness that she now realized that his decision was never in question, although she had been too blind or too ignorant to recognize it. However, she would discuss the matter with him so that there would be no possibility of a mistake. She would decide whether to ask him to see the counselor after her discussion with him.

Sixth Interview: In the sixth interview she reported that she had had several conversations with B in which she asked him what his position would be if the Church made such and such demands, without telling him that she knew definitely what the requirements are. She reported that he "hemmed and hawed" and finally said that if these are the conditions he would have to abide by them for the sake of his family and his future. He told her for the first time that he might get some help from the Church in his academic career, and that it would be foolish for him to jeopardize that, especially since religious observances do not seem to matter very much to her. When she protested against his attitude, he placed the blame on her, saying that she had apparently misled him by misrepresenting her true feelings about her religion, and tried to persuade her to remove the obstacle to their happiness by embracing his superior religion. She declared that she would never accept Catholicism and would never agree to bring up her children in a faith that would alienate them from her; that she was willing to abandon her religion "for a broader humanism" but not, as she put it, "for an even more restricted and more limited religious belief." This only made him more determined in his view and they broke off their engagement.

A was quite bitter about her experience; considered herself very much abused by B, who had not been honest or frank with her; found fault with her father and her rabbi who had failed to make the situation clear to her, but had appealed to her on an emotional basis which she could not accept. Even this counselor had failed her in not presenting the facts in the first interview, but had let her struggle on, all these weeks, with all the unhappiness to which she had been subjected.

It was suggested to her that if this experience was to have any constructive value for her, she would have to re-examine the situation to determine for herself whether everybody had failed her and whether she alone was blameless; that if she is to remain with that attitude without obtaining some objectivity she will be a good subject for other unhappy experiences. She agreed to do so, but doubted whether she could do it by herself and asked for help.

Seventh and Eighth Interviews: The situation was re-examined. She saw, at first with considerable reluctance, but later much more willingly and objectively, that she had been immature in her attitudes toward her father, her religion, her previous convictions, her fiancé, and so on.

Ninth Interview: In the last interview she said that she had now regained her composure and had overcome her resentment. She felt that she had gained a great deal of insight and had "grown up," as she put it.

Follow-Up: She has since married a man of her own faith who entered her father's manufacturing establishment, and from all accounts she is very happy.

Conclusions: This case presents a number of questions and considerations for the professional counselor. Thus it may be asked: What was the counselor's point of view regarding this type of intermarriage? Did he throw the weight of his influence against the marriage rather than try to work through the situation?

But more fundamentally, do this girl's emotionality, her apparent opportunism and rationalizations, her too ready abandonment of life-philosophies and loyalties, her tendency to project her own deficiencies upon others, and her seeking a liaison with someone outside her own faith, indicate a neurotic tendency which could be treated only on a deeper level? If so, is her neuroticism likely to reappear unless treated?

Without attempting to discuss in detail the various symptoms or manifestations of possible neurotic behavior or whether they be only the spontaneous, perhaps somewhat irresponsible, behavior of a young, inexperienced girl who thought herself in love, it should be noted that A displayed considerable self-control, as evidenced by her taking three months to consider B's proposal of marriage. It should also be remembered that this girl came from a cultural environment which places a premium on marriage rather than on a career for a girl. Her taking graduate work was, in her milieu, an inadequate substitute for marriage. At least this was the case in the eyes of her parents, relatives, and friends. Little wonder then, that she was perhaps a little too ready to make some compromises and concessions for marriage, especially since propinquity and other conditions, perhaps in part colored by her dissembling fiancé, made the prospects of a happy married life seem so favorable.

Nevertheless, the counselor was on the alert for deeper therapy requirements. A's subsequent adjustment would seem to justify the counselor's conclusion that a need for deeper therapy was not indicated.

CASE 35

Problem: Cultural differences, complicated by premarital sexual intimacy
Presented by: Professor and marriage counselor (Ph.D. in Sociology) in the student counseling service of a large university

Introduction: This case was handled at the student counseling service of a large university. Students, their boy friends or girl friends, or marriage partners are eligible to come for premarital, marital, or family counseling. A staff of six, all of whom hold academic rank in the departments of sociology, social work, and home economics, spend time in counseling students. No charge is made for these services.

A friend of the student made the initial contact, stating that Mr. A was terrifically upset over his girl friend (Miss B) and that he was talking of killing himself and her. His school work was "going to pot." Counselor Y explained the counseling services to this friend. She talked to Mr. A; as a result, he came for help.

Mr. A was from a foreign land with entirely different cultural backgrounds from those of the American girl with whom he said he was "head over heels in love." Their religious backgrounds were basically different; she was a Protestant and he belonged to a non-Christian faith. The presenting problem was that this boy and girl had gone together for a few months, had been sexually intimate many times, and the girl had recently told him she didn't love him any more and wanted him to "stay away from her." He was desperate and determined to win the girl back.

The Counseling: This case involved one interview with the friend of the client, four interviews with Mr. A, four with Miss B, and one joint interview participated in by Mr. A, Miss B, and the two counselors, Mr. X and Mr. Y. The counseling continued over a period of six weeks. The interviews were limited to 50-60 minutes each.

First Interview, Mr. A and Counselor X: In much detail Mr. A described his relationship with Miss B. It began a few months before and had become an intense love affair almost overnight. He took great delight in describing their intimacies in detail and seemed to gain much satisfaction in depicting what a great lover he was.

He said he couldn't bring himself to accept the fact that she wanted to discontinue seeing him; he felt she was confused. "She said she doesn't love me any more. I know she does, but that's what she told me. I went to pieces completely. I have not been in my right mind since. I told her I would kill myself and her too, if she didn't change her mind. I have cried for days. My heart is broken." He explained there had been other girls in his life, but none that really made him feel as she did.

When the counselor asked about religious and cultural differences, he quickly passed this off by saying, "If you are really in love, nothing else matters."

Mr. A asked if his girl friend could come in for an interview so that the counselor could tell her to go back to him. Counselor X explained that Miss B was certainly welcome but that he would not be able to tell her what to do. She would have to make up her own mind. Mr. A said he would talk to her about this possibility. Arrangements were made for her to see Counselor Y. Ordinarily, in this service, one counselor sees both persons, but in this situation—as in some other special situations—it seemed advisable to use two counselors. It was felt that Mr. A, because of his immaturity and the fact that he was severely upset emotionally, might feel one counselor would take sides against him if only one were used.

Counselor's impressions were that Mr. A is an extremely immature person, impulsive, and one who does not look realistically at cultural differences and their implications. A psychiatrist in the Student Health Service was consulted by the counselor regarding the suicidal threats. His analysis was that since "Mr. A is so open in his threats and is dramatic in the way in which he makes these threats, bordering on histrionics, it is doubtful that any serious consequence will result. The fact that he is able to express himself so freely with reference to intimacies and is so easily verbal in everything, shows that he is capable of acting out or talking through emotions, which, if suppressed, might produce suicidal tendencies."

Counselor concluded that Mr. A is a petulant young man who has never been required to accept much responsibility. He has always had his own way, and now, when things don't go just as he feels they should, he storms about like a child with a temper tantrum. Also his masculinity is being threatened, and he needs help in facing reality and in accepting a more mature responsibility. He needs to accept, intellectually and emotionally, cultural differences between himself and his girl friend. He also needs help in developing insight about his own feelings and needs as well as those of his girl friend.

First Interview, Miss B and Counselor Y: Miss B came on time for her appointment, the day after Mr. A's interview. She was barely seated when she burst into tears, "I hate him now. I have found out that he is extremely selfish and childish." As she proceeded, it was obvious that she had mixed feelings, for soon she was talking about what she could do to prevent hurting him and help him to grow up.

Miss B gave substantially the same story as did Mr. A, about their courtship and intimacies. She then said that about three weeks ago she came to the conclusion that they should quit going together, and she told him so. Since then, he has acted like a child, has cried often, and sometimes has "fallen to the floor dramatically." She said that at one time she was in love with him, or thought she was, but now she knows they could never have a successful marriage of the type she had envisioned. The thought of living in a large house among strangers in a foreign land terrifies her. She explained that she is deeply religious and is a Christian, and he is not. His dramatic mood swings also bother her.

Miss B is an intelligent, unassuming person, with deep feelings of inferiority, who tends to identify with the "underdog" or minority group. She was apparently dominated by her mother, and developed a "puritanical conscience." Miss B is now trying "to live her own life." She indicated that she is deeply ashamed of what has gone on between them, although Mr. A has assured her often that in his country such behavior is entirely all right "if you are in love." She feels so guilty she is sure she will never marry anyone, as it would be unfair in view of what she has done.

Counselor's impressions were that this girl has decided intellectually that she doesn't want to marry Mr. A, but emotionally she is still attached to him. She has deep guilt feelings regarding their intimacies and feels she is a very wicked person. She undoubtedly needs help in working through these feelings, in gaining insight into her reasons for her present dilemma, and in coming to a decision regarding present and future plans.

Second Interview, Mr. A and Counselor X: Two days after the first interview, Mr. A seemed less upset although he claimed that his condition was still critical and that he was "a very weak man." He was encouraged to talk realistically about some of the problems involved in courtship and marriage between persons from the "West and the East." He mentioned that he and Miss B had already discussed some of these factors, such as differences in language, religion, and social customs—particularly regarding premarital intimacies and romantic courtesies. They had begun to see each other's point of view regarding the expression of affection. To her it was a sin, and by losing her virginity she had become an unworthy person. To him, this was a natural way of expressing deep affection and love, in or out of marriage. He spent most of the time describing how he felt about it all. Toward the end of the interview, he said that if he were sure that Miss B didn't love him, he would be willing to give her up. He wondered if a joint interview could be arranged during which he could find out how she really felt. A wall had been built between them, and they seemed to be able to get so far in their discussions but no further—perhaps the counselor could help them.

Second Interview, Miss B and Counselor Y: Miss B spent the hour describing her feelings and in trying to look at both sides of the problem. She said that maybe they should get married since they had been intimate, and she felt she could never marry anyone else because this was so wrong. On the other side, she pointed out these problems: difference in ways of living; trouble in getting along socially with each other's friends; religious differences; his folks are opposed to the marriage (he threatened suicide to them before they gave their consent); she would hate living in his country but knows he would insist on this; and Mr. A is "selfish, childish, and has a violent temper." She was also concerned about how her parents would take it.

Miss B said she understood the counseling service had some tests which if taken, helped in understanding personality and marriageability. Arrangements were made for her to take marriage prediction and personality tests.

Third Interview, Mr. A and Counselor X: Mr. A was less wrought up today than at the previous interviews. He stated he was not at all reconciled to giving up Miss B and talked of new approaches he might use to win her back. He had already tried taking out another girl to make Miss B jealous. Apparently it had not worked.

Mr. A said he could not understand why Miss B wanted to break off their relationship so she could "make things right." Counselor helped him to gain some insight about ambivalent feelings. She had been attracted to him, but she was reared in a deeply religious atmosphere which stressed the importance of chastity.

Third Interview, Miss B and Counselor Y: The results of the two tests were discussed with Miss B. The personality test showed good results except in the areas of "personal freedom," "family relationships," and "feelings of personal worth." The marriage prediction schedule revealed that the chances for successful marriage to each other were poor. Miss B seemed pleased at the result of the test, feeling this gave psychological support to her decision she had made.

She said that since the first interviews there had been no display of affection between her and Mr. A and that she now feels they can separate without too much hardship on either. She still feels guilty about her actions. For the first time, however, she talked a little about future plans, briefly mentioning the possibility of going with some other fellows and maybe even some day marrying someone else. Counselor encouraged her to talk about her feelings in this regard and also pointed out that other young people at times become involved with premarital experimentation. By the end of the interview, she seemed greatly relieved.

Fourth Interview, Miss B and Counselor Y: Miss B came in for an appointment just prior to the joint interview. She seemed to crystallize her own thinking as to what she wanted to discuss in the coming joint conference. She talked some of getting a job in another country, away from everything, but finally said, "I guess that would be running away." She ended the interview stating she was going to tell Mr. A that she no longer loved him and that it was "all off."

Joint Interview, Miss B, Mr. A, and Counselors X and Y: This conference was mutually agreed upon by all participants. Counselor Y took the initiative and explained that the purpose of the conference was to think through together what might be best for all concerned; the aim was not to pit one against the other. Miss B and Mr. A were assured nothing would be divulged that had come up in previous interviews.

Both Mr. A and Miss B participated freely. She told him several times that she was now certain what she felt for him was infatuation—and not genuine love and she believed they should definitely break up. He responded by pointing out that he thought she still loved him and that she was only confused. They talked about several cultural differences in their backgrounds. Throughout the interview Mr. A was quite dramatic. He seized every opportunity to profess his love for her with tender words and deep feeling. She finally made it unmistakably clear she preferred not to see him again, although she hoped they could still be friends. He told her he had a "broken heart" and couldn't live without her; she wasn't swayed at all. The interview ended with Mr. A finally saying, indignantly, "Well, if that's the way you feel about it, let's call it quits."

Fourth Interview, Mr. A and Counselor X: About two weeks later Mr. A dropped in to see the counselor. He was much calmer and more composed than on previous interviews. He claimed he was still in love with Miss B, but had become partially reconciled to their estrangement. He casually mentioned he had dated two or three other girls in the meantime. He also had respected Miss B's wishes and had not called on her.

Follow-Up: Six months later Mr. A had almost forgotten Miss B. He had a "new girl friend" and seemed to be getting along well in school. Three years later Miss B married Mr. C, a man with similar cultural backgrounds and the same religion. It was ascertained that one year later they were getting along satisfactorily.

Conclusions: This case represents the combined use of two counselors, individual interviews, testing, and the joint interview. This total setup seemed to help this young couple ventilate their feelings of love and guilt, gain some insight regarding their own behavior and the behavior of each other, acquire some realistic understanding of cultural differences, and assist them to accept the decision made by one of them to break off their courtship. The counselors attempted to help them to help themselves, not tell them what to do. The girl worked through most of her guilt feelings about premarital sexual intimacies and finally gained enough strength to convince Mr. A she was no longer interested in him as a marriage partner, mainly due to personality, and cultural differences. Within three years she was able to marry someone of her own race and religious faith. Mr. A was given the opportunity to learn more about the American way of life and to contrast it somewhat realistically with his own. He was finally resigned to Miss B's rejection of him as a marriage partner and able to move on to new relationships with the opposite sex. He also recognized his need for a feeling of masculine superiority and adequacy. His adjustment to school improved considerably.

CASE 36

Problem: Contemplated Negro-white marriage
Presented by: Family consultant (Ph.D. in Psychology; graduate degree in Social Work) in private practice in a Western city

Introduction: This case is that of a white girl who was contemplating marriage with a Negro boy. The girl's parents, particularly her mother, were opposed to the marriage, and their opposition threatened to destroy the excellent relationship between the parents and the daughter.

The Problem: This case first came to the counselor's attention through the girl's father, Mr. X, professional man of broad, liberal views on social and economic questions, interested in good race relations, and active in several organizations promoting them. He was a member of the NAACP, the Urban League, and other organizations promoting civic unity. His daughter, a senior in a local university, shared his views, mingled freely with white and Negro classmates of both sexes, and brought them home, with the encouragement of her father, until she announced that she was in love with a Negro boy, a first-year graduate student in chemistry, and that she intended to marry him.

The father stated that Z is an only child, had a fairly happy childhood, was a rather good student in elementary and secondary schools as well as in college where she is majoring in literature with special interest in drama, has a fine social conscience, and has always been interested in the underdog. She has shown considerable interest in minority groups and responded to agitation on the campuses of the junior college and university, opposing discrimination. She resigned from a sorority because of her opposition to discrimination.

He reported that she was not active in church groups and had no special interest in church activity or attendance. The family as a whole is not religiously inclined although the mother would prefer a greater degree of religious identification. The family life was tranquil and happy until this problem arose. Though it has not reached the conflict stage it has caused tension which may result in strife.

The father said he had no objection to racial intermarriage on principle; that he would not oppose the marriage of his daughter to a Negro except that he does not believe that she will be happy, since society is not so constituted at the present as to make it possible for such a couple to be happy. He is deeply hurt by his daughter's accusations that he is insincere in his activities in favor of racial understanding and good will and by her saying that like all good conservatives, he draws the line at intermarriage. She has even charged that he would draw the line at having Negro neighbors.

Mrs. X upbraids her husband with the charge that he is responsible for their difficulties, that she foresaw trouble when their daughter associated with Negro boys and girls and wanted to put a stop to it, or at least to discourage it, but could not stand up against the two of them. She insists that if this marriage goes through she will not be able to face her friends and relatives. Mr. X fears that if this marriage takes place they will have to leave the city, if, indeed, it does not cause his wife's nervous collapse or a rupture in their own marriage.

He was inclined to doubt the depth of their daughter's love for the boy. It seemed to him that at first the relationship was something of an adventure with her and that later it became a "cause." He requested advice as to what to do and how to handle the problem. When it was suggested to him that no advice could be given without discussing the matter with his daughter and perhaps also with his wife, Mr. X doubted whether his daughter would agree to come to see the counselor but thought she might do so because she knows of his interest in interracial problems. He promised to try to get her to come.

Counseling—First Interview: Z, an attractive, high-spirited, intelligent, and somewhat impulsive girl, stated that she knew that her father had been to see the counselor and had no doubt prejudiced him against the marriage, that the only reason she agreed to come was her regard for the high reputation of the counselor on account of his attitude on race relations, but if he had any intention of persuading her against the marriage, he might as well save himself the time and energy. It was apparent that she was aggressively hostile, and that in her present mood little insight could be obtained into her real feelings and motivations. It seemed necessary, therefore, to divert her attention to a different problem, to gain her confidence on a different level, and in a different area. She was assured that nothing was further from the counselor's mind than to persuade her to give up her plan to marry the boy she loves, that I was concerned with a different problem she was facing, perhaps not known to her, on which I might need her help; that it was up to her whether she should discuss the forthcoming marriage with me; that I had no desire to force her confidence and that, in fact, I did not share her father's fears and particularly her mother's conviction, that she would wreck her life with this marriage since I have known several intermarriages which turned out quite happy; that it all depended on the personalities involved and the circumstances. The important thing at the moment was quite a different problem—one which, unless wisely handled, might not only hurt a number of people whom she loved, but might even become a serious obstacle to her own marital happiness.

By this time the girl was considerably calmer, was more at ease and interested in the problem on which I wanted her help. Despite her request that I tell her what the problem was, I told her that I was not yet ready to confide in her, that I would like to know a little more about her, her interests, the kind of books she reads, her outlook on life, the courses she took, and her reactions to them, the insights she had acquired into human behavior, and so on.

We then discussed her courses at the university, especially those in psychology and sociology, her teachers whom we knew in common, books she had read, and so on, so that by the time the first interview was drawing to a close we had established good rapport. She then asked what problem I wanted to discuss with her and how she could help me.

I told her that it was too late to go into that, but I could tell her that the problem concerned her family, that I was especially concerned about her mother, and that I would greatly appreciate it if she would observe her mother most carefully during the next few days and give me the results of her observations and her opinion as to whether there was a problem there, what it is due to, and what can be done about it.

She wanted to stay on and discuss it at once, but it was explained to her that this was both undesirable and impossible. It would be better if she had an opportunity to observe the situation and make up her mind after this special observation. An appointment was made for a week hence.

Second Interview: The second interview with Z consisted mainly of a discussion of the problem presented by the mother, about which the girl had become greatly concerned. She recognized that her mother was facing a nervous breakdown, ascribed it to her own involvement with the Negro boy, was still defiant and insistent that she would go through with the marriage, but was hesitant and deeply concerned about its effect on her mother. She saw no solution because the only thing that would help her mother, she thought, would be to give up her plans of marriage, which she was unwilling to do.

Several times during this interview she asked whether she was not right in her attitude and whether she did not have a right to her own happiness and whether it was right for her parents to interfere. These questions were studiously avoided until she challenged me for an answer.

The reply was that she really did not want an answer to these questions because she knew the answers herself and in fact would most likely not accept anyone else's view on the matter, if it differed from hers. I offered to change places with her and have her answer these questions for me. But since the period was almost up we might leave this subject for our next discussion if she wished to come again. This she was eager to do, and another appointment was made for the following week.

Third Interview: The third interview began with a discussion of the parents' attitude but quickly turned to the questions left unanswered at the last session; that is, whether she did not have a right to her own happiness and whether her parents had a right to deny it to her by interfering with her intended marriage.

Again it was suggested that she answer the questions. At first she was very resistive, but when it became clear that I would not answer them until, at least, she had attempted to do so, she finally yielded.

The first question she answered in the affirmative, that is, that she had every right to her own happiness. Without challenging that right in any way, she was led to re-examine that right when it involved the unhappiness of others. This led to a discussion of her relation to her parents, theirs to her, the interrelation of their happiness as individuals and as a family group, and whether she or they had a right to purchase their own happiness at the cost of the unhappiness of the others.

At the end of the hour she was by no means certain that she would or could be happy if she knew that she would thereby cause extreme unhappiness to her mother or father or both.

Again she was asked whether she wanted to continue to discuss the second question; and so, when she declared her eagerness to continue, another appointment was made for her.

Fourth Interview: The fourth interview began by a review and some further discussion of her right to happiness regardless of its cost to her parents. She said that she had thought about it all week and was very much disturbed by the question and the trend of her own thinking. At several points she started to discuss it with her father and boy friend but could not get herself to do so for fear of being misunderstood or being influenced by either or both. She had as yet reached no conclusion and thought that a discussion of the second question might throw some light on the first.

It was not long before she recognized and freely admitted that never before had her parents interfered with anything she desired or wanted to do when she was able to convince them that she really wanted it; that whenever they resisted her it was because they feared that it was not to her best interests. An examination of a number of incidents made it clear that they were usually right and that where they yielded to her insistence she was usually proved wrong. There was never any "I told you so," and each situation was dealt with on its own merits regardless of how wrong she might have been in the previous one. This naturally made her question whether it was interference on their part or a desire to save her from making a serious mistake. Their greater and more persistent opposition she recognized as due to the seriousness of the step contemplated. This led to the question whether she or they were right and how this question might be answered.

At first she was quite certain that she knew her mind and was sure about her feelings. Her parents, she was convinced, had never been willing to be objective about the matter and always looked on the dark side of the situation. They saw no possibility for a successful marriage in this for her and nothing but heartbreak for themselves. This made it impossible for her to give their objections the weight she otherwise would have attached to them.

Her mother was especially difficult about it. She would burst into tears the moment the situation was mentioned or when she thought about it by herself. She insisted that she would not survive the marriage, that she could not face her friends, and that she did not want to be grandmother to dark children. She had forbidden her home to the young man, which only made matters worse because the daughter was forced to meet him outside the home and developed a strong sense of guilt about it.

Her father was somewhat more objective about the matter and did not resort to the "temper tantrums" that her mother did, but he too was deeply involved and, she felt, took refuge behind the plea that she spare her mother. In fact, this was the first calm and more or less objective discussion she had ever had about her problems and she was grateful for the opportunity. She only wished that she could get some advice instead of doing all the talking.

When doubt was expressed as to whether she wanted advice or confirmation of her own attitude and intentions, she admitted somewhat shamefacedly that she guessed she had not been "too objective" herself and had perhaps "acted like a spoiled brat when crossed." But the problem still remained, what should she do? Was she right or wrong? How could she find out?

This led to a consideration of the problems and issues involved in intermarriage in general and this type of intermarriage in particular. Since the hour was almost up, it was suggested that if she wanted to pursue the matter further she might read up on the subject before the next session and see whether her reading would throw any light on how she might proceed to find out. She asked for some references as to what to read, but it was suggested that she get a list of readings from her sociology professor or the librarian.

Although Z was a little rebellious at the delay, she admitted that this was a good idea and promised to work on this lead.

Fifth Interview: The next interview opened with Z's statement that although she had not yet resolved her problem, she was much clearer about it than she had ever been, and knew now that she must consider it not only from her own point of view and emotional involvement, but from the standpoint of the others involved. She now realized that this type of intermarriage is much more serious in its implications and consequences, whether it proves a success or failure, than other marriages or intermarriages. She had not realized before that she would be practically limited to living in a Negro area, that she would virtually have to give up her white friends and associates, or would have to be prepared to face a life in which she would always imagine herself being pitied or considered peculiar. She seemed particularly concerned about the effect of the marriage on her boy friend and the color of the children born in this marriage. She was no less resentful of society for imposing restrictions and handicaps upon people simply because of the color of their skin, but she wondered whether the best way of fighting this discrimination was by flying in the face of society or whether she could accomplish more by fighting discrimination without being charged with having an axe to grind.

These and other thoughts, she said, made her feel that she had gained more objectivity. She was particularly pleased with two aspects of her new attitude: First, she could discuss the matter with her parents, and especially her mother, without either of them "flying off the handle," so that she was able to reassure her mother that she would not act precipitously, as a result of which her mother has become a different person and something of their former relationship has been re-established. Second, she has come to look upon her boy friend in a somewhat different light. Whereas formerly she saw him as the embodiment or personification of his unfairly persecuted race, she now looks upon him as a person in his own right, and as her future husband, the man with whom she will spend the rest of her life.

But despite her new attitude, she still did not know what to do, or rather, she corrected herself, what would be the wisest and best thing to do, everything and everybody considered. She expressed the wish that it were possible for her to look into the future and see what it holds in store for her.

When it was suggested to her that this might be possible, at least to a limited extent, she was startled and eagerly asked how this might be accomplished. She was reminded that her new attitude which has given her so much satisfaction is not due to anything that anybody had told her, but rather the result of her own thinking. She readily saw that this, too, is something she might think through for herself and that whatever conclusions she arrived at would be more acceptable to her. She agreed to think about it and asked for another appointment.

Sixth Interview: The following interview was devoted to a consideration of a plan she had worked out which would enable her to see what life in a Negro environment, if she had to live in one, would be like. Briefly, the plan called for her to go to an Eastern city, obtain quarters in the Negro section and live there as she might have to live there, after marriage. After further discussion it was agreed that upon graduation, which was only a few weeks off, she would go East, enter a near-by university for graduate study, secure living quarters with a Negro family, and endeavor to live as normal a life as the circumstances would permit. She had acquainted her boy friend with her plan without revealing her purpose in full. He tried to dissuade her, but although she assured him that she would think the matter over, she admitted that she had the feeling that he was afraid that "she couldn't take it" and that this might be the end of their friendship. Hence he tried to keep her from going. His fears only served to strengthen her resolve to do this unless "our discussion should prove a better method of looking into the future."

I promised to facilitate her contacts with Negro people in

the East through several friends who were highly placed in the Negro community. In addition, her boy friend had some relatives to whom he promised to write, although he seemed rather reluctant to do so on the ground that they might misunderstand and think she was out slumming. I told her that I would write my friends frankly the nature of her interests and something of her background. At first she refused to give me permission to reveal her motive, but gradually realized that I could not do otherwise if I were not to violate their friendship and confidence and that in the long run it would also be the best thing for her because she and they could act more naturally than would be possible otherwise.

I saw her only once more before she left. She seemed much better poised and much more certain of herself. She had handled the matter of getting her parents' consent in excellent fashion and had also obtained the active co-operation of her boy friend.

She wrote me several letters. The first few were mainly descriptions of what she did, the people she saw, their mode of life, accounts of the cordiality with which my friends had received and treated her, her utilization of every opportunity to meet and get to know as many Negroes on as intimate as possible a social level, and how much she was learning from these contacts.

Then came a letter in which she announced that she had practically made up her mind that the venture was too much for her and that she did not possess the pioneering spirit which such a marriage required. She said that she did not want to hide behind pious declarations that it was because she felt that she could do more to right the wrongs our society inflicted on the Negro, as she probably would have done some months ago. She preferred to face the situation frankly and honestly by admitting that she just did not have the courage to go through with it. She asked whether she should write her friend of her decision or wait until she came back.

She added that she did not intend to finish the full year at this university but would finish the semester.

My reply neither approved nor disapproved her decision. My only query was whether she was certain of herself and what she wanted to do. It also suggested that the manner in which she should acquaint her friend with her decision must be her choice based on her own sense of right and wrong, her knowledge of the young man's character and personality, which we had not discussed very much.

It only remains to be added that she decided to wait until she returned home and told her friend in person. He made it rather easy for her by saying that he expected this outcome, once she told him that she wanted to go East.

Follow-Up: She has completed her graduate work here and maintains contacts with both white and Negro folks, and sees her former boy friend occasionally. Her mother, too, has regained her emotional balance and has less violent objections to Negroes visiting her home, although she is still not happy about it. The girl will soon complete her work for the doctorate and feels that she is much richer for the experience.

Conclusion: In this case the counselor aimed to treat the situation on the conscious and reality level and to avoid, if possible, prolonged and extensive analysis and deep therapy.

Some readers may feel that the foregoing presentation leaves a number of questions unanswered. What about the boy? Why was he not seen? Was the counselor prejudiced against the marriage *ab initio?* Else, why did he not try to see the mother or win her over to the marriage? In agreeing to the plan proposed by the girl, did the counselor throw the weight of his authority in the direction of a separation because it was fairly certain that the girl would most likely "not be able to take it"?

The psychoanalytically inclined will question whether the

neurotic element in the girl's make-up, which prompted her to seek an alliance with a Negro and which was neither probed nor treated, will not break forth in some other form of neurotic or deviant behavior. Similar questions may be asked about the boy.

Space does not permit an adequate discussion of these and other questions which might be raised. In the absence of a more detailed discussion, it can only be stated that the counselor had and has no prejudice against interracial marriages; that his only requirement is that the social and psychological factors be such as to make possible a happy and successful marriage—a condition required in all premarital counseling. Had he been satisfied that "the girl could take it"—something which seemed doubtful because of her tendency to dramatize herself and her situations—he would have seen the mother and the young man. As it was, the time had not come for it; moreover, it did not seem that the young man was very deeply involved emotionally, but that he was more or less swept off his feet by the girl and the prospect of marrying a white girl of good family with all its implications. Needless to add, this was never mentioned to the girl in order not to prejudice her against the young man.

As for the neurotic trend in the girl which remained unexplored and untreated, this, of course, goes to the heart of the matter. To be sure, it is possible that such a trait exists in the girl. It is possible, also, that had it been inquired into, it would have been uncovered and would have required extensive analysis and therapy. However, a number of years have elapsed since her last visit and since this case was first reported. The girl has secured her doctorate, is teaching in a junior college, is married, and has combined a fairly successful teaching career and motherhood without any neurotic trait having manifested itself thus far. And may we not say that in this case, at least, treating the situation on a conscious level was a service to the client?

EDITOR'S NOTE: Contrary to usual practice, the counselor, in this case, risked stirring up considerable feelings of guilt in the girl about her mother. A more detailed report would undoubtedly indicate at what point the counselor recognized sufficient ego strength in his client to assure a positive rather than negative use of familial attitudes and responsibilities.

COUNSELING THE UNMARRIED

Introduction

Generally speaking, counseling the unmarried differs from premarital counseling to the extent that it is not focused on a relationship with a specific partner. However, it comes to the attention of marriage counselors sufficiently often to be included here, for although the client's focus may not be on *a* marriage, it is on *marriage* and problems of sex adjustment. It also inevitably merges into the whole field of personal and individual adjustment.

Although this type of marriage counseling requires substantially the same kind of knowledge, special training, and equipment as has been noted elsewhere, the situations encountered frequently call for heightened sensitivity to the personalities and attitudes involved, so that one will not too readily assume that the counselee is a neurotic, when in reality the behavior exhibited is the result of some peculiar or particular set of social and cultural circumstances. The counselor needs to be especially fortified by an understanding of and familiarity with the cultural background of the counselee in order to help the client evaluate the situation properly.

14. Some Cases Dealing with Problems of the Unmarried

Cases 37 and 38 are concerned with the problems of the unmarried, younger girl facing a specific crisis. Cases 39, 40, and 41 focus on the problems of the older woman deprived, through divorce or her state of "single blessedness," of a normal marriage relationship.

A type of premarital counseling that is not included here but might well be noted, is that which has to do with general problems of dating and courtship. It has been reported by one of the leading marriage counseling agencies that this type of case represents a decreasing per cent of its caseload—not because it is becoming less important but because as schools, colleges, universities, and community groups develop programs in Education for Marriage and Family Living such questions are increasingly covered in group discussions and conferences.

CASE 37

Problem: The emotional development of a young girl, during the stress of her parents' divorce
Presented by: Marriage counselor (B.D. in Theology; M.A. in Educational Psychology) in a Family Court

Introduction: Teen-age children of divorcing couples who are clients of Domestic Relations Services in Family Courts frequently seek help from court counselors. Such clients want guidance through the throes of their parents' divorce, or help with their own (generally "escape") marriages, or premarital counseling ("our wedding's next month, and we don't want to make the mistakes our parents did"), or what may be designated pre-premarital counseling, or a combination. All counseling relationships in the Court are short-term (that is, they consist on the average of only four or five interviews) since counseling is ancillary to the Court's judicial functions. Persons from families involved in court action who need deeper or more extended help are referred routinely to community mental hygiene or family casework services.

Referral and Contacts: Kay was the daughter of divorcing parents. When first seen she was 17½ years old and in the middle of the first semester of her senior year in high school. Her score on the Wechsler-Bellevue was 110, and her previous grade average was B; but this semester she was failing. Called into conference with the dean, Kay conceded that she was worried over her mother's divorce petition filed nine months before. With encouragement, she unfolded a story of years of discord, of recent open hostility (at this point she broke into tears), of her concern to take sides with neither parent, of her wish after the divorce to live apart from both parents, and of her fantasy-wish ("it just comes and goes—and—and I know it's very silly") just to drop off into a great big hole. The dean, no stranger to the Family Court Center in her city, phoned the marriage coun-selor (hereinafter designated as C). She outlined Kay's predica-ment, with Kay listening on the extension in the next office. Then she hung up, while C talked on with Kay. He described counseling as talking with a temporary professional friend about problems that are too perplexing and too burdensome to be solved alone. Kay made an appointment for the next day. Later the dean phoned C further details regarding Kay's recent out-of-character depressed attitude, school failures, and family. She quoted Kay as saying that she'd felt better after the phone talk with C.

During the next seven weeks, Kay was in C's office five times, twice by herself, twice with her "steady," and once with her di-vorcing parents. During this same period, there were four ex-tended telephone consultations. After a lapse of five months, there was another set of telephone contacts. And thirteen months later, C received a letter, Kay then being 19 years old, one month married, and resident in a distant state.

Kay and Her Parental Home: Dark, slender, 5′ 4″ in height, with sparkling black eyes, upturned nose, a ready smile and an outgoing manner, Kay was the second of her parents' two chil-dren. Her brother, 1½ years older, was a freshman in the local university. He also worked part time in a grocery store. Her half-sister, 5½ years older, child of her mother's first mar-riage, had been married five years previously at the age of 18, six months before the birth of her first child, and soon thereafter had moved with her husband and baby to a distant state. Since the age of 4, Kay had lived in the same six-room house among other blue-collar families. Her father (hereinafter designated F), for more than twenty years a laundry truck driver for the same company, was still paying $54 per month on the mortgage.

Her mother (hereinafter designated M), a practical nurse at a near-by hospital, was employed intermittently and part time throughout Kay's childhood, and for the last three years steadily and full time. Neither parent attended church, although F had been reared a Catholic. At the age of 14, Kay got herself baptized along with the other members of her crowd in a near-by Lutheran Church. Her social and recreational life centered around her neighborhood, her schools, and the roller-skating rink a few blocks from the house. By the age of 10, she was skating several times a week, and by 12, roller-skating had become her passion and forte. While in junior high school she had won several local prizes, and during her middle two high school years she had participated in state and national tournaments and had won several second and third prizes with her partner and "steady." Jimmie (hereinafter designated J), two years her senior, was the second of two sons in a Polish Catholic family. He had dropped out of high school after his freshman year and was working as a roofer's apprentice. Kay had been strongly motivated to complete high school and support herself with an office job.

Kay cannot remember when her parents did not get on each other's nerves. But each made a point of being nice to her brother and herself, especially after their own violent quarrels. Kay remembers picnics and fishing with F and movies with M. There were more good times with F. During early childhood years, she remembers that M was full of complaints and often went to bed for days at a time, that she changed doctors frequently, and that she was a very messy housekeeper. She remembers also that at times F was sullen, and once or twice he was so drunk that he could not stand straight. During the past two or three years, she said, M had spent much time away from home, most of it with one special girl friend, a divorcée. During these years F also had stayed away frequently and for long periods. Her brother, too, went his own way. Frequently she had been the only one to get the meals, and do the cleaning and washing. "It was this way," she explained; "I just could not depend on mother."

The First Interview: Kay and C began their first interview with talk about her school, her good times, and her family. She's always liked school and has dated since the ninth grade. The five steadies of these four years have all been schoolmates except J. As for home, M was cruel. No one ever knew what she was up to or what she would do next. It was impossible to get close to her. She was always doing mean things. She even had the divorce papers served to F on his birthday. Kay herself did not know about them until J told her he saw it in the papers. "Mother always exaggerated everything. She said we kids never loved her. Of course we got fed up, but we loved her, too."

When C suggested that there were reasons in M's experiences and feelings for her behaving as she did, Kay responded, "Yes, I know lots of reasons. Really I pity her. Her folks were killed by a cyclone when she was only two. She was put in an orphanage and she never saw her brothers and sisters for thirty-five years. All four of them were 'Missing' till three years ago. She got married when she was barely 16; three years later her husband died. She's gone through plenty, but she's tried to raise us kids nice. . . . It was terrible after my sister got married and left. My sister was more my mother than my real mother was . . . Um . . . I'm thinking of turning Catholic. You see, the only person I really care about now is a Catholic."

Feeling as she does, C suggested, she seems to have a lot to talk about with people whom she trusts. Kay said that last year she had talked with a Home Economics teacher in high school, but only once. "Of course, J and I talk about everything." And then, after a silence, looking up with a wry smile, "You may think I'm crazy, but I'd die if it weren't for J." When C said that it can mean much to have an understanding friend, Kay said, "Yes, someday after he finishes military service we're going to

get married. He understands me. We've won lots of prizes together. He's a wonderful roller-skater." C nodded.

Kay beamed, and then asked about court procedures. She
said that M is set on divorce, though F still hopes that she won't
go through with it. "My brother and I, we've talked a lot, we
think that they should, and we don't want to live with either of
them. I'm going to drop school." C suggested that she talk this
over with the dean. And then, as Kay got up to put on her coat,
he ventured that M probably didn't often hear from members
of the family such appreciation as Kay had expressed today. Kay
looked at C quizzically. C said he would be glad to talk with
either F or M or both, should they care to get in touch with him.
Kay asked if she could see him again and C answered, "Yes,
anytime, preferably after I have talked with your parents."

C's record of this interview contains the following note: "Kay,
being forced into independence from parents before ready, is
developing overdependence upon J before either is ready to
handle their growing closeness, emotions, and probable arousals
—the kind of situation in which delinquent attitudes and behavior can root and grow."

Interviews with Father: Within 24 hours, F telephoned for an
interview. In give-and-take with C three days later, he poured
out hostility and resentment, and repeatedly expressed the hope
that M would change her mind and continue to make a home for
himself and the children. He confirmed and elaborated Kay's
picture of M's behavior. "That woman's gone crazy because her
big-shot brother (M's recently found older brother was a successful business man owning his own plane) makes such a fuss
over his darling baby sister."

In his second interview, four days after the first, F began with
"It's never been right between us." He told of years of estrangement, during which neither had touched the other nor spoken
civilly. He told how a year and a half previously he had filed for

divorce, when, with no word of her whereabouts, M had remained away from home two weeks. She was finally discovered
in Chicago with her brother, and he had withdrawn the petition.
Slowly then he said, "You see, we had to marry. But it happened only once. We were both drunk. I had the dates changed
so that our son wouldn't know he's a bastard." F brooded. C
remained silent. Jerkily F began to talk about M's breakdown
seventeen years before, after Kay's birth, when for six months
she was resident in the State Mental Hospital. As he talked on,
he softened: "She's taken a terrible beating from life. I haven't
helped. Now, I suppose divorce is the only thing." C commented
that these interviews are a way of walking around the question
of whether or not divorce is the best solution. Shrugging in a
gesture of hopelessness, F commented on his son's success in
school athletics and on Kay's fifteen skating prizes and her good
grades in art courses. Standing to leave, he expressed contempt
for "that mother's boy, J, she thinks she's in love with" and
asked C if he wouldn't please try to do something about it. C
commented that he will gladly talk with Kay about any problem
she brings.

In a long phone conversation with C, a few minutes before
F's third interview, Kay expressed anxiety and helplessness over
the accusations and provocations that F and M were hurling at
each other in the home; and C tried to help her feel that such
hostilities are to be expected at this time when divorce is both
wanted and accepted as inescapable, and yet also regretted and
resented.

In his third interview, the day the date for the divorce trial
was published, F fumed bitterly over his own uncertain future.
C commented only occasionally and briefly. Slowly F softened.
Once again he said he guessed he'd better take the divorce M
wants, forget the past, and "be a better father to my children."

Interview with Mother: Next day M phoned C, and three days
later came in for her first interview. She began by protesting F's

lectures and accusations "from the day we were married." She told of his irresponsibility as provider, of his neglect of her and the children, of his drunken sprees. C's comments added up to "Yes, I know it's been tough." With each story she relaxed a little more, and then suddenly she sighed, "You know, we've both had it tough. He was an orphan and I was an orphan, and that's about all we married on. A tornado killed my parents. I was only two. They put me in an orphanage. For thirty-five years I didn't see my three brothers nor my two sisters. You know (her voice became mysterious and tender), I gave up ever expecting to see them again. I was just existing—then plop, all of a sudden, here they are." She was silent for the better part of a minute. Then, "I wish I had known about you two years ago. But it's too late now." C said that with a counselor a person can learn to understand himself and his family better when he wants to, and more understanding sometimes leads to reconsidering intentions. There was another long silence. Slowly M shook her head, "It's too late now." C said she perhaps hoped another way could be found. Again she shook her head. When at last she spoke, it was to ask painfully formulated questions about the court and divorce procedures. C answered factually. Motioning to end the interview, he said that when children grasp something of the feelings of their mother and father over the years, they are better able to understand and go along with a break-up. M broke into tears, "I've been awfully nasty today. I'm proud of my children. They're sweet children." Silence again. Finally with another sigh, "There just isn't any other way out."

Apparently M conceived the idea of a family conference at C's office and spoke about it to F, for the next day he phoned to say that he was in favor. A few hours later M phoned to ask C what he thought of the idea. C expressed willingness, provided all came freely. At M's request, C put the idea by telephone before each of the children. Both agreed to come, reluctantly. C then informed both attorneys.

Second Interview Involving Kay: At this family interview, M was relaxed from the start, and gracious. In their first comments, F was sarcastic and Kay bitter, but both softened as the hour progressed. Kay's brother was silent throughout, except near the end he grumbled that he would be glad to get it over with. He was going into military service, anyway.

C pointed out that both had wanted to be good parents, and that each had achieved some success. He noted also that each had been progressively disappointed in this marriage and that in the last few years both had felt keenly its emptiness. F said, "That's all true, and now that we understand it, I don't see why we can't turn about. I will, if she will." M's answer was firm, "Without wishing any harm to anybody," she said, "I've just got to get away. We don't have any marriage left any more. There's nothing we can do about it now." Everyone sighed and stared into far corners. Kay was the first to speak. She said she was sorry for both, that she would never take sides, that she had decided to stay in school through the year and then get a job.

C then proposed that they consider their relationships and responsibilities after divorce. Avoiding mention of who should have the house and how the household goods and car should be disposed of, the province of the attorneys, the following was thrashed out and agreed upon: that the court be asked not to make the divorce final until after Kay's 18th birthday; to agree that until they should finish school, both F and M would contribute specific amounts weekly from their respective earnings to the support and education of both children; and to stipulate that through their 21st birthdays legal custody would be in both parents jointly, with the understanding that, if disagreements arise, they would consult a counselor of their choosing.

These agreements, C then said, would be incorporated into his report to the judge and attorneys. A counselor's report (social study of the family) is required by state law in divorce cases where there are children under 14, and this court's judge requests it for all families who use marriage counseling.

A few days later, M's attorney called to say that the two prin-
cipals had met with their attorneys and had worked out and
signed a separation agreement and property settlement "with
none of the bitterness or stubbornness that is usual in such
cases." C also reported progress to the dean, who responded
that Kay seemed to be settling down to her work and now
planned to stay and graduate with her class.

Second Interview with Mother: At her second interview a few
days before the trial, M unburdened hostility against F, and
anxiety over Kay's future. Since the family interview, she said,
Kay had been treating her almost decently. But (her face became
taut and her voice plaintive) she is altogether too intimate with
J. "I am afraid she'll go and do what I did, and her sister, too.
She warned Kay not to make the same mistake, but I can't help
worrying." C stated that Kay has been looking at her upset feelings both with the dean and with C, and that when young people
do this, they generally discern their own feelings more clearly
and behave more wisely. M was unimpressed. She pleaded, "Talk
to Kay like a Dutch uncle." C stated that whenever Kay wanted
to, he would talk with her about her relationship with J.

Third Interview (Kay and Her "Steady"): Recognizing C's voice
when he phoned, without waiting for C to speak, and asking no
questions, Kay said she would like to bring J down to her next
talk. No, she had nothing special in mind, just wanted J to meet
C. Three days later, Kay and J arrived twenty minutes early.
She was serious but comfortable enough to start the conversation. J wore an air of forced joviality. C knew next to nothing
about their relationship or their motives for coming together;
he would have preferred separate interviews. Kay and J sat close
to each other. From time to time Kay patted his knee or laughed
up at his face. At one point, as conversation was warming up,
she took his cigarette, puffed two or three times, and then play-
fully tucked it back between his lips. He responded by putting

his arm around her shoulder where it remained for several minutes.

Kay began to talk about her mother's life, saying that she liked her, and she didn't. C said that M had gone through many difficult experiences, as a growing girl, as a wife, and as a mother. Kay answered, "It's funny, but sometimes when she pats me, I get goose bumps." C pointed out that Kay harbored two very different currents of feeling toward M. Kay pondered and then said with a smile, "Like the fellow you told me about in our first talk, who had to go somewhere, and he didn't want to go, and so he got a sore throat." All laughed, and C commented that it's quite common to have bodily reactions to inner emotional conflicts.

Kay said that her mother is terribly excited "like a little girl starting on a long trip." Then, more thoughtfully, "She's never been exactly normal; she doesn't connect with anyone. But she's tried to be a good mother. This past two weeks she's done some nice things for F, like getting his coffee when he came in late from a long day on the truck. It makes me feel like crawling into bed beside her."

"After the divorce, the dean's going to let me leave school every day at one so I can take care of the house and get the meals." C asked about her plans for after graduation. Came this answer, with an ardent look at J: "Oh, we're going to get married. . . . I mean after he finishes service." J talked about being in the Naval Reserve and his hopes for postponing active service, about how at roofing he and his boss frequently loaf and never get caught, and then about how Kay is tops in art and in roller skating. Kay put in that they'd won several prizes together, but J insisted that she was much better. Turning to C, Kay said, "J has an inferiority complex and I don't know what to do with him." C pointed out that different individuals possess different skills and excel in different ways; that a person often has feelings when he realizes that he is not so good as someone else; and that unless faced and resolved such feelings can be very uncomfortable. And when two young people are getting married, it is important for the girl to know that her man has developed skill on his job and steadiness as a provider. Kay met that one by saying that she wished J would get into a better trade, and that M worries about him, "that is, I mean—about him and me." When C asked what she meant, Kay ventured that her mother is always telling her to be careful and J added that his mother says the same thing. "Yet," said Kay, with a sly wink at J and a toss of her head, "my mother lets me stay at his house overnight; but, of course, his parents are there."

Uncertain as to what Kay was trying to convey, C made note that both seemed more amused and defiant than anxious and guilty. He said that both mothers doubtless realized that Kay and J were pretty close, and that they had talked of marrying someday. Kay nodded. C suggested that there was perhaps another fact back in M's mind; that her older sister had become pregnant when going steady before marriage. Kay put in, "But that doesn't mean we will." J volunteered, "My brother had to, too." C said that this is a problem for every pair of steadies; that our own natures sooner or later put up to us the question, "How intimate are you going to let yourselves be before marriage?" Kay said "Ye-a-a," and J reddened. C talked on about the psychosexual nature of males and females, saying that as closeness grows, a man has to reckon with his inner drive to push petting until there is sexual union; and that although a girl may not consciously want "to go the limit" because of the risks, as closeness grows she may develop the desire to be possessed by her man, and in a heavy petting episode she may not be able to stop, either—that is, unless both have decided that coitus is for after marriage. Kay protested, "I don't like to think of men this way, and besides (giving his knee a pat), J isn't this way." J returned the pat as Kay said pensively, "My mother had to marry, too. I didn't know that until last year." C stated that Kay's F and M were both lonely and that M had lost her first husband by death only a few months before she met F. Kay said,

"You mean they sort of drifted into it . . . um . . . and my older sister, too?" C nodded and went on to say that regrets and complications are less likely if a dating couple who mean a lot to each other understand their own natures and decide together what standards they will set for themselves. Then he commented briefly about marriage as contract and sacrament, and as union and companionship.

Kay appeared thoughtful. J fidgeted, and then broke in with, "I can't marry yet. I haven't finished military service and, besides, I'm not settled the way I should be in a job. I love her all right, but I'm a Catholic and I've decided to stick to my religion. She's taking instructions, so I guess things will work out." Kay shrugged, looked the other way, and then began to talk about a young couple at the rink who would fight furiously and make up fast. The interview ended with discussion of C's draft of his divorce report.

From Kay's material, her open manner, her normally embarrassed responses, C guessed that she had had no seriously upsetting sex experiences, and that there was no abnormally repressed fear or guilt. He wrote this note to himself: "Work with distorted yet still fluid images of self as woman in sex and marriage roles . . . also with emotional security cravings."

Fourth Interview (Kay and Her "Steady"): Three days later Kay and J suddenly appeared again, and C rearranged his schedule to give them some time. Kay plunged in with the observation that M never had been geared to marriage and to making her husband happy. She guessed it was true that she didn't like her mother, but she was sorry for her too, and sometimes felt like comforting her, "getting into bed with her the way I said last time. She'd never clean house and do things right. She never really finished things." When C stated that it looked as if neither parent had been ready to make steady efforts to get along with each other, Kay broke in with "But they both tried to treat us right. But my father kept criticizing and criticizing, till M would go almost crazy." Then with a look at J, "I need appreciation, too." C said that this need is understandable since Kay's parents can say hurtful things, and since Kay is in a way losing them; and that J also may have a special need to feel appreciated since he is the younger brother who dropped out of high school. Said Kay, "We both have inferiority complexes." "I suppose so," said C, "but more significant is the fact that each feels grateful for someone in his life who respects and cares and gives appreciation. And isn't it also true that each tends to lean on the person from whom he gets these things?" Both looked sober. C went on, "Before marriage can be a steady and happy relationship, such leaning has to be outgrown, sort of discarded for self-respect and a freer give-and-take—interdependence is a good word for it." Said Kay thoughtfully, "I know what you're hinting at, we don't do it—not very much." J was silent. C concluded, "A person can develop this sort of thing better by himself. Next time, what about each of you talking to me separately?" Both nodded. Kay reminded C that she had an appointment the day before the divorce trial, and J made an appointment for a few days after.

"This divorce, um-m," said Kay, "my brother is taking it too hard for his own good. I guess he needs appreciation, too. But he's treating me better. We were kidding and wrestling on the floor the other night. This divorce business makes us all feel different." Said J, "I feel restless; I don't really like roofing. My father built up a trucking business. But I'm not like my father. I need someone to push me!" Protested Kay, "There's your old inferiority complex again." J sighed, and Kay turned to C, "We've decided we can't marry till he settles on a job." At the same time she patted his knee, with "Don't worry, you'll get there," and with this aside to C, "You know, I'd die without J." J grinned. C said that their feelings of comfort with each other are understandable, because J is in the process of trying to puzzle out what he's going to train himself for, and so naturally at the moment doesn't feel very settled about himself; and Kay is unsettled, too, having to take care of herself and at the same

time having to give some comfort to her parents, who are breaking up their home. Kay responded with, "I suppose you're worrying about us, too, but I think we're doing all right. We just don't
talk about those things. Married people should, I suppose." C
commented on the great number of things they had to do together, and on the fun they had doing them. He added that this
does not mean that their feelings about themselves and about
each other as man and woman can safely be shrugged off. Kay
commented, "I think I know what you mean. Since I was here
last time I read something in a book at school about how boys
are more vulnerable." J reminded Kay that tonight there would
be an instruction class at the church. C brought the interview
to a close.

Fifth Interview (Kay): Kay appeared at the hour agreed upon
the day before the decretal hearing, and said that J had brought
her and was sitting in the waiting room. C began with the word-
ing of the divorce report. Kay proposed child-support figures
which C noted were the same as those entered by F and M. She
expressed satisfaction, and C thanked her.

Kay then volunteered that M hadn't lived at home for a week,
and that she herself had the house pretty clean and intended to
keep it so. C commented on her combination of school- and
housework, to which she answered, "Oh, I don't mind that, but
I feel restless. I leave as soon as the work's done. My father
doesn't stay home either, nor my brother. I go to J's house and
study there." Then, after a pause, "But I'm restless there, too.
Sometimes I can't even talk with J, and I don't feel like fooling
around with him." Catching C's eye, she smiled in the manner of
a teacher to her charge, "I don't mean it that way. Last summer
he tried to get fresh with me, once, and I wouldn't let him. So
he doesn't bother me. I don't like to think of those things."

C commented that she seems to be feeling pretty lonely when
she is in her parents' house, and only a bit more comfortable
at J's. Kay broke in with, "His mother is nice to me. Sometimes

I like to talk with J and sometimes not. I don't like it when he looks at me that way." There was fear in her eyes. C nodded. "You embarrass me," she said. Puzzling over Kay's neurotic retreat from sex and wondering what he could say that would help her feel more comfortable, C spoke slowly and deliberately, "Step by step, as they are ready, most growing young women think of themselves as being mothers some day, and then, generally later, as being sex partners to their husbands." Kay shrugged. C recalled that she and J and he had talked about the differences in the natures of men and women. He reminded her that home was being pulled out from under her, that this was uncomfortable, that she had said she would die if it wasn't for J, and that clearly J these days is a close and comforting friend. Kay was thoughtful. "But I don't like it when he just sits and hugs and kisses." C said, "Yes, you are more than his friend; you are his girl friend. You are attractive to him as a woman." Kay fidgeted and said she did not want that. C commented that when a couple have agreed that they are going to be married, as the days go by they feel closer and closer, in a way preparing themselves for eventual sexual union. Kay sighed and said grimly, "Sometimes I think I won't ever marry J, but don't tell him. He's an awful baby. He's like my father that way. He won't take any more drafting courses, and he keeps putting off military services. He should really grow up (this with disgust). His mother babies him too much."

C commented that Kay is having to get on all by herself with the business of growing up, since F and M aren't taking care of her any more, although both wish her well, and recently M has been treating her better. Kay nodded, "But what has that to do with it?" C went on, "Well, as you feel comfortable about standing on your own feet, I rather think you'll feel comfortable about being a woman, and you'll be glad that you're attractive to men, especially to the one man that you come deeply to love and respect. And then I wonder if you'll be afraid any more. Kay retorted, "I'm not afraid!" and lapsed into silence. C waited. After perhaps a minute, Kay spoke, "You're trying to help me, aren't you?" Said C, "Yes, to understand yourself, and to feel more comfortable with yourself." The silence that followed was interrupted by a bang on the door. Lurching in, J said, "What is this, anyway? I'm tired of waiting." C noticed the interview had lasted 75 minutes. Kay reached across and shook his hand (something she had not done after previous interviews), turned to J with a wisecrack, put her hand in his, and was off.

Follow-Up: During the *two days before the trial,* M phoned C three times regarding the proceedings and the agreement. The trial was routine. Divorce was granted. The decree incorporated the property settlement and C's recommendations about relationships with the children.

In a telephone conversation *a few days later,* Kay said it was very funny not to have her mother around at all. And then, "J isn't going to keep his appointment tomorrow. When I reminded him, he just grunted and said some things that weren't very nice. I guess you've helped him all you can." C said he would be ready to talk with J at any time, should he ever wish to. (J never wished to.)

Five months later, Kay phoned, said that school had been going well, that she and her brother were taking care of her father, who was much more serious than he used to be. And, by the way, she hoped that C wouldn't mind if she used his name as reference for a job. School would be out in a few days, and she had applied for a kind of art job, and was giving the name of C and the dean as references. Answering C's questions, Kay said that she was feeling fine, that she was graduating with her class, that she had been too busy to enter any more roller-skating tournaments. Then, "Of course, when I start working, I can't see J so often, and . . . and . . . to tell the truth, I'm not going to marry him, only he doesn't know it yet. I'm going to ————, but I've got to work here for a few months first, until my father and my brother get more settled. Mother sent us one letter. It was all full of big doings and surprises at her brother's, just like a little girl. I guess she's happy enough." The following week, Kay phoned again with the news that she had landed the job.

Eight months later, C's Christmas mail brought an elaborate card postmarked ———, and splashed with hand-painted "Noels." Among other things, the written message contained the following: "Thank you again for helping our family, especially me—I hope you remember that I am the girl that came to you from the ——— high school sent by the dean. Everything has worked out wonderfully—I'm married now (*not* to J)—I'm living out here in ——— and keeping in mind ALL your advice on married life. I'll never be able to thank you enough. Merry Christmas! Kay."

CASE 38

Problem: Premarital pregnancy
Presented by: A gynecologist and obstetrician (M.D.) in private practice in a large urban center

Introduction: Miss C was a high school student, sixteen years old. Her father was a hard-working skilled laborer in his fifties. Her mother, in her late forties, was hemiplegic resulting from a postoperative cerebral thrombosis. There were two older children, a brother and a married sister. This married sister brought Miss C to the office because she was "gaining weight too rapidly." On questioning, it was learned that her menstrual period had not appeared for two months. In reality Miss C was over seven months pregnant and had succeeded in keeping this condition from the detection of her family, teachers, and classmates.

Problems That Had to Be Faced: The counseling obstetrician was faced with a number of problems as indicated here.

Informing her family. Permission was requested and obtained by the physician from the patient to tell her older sister, in her presence, what the diagnosis was. A short discussion between patient, sister, and physician resulted in agreement that both parents should be informed without further delay. The solid relationship between the parents and their children made unnecessary using an intermediary, or softening the possible reaction by the presence of a witness. (This was offered, but not urged by the counselor.)

Relationship to the prospective father. This had to be weighed in terms of future values, not by consideration of social attitudes.

The boy was a high school classmate, less mature than the girl. He appeared emotionally incapable of realizing the implications of fatherhood. He was even unready for a well-founded attachment to this girl, beyond the quality of "puppy love." There was reason to doubt whether the present experience would contribute to his early maturing.

The girl who felt warm tenderness for the boy was disappointed by his inability to rise to the situation. Though she would have been prepared to compromise on social and economic standards, her feelings for the boy cooled off as she became aware that here was no "man" to stand beside her.

The family, of course, was very critical of him. When the easily overlooked fact that the man is not the only culprit in such cases was pointed out to the family, they dropped all vindictiveness and decided to let the young father fade entirely out of the picture, as far as they were concerned.

This decision was gladly shared by everyone involved, and this was fortunate as marriage merely for the sake of social approval would have made bad matters worse. Any forced continuation of this premature and exhausted relationship in all probability would have frozen the development of both young people on an adolescent (and resentful) level.

The question of abortion. This was not brought up by any of the people involved. I believe the compelling reason for this, was the already rather advanced state of pregnancy. Aside from legal and medical contradictions, the counselor felt that getting rid of the unborn child would have increased badly the guilt feelings of the young girl whose natural and religious tendencies were strongly for acceptance of her condition. It may well be that this powerful basic attitude had been as much responsible for her secretly carrying on with the pregnancy as her fear of what people would say.

Planning with and for the young mother.

A. Pre-partum Arrangements

With her own home available, things were considerably eased. The school term was near a break and after vacation the girl would not go back to school for the rest of the term. A large hospital in the neighborhood, but not in the immediate community, was chosen for delivery. During the remainder of the pregnancy, arrangements were made for adoption through one of the reputable community agencies. This seemed best in this case as it would spare the patient any possible stigma the rest of her life. One might have given more consideration to keeping the child if the relationship between the boy and girl had had any real emotional significance. Also, keeping the baby in the family was impracticable considering the advanced age of the girl's parents and especially her mother's illness. The young expectant mother herself was involved, as much as possible, in preparatory dealings with the adoption agency. By her practical cooperation she could at least contribute something to her child's future safety.

B. Delivery

According to previous understanding full anesthesia was

applied during childbirth. The doctor felt that the trauma of immediate separation from one's child leads either to unhappiness and guilt feeling, or to callousness and cynicism. For a basically unspoiled young human being it is better never to see the child than to be hurt for the rest of her life. Delivery took place at term. It was normal; so was the puerperal period.

C. Postpartum Arrangements

The patient was not kept in a maternity ward and after a few days with nonobstetrical patients she was dismissed home. Every effort was made to reintegrate her into normal life. Practical planning of day-to-day activities and contact with her peers, mildly forced on her, gave the patient a feeling of purpose, of being accepted.

Fifteen Months Later: It is the counselor's conviction that regular work with immediate purpose and with some future goal is one of the best means of re-establishing a soundly balanced sense of values. The feeling of belonging contributes to the security which is necessary to be able to strive for these values, free of defeatism and of undue aggressiveness.

Convincing proof that these objectives were achieved was given when fifteen months later our young patient came back to present herself with her husband, six years her elder. She had told him all of what had happened before, and his acceptance of the situation could be well understood when one appreciated the girl's development into a mature, well-principled, understanding young woman. The two subsequent pregnancies which I had occasion to handle gave this marriage increasing purpose and strength. The family moved away after four years. An occasional message on Christmas testifies to their happy and successful family life.

CASE 39

Problem: Rehabilitation of a divorcée

Presented by: Social worker and marriage counselor (M.A. from School of Applied Social Science) in the marriage counseling service of a Planned Parenthood Center

Introduction: The family consisting of Mr. Fred Anders, 38 years old, Mrs. Alice Anders, 36, Harold, 13, Jean, 11, Janet, 9, were referred by a court worker. Sexual maladjustment was listed as a factor in the marital difficulties. Mrs. Anders was seen at two different periods. The first time she was threatened with a divorce (which later materialized). Four years later she returned with the emotional problems of a divorcée.

Counseling Prior to Divorce: When Mrs. Anders was first seen she was distressed and sobbed constantly. She had been upset since her recent discovery of her husband's infidelity. He was romantically interested in another woman—and Mrs. Anders was stunned, humiliated, and hostile. She could concentrate only on his wrongdoings, and his actions gave her plenty of provocation. Mr. Anders wanted a divorce to marry his amour and his wife was adamant in her refusal. Mrs. Anders was a woebegone-looking woman. She was overweight, matronly-looking far beyond her years, and her weak self-confidence was thoroughly shattered. The only thing of which she seemed certain was that total tragedy would result if her husband divorced her.

Her own problem engulfed her and she scarcely mentioned the children. She did say that her constant crying annoyed them, but she could not control herself.

Mr. Anders, in contrast to his wife, was a trim, well-dressed man, self-centered, intelligent, ambitious, and impressing one as a person eager to go up the ladder of success. He was impatient with his wife's clinging, felt he needed a woman who was more independent, such as Mrs. Hale whom he intended to marry. He glossed over the problem of support and the six children who were involved in this shift. Mrs. Hale would readily get a divorce and custody of her children, he said, and he confidently foresaw no problems there. The only flaw was his wife's hysteria and once she faced losing him she would "straighten out." He felt the marriage had deteriorated because Mrs. Anders was "too much wife (mother?) and not enough woman." They had gotten along satisfactorily before the children were born; but, frankly, he was "bored with the problems of little ones and my wife is always too tired to be a companion." She irked him because everything had to be done the hard way.

In the early interviews, Mrs. Anders solicited undivided sympathy for herself and censure for her husband. It took her some time to realize that this only repeated what she got from relatives, neighbors, and friends. She was then able to talk about her problems of coping with a reality situation. The couple were living estranged in the same house and she had to face his rejection daily. The fact that she did not insist upon his leaving the home seemed to hint at the picture of a woman who permits painful situations to develop and then suffers for it.

Mrs. Anders was determined to hold the marriage together, but all her focus and energy were geared toward condemnation of the predatory "other woman." She felt some responsibility in the rift because of her sexual problem. She had always been slow to respond, and her husband felt this was a personal affront to his sexual prowess. Too, she suffered from vaginitis and had avoided coitus over a period of time. As we discussed the hostile nature of her sexual problems and encouraged her to obtain some medical aid, the condition eased temporarily but it flared up frequently under emotional stress. Her sexuality seemed to be her one way of feeling superior to her husband—"above this sort of thing."

Mr. Anders was very firm in plans for divorce. He was certain his wife could be influenced to file suit, for he lacked legal grounds. He was irritated by his wife's dependency and he enjoyed the high tension of the present romantic and marital tangle. He seemed surprised that his extramarital life had become so involved, for it started as a harmless flirtation. It was very evident that Mrs. Anders had unconsciously condoned and encouraged this interest in Mrs. Hale. She had been their "best friend" who had free access to the home and was Mrs. Anders' confidante with her personal problems. As Mr. Anders' divorce demands became more insistent, Mrs. Anders made three suicide attempts but each time she informed her husband so that he obtained medical aid. At this point, we arranged to have Mrs. Anders see the staff psychiatrist for evaluation as to whether she needed psychiatric treatment.

The psychiatrist felt that the tension that produced the attempted suicide was under control, and advised that counseling concerning her general problems be continued.

After this emotional peak Mrs. Anders began to shift into a more resigned acceptance of the marital break and to think of practical plans of management. She began to see that her children were suffering. Her routine responsibilities were an aid to her in pulling out of this morass of self-pity and confusion, and she showed strength in this accomplishment, which we recognized and praised. She also began to look more attractive, for she lost twenty-five pounds and dressed in a youthful manner. Her self-pity lessened and she became more dynamic and independent as her focus of attention shifted. Her determined attitude and independence began to attract him, and coitus resumed with mutual satisfaction. He began to waver and show much indecision between the two women. Mrs. Hale openly pursued and pressured him to live up to his earlier promises. By now, her marriage was severed in anticipation of the new union. Mrs. Anders alternately suffered moods of elation and depression as her husband made and changed plans for divorce. Tension was extreme, and Mrs. Anders put the responsibility for the next step upon her husband.

Quite abruptly, Mrs. Anders changed her stand and consented to the divorce. She was tired of the strain and felt Mrs. Hale was "welcome to the whole sorry mess." She felt she had been helped to clarify her own role. She was certain her husband would never be satisfied until he had made the change. Some day he might want her again but now he seemed so swayed by Mrs. Hale and his own desires that her attempts for reconciliation seemed useless.

She felt self-confident enough to proceed on her own and she consulted an attorney. She was planning to get business training and had arranged for day care for the children. She no longer felt herself to be a rejected failure, for she realized she and her husband had both been at fault. She had been helped to see that she was a woman who could experience gratifying sexual response but she had realization that it was oversimplification to blame this one factor and that there were deeper emotional problems involved.

Exploration of her childhood and her husband's showed problems of parental relationship and guilt feelings which seemed to make life hard and hostile. Every situation seemed to challenge her, and she reacted to it harshly.

There was bitterness and humiliation because Mr. Anders immediately remarried and moved near by. The neighborhood gossip was distressing, and Mrs. Anders was determined to flee from her home life by going to work. She felt there was no further need for our service and she was proud of her progress. Our evaluation indicated that she had an impulsive pattern in working out her difficult problems, but she was doing fairly well on the surface level. It was felt, however, that she had little insight into her basic motivations. During this period, Mrs. A had been seen twelve times by the counselor, once by the psychiatrist. Mr. A had been seen four times by the counselor, and once by the psychiatrist. He was evaluated as a self-centered man who was convinced that the marriage was a failure and had been for several years. He was prone to overromanticize the "other woman" and unable to see any part that he might have played in the marital failure. He discontinued contact on the basis that he felt he did not need any help.

Postdivorce Counseling Four Years Later: Four years later Mrs. Anders returned. She was a very slim, smartly dressed, most attractive woman. The counselor scarcely recognized her. During the interim period she had had some difficulties but she had been helped by occasional contacts with a psychiatrist for "nerves and depression" and she had gone further in the exploration of her childhood problems to find the source of her difficulty. She had terminated this contact. She said she saw him only as an emergency measure and was financially unable to continue, nor did she feel the need for psychiatric service. She felt her real problem for which she wanted our help now was adjusting to the loneliness of divorce. She felt that she was doing work that she liked, and the financial picture was better than she had anticipated. However, her former husband was delinquent in his payments for support of the children. He had never accomplished his ambitions or goals as far as his work was concerned. He had told her that his remarriage was a mistake, that she was so much more attractive and interesting now, but she just could not be interested in him. He blamed her for permitting the divorce and said it was only a temporary infatuation. She thought that was ridiculous because he had pressed her so that she was convinced divorce was the only way out for her.

She was missing some of the security of marriage and particularly the sexual life, which surprised her because she never cared too much for it before. Quite suddenly, she said her problem was that she knew only people who were disturbed in marital situations and she wanted to know normal folks. She revealed she was involved in a sexual affair with a married man and was frustrated by this relationship. Her description of his behavior showed him to be very similar to Mr. Anders in his curtness and disinterest. She was amazed to realize the similarity when the counselor commented on it. She was aghast at herself, for she felt she had been hurt enough and wanted no more. The question of returning to the psychiatrist was discussed in an attempt to clarify whether she had discontinued with him at an important time. Her interest seemed geared to practical plans for making and meeting new friends, and enlarging her social life as she did not wish to depend on extramarital affairs. She brought up several lines of interest which were discussed. Further interviews were not planned, but Mrs. Anders requested that she be able to return periodically if she desired.

She came in a year later because of her concern as to whether she was becoming a "tramp." She had experienced several disappointing extramarital affairs and each time felt she only increased her problem. Her affairs were constantly with married men who liked the status quo and did not plan to change their marital status. She seemed to find temporary comfort in her search for affection. She had good sexual response in these relationships but afterward was overcome with guilt and remorse followed by frightening, depressed feelings. She had not returned to the psychiatrist for help and did not desire psychiatric treatment. Finances were a current problem. Mr. Anders was not contributing for the children's support. His financial reverses made it difficult for him to make payments, and she thought there was no point in taking him to court.

The counselor consulted the staff psychiatrist, who felt that in view of Mrs. Anders' lapse of contact with the private physician she could be helped on a counseling level.

Mrs. Anders' constant failure in attaining good relationships with people both personally and at work seems to emphasize her old pattern of feeling that she lives in a very hostile world. Inevitably her behavior courts hostility in return. She becomes involved with people who are certain to hurt her, and this pattern is repeated because she seems to condone these very acts (such as with her husband, her lover).

The psychiatrist suggested that we interpret her depressions to her. We pointed out that her depression actually was an intolerable aggression which she was unable to handle and so it was turned inward. Her relationship with her aggressive mother and her earlier problems of retaliation were reviewed again in relation to the current problem. It was evident that the aggression seemed to be too hard to control when she was around people, but she did very well in impersonal things such as at her work, where she had made great strides. It was readily seen by Mrs. Anders that she has a tendency to act out her own early panic and punishment pattern when her weak father left her alone with her hostile, aggressive mother.

In the past year Mrs. Anders came in intermittently "to talk things over." Her ex-husband is divorcing his second wife, and Mrs. Anders is cold to his attempts to court her again. She thinks more in terms of her children but she still has guilt that she cannot share their interests more sincerely. She shows great strength and capability in following through with serious plans for them such as with her older child's education.

She is glad she did not have the opportunity to remarry earlier, but is beginning to feel stable enough to go into such a relationship. External circumstances do not throw her into panic as much as before and she tends to think out her decisions more carefully. She still slips back into her old pattern, as when she permitted her estranged parents to stay at her home during the holiday season. As expected, the episode ended in stormy tears, denunciation, guilt, and depression. The parents had lived apart for several years, but Mrs. Anders stirred up an intolerable situation when she permitted them to spend a week together at her home.

Her present complaint is that life is dull, flat, and that nothing exciting happens. We pointed out that her quest for excitement usually ends in trouble and it is essential for her to realize this.

In Review: The counseling process seemed to help Mrs. Anders through three difficult phases: (1) the recognition that she and her husband had both failed in marriage and that his divorce demand was inevitable; (2) the depressing emotional impact of his immediate remarriage, contrasted to her own failure to do so; (3) the process of reconstructing her life on more stable economic, social, and emotional grounds with mature consideration of her basic needs, drives, strengths, and weaknesses.

CASE 40

Problem: Postdivorce and premarital adjustments
Presented by: Counselor (LL.B.) at Legal Aid Bureau in large urban center

Introduction: Mrs. S came to the Legal Aid Bureau for counseling concerning a postmarital problem involving the rearing of her child. During the course of the counseling, another major problem concerning divorce and also premarital counseling arose, the latter involving an intercultural and interfaith relationship.

The initial contact was precipitated by the fact that Mrs. S was in fear of having her child taken from her by her mother, Mrs. T, who threatened to force Mrs. S to leave, and leave her child behind with Mrs. T.

Mrs. S is an attractive young woman, aged 18 at the time of her first interview, who appeared extremely upset and anxious to talk about her predicament. She was in great fear of losing her two-year-old son, who was her whole life. She expressed feelings of guilt about her past, but stated that she was trying to be a good mother and would do anything to keep her child.

The counselor permitted her to do most of the talking because of her obvious need to talk out her concern. She then assured her that such action (loss of child) was never taken until the authorities looked into all the facts, and that the law usually favored the rearing of a child by its mother, unless it was in the best interests of the child to be taken from its mother. The counselor also told the client that every assistance would be given her in developing the facts if any such action were undertaken. The client reacted favorably to the psychological support and advice given and appeared more composed when she left.

The Problem as Presented by the Client: Mrs. S, who lived with her widowed mother, Mrs. T and her young son R, had been repeatedly told by her mother that she was unfit, bad, and that if Mrs. S would not do as she was told by Mrs. T, the latter would have her child taken from her permanently. Mrs. S further complained that her mother was impatient with her, and found fault with her all the time. She further stated that in addition to caring for her son's needs many of the household chores were forced upon her when she came home from work. She stated that she contributed one-half of the expenses although her mother earned more than she did and owned property. She never was made to feel that she actually shared the apartment with Mrs. T. She also related that during the past year she went to church regularly, although her mother didn't, and that she sang in the choir, and was giving 10 per cent of her salary to the church; but in spite of this her mother called her a hypocrite and criticized these activities. Her mother was devoted to the child, but when she asked her mother to baby-sit for her, arguments usually ensued. She felt that every effort that she made to improve herself and live a decent life, was futile. Her mother did not permit her to use the living room for dating on the ground that it was depriving her of the opportunity to see television. She also tended to be critical of the young men whom Mrs. S saw.

Background Facts: The background and facts developed in the case consist of the following:

Mrs. S was the youngest of four girls. When she was 18 months old her parents were divorced. She never saw her father after that time. All four children were sent to an orphanage because her mother could not afford to keep them. She didn't like the orphanage and rarely saw her mother during this period. She often broke rules and was severely punished. At the age of 10 she went to the country to live with her grandmother. She was given greater freedom there and enjoyed it, but often her grandmother scolded her and made her feel guilty when she didn't obey her. She was constantly told that she was a problem and hard to handle. At the age of 13 she went to live with her mother who was then running a boarding house in a city where many men in the Armed Forces were stationed. It was located in a rundown area. Many soldiers and sailors came there and she was fascinated by them. They thought her cute, and fussed over her. Her mother had little time to supervise her. She was a truant from school, liked art work, but hated to study, and as a result did poorly in her studies. She had few girl friends, but dated often. She did not get along with her mother. She said her mother was nervous and constantly yelling at her and finding fault.

At fifteen, while still at junior high school, she dated a sailor, Mr. U, who was boarding with her mother. She thought she was pregnant, and communicated this fact to her mother, who immediately insisted upon a marriage to avoid a scandal. Although Mr. U expressed reluctance to do so, Mrs. T threatened him, and he went through with the marriage, and then left the boarding house a week later for an overseas assignment. Mrs. S later discovered that she had mistaken a delayed menstrual period for pregnancy. She rarely communicated with Mr. U, and then only to insist that he notify the Navy of the marriage so that she could get an allotment from him. Several months after Mr. U's departure, Mrs. S met a soldier, age 22, whom she admired and fell in love with after several months of courtship. He was kind to her and made her feel that she was good and wanted. They enjoyed each other's company and planned marriage when she could get her divorce. Her mother approved of the soldier and did nothing to hinder the relationship. She became pregnant, and during the pregnancy the soldier was sent overseas. After the child was born, he notified the U.S. Army that he was the father of Mrs. S's child, and the child received an allotment. Shortly thereafter, he was killed in action. However, Mrs. S was still a minor when the child was born, so Mrs. T was made guardian of the allotment fund for the child.

After that, Mrs. T sold the boarding house and bought her own home. Mrs. S obtained employment as a clerical worker, and boarded the child with a family during the day. Her mother subsequently rented the house she bought and moved into an apartment, and suggested to Mrs. S that she move in and share it with her. She stressed the advantage to both of a reduction in expenses, and said she would baby-sit when she (Mrs. S) wanted to go out. Mrs. S agreed to this arrangement; trouble began almost from the start. Mrs. T took over the supervision of the child, was critical of her daughter's capacity to be a mother, and ridiculed her attempts to make a better person of herself. She especially resented her going out with friends. Her mother claimed that Mrs. S was sloppy and that she did not care for the child as she should. Mrs. T threatened to expose Mrs. S's marital status to her church friends if she didn't listen to her and follow her suggestions.

The Counseling: At the start, Mrs. S was seen weekly at sessions lasting one hour each over a period of two months. Her mother, Mrs. T, was seen at intervals of a month during this same period. Between counseling sessions, both Mrs. S and Mrs. T spoke on the telephone to the counselor quite frequently.

Immediately after the first interview, the counselor made inquiry of the Veterans Administration and learned that Mrs. T was merely custodian of the funds of Mrs. S's son, and that Mrs. S retained custody of her son. The counselor inquired of the Navy and learned that Mr. U had been discharged and re-enlisted and that he was then overseas. The counselor also learned that when he re-enlisted he had made no mention of the fact that he was married. The counselor then wrote to Mr. U to determine whether he had instituted any divorce or other proceedings. He answered that he wished a divorce but was waiting until he returned to the States. He said that he had no interest in Mrs. S and if she applied for any allotment, he would mention the birth of her son, which fact he had learned some time ago.

During this early period of counseling, Mrs. S thought through, with the assistance of the counselor, the advisability of setting up a home for herself and child as against remaining with her mother. She decided that if she could get along with her mother better, she would like to remain because of the impossible financial situation she would have and the fact that the person taking care of her son was good and lived near where she was at present living. Her son was also attached to her mother, and she thought that having a doting mother and grandmother was good for him. She gave thought during this period to her role of mother and the needs of the child for her companionship and attention. She agreed to plan her free time so that she could use it to the best advantage of the child. We spoke further in terms of health and cleanliness, and that although some of the chores involved were tiring yet they were necessary, and that in setting up routines some of the tasks would be simplified. She agreed to work at this and not to be discouraged if things didn't work out exactly as planned. She seemed to gain confidence in herself, and was pleased with some of the good habits she was instilling in her child. She expressed a great need to be accepted by decent people, by her minister, and by her choral group. She felt that she was making progress in meeting the right kind of people. She wasn't doing too well at her job and felt it was because her mother upset her.

As we progressed, she seemed better able to accept herself and feel less ashamed for what had happened. She began to gain insight into the contributory causes of her truancy, willfulness, need for male companionship, and desire to break away from her mother, and yet to feel dependent upon her. We discussed factors which contribute to a wholesome personality development, such as mother love, guidance tempered with love, training in responsibility, a need to belong, and self-recognition, which she had lacked in early formative years, and which she could not control; and also the fact that her mother in her own way could not assume full responsibility for her inadequacies. She learned that by giving her mother understanding, and letting her mother know in various ways that she loved her, her mother would respond, for she too needed love, and attention. Part of her mother's hostility toward Mrs. S was the fact that she too wanted to be a good mother, which she hadn't been to her own children because of her marital difficulties. She realized that she wasn't co-operating with her mother and that many of her actions were due to her resentment of her mother.

Mrs. T learned during the counseling sessions that she was treating her daughter as a rival in being a mother to her grandchild, and that her real role of grandmother could be very satisfying. She agreed with the counselor that she resented the fact that her daughter was dating and that this was due in part to the fact that she herself had no companionship with men. She lacked such companionship as a result of her divorce at an early age, which in turn was due to the fact that her husband hadn't fulfilled her needs. She also agreed that her daughter, in spite of her experiences, was still very young, needed guidance and warmth, and that she could help her daughter greatly to grow into a successful mature woman. She recognized that her daughter was really of an age when most young women were just finishing high school and perhaps she was expecting too much of her because of her great desire to feel competent as a mother.

During the ensuing months, Mrs. T became more patient with her daughter and permitted her more control over her child. She found that this eliminated much argument and that they both were happier. She gained insight into the contributing causes of her daughter's behavior, and felt that it was not too late to help her grow. Mrs. T realized that she herself needed recreation because her job was boring and she felt nervous being alone at night. Subsequently, she told the counselor that she enrolled at one of the social dancing schools, and was enjoying it very much. She met some very nice people there, male and female, of her own age. She also enrolled at one of the reducing schools, and was making progress in losing weight. She remarked that she thought this was more effective than going to a psychiatrist.

She no longer resented her daughter's dating and thus staying home with the baby at night. She said that she would like to see her daughter get a divorce and some day marry and have a home of her own. She also felt that her grandchild needed a father to guide him.

Mrs. S brought up the subject of her desire for a divorce in terms of her dislike to pretend that she was a widow, and because the marriage was one without meaning to either herself or her husband. She wrote to him and he agreed that she go ahead and get a divorce, and that he would help her financially. After ten months the decree of divorce was granted.

During the divorce proceedings, Mrs. S met a young man who had arrived a year earlier from a South American country. He was of another religious faith and his skin was much darker than hers. He rushed Mrs. S, seeing her three times a week, and declared his love and desire for marriage. Mrs. T called the counselor, and was much distressed over the relationship, because she feared that the grandchild would be taken away from her if they moved to a foreign country. She also considered foreigners below her accepted standards. She felt that the relationship should be ended quickly. She called him a halfbreed when talking about him to her daughter; she also said that all foreigners were dirty, and not to be trusted. She and Mrs. S started arguing again.

The counselor discussed with Mrs. S the need to give serious thought to any marital relationship that she considered, not only because her future was involved, but also that of her son. She agreed that she would not rush the situation, and would see her friend, Mr. B, only once a week, until her divorce became final, and that after that she would bring him in for a counseling session. She was very anxious that the counselor meet Mr. B; she felt that he would make a good impression. We discussed the reason for her mother's fears, and Mrs. S agreed to be more patient. She emphasized to the counselor that she respected Mr. B and that he was a kind and yet a very strong personality, from whom she enjoyed taking advice. He called her a princess. He attended a mechanical school part time and worked in his specialty the other part of the day. He shared an apartment with his brother, who had an important position with the government. He was cultured and took her to foreign films, and introduced her to refined people, who treated her very nicely. She also informed the counselor that Mr. B came from an excellent family, and that his father was a high official in his government and would be arriving in the United States shortly on a foreign mission.

The counselor subsequently saw Mr. B and was impressed with his sincerity and affection for Mrs. S. We discussed his background and pointed up differences in the mores of the two countries and the need to adjust to these. He felt that he wanted to be like an American husband and he admired the partnership relationship that he observed here. He discussed his affection for Mrs. S's child and his desire to be a real father to him. He said that he felt that his family would accept Mrs. S; he was waiting until they arrived, and after Mrs. S's divorce was final, before announcing their engagement. He said that he wanted to remain in the United States and that he could get a full-time job. The fact that she was anxious to adopt his religion pleased him. He agreed that it was best to see her less frequently and hold up marriage plans until more of the hurdles were overcome. After the divorce became final, Mr. B's parents arrived in the city where he was living and met Mrs. S and her mother. They liked Mrs. S and her son. They were under the impression that she was widowed. Mr. B felt that it was best to keep the divorce from them until after he and Mrs. S were married. After Mrs. T met Mr. B's parents, her attitude toward her daughter and Mr. B changed. She realized that he was actually in a social class superior to her own, and that his people were cultured and well-mannered. She also admired their standard of living. She was proud of the way that they treated her and her daughter. They were very generous with gifts for the whole family and loved her grandson. Mrs. S took instruction in the religion of Mr. B. She felt that she was making a good start toward a happy marriage.

The entire counseling period lasted one year and four months. During the divorce proceedings, the counselor saw Mrs. S about once every two months.

Conclusions: The counseling served to help Mrs. S feel more adequate and less guilty about her past, and to accept her role as mother and daughter. Mrs. T was aided greatly by the insights she gained concerning her treatment of her daughter and the improper role she attempted to play with her grandson. She gained greater respect for herself and had less fear of the future, and her ability to make a life for herself. The strength of the counseling was due to the wonderful co-operation and rapport between clients and counselor and the intelligence that both mother and daughter displayed.

The weaknesses lay in the lack of opportunity to counsel the former husband, because he was bitter and was left with a feeling that he had been used by Mrs. S and that she was a bad person.

The counselor regrets the fact that greater pre-divorce counseling opportunities were not had.

CASE 41

Problem: Counseling the middle-aged single woman
Presented by: A psychiatrist (M.D.; LL.B.), specializing in Marriage Counseling in private practice, in a large urban center

Introduction: At times a counselor will be consulted by women who have reached middle age without marrying, yet who continue to have an active interest in the possibility of marriage. They may seek counsel either about a relationship with a particular man or about problems in their relations with men in general.

These women are likely to present several characteristics that are significantly different from those of younger women. In particular, they are not concerned with having children (being near or past the menopause); they give relatively high value to male companionship and low value to erotic satisfaction; they may evidence exaggerated defensiveness in relating to men; they are likely to have firmly established habits of life that make for difficulty in adjusting to a man's habits and emotional needs; and many display emotional instability due to endocrine imbalance associated with the menopause. Some women in the group have such rigid personalities, are so seriously neurotic, that very limited benefit is possible through counseling and the wisdom of undertaking deep-level therapy may be gravely questionable. But in other instances they may be considerably helped toward a happier way of life and a less lonely old age. This is a report of such a case, seen in private counseling practice over a period of seventeen years, for a total of sixty-nine sessions.

Description of Situation Prior to First Contact: I shall refer to the client as Elsa. She was sent to me by a colleague whom she had consulted in another city about a medical problem. When I first saw her she was fifty years of age. She was a woman of good appearance except for a noticeably shy, self-effacing manner and an obviously indifferent attention to her clothing and personal grooming.

Elsa started by saying that she had recently become involved in an unhappy relationship with a well-educated but unemployed and irresponsible bachelor of her own age. Also, she complained of being discontented at her office, feeling herself the victim of persecution and discrimination and feeling powerless to cope with superiors whom she hated.

A routine history disclosed that Elsa was born in an English-speaking foreign country where she had been raised to the age of eighteen. Her father was a minor government official who died from natural causes when she was only two years old. She had three brothers, all older than she. Following the father's death, her mother had a rigorous struggle raising the family, and the boys were mostly in the custody of relatives. The mother appears to have been an extremely aggressive, forceful person, with fixed moral and religious convictions. Elsa remembers her as a grim, unsmiling person who found little in life to enjoy and much to worry and complain about.

After the father's death Elsa seems to have become her mother's central object of affection. Her mother repeatedly stated that Elsa must try to provide the affection which she had lost with the husband's death. Elsa recalls that at times there was a disturbingly erotic quality in the physical affection which her mother lavished upon her. The boys seem to have been regarded as a burden to be dutifully tolerated, while Elsa was her mother's pet. As Elsa was growing up her mother spoke several times of receiving proposals of marriage which seem never to have interested her. Elsa suspected that her mother got a morbid satisfaction from preserving her status as an unhappy widow and fastening her emotional needs upon her daughter.

At the age of eighteen Elsa graduated from high school and came to the United States. She went to college here and graduated, majoring in economics. During her college days she was intensely religious and made up her mind to accept a foreign missionary assignment. This she did, and for sixteen years served in a Middle-Eastern country, where she became proficient in the native language and a keen student of the culture. She found the missionary experience highly disillusioning in respect to her religious hopes and ambitions and upon her return to this country felt that the "heathen" had made a much more significant impression upon her than she upon them. This was probably a good prognostic sign, indicating that she was capable of considerable faith in realistic human values and that her sense of security was not overly bound to religious dogma.

After returning to the United States she took postgraduate work as a statistician. But in the financial depression of the 1930's she had a hard time making a living and when she first saw me, she was making only a hundred dollars a month.

The Counseling: In the first year of our contact I saw Elsa a total of six one-hour sessions. She revealed that the involvement with her current man friend was the first of her lifetime. Prior to this affair, Elsa had never kissed or embraced a man. She had been having sexual relations with her friend for about a year and said she enjoyed his companionship and affection but was not responsive in intercourse. The man presented a severe problem of premature ejaculation on all occasions. In addition, he was often cynical and depressed and seemed more concerned with his own troubles than with spontaneous enjoyment of his relations with Elsa. She was grateful for the limited pleasure she found in his company but was getting fed up with his moody, undependable, inadequate behavior and his obvious inability to find contentment in their relationship. Also she sensed that his sexual functioning was seriously inadequate. It is probably significant that this, her first real emotional involvement with a man, occurred not long after the death of her mother.

By the end of our first six hours of counseling, it was established that Elsa's friend was so neurotically handicapped as to offer her no future satisfaction and she gave him up. He was unwilling to accept counseling or therapy for himself when she suggested it.

Therapy: Elsa agreed with my judgment that she should undergo psychoanalytic therapy and this was begun. She came for twenty-seven sessions, after which she felt herself enough improved and armed with insight to render further therapy unnecessary.

The expenses involved were also a heavy factor in her decision, for although she was charged a small fee, her salary was very small and she had no financial security for later years. It was my judgment, furthermore, that any prolonged analytic therapy could not be tolerated, for the pressure of analysis tended to bring out extreme anxiety in her dreams and some delusional tendencies in the waking state. Since the termination of her brief analytic therapy, I have seen her in counseling sessions at odd intervals ever since, sometimes not seeing her at all for as much as two or three years and then perhaps for several sessions close together. During much of the seventeen years of our contact, she has been under endocrine treatment, a very important supplement to her psychotherapy, since it was found effective in controlling hot flushes and depression.

Elsa's twenty-seven hours of analytic therapy were devoted to a combination of free association, dream analysis, and discussion. As a result of these sessions, it became apparent that she was still greatly dependent upon a domineering mother image who also merged with her ideal of a father of whom she had no actual memory (since his death occurred when she was only two years old). Also her mother image was closely associated with the conception of God that had developed in her religious thinking.

During Elsa's childhood her mother filled her with terror of masturbation, often stressing that it would cause insanity. When she was twelve, a girl friend gave her some idea of the relationship of intercourse to pregnancy. She reacted to this information with an acute anxiety that she might be pregnant from a fumbling attempt at intercourse with a brother when she had been six years old. Her fear was so overpowering that she confessed the situation to her mother, who appeared indifferent and gave her only partial reassurance. It would seem significant that Elsa's reactions to both adolescence and the menopause were of a markedly disturbed nature. This would appear due to her weak ego structure, stemming from excessive dependence upon and fear of her mother, and her consequently weak ability to cope with her own assertive impulses, especially the hostile and erotic ones.

During the period of analytic therapy Elsa was able to adopt masturbation as an erotic outlet, but only after a hard inner struggle, as revealed by her dreams. Eventually she was able to masturbate, with heterosexual fantasies, and was a much calmer person after this struggle had been won. The attainment of the masturbation outlet enabled her to pursue her erotic feeling to relaxing orgastic expression instead of using these feelings to promote endless anxiety and tension, as she had been doing previously.

As a result of the analytic digest of her childhood experience Elsa gained a new and less fearful general orientation toward sex. Also, her sense of being persecuted at her office greatly abated and her timidity about social participation lessened. She became noticeably more self-confident and took many steps to improve her social life. She began to take pains with her personal appearance, to dress smartly, took dancing lessons, joined a social club and a liberal church group which fosters social activity among its members. She was encouraged in these ventures as a part of her therapy.

Fifteen Years Later: During the fifteen years since her intensive therapy ended Elsa has had emotional and sexual relations with several men. None of these affairs has proved to be sufficiently satisfactory on both sides to result in marriage, yet her life has been brightened by these experiences and they have helped her to become a more mature and self-confident person. At her office, she has had several promotions and now feels that she is respected as an able and friendly member of the office team. She has succeeded in establishing job tenure, with professional status, and is assured an adequate retirement income. Her retirement is realistically planned and she looks forward to it with zest. It is a rather amazing thing that today Elsa actually appears much more "alive" and attractive than she did seventeen years ago.

At times, she has periods of mild depression, but they are transient and she has confidence that they will be successfully weathered. Without therapy and counseling, I believe that Elsa would have had a severe breakdown, probably a psychotic reaction. It cannot be said that she has attained an ideally complete adjustment through her therapy and counseling, but I feel it to have been very much worth while that her regressive tendencies were arrested and that she now deals with life on a sufficiently realistic and comfortable basis to insure that her remaining years will be enjoyable ones, whether she marries or not.

Concluding Diagnosis: For the sake of the professional record, it may be desirable to state a psychiatric diagnosis of Elsa's case, although psychiatric labels often tend to blunt rather than sharpen effective grasp of the dynamics of personality disorders. Following conventional nomenclature I would classify Elsa as an inadequate personality, with schizoid reaction, paranoid type, complicated by a menopausal syndrome. She seemed to me on the border line of psychosis, yet with enough ego strength to respond quite well to partial psychoanalysis and prolonged supportive therapy, plus indicated endocrine treatment.

The nonmedical counselor who handles a case such as this would be wise to seek medical collaboration in respect to the endocrine and other medical complications that are likely to be present. In some instances, it may be prudent to seek psychiatric consultation. But it is a kind of problem that should not dismay a well-trained counselor who is prepared realistically to do the best that can be done in the face of discouraging odds.

PART THREE

MARRIAGE COUNSELING

TODAY AND TOMORROW

---

15. Method and Process, a Recapitulation

Theoretical problems and actual practice in marriage counseling have been presented in Parts One and Two of this casebook. Part One dealt with the general concepts underlying the processes of marriage counseling; Part Two presented a series of 41 cases, illustrative of the methods and processes actually employed by a number of different counselors from a variety of professional disciplines.

In this chapter an attempt will be made to explore the extent to which the principles and concepts suggested in Parts One and Two correlate with the actual practice of marriage counseling as represented in the selected cases. In the final chapter, 16, the lines along which marriage counseling is likely to develop will be briefly sketched together with suggested programs for the future.

In discussing the cases presented in Part Two of this volume it should be recalled that the Foreword explains the factors which governed their selection. In considering the analysis which follows, it should be borne in mind that these cases were selected in part for content, because the Casebook Committee sought a variety of counseling problems, but priority was accorded to cases in which the counselor described in detail and with clarity the counseling methods and the theoretical processes involved.

There is a natural interest on the part of both professional and lay persons in knowing how those wanting help with a marriage situation get to a marriage counselor. This is of practical importance to the troubled individual as well as to the counselor or marriage counseling service. A review of the sources of referral in these forty-one cases shows a wide dispersion. In some 40 per cent, they came from professional agencies, from physicians, lawyers, teachers, courts, and a county medical society; in another 40 per cent, from educational sources such as college classes, magazine articles, books, and other communication media; and in the remaining 20 per cent, from self-knowledge, former clients, friends, and relatives.

Because of the selectivity of the cases and the comparatively small number of counselors represented, these figures may not be representative of practice in general throughout the United States. Obviously, referral to any one marriage counselor will vary in accordance with the professional status, affiliations, and personality of the individual counselor. An analysis of 1,559 consecutive marriage counseling cases seen at one marriage counseling service during the years of 1936 to 1949 showed the sources of referral to be as follows: 36 per cent from professional individuals and agencies, 27 per cent from educational sources, 34 per cent from lay individuals and 3 per cent from other sources.[1]

Methods

Counseling with One or Both Partners: Should the same counselor see both partners? One of the suggested principles in marriage counseling mentioned in Chapter 2 was that the marriage counselor should see both partners. This was considered dynamically important in the counseling process. In the main this appears to be general practice in marriage counseling as exemplified in this casebook.

[1] Emily H. Mudd, *The Practice of Marriage Counseling* (New York: Association Press, 1951), Ch. 5, Table 3, p. 77.

An analysis of the histories shows that in sixteen of the twenty marital cases and in eight of the sixteen premarital cases both husband and wife or young man and young woman were seen by the same counselor. In only two cases (15, 18) did the counselor feel that it would be better for the other partner to be seen by a different counselor.

It appears that in the practice of marriage counseling, when an individual or a couple comes with a marital problem, the marriage is regarded as the patient, and every effort is made to see both partners. When both are available, it is also apparently deemed best for the same counselor to work with both partners. Although both partners often avail themselves of counseling, every marriage counselor is undoubtedly familiar with situations in which one partner seeks help and the other is not interested or refuses to co-operate. Under such conditions, the counselor can still focus on the marriage and serve the client constructively even though the situation is not ideal.

In certain instances in addition to counseling with both partners, it is necessary and helpful to interview other persons connected with the case in order to obtain adequate information and perspective about the situation. In several cases (18, 37, 38, 40)—the three latter involving the counseling of single people—other members of the family, a mother, father, et cetera, were brought in for a consultation either in order to give the counselor a clearer understanding of the situation or because these persons were directly involved and were needed to participate in the counseling process and plan. This was recommended in Chapter 11 as a guiding principle. In a recent paper on marriage counseling, Robert W. Laidlaw, a psychiatrist and former president of the American Association of Marriage Counselors, stressed this point. "Contrary to the usual clinical procedure (in psychiatry) of working only with the patient," he stated, "marriage counseling techniques frequently bring in other individuals who in some way impinge upon the patient's presenting marital problem, such as . . . members of the family, friends, the other man, or the other woman." [2]

Joint Interview: Another point stressed in Chapter 2 is concerned with the value and dangers of joint interviews with both partners. It was pointed out that joint counseling can become a valuable technique but that it should be used with utmost care. In this series, joint interviews were held from time to time in eight of the twenty marital and in eight of the seventeen premarital cases. In the paper already mentioned, Laidlaw wrote as follows about the usefulness of the joint interview. "There will be times when the counselor will wish to bring two or more individuals in the constellation together for a conference with him. Such a conference usually takes place after the counselor feels that he has a good understanding of the various facts in the marital problem and is in a position to begin to approach it therapeutically. . . . In a discordant marital relationship there are painful areas which the marital partners either have shied away from entirely or have found impossible to discuss without acrimony. From his neutral vantage point the counselor is able to direct the discussion to those areas. . . . With his previously gained understanding of the inner state of each partner, the counselor skillfully asks leading questions first of one partner, then of the other, in a way to open up these silent areas and to create a new communication between the two. This may have great therapeutic impact." [3]

Duration and Timing of Counseling: How long does a marriage counseling case take? This question is of immediate concern to the individual or couple who seeks guidance in this area. Many people are of the opinion that one or two visits to a marriage

---

[2] Robert W. Laidlaw, M.D., "Marriage Counseling," chapter in *Understanding Your Patient,* ed. by Samuel Liebman, M.D. (Philadelphia: J. B. Lippincott Company, 1957). Used by permission of the publishers.

[3] *Ibid.* Used by permission of the publishers.

counselor will resolve their difficulties.[4] Often they are surprised to find that it may require a series of interviews before the problems can be adequately brought to an acceptable solution.

The duration of a marriage counseling case obviously depends on a number of factors—the nature of the situation, the frequency of the interviews, the willingness of the partners to continue. In some instances a single interview may suffice. The counselor may be able to give needed factual information, initiate new points of view, or effect a referral to another source of aid, at the first contact. Usually, however, a series of discussions with one or both partners, and sometimes joint sessions, may be necessary.

An analysis of this series of selected cases shows that the duration of counseling, not including follow-up contacts, varied from one month in four cases to over three years in two cases. Continuously or intermittently, seven cases had contact with the counselor for two months, twelve for from three to six months, six for from six to twelve months, and eight for from one to three years. In two instances the counseling process extended for a longer period: in Case 15 for four years, and in Case 41, which included both psychiatric and medical therapy, for a total of seventeen years.

The total number of sessions per case varied from one interview with each partner, in one case, to six hundred with one individual client in another. In the large majority of cases each individual partner had between six and thirty interviews.

In twenty-three instances interviews were held weekly, in seven at more frequent intervals, and in eleven once every two weeks or even less frequently. As the case drew to a close, the interval between visits usually increased. As might be expected, the number of interviews per case was higher in the marital than in the premarital group. In the latter, the average was from two to ten interviews, and no case extended beyond eight months.

[4] See David R. Mace, *What Is Marriage Counseling?*, Public Affairs Pamphlet, No. 250, June, 1957.

Fees: Whether a fee should or should not be charged for marriage counseling services is now perhaps an academic question. A survey made by the American Association of Marriage Counselors in 1952-53 of functioning marriage counseling services showed that, with a few exceptions, a nominal fee or one based on the client's income was charged in most of the then functioning centers. This practice was based in part on the psychological premise that an individual places more value on something in which he himself has to participate and therefore a fee can be dynamically useful in the counseling process; and in part also on the fact that the cost of marriage counseling services was high and it was felt suitable by boards of directors therefore that the expenses of the service should be covered at least partly by clients' fees.

Fees in marriage counseling centers were found to range from $1 to $10 per interview, with occasional well-to-do clients paying considerably more. In no center surveyed was it found that a client unable to pay even a nominal fee was refused service. The average fee classification in centers was around $5 although the average collected was almost uniformly less than this figure.

The marriage counselor who functions in private practice obviously must charge for his services. Although we have no systematic information on the range or the average fees in private practice, reports indicate that usually they vary from $5 to $25 or over per interview of approximately an hour.

We have no systematic information on how fees were handled in the group of cases presented in this book. It appears that fees were charged in many instances either in accordance with the directives of the counseling service or the patterns of private practice.

Process

How did the counselors proceed with their cases? What were the techniques employed by them? What general concepts or principles were utilized in the achievement of the reported results?

Some of the theoretical principles of marriage counseling were discussed in Chapter 2. Here an attempt will be made to analyze the cases presented from the point of view of the processes and techniques reported in the case presentations as actually employed by the different counselors included in this report. This summary should indicate how closely practice relates to theory in these particular cases and may be considered suggestive in connection with the current practice of marriage counseling.

The Initial Interview: The way in which the client-counselor relationship is established in the first interview is important psychologically as well as practically. Almost every experienced counselor evolves his own procedure on the basis of what seems most comfortable and efficient for himself and his client. The goals of this first contact are similar for counselor and client in three major respects: each hopes to end the hour with a picture of what the focus of the problem is, to ascertain whether the counselor through his specific agency or private practice is equipped to deal with the situation, and finally to decide whether the client is sufficiently motivated to work out a mutually acceptable plan for counseling.

In this first contact some clients pour out their story with such vehemence that the counselor can do little but interrupt occasionally to keep the flood of words focused on relevant material and finally to allow time for discussing a plan of counseling. Other clients may be so upset it is extremely difficult for them to talk at all, let alone organize their account. In each and every situation it is the counselor's most important job to help the client feel comfortable, to let him know the counselor is interested and wants to be of assistance. This is referred to in Chapter 2 as the "Establishment of Rapport" and may be considered an important area. Often some simple question or statement breaks the ice. "How did you hear about marriage counseling?" or "Why don't you just begin to talk about what you most want me to know; we can fill in the details later."

Sometimes, in spite of how it may be suggested, couples come separately for the first interview; sometimes they come together. Some counselors plan, if possible, to see a couple together for ten minutes or so; then to see the man and woman each separately for about thirty minutes, and finally to spend the last fifteen minutes with both again jointly in order to set up a plan. Such a process enables the counselor to get a glimpse of the interaction between the partners, to find out if they are concerned with the same or different problems, and to estimate whether one or both are committed to a plan for participating in the counseling.

In our group of forty-one cases, the clients were seen individually in 37 cases—the large majority; they were seen jointly in eleven cases and in seven instances they were seen both individually and jointly.

Opening Communication Between Partners: One of the most useful processes in marriage counseling is to encourage, when it is lacking, fuller and freer communication between the partners. As was pointed out in the discussion of the joint interview, this may in itself have great therapeutic value. At the root of many marital difficulties lies the inability of husband and wife to talk about their problems without great tension and hostility. "We never talk," a wife or husband may say, "we always argue." "It is impossible for us to communicate," a husband comments, "we just knife each other." Changing argument to discussion, changing destructive undermining to the beginning of mutual support, may help a couple to new patterns in the resolving of their conflicts.

Case 6 is especially illustrative of a marital conflict caused by a breakdown of communication. During the first joint interviews the husband and wife were continually "dueling." As the counseling processes progressed, jointly and individually, the couple began to communicate with one another more freely without the pattern of constant attack and counterattack, and, though argument still continued, at times, the sequelae were much less disturbing and lasting.

In Case 13, too, the ability to talk more freely to each other aided in the resolution of their problem. "They felt," says the counselor, "that they now wanted to try to work on their problems together, because they had learned for the first time they could share feeling with each other and thus work on their own relationship."

The establishment of better communication is one of the goals of marriage counseling. When a husband and wife are able to talk over their different ideas and feelings together, as pointed out in Chapter 2, they will be more apt to modify their activities and adopt new ideas and new patterns of behavior in their interpersonal relations.

Ventilation and Catharsis: In Chapter 2, stress was laid on the value of "listening" as a counseling technique and the reduction of hostility as a therapeutic measure. A consultation with an understanding, sympathetic, nonjudgmental professional person can, in itself, be a constructive therapeutic measure. It gives an opportunity for the troubled and distraught individual to ventilate his grievances, to discharge his emotions, to free himself from accumulated resentments and hostilities. This is the process of ventilation and catharsis which is a basic part of psychotherapy. How often (as in Case 22) does a counselor hear the statement after the first interview: "You know, I feel so much better for having talked to you." This "feeling better" may not carry over for long, but it is an indication of the value of the release of emotional tension.

In the cases in this book, the effect of ventilation of feeling is mentioned directly or indirectly by the counselor in many instances (Case 1, 3, 5, 10, 13, 15, 21, 23, 24, 27, 32, 34). In each of these records, the counselor speaks specifically of the value to the counselee of the release of emotions and tensions. In all the other cases, however, this process is implicit in the description of the interviews.

Emotional Support: In practically every case presented in this series, emotional support and reassurance was an important part of the counseling process. The objective of the counselor throughout was to build up the ego strength of the counselee, by developing his self-confidence, his ability in handling reality, and by giving him reassurance when indicated. Supportive therapy is a well-recognized aspect of psychotherapy generally, and plays an important role in marriage counseling.

Clarification and Interpretation: Often a discussion with a counselor helps the client to understand more clearly the difference between his own and his partner's needs and the causes of the marital difficulties. In over half the cases in this series, clarification was a part of the counseling technique.

Interpretation goes further and demands considerable psychotherapeutic skill and additional responsibility on the part of the counselor. In this process the counselor attempts to interpret for the counselee some of the motivations for his own and perhaps even for his partner's actions. This procedure too, is used by the counselors in the majority of the cases in this book.

Insight: Development of insight as a part of the process of marriage counseling is mentioned as one of the aims in Chapter 2. Many of the counselors in these case records specifically refer to this factor as a part of their procedure. In other cases this process is implicit in the histories. Through interpretation and sometimes suggestion, an attempt is made to enable the client to achieve a deeper insight into the underlying reasons for his own or his partner's behavior. Marriage counseling attempts to aid the counselee to develop a greater understanding of self without necessarily aiming at a reorganization of the individual's personality. "Insight therapy" which includes intensive use of interpretation may belong to the realm of prolonged therapy, and obviously needs to be used with a great deal of caution in marriage counseling unless the counselor has special training in psychotherapy. A specifically trained and well-equipped marriage counselor, however, may utilize this measure as a part of his therapy in marital disturbances.

Bibliotherapy: Part of the marriage counseling process may be the recommendation of books, pamphlets or articles that may be pertinent to the particular case. Books are sometimes recommended for specific purposes as an adjunct to the counseling and are discussed by the counselor and counselee during subsequent interviews. The counselor may wish to illustrate certain areas of information or discussion by enabling the client to see how someone else describes this. Often the written word is reassuring and carries conviction. Some counselors may hesitate to recommend any specific reference, feeling that this may represent their own bias. Under such conditions, the counselor will refer his clients to a college or public library or suggest they obtain references for reading from their teacher or minister or physician.

Literature recommendations were made in a number of cases in this series (Cases 2, 3, 7, 8, 9, 20, 24, 25, 34, 36). It is likely, however, that suggestions for reading were also made in other cases, though this was not specifically mentioned in the histories. Study of these cases indicates that recommended reading should not in itself ordinarily be considered as an answer to a problem. It should be looked upon as a potentially helpful adjunct to the counseling process to broaden horizons, educate, and re-educate and also assist in emotional release. It need hardly be mentioned that the skilled and experienced marriage counselor recommends only reading material with which he is personally acquainted.

Information Giving: Although the client can obtain information through supplementary reading, an important element in marriage counseling is the provision directly by the counselor of specific information needed by a client. In this series, information giving played a definite role in nearly three-quarters of the cases. Often it helped the individual to gain a better perspective of the total situation. In some instances, the information related to cultural and religious differences and their effects upon the marriage (Cases 1, 32, 34, and 36). In Case 1 the information dealt with budgets and menus. In others, it dealt with the physical factors of sex and reproduction (Cases 5, 15, 16, 21, 23, 24, 25, 26, 37, and 41); with contraceptive techniques (Case 20); with the facts of pregnancy and childbirth (Case 38); with emotional relationships between partners in marriage (Cases 7, 8, 9) and between parents and children as well as the partners, (Cases 15, 18). In all these cases the counselor found it constructive to provide factual information to the counselees in the belief that this, along with the other aspects of the counseling relationship, might enable them to meet more adequately the various physical and emotional demands in the marriage.

Practical Aid: In addition to information giving, some counselors also provide practical aid. This area in counseling has received little attention in the literature, although it has long been recognized as an important part of medical and social work. Often and quite naturally this practical assistance is related to the special skills of the counselor. An interesting example is found in Case 36 in which the young woman client who is considering an interracial marriage is given introductions to a Negro community. Many other types of practical aid can be found in Cases 4, 7, 9, 10, 16, 17, 18, 19. From a review of these, it is obvious that "practical aid" is becoming an integral part of the practice of marriage counseling.

Referral for Additional Help: In Chapter 2 it was suggested that the counselor should utilize other professional skills when this seems indicated, and that he should readily accept the natural and inevitable limitations of his particular training and of both his professional and personal experiences. Any counselee may at times need general or specific assistance which the counselor may not be equipped to provide. Thus the counselor should be responsible for knowledge of the community in which he works and ready to make an appropriate referral to other professional facilities and community resources whenever this seems to be needed by the counselee. Obviously, discussing additional sources of help when appropriate with a client in such a way that the client becomes interested in the possibility and desirous of putting it into effect requires skill, tact, and sound judgment. It is one of the important processes of counseling.

In this series of cases, referrals were suggested and actually effected in seventeen instances. Through the assistance of the marriage counselors, those clients were able to obtain services which included medical examinations and treatment; premarital examination (Cases 20, 23, 24, 26); psychiatric consultation or care for themselves (Cases 33, 39) or their children (Cases 18, 19); psychological tests, (Cases 19, 25); child placement for adoption (Case 38); and religious advice (Case 2).

Psychosomatic Symptoms: It is of interest to note that in this series of forty-one cases reported by a variety of counselors from many disciplines, somatic symptoms of one kind or another are recorded in nearly half of them. Among the more frequent were dizziness, fainting, chronic headache, tension, insomnia, anorexia, gastrointestinal disturbances, impotence, dyspareunia, and suicidal attempts. Somatic symptoms are not infrequently the result of emotional disturbances which stem from marital maladjustments. "The origin of my own interest in marriage counseling," writes Dr. Kenneth E. Appel, Professor of Psychiatry at the

University of Pennsylvania's School of Medicine, "was my discovery of the extent to which marital maladjustment appeared in patients, masquerading or expressing itself unconsciously in unhappiness, vocational ineffectiveness, alcoholism, psychosomatic symptoms, nervous illness, mental disease, and even suicide." [5]

Many of these people had had thorough medical examination and were found to be free from organic disease. Some of them, in fact, were referred by their own doctors for marriage counseling (Cases 8, 16), and in several cases the symptoms cleared up during the therapeutic course of the counseling. In Case 5, for instance, Mrs. R stated that for years she had had a choking sensation in her throat, as well as palpitation, especially when she was angry and under tension. Physical examination had apparently been negative. During the course of the counseling interviews her symptoms completely cleared up. In Case 17, reported by a psychiatrist, the wife, among other things, complained of a writing difficulty. She found it difficult to write or sign her name or her employer's name to documents. During the course of the therapy, the patient obtained considerable insight into the pattern of her behavior and the reasons for her trouble, and her writing difficulty subsided quickly and did not return.

Somatic and psychiatric complaints obviously belong in the domain of medicine, and the marriage counselor, unless he be a physician or a psychiatrist, will not undertake to care for them without appropriate consultation. Sometimes, however, these symptoms clear up spontaneously as a result of the counseling process.

Follow-Up: How successful is marriage counseling? In what per cent of cases is the situation improved? There is an unusually good opportunity to answer such questions from these records

[5] "Problems with Which People Want Help in Sex and Marriage," Ch. 1 in *Man and Wife,* ed. by Emily H. Mudd, Ph.D. and Aron Krich, Ed.D. (New York: W. W. Norton and Company, 1957).

since 39 out of the 41 cases have follow-up notes extending over varying lengths of time after completion of the counseling process. Results found in these follow-up contacts indicated that the clients had obtained partial or complete relief from the problems for which counseling had been sought in 97 per cent of the cases. It must be remembered that for this book the cases were especially selected by the various counselors for presentation, partly because of their special interest, partly because they had obtained a follow-up and partly, no doubt, because of the successful results obtained. These results appear favorable in a much higher proportion of cases than in an average group seen in any one marriage counseling service or by any one individual counselor. In contrast a survey of results from one marriage counseling service made in 1952 showed that in some 66 per cent of the cases the problems for which aid was sought had either entirely cleared up or were partially improved after counseling, in 29 per cent no change had taken place, and in 5 per cent the situation had apparently deteriorated.[6]

How long does improvement, if there is any, last? Will they "live happily ever afterward"? In general, the length of contact, including follow-up, varied from 5-6 weeks (Cases 18 and 20) to as long as 8 years (Case 10). In the latter case, the counselee, who was by then in her late thirties, wrote to the counselor eight years after her last visit: "We are getting along fine with an understanding of each other we never had before," and have "nothing but contentment." Six months later this client came to discuss with the counselor the problem of her children's masturbation. At that interview she stated that her previous counseling sessions had been helpful to her, not only in her own relationship with her husband but also in her relationship with her children and her realization of responsibility for their proper sex education.

In another case (22), a father, who had originally referred

---

[6] Malcolm G. Preston, Emily H. Mudd and Hazel B. Froscher, "Factors Affecting Movement in Counseling," *Social Casework*, March, 1953.

his daughter for counseling because of an unsatisfactory engagement, the breaking of which had been very traumatic for her, wrote years later, following her marriage to another man: "They are radiantly happy, have a lovely home, and are extraordinarily congenial." And again, after the birth of the first baby, five years after the close of the case, this same father wrote: "I suppose you marriage counselors cannot keep in touch with your boys and girls the way a minister who married them does, but there must be many all over the country who feel as my daughter does."

In most instances, the follow-up contacts were with the counselee himself or herself by personal interview. In some instances, it was with a spouse, parent, friend, or with the source of the original referral. By maintaining contact with their clients, individual marriage counselors and, through them, students in the field, may have an added opportunity to evaluate their techniques, their attitudes and their general philosophy of practice.

In spite of the obvious value of ascertaining the results of marriage counseling, there is little probability that follow-up contacts, except for a few research projects, are either routine or systematic in the over-all counseling load of marriage counselors in agency work or in private practice. Such efforts are time consuming, expensive, and sometimes even questionable from the point of view of the client's welfare and anonymity. It is usually in those cases where the client takes the initiative, where there are some particular conditions, or when the case is reopened that contact is maintained between counselor and client.

In all probability, there is not a counselor who has not at some time been surprised by what has happened after counseling. Perhaps a case in which he felt discouraged and pessimistic showed a more favorable outcome than was anticipated; or else, a case which he had reported with sincere pride as a success was found, two years later, to be badly on the rocks. Marriage counseling is still far from being based on precise scientific data, and its variables are as complex as human nature itself. The counselor whose expectations of success are too high is not facing his practice and its potentialities realistically and the counselee who believes that he can obtain a "sure cure" for an ailing marriage is also unrealistic in his expectations.

The Intangibles: No matter what the process or technique used by a counselor may be, there is an intangible quality in marriage counseling which cannot be described in specific terms of method or process. The personality of the counselor himself, the relationship which he establishes with the counselee, the understanding, the sympathy, the interest, the warmth which he possesses, profoundly affect his counseling and its results. In writing on the philosophy of marriage counseling many years ago, Emily Mudd stated as follows:

> It takes time to change, to grow, to make adjustments, to develop competence. Therefore patience is necessary and not hastiness, sympathy not indulgence, tolerance not criticism, faith not pessimism. People do not want too much fuss made over them; neither do they want to be pitied. They have to feel their way. Many will find themselves through trial and error. The counselor should not argue, blame, criticize, moralize, or tell the other person that he is wrong. He should not humiliate or tell the counselee to be ashamed of his unusual or erratic behavior. He should express approval for real effort to become more adequate, even though success is not immediately forthcoming, and above all, he should show a warm human responsiveness, a sympathy with human differences and an understanding of them, and an awareness of spiritual values. The goal of counseling is to help people over the spots that seem rough to them and through this process enable them to help themselves and those with whom they are most closely associated.[7]

[7] Emily H. Mudd, "Counseling, a Philosophy and Method," in *The Cyclopedia of Medicine, Surgery, and Specialties* (New York: T. A. Davis Co., 1945), pp. 450-460.

Conclusion

When the Committee undertook to prepare this casebook there was no evidence available as to whether or not there were common denominators between theory and practice in the field of marriage counseling. Nor was it known how specifically any school of psychological thought might affect or differentiate methods and techniques employed by counselors with their clients.

The close relationship between some of the more general principles and procedures in marriage counseling, on the one hand, as stated in Chapter 2 and, on the other, the methods actually used by marriage counselors in practice as presented in the case material seem to have important implications for the present status of marriage counseling as well as for the future development of this field. The high degree of correlation between these general principles and the case material indicates that although the field is relatively new there has already been developed a considerable amount of generally accepted practice, whether such practice is consciously related to formulated theory or not. This demonstrates the teachability of marriage counseling and the need for developing accredited courses for future marriage counselors so that they may profit from the accumulated thought and experience already available.

The high correlation between theory and practice as presented in this volume has equally important implications for the future. For it would seem to be self-evident that if, at this stage of development of the field, theory and practice are essentially closely interrelated, much more can be accomplished through concentrated effort on research. Research must be based on practice, and practice should be modified by the findings of research. Such interdependence would assist each in contributing to the advancement of the other. This task can be performed only if teachers, researchers, and practitioners maintain close communication and learn to take from as well as to give to each other.

16. Programs for the Future

This casebook has been concerned primarily with the problems arising from the interpersonal relations between men and women before and after marriage, some of the main factors responsible for marriage disorganization, and what marriage counseling can do to contribute to greater interpersonal competence. The purpose of marriage counseling is the promotion of better marriages. In this final chapter, therefore, it seems appropriate again, as was done in Chapter 1, to view marriage as the core of family life and further to relate marriage to general family well-being and stability.

In a memorandum on Strengthening Family Life, prepared for the Social Security Administration of the Department of Health, Education, and Welfare, Emily Mudd and Reuben Hill write as follows:

> The climate of opinion in the United States is highly favorable for the support of marriage and family life. There is today widespread affirmation of the values associated with both marriage and parenthood. Well known as the most marrying people in the world, a higher proportion of the population in 1955 was married or remarried than ever before in our history. Despite a relatively high divorce rate, the proportion remaining divorced is only two per cent of the population—the married status is the preferred status of most Americans. Childbearing has likewise stabilized around a

norm of medium-sized families, two to four children. This is most apparent among the college educated style-setters making it fashionable to have four children rather than one or two. This, coupled with continued high residential construction of individual family homes (45 per cent of all construction, 1946–50), suggests a mode of living in America that is comfortably family oriented.[1]

If the family thus remains the basic unit of our society, any social or professional practice which helps to maintain competent marriages should in itself contribute to the strengthening of family life and indirectly of society. Long ago Confucius pointed out that good families are essential to good communities, and good communities to a good national life. What then constitutes a good family? In the memorandum mentioned above, a *Good Family* was defined as one which "stresses growth and development of children and parents, has achieved happiness, strong bonds of affection, mutual enjoyment and co-operation, is characterized in practice by democratic give-and-take and high togetherness, is actively contributing to the community and is crisis-proof because rooted in spiritual values." Expectations both in marriage and family life are in the main high in our American culture. They go well beyond economic security and adequate physical care. They stress the importance of affection, of equality within the home, of a mutually supportive emotional and physical relationship, and of wholesome and understanding parenthood.

Education for Family Life: Among the proposals for strengthening family life recommended in the memorandum, in addition to the availability of counseling, social, and medical services at all stages of family need, major emphasis was placed on family life education as one means of prevention of difficulty and promotion

[1] This memorandum was prepared in the spring of 1956 for administrative use only and is referred to here and later in this section by permission of Commissioner Charles Schottland of the Social Security Administration, Washington, D. C., and of the authors.

of competence. Such education, the report continues, should be given to those about to be married and to those already married and should include adequate factual information, as well as an appreciation of the values of good interpersonal relationships and of the skills needed in maintaining such relations. Education for marriage should begin in the home because children develop their attitudes toward marriage and family living in the early years of life and it should continue as a part of the total education of the individual in school, church, and community. Specific information should be given expectant parents about infant and child care; to parents of preschoolers about dealing with questions children ask; to parents of teen-agers about adolescence and the physical and interpersonal problems that arise in this period; and to parents of young adults and young adults themselves concerning facilities for meeting suitable persons of the opposite sex and methods of evaluating their potentialities as marriage partners. Such education should, of course, involve preparing engaged couples to deal with the natural adjustments of early marriage.

In many of these areas the marriage counselor has a specific function. Many of the cases presented in Part Two illustrate the role of the counselor in preparing young people for marriage and in helping them to resolve some of the perplexities which may arise later.

Training: What of marriage counseling in the future? Who will be the marriage counselor of tomorrow, and what will the major functions of counseling be? In a paper on this subject published in 1950,[2] Dr. Stone pointed out that "as more people are trained for this practice and as better techniques and methods are evolved, marriage counseling will widen its horizons and field of usefulness. The counselor of tomorrow will be well grounded in the psychology and sociology of marriage and human relations, in the anatomy and physiology of sex, as well as in the skills and tools of

[2] Abraham Stone, M.D., "Marriage Counseling Today and Tomorrow," *Marriage and Family Living,* Vol. XIII, No. 2, May, 1950.

counseling. He or she hopefully will be mature, well-balanced and well-integrated and prepared to deal with many types of marital disabilities, recognizing, however, his or her own personal and professional limitations." [3]

In the future, too, as demand at all levels increases, more universities will probably provide specialized courses on the graduate level to meet the academic requirements of advanced students in this field. In-service, supervised training for the acquisition of clinical experience, skill and insight will become more readily available in adequately qualified marriage counseling centers.

Eventually some form of certification may be indicated for qualified persons. When a new area is opened, many prospectors exploit its resources for their own benefit with little regard for social values. To prevent such exploitation and to develop marriage counseling on high professional and ethical standards will be the aim of both governmental agencies and professional associations.

Research: Of utmost importance for the future of marriage counseling is continued evaluation of its objectives and accomplishments through systematic study and research. As of today, the Unknowns in marriage counseling, as in many other aspects of the behavioral sciences, far outweigh the Knowns. Recent critical reviews of marriage counseling and of family and mental health programs indicate that, to quote from Dr. Mudd, "we have not yet verified or refuted many of our constantly applied assertions and theories . . . we do not know scientifically that the use of one type of analytic, psychiatric, psychological counseling or guidance procedure is actually of greater benefit than another to a person with troubles. We cannot even be completely sure that any

[3] The requirements thought necessary for marriage counselors have been spelled out after many hours of thought by a combined committee of the American Association of Marriage Counselors and the National Council of Family Relations and are available at the headquarters office of the American Association of Marriage Counselors, 104 East 40th Street, New York 16, N.Y.

type of help, on the basis of evaluation ten years hence, brings better results than if the person had received no therapy from a professional source." [4]

Clearly, then, much research is still needed in all areas of marriage and family living. The main goal of such research should be the development of a theory of marital interaction and family living that would be cultural in perspective and from which a more adequate philosophy of the practice of marriage counseling might develop.

Summary

In summary, contemporary marriage counseling practice has been reviewed in this book. This has been accomplished through an analysis of the cultural background in which marriage counseling has emerged, an exploration of methods, procedures, and philosophies of the various schools of thought which apply to marriage counseling, and the presentation and analysis of selected cases representative of the problems brought to marriage counselors who meet the professional qualifications of the national association. In the last chapter, the Committee has attempted to relate marriage counseling to the strengthening of family well-being in the future.

The work of preparing this manuscript was undertaken by the Casebook Committee and the American Association of Marriage Counselors in the context of general affirmation of the values of marriage and family life. Detailed examination, at least in part, of the practice of contemporary marriage counseling reaffirms and enhances the importance of these values for the future.

[4] "Knowns and Unknowns in Marriage Counseling Research" by Emily H. Mudd, *Marriage and Family Living*, Vol. XIX, No. 1, February, 1957.

APPENDIX

The American Association of Marriage Counselors

The American Association of Marriage Counselors is the only existing national organization exclusively concerned with marriage counseling. Historically it developed from the expressed interest of members of the Groves Conference and of Dr. Groves himself, who, in 1939, appointed a Committee on the Protection of Professional Standards. Lester Dearborn, a member of this committee, had previously in 1934 and 1936, discussed the possible need to organize a group "for the purpose of establishing standards, exchanging information and helping in the development of interest in this field . . ." with Drs. Emily H. Mudd and Abraham Stone.[1]

Concurrent with the exploratory work of this committee on "Protection of Standards," Dr. Robert L. Dickinson, in New York, had organized a committee on "Socio-Sexual Relations of Men and Women," which had been meeting at irregular intervals to exchange data and information.

Conferring with Dr. Robert W. Laidlaw (a member both of the Groves Conference and of Dr. Dickinson's committee) Mr. Dearborn (also a member of both groups) invited the following persons to a meeting which was held in Dr. Laidlaw's office in New York on June 20, 1942: Dr. Ernest Groves, Mrs. Gladys Groves, Dr.

[1] Lester Dearborn, March 18, 1957 (letter).

483

Robert L. Dickinson, Mrs. Stuart Mudd, Dr. Abraham Stone, Dr. Valeria Parker, and Dr. Robert W. Laidlaw. A second meeting was held with a small but carefully expanded invitation list in October of that year. And on April 30, 1943, the first clinical session of the group was held.

During this early period, and up to the spring of 1945, Lester Dearborn was chairman of the group. In April, 1945, the following officers were elected: President, Dr. Ernest Groves; First Vice-President, Lester Dearborn; Second Vice-President, Mrs. Stuart Mudd; Secretary and Treasurer, Dr. Robert W. Laidlaw. The presidents of the organization since then have been Dr. Bernard S. Wortis, Dr. Abraham Stone, Dr. Robert W. Laidlaw, Dr. Emily H. Mudd, Dr. Lewis Sharp, and Lester Dearborn.

It may be noted from early records and correspondence that of this small group of professional persons who were especially interested in problems of sex and marriage, fifty per cent came primarily from the medical specialties with a few individuals invited from social work, psychology, and sociology. It was informally organized to exchange clinical information and pool experience; and to aid in the progressive development of counseling techniques, and the study of the results of their use. By 1943 it became more formally organized with some attention paid to membership requirements and the development of a formal statement of purpose. It was incorporated in 1947.

According to a statement by its first formally elected secretary and later president, Robert W. Laidlaw, M.D.:

> It is a professional organization which concentrates its work specifically on marriage counseling. It has this stated purpose (taken from the by-laws): to establish and maintain professional standards in marriage counseling. This purpose shall be furthered by meetings, clinical sessions, publications and research. Its membership is open to those who meet its detailed requirements for clinicians in the field or for affiliates whose work in this or related fields is outstanding, and for associates whose background, training and beginning practice

are sufficiently advanced to enable them to gain professionally by meeting with the more experienced counselors.[2]

No marriage counseling services per se function under AAMC auspices, nor does it perform any certifying procedures. However, on written request to its headquarters office,[3] the names and addresses of professionally qualified persons, who are either members of the AAMC or of related recognized professional organizations, are made available.

Since its inception, there has been continued and consistent interest in the definition and redefinition of membership requirements. At present writing, there are six classifications of membership: Active, Associate, Affiliate, Foreign Corresponding, Honorary, and most recently (June, 1955) Associate-in-Training. There has been but one Honorary Member—Robert Latou Dickinson, M.D.—to whose inspiration and leadership the Association and each individual member who knew him, is lovingly indebted.[4]

The composition of the AAMC membership reflects the interdisciplinary character of marriage counseling. In 1955, a breakdown of the active members indicated that the medical profession still predominated, representing 31% (gynecologists, 12%; general medicine, 9%; psychiatrists, 9%; urologists, 1%). In addition, 18% of the membership are educators; 11%, ministers; 13%, psychologists; 16%, social workers; 11%, sociologists. (The indicated profession refers to the academic field in which initial training and advanced degrees were obtained.) However, when this is corrected for 1957 to include all classes of membership a slight shift, which may or may not be sustained, is reflected: social workers, 20%; physicians, 19% (gynecologists, 8%; general medicine, 6%; psychiatrists, 5%); educators, 16%; minis-

[2] Emily H. Mudd, Ph.D., *The Practice of Marriage Counseling* (New York: Association Press, 1951), Ch. IV, p. 50.

[3] American Association of Marriage Counselors, 104 East 40 St., New York 16, N.Y.

[4] Dr. Dickinson died in November, 1950. Subsequently, a Robert Latou Dickinson Memorial Fund was established, which constituted the basis of the Fellowship Fund, designated December 6, 1950.

ters, 15%; psychologists, 14%; sociologists, 12%; lawyers, 4%.

In addition to clinical programs and regularly scheduled membership meetings, the Association's announced concern for establishing and maintaining professional standards has been implemented by two special projects.

In 1948, the American Association of Marriage Counselors together with the marriage counseling section of the National Council of Family Relations, jointly released a statement of standards for "acceptable and recognized marriage counselors."[5] These were presented in terms of (1) academic training, (2) professional experience and qualifications, (3) personal qualifications. They are at present in the process of revision.

In 1954, at its annual meeting in Philadelphia, the Association formally accepted the report of the Committee on Criteria for Marriage Counseling Centers. This report,[6] accepted item by item by the membership, was based on a survey of marriage counseling centers and services existing in 1953-54. It made specific recommendations for minimum standards for organizations which, either exclusively or as a specialized part of a total service, offered marriage counseling. These dealt with matters relating to organization and structure, qualifications of professional staff, provision for staff case-conference, supervision, consultation, and referral. It also dealt with the question of records, with confidentiality of materials, and with the whole problem of fees. A separate statement emphasizing the same professional standards of training and experience for marriage counseling in colleges and universities was attached. It was further voted by the membership that an appropriate committee be appointed to explore ways and means of implementing these recommendations.

[5] Copies of this statement may be obtained by writing to The American Association of Marriage Counselors, 104 East 40 Street, New York 16, N. Y.

[6] Copies of this report may be obtained by writing to The American Association of Marriage Counselors, 104 East 40 Street, New York 16, N. Y.

Definition and clarification of the field of marriage counseling is a major objective of the Association and especially of its *Program and Development Committee*. In the meantime, pending further exploration, the definition of marriage counseling most generally acceptable to Association members, is the one presented by the Criteria Committee:

> Marriage Counseling is a specialized field of family counseling, primarily concerned with the interpersonal relations of husband and wife, wherein the client is aided to a self-determined resolution of his problem.

Emily Mudd makes a further nice distinction when she writes: ". . . the focus of the counselor's approach is the relationship between the two people in marriage rather than, as in psychiatric therapy, the reorganization of the personality structure of the individual." [7]

Although in no way offering "accredited" standing, membership in the Association is meaningful in so far as it represents a screening in terms of training, experience, and personal qualifications. Training and experience both initially stem from the original disciplines of the candidate or member. However, it is increasingly apparent that in addition to basic requirements there is a common body of knowledge, techniques, and qualifications that cross-cuts all the professions involved. To define those needs and to help provide in-service training which supplements the basic skills and is focused on marriage counseling, is the responsibility of the *Committee on Training* working closely with the Fellowship Committee.

The Association also has appointed a committee to explore the possibility of developing a Code of Ethics for Marriage Counselors. According to its chairman, that committee has been at work on developing a Code for Marriage Counselors consistent with

[7] Emily Hartshorne Mudd, Ph.D., "Psychiatry and Marital Problems," *Eugenics Quarterly,* June, 1955, Vol. 2, No. 2, pp. 110-117.

the practices of the professional groups composing its member-ship.[8]

Without attempting to resolve the whole complicated area of the relation of psychotherapy and counseling, the Association has made it clear that in no sense are psychotherapy and counseling to be considered synonymous. Members of the AAMC may do psychotherapy—many of them do—but not by virtue of their work in marriage counseling. This activity derives from their own individual basic training, and unless they are so trained and so qualified, marriage counselors per se are not considered to be psychotherapists. This is of special importance in relation to the question of the private practice of nonmedical counselors. Some members of the Association feel that marriage counseling by non-medical personnel may be most efficiently accomplished within the policies and procedures of an established agency. Others, al-though they recognize the difficulties, feel that every effort should be made to strengthen and develop standards of training and experience, ethics, and regulations which would eventually lead to licensing of marriage counselors in private practice. With these differences in mind, the Association (in 1955) appointed a committee, *Private Practice Committee,* to study and explore this controversial subject.

[8] Maurice J. Karpf, April 18, 1957 (letter).